Lucky Luciano

Lucky Luciano

The Rise and Fall of a Mob Boss

WILLIAM DONATI

McFarland & Company, Inc., Publishers
Jefferson, North Carolina, and London

Library of Congress Cataloguing-in-Publication Data

Donati, William.
  Lucky Luciano : the rise and fall of a mob boss / William
Donati.
     p.   cm.
  Includes bibliographical references and index.

  ISBN 978-0-7864-4666-7
  softcover : 50# alkaline paper ∞

  1. Luciano, Lucky, 1897–1962.   2. Criminals—New York
(State)—New York—Biography   3. Organized crime—
New York (State)—New York.   4. Mafia—United States.
I. Title.
HV6248.L92D66   2010
364.1092—dc21   2010012989
[B]

British Library cataloguing data are available

Front cover: Brooklyn Bridge and New York City skyline ©2010
Shutterstock; *background* Luciano Mug Shot, April 4, 1936
(New York Police Department)

Manufactured in the United States of America

McFarland & Company, Inc., Publishers
  Box 611, Jefferson, North Carolina 28640
    www.mcfarlandpub.com

To John Romano,
citizen

*"I respect you because you are an old man
and if you weren't, I would have you beat up."*
— *Jean*

"You have got to kill me."
— *John Romano*

Contents

Acknowledgments

Special thanks to the following: Ken Cobb and his staff at the New York City Municipal Archives; Karl Kabelac, manuscripts librarian, Rush Rhees Library, University of Rochester, and his successor, Nancy Martin; Mark Palmer, crime historian of Hot Springs, Arkansas; the Garland County Historical Society in Hot Springs; the New York Public Library; the Billy Rose Theatre Collection; the Harry Ransom Humanities Research Center, University of Texas at Austin.

Commercialized Vice by George Kneeland is a prime source of information. The reformers conducted a masterful and thorough investigation. Their vice reports were meticulously documented; first-hand observations were designed to reveal the miserable life endured by prostitutes and the moral corruption and health problems *the trade* generated. The reformers meant for the hidden world to be exposed. Kneeland's narrative weaves an invaluable text, which I reproduce. A madam's offer to sell young girls on "bargain night" was a shocking revelation in 1917, just as it is today. The factual descriptions and detailed statistics are invaluable in establishing the true depth of *the social ill*.

I have remained faithful to the sources; however, judicious editing was necessary, especially of the voluminous grand jury and trial testimony. The scholar intent on studying the documents in the Lucania File must have the precious gifts of time and patience. The trial testimony of major witnesses is found in Boxes 51–56.

The success of Thomas E. Dewey and his staff in developing a solid case against the members of the vice underworld in a matter of months is astounding. Dewey had the added burden of depending on the testimony of underworld denizens, devious and morally corrupt, but ultimately knowledgeable about the illegal realm in which they existed.

While Luciano's trial provides a great deal of information, the raw record developed by Dewey's staff establishes numerous crimes beyond prostitution, especially narcotics trafficking, a major source of revenue for Luciano. The records were impermissible in court, though the reports stand as significant historical documents, shedding light on organized crime. The records also bring a human face to the bookers, prostitutes, pimps, thieves, and hoodlums, a linkage of crime which became the combination. The documents contain poignant scenes: Young Paul being rejected by his mother, who prefers instead a brutal pimp; wiretaps revealing a young prostitute who dutifully sends money to her parents; Cokey Flo writing warm letters to Barent Ten Eyck, only to betray him soon after; Lucky Luciano, finally attaining a position of wealth, residing at the plush Barbizon-Plaza, but forced to live under a false name. I give readers the records as they exist; not a single line of dialogue has been invented.

Despite the voluminous material presented, some mysteries remain. What became of Lucky's vast wealth? Dewey could never find any bank accounts; so Lucky cleverly managed to hide his cash. Funds were delivered to Italy after his deportation; however, the likelihood exists that he spent money as fast as it came in. Luciano was a gambling addict and, in my opinion, high sums were wagered at the tracks and in card games.

And what of the trio's betrayal? Did Flo, Mildred, and Nancy tell the truth during the trial? In my estimate, they did. The trio had direct access to important members of the combination. The women were the mistress-prostitutes of Lucky's underlings. Historians have never challenged the guilty verdicts of combination members. But Lucky Luciano's involvement was questioned decades later by crime writers, those who echoed Joe Valachi: "Charley Lucky wasn't no pimp. He was a boss." Lucky was, without question, a *padrone*, a crime boss, but he always accepted illegal funds. Nancy Presser said Lucky had been the pimp of Betty Cook. If Nancy wished to lie, why not just invent a prostitute? Betty Cook actually existed. The defense team located Betty Cook. Although she denied Nancy's story, she never testified in court, subjected to a withering cross-examination under oath. Like the women, Cook was likely terrified and denied the truth. The records make it clear that the combination never made a lot of money on the prostitution takeover; nevertheless, Luciano gave his approval for underlings to organize the bookers and prostitutes. Lucky expected to eventually make money. The *padrone* was indeed guilty.

Is it possible that Nancy Presser embellished details? Lucky's telephone records fail to indicate that he had called Nancy at the Emerson Hotel. Yet, Nancy testified Lucky had called her. Could he have telephoned her from a different phone? Or did she invent the visits to his apartment, as the defense claimed? Nancy certainly knew more details than the other informants.

Weighing the evidence raises questions. If the women were outright liars they could have concocted far more damaging circumstances, such as seeing Lucky being handed prostitution money. The trio's stories are highly credible; in fact, as Dewey stressed, the jury believed their testimony.

Thomas E. Dewey has slipped to a minor place in history, mainly remembered as the boyish, mustachioed candidate who lost the presidential election to Harry Truman. But Dewey deserves to be hailed as a great American. He was the special prosecutor of the people, and he served the honest citizenry well, very well. At a time when New York was overwhelmed by organized crime and corrupt politicians he brought hope and action. He restored confidence to New Yorkers and inspired the nation. Dewey's prosecution of Lucky Luciano remains one of his greatest achievements. The Lucania File contains a statement that "this collection exists in the hope that the records of the Luciano trial may be presented for all time." And rightly so.

Americans of Italian heritage can only cringe at the atrocious conduct of Italian criminals, the gangsters who terrorized their fellow immigrants and shamed decent newcomers in America. Films and novels have romanticized the Mafia; contemporary citizens lose sight of the fact that the Mafia was nothing more than a loose confederation of criminal gangs, devoid of real honor, and unified only in self-preservation, greed, and brutality; fiction has created historical confusion and moral ambiguity. Hopefully, this non-fiction text penetrates the deep shadows and exposes brutes such as Charley Lucky, Jimmy, Davie, a triumvirate of terror. The members of the combination were vermin; their societal transgressions merited prison.

Let the historical record demonstrate the integrity of Italian-American John Romano, an average citizen who refused to be intimidated by threats from well-protected madams. "I am not tough," he told investigators. However, Romano was the epitome of citizen courage. He boldly challenged the political corruption that protected the vice underworld. Dewey understood Romano's basic desire to live in a decent neighborhood. The citizen and the prosecutor shared a common vision for a stable and moral society; it was that simple.

Dewey risked his life to defend the rights of citizens. New Yorkers should erect a statue in his memory in Times Square to recall when mobsters lurked in the shadows, eager to bribe, extort, and murder. But Dewey prosecuted thugs and crooked politicians who violated the social contract. As governor he was just as fearless when he endorsed anti-discrimination measures long before the federal civil rights laws of the sixties. A statue of Thomas E. Dewey would indeed be a fitting tribute to a fine public servant.

Preface

On a gray winter afternoon I visited St. John's Cemetery. The realm of the dead was shrouded by a faint mist. Within the cemetery all was quiet. There was a sense of separateness from the outer world. Etched on marble and granite stones were the last remembrances of those who sleep the eternal sleep. The trail to the boss of bosses led to the Lucania mausoleum. Lucky's real name was Salvatore Lucania. Behind the bronze doors he was hidden in a stone crypt; the drama of his life was buried with him but not the legend. Mobsters have ghostly footsteps that echo through time. The public is entranced by the fictive and the factual. Exactly who was Lucky Luciano?

For decades, Feder and Joesten's *The Luciano Story* (1954) has been the main source of the career of the infamous gangster, but the book has questionable value. Lucky was supposedly present at the Nuova Villa Tamaro Restaurant when Giuseppe Masseria ate his last meal. "A little cards, Giusepp?" asked Lucky. When bullets ripped into Joe the Boss, Lucky was in the washroom; at least this is how Feder and Joesten told the tale. But the reporters of the day make no mention of any final conversations between Lucky and Joe; nor do they write that Luciano was anywhere near the restaurant. If a reliable source provided the authors with the information, nothing is documented. Or was the line simply invented? In *The Valachi Papers*, published in 1968, Luciano was again supposedly in the Villa Tamaro when police arrived. But newspaper accounts report that only the hats and coats of Masseria's unidentified companions were found. Valachi certainly had insight into criminal conversations and activities pertaining to his own crimes, but Valachi loses credibility when his version is weighed against the published news accounts and the unpublished police reports.

In 1974 George Wolf and Joseph DiMona produced *Frank Costello*, a slim but interesting biography that lacks a bibliography or sources. According to

1

Wolf and DiMona's text, Lucky was present when Joe the Boss was executed. "Got a deck of cards?" he supposedly asked a bartender. The comment comes very close to Feder and Joesten's "A little cards, Giusepp?" Did Wolf hear the words from Lucky's lips, or was the source *The Luciano Story*? If Wolf knew so much, why couldn't he supply more conversation than a single line? The most solid source is the police file on Salvatore Lucania. There is no mention in the police files of Luciano being present at the murder of Joe Masseria.

The historian delving into the past must establish a foundation for judgment. Since the voices of the distant decades are stilled, only the paper trail remains. Sid Feder and Joachim Joesten and others had limited access to important documents, but the definitive archival files are now examined in detail for the first time. Even though Luciano is discussed in political books about Thomas E. Dewey, Luciano's prosecutor, most portraits of the mobster are merely general accounts of his life; existing texts certainly do not descend to the lowest depths of the underworld to present the full picture of the vice takeover. After Dewey's death in 1971 articles posited an unsettling condition: there was sympathy for Luciano, a deported exile who claimed that he was the innocent victim of a Dewey frame-up. In addition, the film *Hoodlum* depicted Dewey as a corrupt prosecutor, an accusation that was vigorously refuted by Dewey's family as fiction.

Dewey's case against Luciano depended on the testimony of underworld figures, specifically, a knowledgeable core of pimps and prostitutes. Florence Brown, Mildred Balitzer, and Nancy Presser led sordid lives, but their court testimony carried the most weight in placing Lucky at the pinnacle of the vice chain. The trio later recanted their testimony. Why?

History is made by the actions of individuals; usually, it is the powerful and prominent who receive the most attention. This book explores the vice underworld, a shadowy region where the decadent did as they pleased. They had their own reasons for societal transgression and, even though they were condemned for their deeds, they have a voice in this narrative. When questioned by authorities in the Luciano prosecution, those in the vice chain were allowed to speak—combination members, underlings, bookers, madams, pimps, and prostitutes—all had an opportunity to disclose their past lives, to explain what brought them to such degradation. Their stories are tragic yet fascinating. Most citizens will never engage in such lifestyles, but we are curious. About Dewey, much is known; unfortunately, a great deal has been forgotten since the glory days of 1936.

The Lucania File in the New York City Municipal Archives is quite voluminous. Luciano's trial alone comprises approximately seven thousand pages. In addition, there are thousands of pages of archival material relating to the investigation and prosecution of the combination. These documents include wiretap transcripts, police reports, witness interviews, extradition papers, grand jury testimony, defense appeals, and miscellaneous documents. The Lucania File is stored in boxes that lack specific organization. I personally analyzed each document in every box. I searched for bits and pieces to augment the larger picture of a fascinating chapter in American history. I made over six thousand photocopies to capture the essence of the prosecution, arrest, and conviction of the combination.

The purpose of this book is to provide a full and accurate history of the investigation, arrest, and conviction of Lucky Luciano. Due to the seamy nature of the trial, portions of witness testimony were omitted in reportage, but it is amazing how much actually did reach newsprint. Luciano's trial was one of the most sensational courtroom dramas of the 1930s. I have made a conscientious effort to obtain and convey the factual evidence. I have examined over 40,000 archival documents. I also examined numerous books and articles. A debt of gratitude is owed to the great reporters of the past. I have relied on their journalistic probity to reach conclusions. I was not there, so I present the reproduction of the written word. I give you what I uncovered. The silent mausoleum reveals no secrets; the blood-stained trail leads to archival shadows. This is where the truth hides.

We have come to the place
  Where I said
You will see sorrowful people
  Who have lost the good of their intellect
                              — Virgil

And then he took my hand
  With a confident face that comforted me
And drew me within that secret
  Unknown world
                              — Dante
                        Inferno, Canto III

*   *   *

Mildred Curtis, Tommy's seventeen-year-old addict-mistress, wanted to know how "Abie the Jew" got in the Combination: "I thought the Combination was only of Italians."

"We let Abie in because we needed the money and he had the money to give."

Tommy told Mildred of the secret narcotic shipments and occasionally asked favors: "I got about seven ounces of heroin. I want you to take it uptown."

Introduction:
Charley Lucky

Anybody might be assaulted

On the night of October 16, 1929, a Staten Island police officer stood watch on Prince's Bay Avenue. Just before midnight, the guard observed someone staggering along the sidewalk; closer inspection revealed a gruesome sight. Beneath a dead white face was a crimson throat. The bloody man had walked almost a mile, from a desolate strand near the waterfront, he hoarsely whispered. Though somewhat dazed, he tried to explain. The roar of the surf had awakened him from a nightmare. He discovered that his throat had been cut. When the officer reached for a telephone, the victim removed a wad of bills from his pocket. Though dripping blood, the man waved fifty dollars, just for the cop to let him disappear. Instead, the walking corpse was taken into custody and transported to Richmond Hospital where a surgeon stitched the deep facial and throat wounds. Afterward, at the 123rd precinct station, detective Charles Schley questioned the bandaged victim as curious officers listened. He identified himself as Charles Luciano and told his story. While waiting for a girl in Manhattan, around 6:30 P.M., he had been abducted. A limousine with curtained windows rolled to the curb. Three men stepped out and handcuffs were suddenly snapped on his wrists. At gunpoint he was forced inside the car; adhesive tape sealed his eyes and lips. Fists beat him into unconsciousness. He awoke in the woods near Huguenot Beach. The assailants were all strangers.[1] The police smiled knowingly. Luciano had been taken for a ride. In most death drives the trip was one way, but he had survived. The police believed he had been taught a brutal lesson. The victim became angry.

"Don't you cops lose any sleep over it," Luciano sneered. "I'll attend to

5

this thing myself."[2] Detective Schley understood the criminal code of silence: thugs kept their mouths shut because *squealers* died fast. Luciano said nothing more.

The officers located a police file on Salvatore Lucania. Informers said he was a killer, a gunman whose dirty deeds were undertaken in darkness. In the sunlight he called himself Charley Luciano and assumed different identities: salesman, sportsman and chauffeur. But the truth was in the file. Luciano had been arrested for selling morphine. He was a close friend of notorious gangster Jack "Legs" Diamond; both hoodlums were former bodyguards of murdered gambler Arnold Rothstein. Luciano had been a pal of Thomas "Fatty" Walsh, too, until Fatty was shot to death during a card game in Coral Gables. Known in the underworld as Charley Lucky, Luciano was a driver and gunman for Giuseppe "Joe the Boss" Masseria, one of the most vicious gangsters in New York City.

Detectives searched the area where Luciano had been dumped, which was near the Terra Marine Inn. They discovered pieces of adhesive tape saturated with blood. In Manhattan, at the corner of Third Avenue and Fiftieth Street, shopkeepers knew nothing about the kidnapping, but informants whispered to police that Charley Lucky had been beaten by drug racketeers. Charley had failed to pay $10,000 in a narcotics deal that went sour. Legs Diamond was also involved in the aborted transaction. The abductors had been searching for Legs Diamond, but Lucky wouldn't talk, so he was punished. The police decided to administer a lesson of their own. Luciano was arrested and led to a jail cell, stunned to discover he was being charged with auto theft; bail was set at $25,000. Despite the turn of events, Luciano maintained an icy calm. He had slipped through police nets before and had a peasant-like belief in his good fortune. On the morning of October 29, the prisoner was escorted to the Staten Island Courthouse. Members of the grand jury watched as the kidnap victim entered. They observed a dark complexioned Sicilian with slick, pomaded hair; ugly scars marred his neck and chin. An eyelid drooped slightly, the result of the slashing. Was he simply an innocent victim? Or was he hiding his involvement in a narcotics deal?

District Attorney Albert C. Fach prepared to grill the 33-year-old hoodlum whose face was a mask of subdued ferocity. Fach was a seasoned prosecutor; there was the possibility Luciano would trip and stumble, spilling the truth about his kidnapping. Why did he call himself Luciano, he was asked. Since people mangled his true name, he told the court he preferred to be known as Charles Luciano. He swore to tell the truth. After the oath he sat before the jurors.

"Have you ever been known by any other name?" asked Fach.[3]

He had a nickname, he admitted, "Lucky ... Charles Lucky."

Luciano testified that he was unmarried and lived alone in Ulster County, though his parents resided at 265 East Tenth Street in Manhattan. When he gave his occupation as a chauffeur, driving his own 1928 Lincoln, the district attorney smelled a lie.

"Have you a taxi license?"

"No."

"Then you have been violating the law, haven't you?"

"I don't know."

Fach demanded to know the names of his clients.

"I couldn't answer that."

How exactly did he earn his living? Luciano responded that he owned a restaurant at 232 West 52nd Street, but it had closed eight months earlier. The witness repeated the story of the assault but added details. While waiting for Jennie, a girl he had met an hour earlier, a trio claiming to be policemen kidnapped him. District Attorney Fach was curious about Jennie. "What was the purpose of making the date, friendship?"

"Yes."

"For sexual purposes?"

"I don't know, for company's sake."

The prosecutor asked about the three hundred dollars in his possession during the beating, as well as an expensive watch. The witness displayed the watch with its diamond-studded platinum chain.

"What did you pay for it?"

"About four hundred dollars."

"So we can eliminate any thought that their purpose was to commit robbery. Is that correct?"

"Yes."

Luciano professed bafflement over the kidnapping. He insisted that he was not involved in any crimes and had no enemies. The district attorney queried him about the arrest for narcotics.

"What was the nature of these drugs?"

"I don't understand."

"You know what I mean."

"That is too far back."

"Convicted of selling them?"

"Yes."

"Where?"

"Pennsylvania."

"Sent to jail."

"Yes."

"From where?"

"New York."

The witness admitted that he had been arrested for carrying a loaded revolver. Though he had a gun permit, he could not recall who issued the papers.

"Why did you have to have a revolver?"

"For protection."

"Did you suspect you might be assaulted?"

"Anybody might be assaulted."

Luciano discussed his residence in Ulster County. The house was on Tucker Avenue and a family named Skip looked after it while he was away. He denied telling the police he would deal with the assailants in his own way. He assured the district attorney he had always given his true name when interrogated by law officers.

Fach hammered away, trying to squeeze information from the reluctant witness with the weak memory. Once again, the D.A. probed Lucky's income. Where did his money originate?

From the failed restaurant, he explained. Oh, there was a partner, Ignatz Coppa, but the place had gone out of business.

The restaurant was probably a speakeasy, noted the district attorney, who then cast his final net.

"Engage in the liquor traffic?"

"No."

The interrogation had been a futile fishing trip for the law. The mystery of Luciano's kidnapping remained unsolved, at least publicly. As for the auto theft charge, Magistrate Kroak dismissed the complaint due to lack of evidence. The reluctant witness vanished from the courtroom. His good fortune had returned. Despite the humiliating abduction, beating, and scars, the gunman's ascent to power was underway. Newspaper accounts of the death drive had brought unwanted attention for the gunman, but he would return to the shadows where he worked his dirty deeds. Charley Lucky had ruthless ambition. Associates heard his boast that he could outsmart dumb cops any day, and he had a plan to reach the throne of crime. Lucky Luciano would become the most feared mobster in New York City and the sultan of vice. Narcotics trafficking, loan sharking, sales of stolen property and prostitution would bring him enormous wealth. But prostitution would lead to his downfall. Yet, how could he foresee that in 1929? Prostitution in New York City had been around for a long time. Despite the many attempts to end *the trade*, men wanted women for hire, to service their sexual needs. And thousands of women, whether by choice or necessity, complied. *The trade* always flourished.

CHAPTER ONE

City of Vice

I am what men have made me

From Colonial times prostitution had flourished in New York City. By 1869 there were estimates of five hundred brothels. The police did not bother the bawdy houses unless they disturbed the peace or became a public nuisance. While the brothels did a thriving business, the streets offered the cheaper rates.[1]

Before midnight, men congregated at the corner of Houston and Greene streets and observed the parade of "prowling prostitutes."[2] For 50 cents a woman would escort a client into a nearby garret or cellar. But at the corner of Amity and Greene streets the *night-walkers* were more refined in appearance and dress. They were easy to detect. The women lacked male escorts and gave men a direct stare, a sexual leer that invited advances. Rather than the blunt invitation to accompany them home, as the inexpensive whores offered, these women politely asked, "How are you, my dear?" These women were more expensive, since they usually rented a pleasant room in a modest hotel.

There were other vice neighborhoods. Women paraded at Broadway and Washington Place or at Broadway and 24th Street. These women were attractive, stepping quickly, without male escorts, looking neither left nor right. It was contrary to social custom for women to be out alone at night, unless there was an emergency. Thus, a gentleman could offer to escort an unaccompanied *lady* to an unknown destination. But when she stopped before a door, the prostitute revealed herself. There would be an invitation to accompany her inside. From the hallway, the woman entered a private room. Once inside, she locked the door and the cool reserve vanished. After the sexual encounter, the man left the bed and searched his clothes for payment. Often, the client discovered he had no money. He had been fleeced. An accomplice, known as a *creep,* had slipped through a wall panel and searched his clothes. The prostitute and thief had robbed another victim. The disreputable circumstances prevented complaints to authorities, especially if the man was married.

A common ruse was for the woman, after having turned the lock, to become frightened when a knock boomed. She expressed terror that it was her husband or lover. Feigned conversation occurred between the woman and her accomplice, while the victim hid, only to discover that once the pair had disappeared, so had his clothes and money.

The wary male, to prevent trickery, preferred the parlor houses. In Greene and Wooster Streets several blocks were filled with popular brothels that boasted young and refined women. Some were married and worked to supplement family income; others were girls driven by destitution to sell themselves to a casual buyer. A young girl, captured in a raid, told police, "I am what men have made me."[3] Those who were convicted in court were sent to the workhouse. Over the decades, citizens tried to assist prostitutes. As early as 1833, the Magdalen Society started a home for those who wanted to leave the business. But *the trade* flourished. Without a political vote, education, and economic independence, many women were forced to accept menial positions and, disgusted with their poverty, prostitution was always a lure, and vice agents exploited misery.

The immorality of New York City aroused the wrath of Anthony Comstock, a reformer who became famous as the secretary of the New York Society for the Suppression of Vice. In 1868 Comstock discovered that a large number of obscene books and pamphlets were being sold through the mail. Bald and portly, with mutton-chop whiskers, Comstock became a familiar face in the state legislature as he successfully lobbied for anti-obscenity laws. The legislature passed an act that incorporated the Society as a legal body with the power to enforce vice laws. Comstock began a long career as an investigator responsible for numerous prosecutions. In 1873 he lobbied Congress for severe federal legislation; five laws were passed that rendered illegal the importation, dissemination, and purchase of obscene articles by mail. Comstock was named a special agent by the postmaster general. In 1878 Comstock entered a brothel on Greene Street and witnessed sexual acts, known in the trade as *circuses.* Comstock was shocked when three women disrobed before patrons and placed "their faces and mouths between one another's legs."[4] The Society sought to enforce laws eliminating not only obscene literature and photographs but prostitution, gambling, and lotteries. In 1877 the Society for the Prevention of Crime was organized. There were numerous organized efforts to eliminate brothels and gambling dens. The most famous crusade was led by the Reverend Charles H. Parkhurst in 1893. The minister blasted the police for failure to prosecute vice.

When the new century came, not much had changed. In 1907 investigators determined that brothel income was substantial. In fact, a single house with 35 women raked in $3,500 per week. The same year, at the age of 14, entertainer Jimmy Durante started his career as a pianist in a Bowery saloon, "run for the boys with five finger marks on the hip. You know the la-de-da lads who are that way about each other."[5] Durante only worked a few nights, until a half dozen cops stormed the saloon and began smashing the patrons and furniture. Known as "Ragtime Jimmy," the young man continued to perform in Bowery and Coney Island dives. The saloons offered cheap food, but the main attraction was booze and prostitutes. Nearly every waiter in Coney Island had girls working for him. If the women didn't deliver enough money each night, they got a beating. Durante was nightly solicited for money, so a girl could keep a pimp from pounding her: "There wasn't anything I could do to change the system, so if I wasn't broke I'd hand her the two dollars."

By 1908, Comstock was still active. In that year alone the post office assigned 235 cases for obscenity investigation. From 1873 to 1908 the Society's records reveal authorities had seized 2,658,687 images and photographs regarded as obscene; 7,768 charms, such as medallions and knives, were confiscated due to microscopic obscene pictures. In addition, 129,720 advertisements about to be mailed had been seized. Those targeted for material numbered 1,344,318. The Society arranged for the prosecution of 721 individuals under federal law and 2,551 under state law; 195 were released by magistrates, but 2,408 were convicted or pleaded guilty; 2,015 received prison sentences and 66 fled. Fines amounted to $219,961.25. Nevertheless, despite its many successes, abundant vice remained in New York City.

In 1908 the Bureau of Social Hygiene attacked prostitution as a result of a special grand jury investigation into "the white slave traffic." Two years later, the Committee of Fourteen issued a research survey. The paper began with the premise that it was possible for reformers to rid the streets and tenements of *the social evil*. The same year Congress passed the White Slave Traffic Act in the wake of nationwide news about forced prostitution. The bill's sponsor, James R. Mann, a Chicago Republican, designed the law to prosecute men who transported women across state lines for sexual activity. In 1912 anti-vice activists sent members throughout New York City to document immorality. The investigation was led by George Kneeland, a reformer who had previously directed a vice commission in Chicago. The public was shocked by the meticulous report. In Manhattan alone there were 142 parlor houses. The investigation detailed the brothels: 34 locations were five and ten cent houses; 20 houses charged 50 cent fees; 80 were one dollar houses; six were two dollar houses; several were unknown. Many were located on Sixth and Seventh Avenues and in nearby residential side streets.

Below East 14th Street there were many 50 cent houses with low ceilings and tiny windows. A *lighthouse* stood outside and procured trade and shouted warnings if police approached. Lower East Side tenements had basement *cider stubs* where immigrant girls worked as waitresses. They sold glasses of cider and soft drinks to men, but the real business came in propositions to enter back rooms. In the sex business a moneymaker was known as a *star*: "The secret of their popularity lies frequently in the perverse practices to which they resort," reported an investigator. To tally customer encounters, a madam punched a hole in a square piece of cardboard; on a specific date, July 9, 1912, the highest number was 30. Clients were assured the girls had no venereal diseases and medical certificates attested to the good health of the women, but the documents were usually worthless, concluded the investigators.

Business rivalry was intense, as parlor house madams, who passed along bribes, complained to police about common streetwalkers and phony massage businesses. The madams were adept at maintaining *the trade*, apprising regular customers of new selections by mailing advertisements: "Beautiful Spring Stock on View." Business cards were distributed at factory entrances, trade shows, and department stores. Cabbies lured customers to vice houses, whispering, "I know where there are a lot of chickens." Many girls lived at home, but never revealed to families their true profession.

In mid–July an investigator entered a building on West 28th Street; 264 men sat in sweltering heat awaiting their moment of pleasure. The madam had left for a resort and a housekeeper was in charge. The owner was furious because prostitutes were not available the previous night. The fierce heat kept them away, replied the housekeeper. The brothel owner, fat and well-dressed, cursed and tossed a teacup at the housekeeper. "The trade must be taken care of!" he shouted.

Circuses were still available in the parlor houses, despite Comstock's earlier shock. George Kneeland could only relate that "these exhibitions were too vulgar and degrading to be described." They were also expensive, at $50 a session. The women were young, refined, and supposedly without disease. Lavish dresses and jewelry gave the women the image of elegance. In a parlor house in West 15th Street a rich client stayed for four days and spent six hundred dollars, wrote an investigator. In Diamond Fanny's house on West 40th Street all types of women were available — short ones, tall ones, thin or stout, and "just kids."

On a chilly February night an investigator was driven to an exclusive house by a chauffeur who received a commission for every customer he delivered. A maid in a white apron ushered the arrival to "the stock." The prospective client observed plush carpets, gold-trimmed furniture, and expensive paintings. In the library the customer was offered "new books" and expensive bottles of wine. If requested, drugs could be found. Once in the parlor, the client was shown fifteen young and attractive women, attired in silk evening gowns. The madam approached him, "Every Saturday night is bargain night, and next Saturday I shall have twelve young girls and guarantee them not to be over sixteen years of age. Come early and get one of the bargains."

At *call houses* clients were shown a photograph album. Each picture had detailed physical measurements and prices. The girls were summoned by telephone. Madams were well practiced in luring young women, noted investigators. Lonely girls were spotted in restaurants and offices. A conversation led to friendship, theatre tickets, fine clothes, and then business opportunities for pleasure and money. During the probe an investigator documented how a madam had telephoned a girl named Irene, a girl who had a day job in a Brooklyn department store. When she arrived, Irene revealed that she had only been in the business a few months. Her sweetheart, a shipping clerk, was unaware of Irene's second job. Irene said she lived with her aunt and dutifully arrived home each night at 10:00 P.M. The investigator asked for another girl. Margie spoke up and offered "a kid" for ten dollars. Margie lived at home in Brooklyn. Her parents thought she was employed in a clothing store. The kid was her sister.

Many hotels were vice centers. In 1912 investigators examined smaller, ten-room hotels, those advertised as *for men only*; 103, nearly a fourth, were identified as "assignation parlors." A prostitute booked a room for two dollars, and was usually handed back a dollar for being a regular guest. There were numerous incidents of robbery. Prostitute-pickpockets, called *gun molls*, lifted wallets from their sleeping clients and slipped away.

Prostitution was rampant in the massage business. Anti-vice spies documented three hundred massage parlors in Manhattan, many on the upper floors of buildings on Sixth Avenue and Columbus Avenue. Newspaper advertisements sought young female employees; with fees and tips, the female prospects were told, they could "coin money."

George Kneeland personally investigated a delicatessen on Seventh Avenue; it was a gathering place for madams, prostitutes, pimps, and lighthouses. There were loud quarrels over profits, purchases, trades, and share selling. Upstairs, the owner's wife cared for the children. A 17-year-old daughter, dressed in white, conversed with a handsome procurer, and was fawned over by the madams.

Handsome pimps easily ensnared victims, asserted Kneeland. Polite and well-mannered, the suave seduced the naïve into *the trade.* Pimps, known as *cadets,* could be found in cigar stores, pool rooms, and cheap cafés. They awaited telephone messages from their girls or planned *lineups,* the process of breaking in *young chickens.* Prostitutes with money strutted wherever men gathered. They paid young boys to drum up trade and collect fees. Many whores and pimps had been childhood friends; if one succeeded, the other joined the business, noted an investigator. Hairstylists sent attractive young women to madams, who were always in search of new flesh. At a dance a teenage girl gave a boy a card advertising a party. When the card was folded it formed a sexually suggestive title and picture, and was actually an advertisement for a brothel. In the Tenderloin District, between West 24th and West 40th Streets, 15 business entrepreneurs formed a *combine.* Their financial venture controlled 30 houses.

In 1912 George Kneeland determined the number of prostitutes in New York City was 14,926. The report stated that 6,759 women worked the streets; the remainder preferred parlor houses. Investigators questioned 1,106 women regarding their native countries; 762 said they had been born in America; 344 were foreign-born. Another group of 487 women were asked about their employment history, the responses revealed that 117 had been department store clerks; 28 store clerks; 25 office workers; 31 stenographers; 9 telephone operators; 72 had been on the stage and 16 still worked as actresses. Brutal labor conditions forced some to choose a whore's life. As a former servant said, "I'd rather do this than be kicked around like a dog in a kitchen by some woman who calls herself a lady." Sixty-two percent of the women were white, 13 percent colored, 25 percent were immigrants; 11 percent of the street prostitutes were illiterate.

In 1912 domestics earned $5.55 per week, plus food and lodging; factory workers earned between $3 and $17 per week; shop girls made $8.24 per week; teachers earned $80 a month. Former domestic servants raised their weekly income from $26 to $38 by selling their bodies. The average girl was 17 and life as a professional prostitute was approximately five years. In the lower houses, the 50-cent dives, the clients were coal haulers, soldiers, sailors, truck drivers, and longshoremen. The next level, the one and two dollar houses, were popular with clerks, barbers, tailors, waiters, and bank messengers. Prostitutes usually engaged in 10 and 15 sexual encounters a day. In 1912 six percent of all hospital patients had illnesses caused by venereal diseases; these were documented as 5,380 patients.

In New York City compulsory prostitution was punished by a minimum fine of $1,000 and a maximum of $5,000, with a prison term of one to three years. Those convicted of "seduction under promise of marriage" received a similar punishment.

According to legal statutes, children under 16 could not enter dance halls, saloons, or movie theatres. Minors were prohibited from working more than 54 hours per week or more than nine hours in a single day. But young boys ignored laws in the vice underworld. Late at night, delivery boys often brought alcohol to parlor houses, arriving with quarts of Mumms Champagne, and a bill for $2.70. The boys received big tips from the houses, from 25 to 50 cents. Many delivery boys became *steerers* and distributed cards for brothels. But the reformers were determined to end *the social evil*.

The Prophylaxis Society, the National Purity League, the Consumers League, Travelers Aid, immigrant aid groups, and state probation associations worked to end prostitution. The Committee of Fourteen and the National Vigilance League, both comprised of prominent citizens, sought legislative action. Other active groups were the County Medical Society, the Society for the Prevention of Cruelty to Children, and the Society for the Prevention of Crime. Laws were passed that made tenement owners subject to arrest if prostitution existed on the premises; if convicted, the landlords were sentenced to six months in the workhouse and made to pay a fine of $1,000.

Rules were strict for police officers; precinct captains had to report all disorderly houses; furthermore, captains were expected to charge with neglect any patrolman who allowed prostitution while on duty. Despite the anti-prostitution laws, the Committee of Fourteen discovered that brothels proliferated. It was apparent there was minimal enforcement. Not only were police officials being bribed, but there was also an elaborate payoff system; sums ranged from $400 to $600 per month for protection. The elite houses slipped bribes to officers, with a hierarchy of payment: detectives, $205; patrolmen, $184; inspectors, $100; sergeants, $50. A former police commissioner estimated that 1,500 to 2,000 officers were corrupt; this amounted to 15 percent of the force. Failure to report a disorderly house was common, but neglecting to report a dead cat resulted in a reprimand. The parlor houses were usually left alone. Despite laws and occasional raids, reformers were appalled by how little had changed and blamed police corruption.

The reformers were also critical of dance halls, especially those where liquor was served. Dancers were prohibited from sitting at tables, unless drinks were ordered. Minors were usually present. Seventy-five dance resorts were investigated; only five were deemed to be reputable. Though well-lit, with good music, and excellent dance floors, many halls were frequented by procurers. At night crowds flocked to the dance halls for excitement, to dance *the spiel*, a risque favorite. Expert dancers were known as *spielers*. Due to the "twirling and twisting" between men and women the Committee found *the spiel* objectionable. Dances lasted from three to five minutes. There were also female *spielers*, usually under 20 years of age; they were regarded as immoral. A girl seeking romance often met a pimp. From dance halls, girls were often lured to nearby hotels and, for some, to a life of prostitution.

Dance academies, where most clients were teenagers, were condemned by the more severe moralists. On the East Side, beginners in dance schools paid $5 for 24 lessons. The Dancing Teachers Association despised the academies because "*the bear hug* and the proximity of faces during a waltz are frowned upon. In the first place they are unhygienic."

Petty thieving in a street gang was risky and often resulted in arrest, but pimping was easy money and jail time was almost unknown. In three years, from the passage of stiff laws from 1906 to 1909, 265 men were arrested and prosecuted for living off the proceeds of prostitutes, but only two were charged with compulsory prostitution and subjected to the most severe penalty. During five months of 1908, 1,217 women were arrested for prostitution. The reformers also condemned abortion.

In 1906 a report on midwives stated that 100,000 abortions were performed annually in the city. Prior to 1908, the Society for the Suppression of Vice had destroyed 42,233 boxes of pills and powders used by abortionists. In 1908, 53,000 circulars, and 142,000 booklets that advertised abortion pills were confiscated, along with 5,572 boxes of pills. What the authorities removed from drug stores were pills of tanzy, pennyroyal, and ergot. Some abortion pills were marketed as *Elamef* in drug stores, a sly method of alerting buyers, as it was *female* spelled backwards. From 1908 to 1910 there had been 25 abortion cases in court with five convictions. The maximum sentence could result in 20 years in prison.

Prostitution and drugs were inextricably intertwined, believed social reformers. New York City had both opium dens and drug stores dispensing narcotics. The sale of cocaine brought a felony conviction, punishable by a maximum sentence of a year in prison and a fine of one thousand dollars. During the first six months of 1909 there were 23 prosecutions for possession of illegal drugs. One individual was fined, 12 were sent to prison, three went to a reformatory, three were acquitted, one person disappeared, and three were given probation. The highest fine amounted to five hundred dollars.

A druggist on West 8th Street pleaded guilty to selling cocaine to an elderly man. He was fined $250 and sent to prison for five months. According to the Committee, drug use began with cigarettes, then came opium, easily found in the decadence of Chinatown.

The splendor and squalor of Chinatown began at Chatham Square, embracing Bayard, Doyer, and Mott Streets. Shortly before the Civil War, Orientals settled in the crooked, narrow, winding streets leading off from the Bowery. By 1890 there were one thousand Chinese residents. On Mott Street there was an abundance of *joss* houses, religious temples where candles burned on golden altars and guided spirits to the afterworld. In Chinatown crowds scurried to markets and bought dried fish, lichee nuts, water chestnuts, bamboo shoots, and fragrant teas. The smell of incense led to white-tiled entranceways where diners sat at mother-of-pearl topped tables beneath illuminated paper lanterns. Pigtailed waiters brought jasmine tea and ginger almond cakes. Doorways led to the underground world of gambling, illicit sex, and opium smoking. Criminals known as *highbinders* controlled crime and violence. Secret initiations were held. A new member knelt in silken robes, while a jeweled two handed sword was pressed against the throat. The neophyte pledged loyalty to the *tong*. Flowing robes with wide sleeves hid revolvers to be reached in seconds. Murders were common in Chinatown.

By the turn of the century, deadly battles were fought over control of fan-tan and pi-gow gambling. At the corner of Mott and Pell Streets, the On Leongs and the Hip Sings, rival tongs, battled for dominance. Red and white posters, covered with Chinese characters in orange and black, warned passersby whose territory they entered. Alleys in Chinatown led to opium dens where addicts could be found "hitting the pipe." Smokers were not only Chinese but young thrill seekers, many from prominent families, who identified themselves as "hop fiends" or "pleasure smokers." The opium rooms were lit by small candle lamps and were usually gloomy and filthy. Smokers eagerly reached for the black pill the size of a quarter. They retired to private cubicles to cook the molasses-like opium until it bubbled and swelled. Reclining comfortably, head placed squarely on a wooden block, the smoker sucked the ivory mouthpiece of the bamboo pipe and inhaled deeply until the heavy white smoke with a fruity odor transported them into a state of euphoria and contentment, a transcendent realm where dreams were wonderful, as a contemporary, but anonymous poem documents.

> *He owned houses and lots, cattle and sheep*
> *And a million ships that sailed on the deep*
> *He was king of the world, whom all obeyed*
> *And was in the most gorgeous garb arrayed...*
> *He had a thousand wives, all pretty and rare*
> *All dressed in the finest, with golden hair...*
> *He kept on dreaming, until he awoke*
> *Only to find he had run out of dope*[6]

The visions of pleasure ended all too soon and bitter craving began once again. "I've got the yen-yen terrible," was a common refrain of the addicted. Women would often disappear in the opium dens for weeks. When their money disappeared, they sold their bodies for the precious pipe.

By 1912 many opium smokers had switched to morphine injections. In 1914 the Harrison Narcotics Act ended the legal supply of opiates; addicts were now regarded as morally weak, rather than sick patients. Thereafter, the addicts could no longer obtain narcotics from licensed physicians and were driven to the streets for drugs. Whether it was narcotics, women, or stolen goods, the vice underworld was ready to do business.

CHAPTER TWO

Rise to Power

Little is known of the new boss

By the turn of the century, Mulberry Street was the heart of the Italian community. Beneath awning-covered pushcarts, vendors with oiled hair hawked fruit, vegetables, and clothing. The loud, rapid-fire voices of sellers and buyers pierced the air with haggling over prices. From cafes the scent of fresh bread and savory spices enticed customers. Along the street young men with dark moustaches admired passing beauties whose eyes sparkled. In the tenements above, dark faces watched the crowd. From a window a man would extend his fingers, another man below understood — a secret code of communication closed to outsiders. On religious days Mulberry was decorated with colored lights. Priests led processions and bestowed blessings; the devout crossed themselves when the statue of the madonna passed. Around the corner was Chinatown; nearby, Delancey Street teemed with Jewish immigrants, but Mulberry, Baxter, and Elizabeth streets belonged to the Italians.

America was in the midst of industrial expansion, and unskilled labor was in demand. Immigrants came from northern and central Italy, but the poorer regions of southern Italy were drained. Between 1899 and 1910 there were 1,502,968 southern Italians who booked passage to America, streaming through Ellis Island and into tenements, often alongside family and friends from their native regions of Sicily, Abruzzia, Calabria, and Apuglia. Labor bosses welcomed the newcomers, poor Italians who often paid for a job in advance, then were lodged in a slum dwelling, and escorted to backbreaking jobs. But there were opportunities in New York City. Four thousand Italian laborers found work building Manhattan's subway system, removing tons of rock and soil all the way from Chambers Street to 59th Street. The Italian crews cheered when the subway system opened in 1904.[1]

America was the land of promise, the land of hope, and a country of freedom. The Society for the Protection of Italian Immigrants assisted new arrivals. Immigrants were greeted at Ellis Island by the society's representatives and escorted across Battery Park to an office at 17 Pearl Street. Representatives provided help to locate railway stations, reputable lodging houses, and relatives for a small fee. The Mulberry Community House at 256 Mott Street organized English classes. Prosperous Italian merchants operated grocery stores, butcher shops, restaurants, and ice and coal businesses. The Italian-American Society was founded to create friendship between nations. With headquarters in the plush Waldorf-Astoria, the society sponsored lectures, literary readings, awards for study abroad, art exhibits, and musical performances. The fame of Italian artists permeated New York cultural life. In 1908 Giulio Gatti-Casazza, formerly of La Scala in Milan, was appointed manager of the Metropolitan Opera Company. He brought Giacomo Puccini and Arturo Toscanini to the Met's stage, ensuring further glory for Italians.

While the surface world sparkled with the cultural gems, fostering admiration from Americans, the dark deeds of the criminal class generated hatred. The old customs remained, difficult to change, especially the ingrained idea of the *padrone,* the man of power and authority. And the Mafia, the secret society of Sicilian criminals, had already planted its poisonous roots in America. *La mala vita,* the criminal life, had thrived in western Sicily, around Palermo and Agrigento. The *stoppaglieri* was a hidden group that engaged in criminal activities. Sicilian peasants immigrated to America, Brazil, and Argentina, not only for a better life but to escape criminal extortionists at home. Americans were wary of immigrants but came to accept them, unless, like in New Orleans, community outrage brought mob violence.

On March 14, 1891, enraged citizens in New Orleans had stormed the Parish Prison, hanging and shooting Italian prisoners after a jury exonerated those accused of murdering David Hennessy, the respected chief of police. The mob was formed after a trial failed to convict Joseph Macheca, a wealthy fruit importer, and others of murder and conspiracy. The jury had been bought, shouted outraged citizens. According to the prosecutors, the terrible tragedy allegedly started in a feud between the Provenzano and Matranga stevedore firms. The Provenzano brothers had reaped the profits of unloading vessels on the docks of New Orleans; unexpectedly, shippers awarded the Matrangas the lucrative work. Joe Macheca supposedly controlled the docks. In July 1881, David Hennessy arrested Giuseppe Esposito, a notorious Sicilian bandit who had murdered six men and sliced off the ears of a kidnapped Englishman. Esposito had secretly lived in New Orleans until Antonio Labousse revealed the bandit's identity to authorities. Three days after Esposito's arrest, Labousse was shot dead. Years later, as Hennessey walked home late one night, shotguns cut him down. Was it a vendetta murder by Esposito friends? Or was it because Hennessy was thought to be sympathetic to the Provenzanos? Or did the police chief have other enemies? After the surprising verdict of innocence, a lynch mob stormed the prison and murdered eleven Italian prisoners, still in jail awaiting the dismissal of the charges. Joe Macheca died. The vigilantes murdered four men who were not charged with Hennessy's death. The Committee of Fifty was asked to investigate. The report concluded that "for years the Mafia has terrorized the Italian population of this city."[2] The Hennessey murder was never resolved, but the aftermath led Americans to fear the secret criminals known as *mafiosi.*

Joseph Petrosino met the same fate as David Hennessey. Born in Calabria, Petrosino became a famous detective in New York City. Petrosino had solved the horrific death of Benedetto Madonia. Ignazio Saietta, known as Lupo the Wolf, and his partner, Giuseppe Morello, were counterfeiters. The Morello brothers, along with the Saiettas, conducted a reign of terror. The gang made their headquarters in a saloon at 8 Prince Street. On April 14, 1903, the body of Benedetto Madonia was discovered in a sugar barrel. Detective Petrosino raided a cafe at 220 Elizabeth Street and the gang was caught with counterfeit currency. Over the years Petrosino arrested numerous Italian criminals. In 1909 the detective sailed to Italy to obtain criminal photographs and dossiers. While alone in Palermo, after dinner, Petrosino walked through Piazza Marina. An assassin stepped from the shadows and fired and murdered the detective.[3]

In America, the *Unione Siciliana* had originally been a fraternal organization, established in large cities to assist immigrants, but it was taken over by criminals. The *Unione* became synonymous with terror. Gangsters pounced, sucking money like parasites; victims who disregarded *omertà,* the conspiracy of silence, faced violence. Some things never change, shrugged the fearful; it was wiser not to complain, even though Little Italy stood in the shadow of police headquarters, located at 240 Centre Street. The police were avoided. Could the police protect citizens from having a child kidnapped? Or prevent a store from being burned? Or shield an honest man from a pistol fired in the dark? Terror protected the swaggering criminals, especially in the neighborhood where the Lucania family lived. Once a miner in Lercara Friddi, Antonio Lucania worked as a carpenter on New York's Lower East Side. The Lucania family resided at 511 East 13th Street, a dingy tenement building in a tough neighborhood. The Lucanias had abandoned Lercara Friddi, near Palermo, where the grim sulphur mines were the salvation of the impoverished village. Antonio and Rosa had three sons and two daughters. Salvatore was born on November 11, 1897. While attending Public School 19 Salvatore became known as Charley; the boy wanted to be an American, and a rich one.

Antonio clashed with his son, an adolescent who was always in trouble for truancy. Charley eventually served time in the Brooklyn Truant School in 1911. The following year, at age 14, he quit school to work as an errand boy and was later hired as a shipping clerk at the Goodman Hat Factory in Greene Street, for a salary of $5 a week. The clerk position would be the only honest employment he could ever verify.

The same year, the *New York Times* recounted the "Black Hand Crimes" in the Lucania neighborhood. There were murders, extortions, bombings, and kidnappings. Victims were sent threatening messages, accompanied by a drawing of a black fist, *la mano nera*, a symbol of brutality and terror. The Lucanias later moved to apartment five, at 265 East 10th Street, but the family was still in the slums. Detective Abe Shoenfeld reported that "Italian black-handers"[4] had hangouts at 418 and 430 East 11th Street. Tompkins Square Park was a meeting place for thieves. There were dozens of dope dealers in the area. Dreyfus Drug Store, at the corner of Second Avenue and 14th Street,

265 East 10th Street, New York City; the Lucania family lived in apartment 5.

sold illegal cocaine for 50 cents a package.

The shipping clerk had another life. He thrilled to the excitement of street craps as corner gamblers tossed the dice excitedly. His skill at winning brought the nickname Charley Lucky. Faintly pockmarked, with a lean body and dark curly hair, the teenager had a violent streak, which made him a leader. Charley observed the secret market in stolen goods, extortion threats, drug deals, brothels, and backroom gambling parlors. Crime paid handsomely. Pistols, blackjacks, and brass knuckles encouraged prosperity. The *wise guys* strutted like peacocks, dressed in fashionable clothes. Their pockets were filled with money from the empire of vice.

The law of the streets was enforced in slum neighborhoods; fight or expect a beating; neighborhood and nationality predominated. Teenage Italians chased and beat Jewish boys who strayed into their territory, unless tribute was paid. On one occasion, Lucky ran down a lone Jewish youth, but he admired the boy's fighting spirit, and a friendship developed. Meyer Lansky would remain a lifelong friend.[5]

At age 18, Charley tired of working as a shipping clerk. Beyond the grimy tenements was a luxurious life. Only *crumbs* labored. Luciano was associated with the Five Points Gang, led by Paolo Vaccarelli, a gangster later known as Paul Kelly. Al Capone and John Torrio also were involved with Vaccarelli. Paul Kelly later became the vice president of the International Longshoremen's Association (ILA).

Charley Lucky realized there was a fortune to be made in dope. He bought an eighth of a bottle of liquid morphine and sold small portions to an addict, who returned 15 times for more. It was easy money, until he was arrested. On June 27, 1916, Salvatore Lucania was convicted and sentenced to eight months at New Hampton Farms Reformatory.[6]

Once released, Charley, as he was always known to close friends, returned to the Goodman Hat Company, but two years later he walked away from the job. Charley and Joe Gould operated a floating craps game. They circulated the dice game through the city and upstate New York. Lucky was introduced to gambler and financier Arnold Rothstein, a mysterious figure who was rich from high stakes poker, sports betting, and narcotics deals. In Rothstein's card games a half-million dollars could change hands. Legs Diamond and Charley Lucky were hired as bodyguards, to make certain that no one robbed the wealthy gambler. The suave and successful Rothstein became their mentor. Rothstein was the son of a respected Jewish merchant. Dapper and charming, he allowed the press and public to observe the colorful side of his life. Beneath the gentle smile, Rothstein was ruthless. Lucky saw the man behind the mask, the shrewd criminal who raked in money from gambling and drug deals. Charley Lucky watched and learned. Opportunity was just around the corner.

January 15, 1920, was the last day for legal drinks. The following day, The Eighteenth Amendment, and the Prohibition Enforcement Act (Volstead Act) went into effect. The saloons closed, but a new industry began. The city's 15,000 pre–Prohibition taverns were soon replaced by 32,000 speakeasies. Bishop James Cannon denounced New York City as "Satan's seat."[7] Thirsty citizens shrugged. Lucky shrewdly scrambled to control grape growers in upstate New York. He hired the "the Bugs and Meyer mob" to protect booze trucks headed for the Lower East Side. Meyer Lansky and Ben "Bugsy" Siegel became bootleggers themselves. Franceso Costiglia, alias Frank Costello, was raking in thousands of dollars a week. Costello imported quality liquor from Nassau to the island of St. Pierre, off Newfoundland. Freighters unloaded fine whisky, liquid gold, purchased at eight dollars a case and sold for hundreds of dollars in the states. Costello was a bribe master who successfully bought high ranking Coast Guard officials.[8]

The Eighteenth Amendment created markets for the industrious. Grapes were fermented and pressed in the basement of tenement dwellings. Bottles of wine and alcohol were sold out of candy stores and other legitimate businesses. Lucky rented a garage at Centre and White Street. A phony real estate sign was painted on its window. The building was merely a front for the sale of booze and *swag,* merchandise stolen from trucks and warehouses, usually clothing and cigarettes. Along with his partner, John Manfredi, Lucky spread the word where cheap goods were available, and lots of booze as well. Along the streets of Kenmare, Broome, Grand, and Elizabeth bootleggers gathered to sell or exchange different brands of alcohol. A familiar face in the curb exchange trade was Tommy Pennochio, a rotund dealer known as Tommy the Bull. But the true overlord of the illegal trade was Giuseppe Masseria.

Joe the Boss was a vicious *padrone.* Born in Sicily, Masseria came to America at 16 and grew up in the Mulberry Bend district. He was first arrested for attempting to extort money from an Italian shopkeeper. His name became familiar in criminal records as an aggressive hoodlum. The police charged him with assault, burglary, and extortion. In 1913 he dynamited a safe in the Simpson Pawn Shop in the Bowery but was caught and sentenced to serve time in Sing Sing Prison. On his release he organized an illegal lottery game popular with the Italian community. As a cover for his criminal activity, Masseria operated a car dealership and an imported food business; spaghetti, olive oil, and wine grapes were monopolized by his company. Though balding and portly, with a sly charm, Masseria was suspected of 30 murders.[9]

Frank Costello became a Masseria associate. Costello paid a fee to distribute alcohol in Masseria's territory. Joe the Boss expected tribute from every bootlegger; those who failed to provide financial gifts faced death. Reporter Thomas J. Randall described Masseria as "the monster."[10] Charley Lucky joined Masseria's gang. In Little Italy he developed a reputation as an *enforcer.* Narcotics, alcohol, extortion, and gambling were the cornerstones of Masseria's empire. Lucky gained the confidence of Masseria and rose to the rank of *capo.* Luciano was quiet. He said little but took in everything; the ideal lieutenant, cold and efficient. But life was dangerous for Masseria; there were always contenders for the illegal money.

Ciro "the Artichoke King" Terranova had fought with Masseria. Ciro extorted money from grocers and pushcart vendors on the Lower East Side. Terranova was suspected by police of dozens of murders. But Terranova and

Masseria made peace. They avoided bloodshed by dividing territories. Frankie Uale, known as Frankie Yale, was allowed to rule unmolested in Brooklyn.

Life was peaceful until Umberto Valenti decided to occupy Masseria's throne in 1922. But Masseria struck first. Valenti's speakeasy partner, Salvatore Mauro, was murdered at 222 Christie Street. Police arrested Masseria but the charge was dismissed for lack of evidence. Joe the Boss had important friends. Judge Selah Strong had issued a gun permit to Masseria. The judge personally wrote in red ink on the permit—*unlimited*. The permit allowed Joe to carry a gun, anywhere, despite his criminal past.

On a warm spring day, Masseria and his gang drove to Grand Street, just a block east of police headquarters. Joe set up an ambush of Umberto Valenti and bodyguard Silvio Tagliagamba. As the duo approached, the assailants took aim from a doorway at 194 Grand Street. Valenti escaped, but the bodyguard was fatally shot in the chest. Six innocent bystanders were wounded in the gunfire. Masseria's hit squad ran inside a tenement and escaped. Joe the Boss fled the scene, but police cornered him, and he was blackjacked into unconsciousness.[11]

The disclosure of Masseria's gun permit brought an uproar. Justice Strong told the press he had been duped. The permit papers vanished. After several court postponements, the murder charge against Masseria was quietly dropped, but retaliation came fast. When Masseria left a building at 80 Second Avenue shots rang out. Joe was caught in a crossfire of bullets. Masseria bolted inside Heiney's Millinery Shop as bullets creased his new straw hat. Inside the store, he dodged an assassin's blazing pistol. Two days later, a truce was called. A meeting was arranged at John's Restaurant on 12th Street. When Valenti and Masseria left the restaurant, a fusillade exploded. Valenti ran for a waiting taxi but just as he gripped the door handle, bullets ripped into him. No witnesses came forward. Word spread that Charley Lucky was Valenti's executioner.

As Masseria's deadly power grew, so did his wealth. Joe the Boss had a lavish apartment at 15 West 81st Street and a summer residence in the Berkshires. Joe rode regally in a chauffeur-driven, armored-plated limousine. With increased prosperity, Joe delegated duties and criminal concessions to underlings. Charley Lucky had his own enterprises, including pimping. Betty Cook, his prostitute-mistress, was expected to hand over a weekly sum, and other prostitutes did the same.[12] A compulsive gambler, Lucky won and lost high sums in card games and the race track. Daily cash became an obsession.

On June 2, 1923, Lucky sold a two-ounce box of narcotics, known as deacetyl morphine hydrochloride to John Lyons. Three days later, his customer returned to 133 East 14th Street to buy an ounce of heroin. After Lucky sold the dope, officers arrested him. Lyons was an undercover agent. The family apartment on 10th Street was raided. Agents uncovered two half-ounce packages of morphine and two ounces of heroin and opium. Faced with imprisonment, Lucky squirmed. He gave a secret statement to chief agent Joseph Van Bransky that a trunk of dope could be found in the heart of Little Italy, at 163 Mulberry Street. Lucky escaped prosecution. Despite his allegiance to Masseria, Lucky had to satisfy his gambling addiction, so criminal alliances were formed almost daily to provide ready cash.

Lucky Luciano as a young man. This is an undated photograph that was confiscated by police, circa 1931 (courtesy NYC Municipal Archives).

In July 1926, Detective Charles Kane of the Gun Squad stopped an automobile at First Avenue and 24th Street. Inside were Lucky, Joseph Scalise, and Christopher Lopinto. Lucky and Scalise had revolvers and a Remington shotgun with 45 rounds of ammunition. Though both had gun permits, they were arrested for carrying concealed weapons. The prisoners were arraigned in Fourth District Court, but the charge was dismissed by Magistrate McHenry. A few days after Christmas, Lucky was arrested for shooting Al Levey, who lived at 105 Central Park West. The charge was dismissed. In the midst of Prohibition, citizens were shocked as gangsters fought for control of beer and booze territory. Between 1923 and 1926 gangsters murdered 215 fellow thugs. In Chicago Scarface Al Capone assassinated dozens of rivals, including powerful mobsters Dion O' Banyon and Hymie Weiss.

In January 1927, Lucky purchased a house and a small strip of land for $5,000 in Ardonia, New York, a community where Italians harvested legal wine vineyards. The Ulster County Savings Institution held a $3,000 mortgage on the property. Two yearly notes of $82.50 were always paid by money order. Local police kept him under strict surveillance and observed that his friends were notorious criminals. Lucky formed a partnership in high-stakes craps games in White Plains with gamblers Fred Bachmann and James Borisia. A familiar face at racetracks throughout the state, Luciano organized high-stake poker games with racetrack gamblers. As always, there was an incessant need for cash.

In February, Joseph Corbo reported to police that his truck had been hijacked on Duffield Street in Brooklyn. Three armed men had stolen the Mack truck, valued at $2,000. The truck belonged to the Industrial Alcohol Company; its cargo was 27 cases of grain and denatured alcohol valued at $3,458. The driver was forced inside a sedan later found at Seventh Avenue and 22nd Street. The car was traced to Anthony Scalise, who confessed to the robbery. John Manfredi was charged with receiving stolen goods at a garage at 134 Centre Street. Police arrested Lucky, since he was Manfredi's partner. After winning an appeal, Manfredi was found not guilty in a second trial. Soon after, Lucky was arrested for disorderly conduct and violation of parole. He was released on $5,000 bail. Both charges were dismissed.

Lucky teamed with Louis Buchalter and Jacob Shapiro in labor racketeering. The mobsters provided the labor muscle to intimidate businesses in the garment industry; to insure labor peace they extorted a percentage of the company profits. In October 1928, Arthur Davey was robbed at Central Park West and 81st Street by two unknown men. The company payroll of $8,374 was taken. Police arrested Lucky, James Walsh, and George Uffner. Witnesses viewed a lineup, but were unable to make positive identifications. Lucky would team with anyone who could produce an illegal dollar. He always dodged jail and death, unlike others.[13]

Arnold Rothstein was found writhing in pain at the Central Park Hotel on Seventh Avenue. He owed $300,000 on an unpaid gambling debt, incurred after an unusual losing streak. Rothstein protested that the poker game had been fixed and refused to pay. He died from a gunshot wound to the stomach. In a black memorandum book were records of loan transactions to Frank Costello. All the debts had been repaid except for $6,500. Costello quietly wrote a check that went to Rothstein's estate. When Costello took over Rothstein's bookmaking operation in New York, he inherited "Dandy Phil" Kastel, a Rothstein associate who had been convicted of stock swindling. Costello and Kastel soon unveiled their slot machines; the slots dispensed candy mints and, for the winners, tokens that were redeemed for cash. Costello and Luciano became close friends, each admiring the daring of the other. Both pledged loyalty to Joe Masseria.

On December 5, 1928, police in Cleveland arrested 27 men at the Hotel Statler. The arrested were described in newspapers as "the Mafia Grand Council." A meeting had been called to discuss national territory. Joe Masseria, the boss of New York, had sent his trusted lieutenant, Charley Lucky, as a representative, but Luciano avoided arrest.

Back in New York City, Lucky arranged to buy stolen jewelry from Joe

Bendix, a hotel thief. Bendix had slipped inside a ninth floor hotel room at the Ritz Carlton and walked out with an emerald necklace, bracelets, rings, and brooches. Al Friedman, a jeweler and *fence,* appraised the jewelry at $50,000, and agreed to hide several pieces in his shop at the corner of Fifth Avenue and 44th Street. Bendix arranged a *meet* with Charley Lucky in front of Moe Ducore's drug store on Seventh Avenue. A taxi was hailed. As they drove through Central Park, Lucky examined the jewelry, and the men discussed prices. Lucky wanted an appraisal by Bernie Cohen at the Jeweler's Exchange near Canal Street. A few days later, they met again at Ducore's drug store and walked to the Chesterfield Hotel. They slipped inside the gentleman's restroom; inside a pay toilet stall Lucky carefully examined the jewelry. Satisfied, he handed Bendix $24,000 in a brown envelope.[14]

The same month, machine guns raked gangster Frankie Yale as he drove in Brooklyn. Crime reporters speculated Al Capone was involved. But police had another suspect: Salvatore Maranzano, a high ranking Sicilian *mafioso* who had fled to America in 1925, driven from Sicily by Benito Mussolini's attempt to destroy the Mafia. Maranzano was a former seminarian who spoke Latin. He gave the impression of being a cultured businessman, someone who was knowledgeable about international trade and Roman history as well. But Maranzano was actually a brutal cutthroat who planned to make himself crime king of New York City.

Police surveillance observed Legs Diamond paying a visit to Lucky's residence in Ardonia.[15] Undercover officers were certain Luciano and Diamond imported heroin from Europe; the partners had been financed by Arnold Rothstein in narcotics deals. An international search began for incriminating evidence. Jack Noland, alias Legs Diamond, had acquired his nickname as a teenager, after he lifted packages from trucks, and bolted away. Diamond, a survivor of several murder attempts, was a brutal sadist. Diamond forced tavern owners to purchase bootleg beer. Those who resisted met the fate of Grover Parks, a truck driver who was kidnapped by Diamond. Parks was hoisted by his wrists until he dangled from a garage rafter. Diamond then burned the soles of his feet with a blowtorch.[16]

In March 1929, a citizen complaint was filed against Lucky, for shooting pheasants out of season.[17] The next day a game official, accompanied by a state trooper, arrested Luciano. He was convicted of the violation in a courtroom in Platterskill, New York, and fined 50 dollars. Police determined the gun permit had been issued on the recommendation of Frank Marino, a merchant in the town of Hylan, and authorized by Justice of the Peace William Carpenter. The gun permit was revoked. Angry over the constant police surveillance, Luciano sold his home in Ardonia and moved to a secret apartment at 40 Oswego Avenue in Long Beach.

Whenever police questioned him, Lucky always lied. He told officers that he was a married businessman, a salesman, fruit dealer, or real estate agent. He drove a new Lincoln and often claimed to be a chauffeur. As his residence, he listed the family apartment on 10th Street, though he lived in hotels, constantly moving. In Newark, Lucky made money by issuing forged stocks and bonds.

Luciano served Masseria well. He skillfully supervised illegal operations and organized high stake card games for the *padrone*. On the Lower East Side, Lucky's status was acknowledged. Gangsters were killers and parasites but *meno si dice, meglio è*— the less you say, the better, shrugged frightened immigrants.

Charley Lucky had an intimidating appearance; the hooded brown eyes were piercing and cold; the drooping eyelid was especially unsettling. The scar from his eye to his throat reminded observers his life was violent. Anyone brave enough to resist mob dominance was beaten or found a new home — at the city morgue.

Mobsters got their hands in everything; even annual parish feasts in Little Italy. Charity gambling was licensed by the city for religious holidays and festivals. The religious celebrations generated high profits, mainly from gambling and food concessions. Italian thugs demanded a piece of the action. No one dared to resist.

By 1929, mobsters were on a nationwide rampage of murder. On Valentine's Day seven hoodlums were lined up and massacred by machine gun fire in Chicago. Bugs Moran's gang was wiped out. The nation was shocked by the horrendous executions. Frank Costello financed a nationwide meeting at the President Hotel in Atlantic City. Bosses of bootlegging syndicates attended. The aim was to stop violence and discuss territorial authority to avert bloodshed. Al Capone was creating a national uproar. In the conference room Johnny Torrio spoke first. Torrio pleaded for cooperation around the country; city bosses had to work with each other. Frank Costello addressed the group, condemning the bloodshed. "From now on nobody gets killed without a commission saying so."[18] Big Al had to avoid Chicago. Costello warned that more warfare would result in federal intervention. Torrio told Capone that he had to go to jail and allow the situation to cool. Capone reluctantly agreed. Days later, Capone and Frank Rio were arrested for carrying concealed weapons. Capone was sentenced to a year in jail.

In December, an event took place that shocked even jaded New Yorkers. The Tepecano Democratic Club had rented the Roman Gardens Restaurant in the Bronx for a lavish dinner in honor of Magistrate Albert Vitale. The event was secretly organized by crime boss Ciro Terranova; among the 40 guests were gangsters, politicians, and police officers, including detective

Art Johnson. Magistrate Vitale was controversial. Published reports documented that he had "borrowed" $20,000 from Arnold Rothstein. Yet, Vitale was so politically important that he had directed Jimmy Walker's mayoral campaign in the Italian community. In the middle of the dinner men waving guns suddenly appeared. Guests were robbed of cash and jewelry. When the robbery was reported in newspapers, shockwaves permeated the city. The friendship between the prominent magistrate and recognized hoodlums appalled citizens. Stories circulated that Salvatore Maranzano was behind the robbery, calculated to humiliate Ciro Terranova. Most of the stolen items, including Art Johnson's detective badge, were later returned to Magistrate Vitale. A few weeks later, police raided a Harlem nightclub owned by Louis and Frank Saccarona. They were arrested for distributing narcotics. Financial records tied the Saccaronas to Tammany leader James J. Hines, Joe Masseria, Lucky Luciano, and Magistrate Vitale.

Joe Masseria led the most powerful crime gang among Sicilians. When other mobs showed their muscle, the iron fist struck without mercy. In a display of sheer greed, Joe the Boss demanded $10,000 from Cola Schiro as tribute. Schiro paid. Joe the Boss asserted his authority even further and arranged the murder of gangster Vito Bonventre. Then Salvatore Maranzano declared open war against Joe the Boss.

On February 26, 1930, Gaetano Reina was shotgunned to death in the Bronx. Masseria was suspected of the murder. But Joe the Boss had a solid alibi. At the time, he and Lucky had been in Miami, hosting an all-night, high-stakes card game.[19] Seated around the green baize poker table were 19 New York gamblers. Deputies with drawn pistols crashed the door of the smoke-filled hotel room. In Lucky's hands was a huge roll of money that resembled "a cabbage head," in the amount of $60,000. Lucky was winning. The deputies counted only $13,000 among the other players. Lucky gave the deputies his true name. The game had been going all night, he said. As the only player with a gun, he was charged with carrying a concealed weapon. Masseria and Luciano were arrested as operators of the illegal game, and fined $1,000. All the gamblers were advised to leave town.

The next month, Masseria and his gang met for a conference at the Alhambra Apartments on the Pelham Parkway in the Bronx. As Joe the Boss left the building, gunfire exploded from a window. Stephen Ferrigno and Alfred Mineo were fatally wounded. Newspaper accounts reported that Joe Masseria and Ciro Terranova had received demands from rival thugs who wanted to be "cut in" on the sale of wine grapes.[20] The *Daily Mirror* informed readers that Masseria and Terranova belonged to the Unione Siciliana, as "members of the national organization."[21]

Three days later, Antonio D'Amico walked along Elizabeth Street, between

Broome and Grand. A black sedan slowly trailed him. A man suddenly stepped out from the car. After heated words, D'Amico dropped with three bullets in the abdomen and two in the head. D'Amico was a Brooklyn resident previously arrested for suspicion of kidnapping and attempted murder. Police believed the dead man had been trying to cut in on the East Side alcohol sales.

Warfare exploded.

In August, Masseria's ally, Giuseppe Morello, was shot in his office at 362 East 116th Street. Ciro Terranova's nephew, Joe Catania, was shot next. While Joe the Boss wintered safely in Florida, Maranzano arranged a secret meeting with Lucky Luciano. Once Joe the Boss was dead, peace would reign. Lucky agreed. On April 15, 1931, Joe Masseria drove his steel-plated car, with windows an inch thick, to the Nuova Villa Tammaro restaurant, at 2715 West 15th Street in Coney Island, accompanied by a friendly trio. He had lunch and was playing cards when a Cadillac pulled to the curb. Two gunmen entered and shot Joe the Boss twice in the head and once in the heart. When police arrived they found the ace of diamonds in Masseria's right hand. The owner, Gerardo Scarpato, said he had been out for a walk, and his mother-in-law, Anna Tammaro, had been in the kitchen. Four hours later, the Cadillac, reported stolen, was found abandoned on West First Street, near King's Highway in Brooklyn; on the rear seat were three pistols. Two more guns were found in an alley alongside the restaurant; inside, three hats and coats had been left behind. Scarpato was identified as an extortionist and a vendor of illegal lottery tickets. Scarpato was so terrified that he pleaded with police to take his fingerprints, so in the likely event of his death at least his body could be identified. At first, police suspected an ethnic gang war on the Lower East Side. For two months warfare had existed between Masseria and Abe Wagner, leader of a "Jewish dope-booze mob."[22] Gunfire had erupted in the Hatfield House at 103 West 29th Street; Abe Wagner had been wounded, and his brother was killed. A dozen mobsters had already been slain.

Reports circulated that Al Capone had Joe the Boss murdered; then another story surfaced: Masseria's own gang betrayed him. A week after the murder, the *Daily Mirror* reported: "And Charley Lucky Luciano, whose name never before has been writ large in the roll of gang leaders, will have his brief day. He is already the real boss, successor to the bloodthirsty Masseria."[23] The Brooklyn Homicide Squad was soon after Luciano for questioning in Masseria's murder. "Little is known of the new Boss," wrote reporter Thomas J. Randall, "beyond the present indications that he has been increasing his power for the past year or two in a quiet manner, operating exclusively in Manhattan and winning popularity among Sicilian extortionists by presenting a defiant attitude toward Scarface Al Capone."[24] Newspaper reports identified Lucky as a friend of George "Humpy" McManus, a gambler acquitted in the unsolved murder of Arnold Rothstein. Joe the Boss had enjoyed a long and brutal reign. The funeral procession for Joe Masseria numbered 69 automobiles, including 16 cars filled with flowers.

Salvatore Marazano moved to consolidate power. A party was arranged at a hall on Washington Avenue in the Bronx. Maranzano had a plan to ensure the success of *la cosa nostra—our thing*: survival required enforcement of a rigid code, a chain of command, and unlimited respect for the boss; gangs must discipline their own members; permission for *undertakings* must be given. At the victory party Lucky handed over tribute of $6,000 to the new *padrone*. In May 1931, Maranzano arranged a meeting at a resort near Wappingers Falls. Three hundred men from around the country gathered. Maranzano proclaimed himself the leader of *la cosa nostra*. Later in the month, another meeting was held in Chicago, hosted by Al Capone. The agreement reached was that Capone would run Chicago, while Maranzano ruled New York.

Lucky was in Cleveland in July, enjoying the Stribling-Schmeling world's heavyweight title fight. He sat at ringside with Joe Biondo and Tommy Lucchese, until police led him away to be questioned "on suspicion."[25] As usual, he dodged prosecution.

As time passed, it was apparent that *our thing* was actually for Maranzano alone, observed gangsters. When fighting erupted in the Amalgamated Clothing Workers Union, Maranzano tried to seize control. He backed a faction against Lucky and Buchalter's group. After Lucky's alcohol trucks were highjacked, Maranzano was the suspect. Maranzano had plans for Charley Lucky. He would be murdered along with other rivals. But Charley had plans, too.

On September 10, a quartet of gunmen entered the Grand Central Building at 230 Park Avenue. On the ninth floor, they flashed badges and ordered seven men, as well as a secretary, to line up against the wall. Shots rang out. The gunmen ran from the inner office. Slumped in a chair was Salvatore Maranzano, dead of knife and gunshot wounds. Police recovered handguns in the building stairway. Maranzano's family insisted he was merely a businessman who operated a fishing fleet at Sea Isle, New Jersey. Police told reporters the dead man had been involved in an alien smuggling operation, and had revealed names, resulting in their arrests three days earlier. The *Daily Mirror* reported Maranzano's tongue had been slit, "the Sicilian mark of the squealer."[26]

The following day, worried residents of Windsor Place in Brooklyn called police. A sedan had been parked on the street days earlier. In the trunk was a body in a burlap sack. The victim had tattooed his name on his arm. It was

Gerardo Scarpato, trussed with sash cord, his feet pulled up beside his ears. He had been strangled, the same method employed in seven recent sack murders.[27] In response, Mayor McKee ordered police in Brooklyn to raid gambling houses where craps, sports betting, and poker games were nightly events; 156 people were arrested, mostly from Brooklyn where Frank Costello's illegal slot machines were in hundreds of businesses.

On September 14, the bodies of hoodlums Samuel Monaco and Louis Russo were found floating in Newark Bay. The *Daily Mirror* reported they had defied an ultimatum issued by "the new chief of the powerful Unione Siciliana, Charley Lucky Luciano." Monaco, a New Jersey mobster, had farmed out alcohol production among hundreds of homes, making him wealthy, but when Lucky ordered him to raise the price of New Jersey booze, Monaco sent an insulting refusal. Monaco and Russo had operated a coal and ice business as a front with a third partner, who had disappeared.

The next day, on the Lower East Side, bootlegger Frank Plescia walked among the crowded pushcart market at First Avenue and 13th Street. Plescia had been arrested the previous week, while driving an auto containing a trunk with a false bottom which concealed 15 five-gallon cans of alcohol. Smartly dressed, the bootlegger strolled along with a can of grain alcohol in hand. Two men slipped behind him and bullets tore the man's head and face to pieces. The gunmen disappeared. Frightened whispers spread the name of the new *padrone*. Little Italy was terrified, aware that Lucky Luciano now ruled with brute force.

Power in Maranzano's family was assumed by Joe Bonanno. A truce was arranged. Lucky said he had acted in self-defense, that Maranzano had hired Vincent Coll to murder him. Bonanno was aware of the dispute over union control in the garment district; both men planned the other's execution, but Lucky struck first. Joe Bonanno did not retaliate. Peace was chosen instead. The bosses agreed the gangs would exist as equals, with regular meetings, to avoid disputes. The dominant gangsters were Lucky, Joe Bonanno, Vincent Mangano, and Joe Profaci. The syndicate of crime was born. Word spread that there was a new *Unione Siciliana*.

Police learned of a secret loyalty banquet, arranged for Lucky at the Villa Tammaro Restaurant, the very place where Joe Masseria was riddled. Tributes of money were handed to the new boss. His high status brought wealth and undisputed power. Rothstein and Masseria had been his tutors in crime. By day, Lucky would model himself on Arnold Rothstein, acquiring the persona of a dapper gambler. By night, he would rule the underworld. Joe the Boss had taught him the value of brute force, but Lucky agreed with Frank Costello that daily murder was bad for everyone; yet, if necessary, the new *padrone* passed along an execution order.

Lucky had inherited a gang of ruthless underlings who would do his bidding. Vito Genovese introduced a new recruit. Though he had been with Maranzano, Joe Valachi was accepted and placed in the crew of "Tony Bender" Strollo. After entering Lucky's gang, Valachi married Mildred Reina. Her father had been murdered by Joe Masseria. As a wedding gift Lucky sent an envelope with cash inside. Soon after, Tony Bender gave Valachi a contract. Years before, explained Bender, two brothers in the Reggione family had been eliminated by Lucky and Vito. The new boss feared retaliation. Valachi set up a hit, befriending Michael Reggione in a coffee shop on East 109th Street. One night Valachi casually mentioned a nearby craps game. As Reggione stepped inside a tenement hallway, guns exploded. Police found a body with three gunshot wounds in Reggione's head.[28]

As *padrone*, Lucky's hands no longer pulled the trigger. He preferred the good life, indulging in lovely women and expensive nightclubs. In nightspots and restaurants Charley Lucky rubbed elbows with those he aped. During thoroughbred season in Saratoga and Hot Springs, Lucky mingled with the racing crowd as a *sportsman.* The elite came to know him as a gambler, fond of the racetrack and high stake card games.

The new boss liked to strut through Little Italy. At 32 Mulberry Street the riff raff were excluded. Monetas was patronized by judges, politicians, and the rich. Papa Moneta welcomed the distinguished, including Will Rogers, David Belasco, and George Jean Nathan. Patrons dined on zuppa di pesce, veal marsala, and ravioli. Lucky Luciano came too, death's head at the feast. Seated at the white linen table, he appeared respectable. But his was an ugly face with wary eyes. There were secrets that had brought him to the pinnacle, secrets that would never be revealed. Cocksure and cunning, he had yearned for an easy life. Now he had attained his goal.

Flanked by bodyguards, the *padrone* sauntered along Mulberry Street, past red brick tenements with iron fire escapes, past open windows where honest Italians watched silently. If they disliked the *porco stronzo*, they averted their eyes; they never dared tell him he was a pig who dirtied the reputations of New York Italians, and that Italy, too, an ancient nation whose culture had given the world everything worthwhile, was being sullied by mobsters like him.

By 1933 the *mafiosi* gangs ruled their own turf; an uneasy peace was established. Prohibition's demise would soon end the lucrative booze market; new sources of revenue had to be found. As usual, any illegal dollar was fair game. A *meet* had been arranged by Davie and Tommy. They had big plans they wanted to share with the *padrone.*

Lucky arrived at a small pastry cafe at 121 Mulberry Street. The cafe was Dave Betillo's hangout.[29] Little Davie was the gang's ranking lieutenant and a strict enforcer of Lucky's rule. Behind the cafe was a building for conferences. Lucky's gang members secretly met here to discuss how to get their slimy hands into the pockets of the honest, to discuss how to reap the biggest reward for the smallest effort. Dave Betillo and Tommy Pennochio handled drug deals and loan sharking; both men were killers. Jerry Bruno ran a gambling den and a nationwide bookmaking operation; Vito Genovese handled extortion, lottery tickets and stolen merchandise. Lorenzo Brescio was a trusted bodyguard. This was the inner circle. These underlings had a voice, but Lucky's decision was final. Davie and Tommy pressed their plan. The Luciano mob would take over pimps who were demanding money from madams. The pimps called themselves a *combination*. The group had approached Jerry Bruno for protection and explained their new operation. The madams and prostitutes would make weekly payments, as bail bond money. In the event any prostitutes were arrested, a ready fund was available for bail. Let's get rid of the pimps, suggested Davie. The Luciano mob would control all the whorehouses. There might not be much money in it at first, he conceded, but it will be a lucrative project in the future. The prostitution business would be a real moneymaker.

When deep in thought Lucky had a habit of stroking his nose with his index finger. But it didn't take him long to decide. It was a fine idea. Like bloodhounds, men always pursued women. Men always wanted sex and, if desperate enough, they paid for it. Betty Cook had been a good source of revenue. Peggy Wild's brothel was a good house. Lucky knew because he was a customer. First the madams, then the girls—they'll all work for us. Why not? The whorehouses could operate like a grocery chain, enthused the *padrone*.

And the whores will buy dope, added Tommy. Sure they would, agreed Lucky. It was a fine idea. Lucky gave his approval. The Luciano mob would control the vice underworld.

CHAPTER THREE

Love's Illusion

I will be right up

Fifteen Luscious Peaches on the Illuminated Runway of Joy

Or so claimed the poster near the Grand Street subway station. The advertisement promoted *burlesque*, a legalized striptease that featured hefty women with large bosoms. The Houston Street Winter Garden, at the foot of Second Avenue, was always packed with leering men. The audience watched as strippers shed their clothes until all that remained were jiggling, tasseled breasts and a gossamer triangle of white linen. Between revues comics told jokes, but the male audience came to see the female form. New York's vice squad permitted such entertainment, provided full nudity never took place.[1]

If burlesque shows were unappealing, lonely men seeking female companionship could frequent Blossomland. Lonely patrons could pay for foxtrots and tangos. Tickets were 35 cents and each dancer received a 25 percent commission. Young women with penciled eyebrows smiled professionally and kept partners at arm's length, unless tipped, then men could dance closer, and embrace a partner. If lonely males didn't care to hire dance partners, they could go to Roseland on Broadway. If it was masquerade night, patrons could dance to Fletcher Henderson's Orchestra, dressed as pirates and gypsies. Amidst the noise and crowd, lonely people could find companions.

If the night was still young, and there was money to burn, then a nightclub was the next stop. Nightspots featured lovely women in dance routines; hidden entrances led to gambling rooms, where roulette wheels and craps tables fleeced the gullible.

During the prosperous times of the 1920s, Texas Guinan was the Queen of the Nightclubs. "Hello, suckers!" she shouted to patrons of The Padlocks, a nightspot named after the many closings she had suffered due to violations of the Volstead Act.[2] When Texas Guinan blew a police whistle, the party atmosphere intensified; waiters began rattling clappers, the band played louder, and balloons dropped. Champagne was kept chilled in silver buckets under tables. Cigarette girls in satin blue pajamas smiled, and men ogled the troupe of scantily attired dancers who sang a song about cherries. They circulated with leers and ruffled men's hair. Texas Guinan grew rich selling entertainment and expensive alcohol.

Prohibition was underway, but alcohol practically flowed in the streets. Passwords allowed easy access to speakeasies. Simply ask a policeman where a good drink could be found, joked New Yorkers. There were thousands of choices. In the better nightspots a shot of Bacardi cost $3.00; it was supposedly genuine. Apricot brandy went for $3.50 a drink. In streets off Fifth Avenue, speakeasies served absinthe frappe for a $1.00; a double whisky known as *blackfall* was guaranteed to make the pavement meet your face before a city block was walked.

Although the temperance reformers had triumphed, many citizens simply ignored the unpopular law. It was fashionable to carry a silver flask. America's moral streak clashed with hedonistic desires. Paying to have one's emotions aroused was easy. If a night of burlesque, dancing, and nightspots was not enough sensation, male loneliness could be banished by hiring a prostitute.

The houses were everywhere. Fliers were flagrantly passed out in the city streets. Men knew where to find prostitutes, and so did the police. Many houses of prostitution were protected by precinct patrolmen who were bribed to avoid them. Occasionally, vice raids occurred.

In June 1931, an anonymous letter was sent to the police. The author wrote for "the benefit of the unfortunate women," including his sister, a former prostitute. She had been saved "and is now happily married.... I have some information and addresses of disorderly houses, also an agent of these women who sends them out to work, also the lieutenant and helper." The vice ring was suspicious of strangers, so the writer suggested a wiretap and gave a telephone number.[3]

On a hot August morning plainclothes officers maintained surveillance on an apartment on 64th Street in Brooklyn. As expected, a 57-year-old man with a partly closed left eye emerged. The officers tailed him to a three-story brick building at 2925 West 22nd Street, Coney Island. Their prey entered a restaurant on the lower level operated by a woman named Yedis Porgamin, the building's owner. Arrests on the premises had already been made for illegal liquor, prostitution, and gambling. Austrian-born Lou Weiner, alias "Cockeyed Lou," was a notorious procurer of women. Shortly after his arrival at the restaurant, Cockeyed Lou and his assistant, Al Lutz, began making telephone calls.

Policeman Samuel Morris was also at work. Morris had been assigned the task of eavesdropping. Headphones in place, he was ready to record all conversations to or from the restaurant's pay telephone. At 12:30 P.M. an incoming call was overheard.

"Hello, Louie, this is Esther from Madison Avenue."[4]

A heavily accented voice spoke. "Hello, dearie, how are you? Why did you let her beat it on you when she was good to make $50 or $60?"

"Listen, Lou, I didn't leave her go. I went to the baths and when I came back she was gone. Louie, I can't talk any longer. I have four fellows waiting."

"Why did you go to the baths?"

"Louie, I want to go back to work."

"I'll try and get you a job."

"Will you call me when you want me, at University 4-89?"

"When I want you, I will send for you, you're in apartment two. Goodbye."

At 12:40 P.M. another incoming call was overheard.

"Hello, Louie. I want somebody to stay in a place in Long Island. It's a wonderful place and they will have to stay all night."

"I sure will, dear."

Then Cockeyed Lou placed a call. "Hello, Shirley, this is Louie. How are you, dear? I have a job for you out on Long Island."

"Aw, gee, ain't you got nothing in New York?"

"Christ, that's the worst of you girls; get a job and you don't want to go. It's a good job, you will get paid plenty of money and you can stay all night."

"You know I like to be home in the evenings."

"You know I like to do the best I can for you."

"Yes, I know you do."

"You think it over and I will call you later."

Throughout the day Officer Morris noted each conversation. There was no doubt that Cockeyed Lou was lining up women for sex. The next day's wiretap was even more conclusive.

"Hello, Louie?"

"Yes."

"This is Peggy. What kind of place did you send me? I don't have to go if I don't want to. I don't like to go with anybody to anyplace he takes me."

"Call her up and tell her you don't feel well. You don't have to be ashamed to tell her you don't want to go there. How much money is coming to you?"

"Six dollars."

"Is Florence there? What kind of a joint is she running on Long Island?

Call Jennie, Orchard 5536. Tell her to give you the money. Jesus Christ, what is the difference? Some days is good and some days is bad."

At 12:45 P.M. Abe called. "She did not come yet. I got seven men waiting."

"I got one now. I will send her over right away. I will send Peggy. Tell them to wait 15 minutes. Jesus Christ, you talk and talk and talk. I have more madams. I am not interested in your business. God, God, God, can't you get out of the Jewish habit? Wait. She will be over in 15 or 20 minutes."

Officer Morris noted that Cockeyed Lou spoke with the girls in English, but his conversations with the madams and pimps were in Yiddish. Weiner started drinking and handed the telephone to Josie, one of his many madams. She telephoned Rose. "Louie wants to talk to you. I had an argument with Abe."

"Let him go to hell. Lou says I have a nice big—*ich up a grosser stick*—I have a great big piece."

Rose dutifully discussed a new girl. "She is some worker. She is poor; she has not got any pajamas. Treat her good. Take care of her and give her plenty of work for she can take it. She is a good worker. I will send one of my other girls away. She is a big troublemaker, talks too much."

As the days passed, the wiretaps revealed rich veins of incriminating evidence. Each call that Weiner made was placed through an operator, and Officer Morris always registered the number. By September 2, more details were unfolding as Cockeyed Lou checked on his supply of women. At 12:30 P.M., the start of his workday, he asked the operator to dial President 3-3622.

"Hello, Mary dear. How are you, alright? How do you feel, honey?"

"Alright."

"Are you still sleeping?"

"No, I just came out of the bath. I'm still wet."

"Did you like the work there?"

"Yes."

"Nice place, isn't it?"

"Yes, alright."

Then he telephoned Sarah. "How is she?"

"She is a fine girl, a nice quiet girl."

"How is business?"

"If I had the business I could work all night."

"Are you going to work Rosh Hashana and Yom Kippur?"

"Give me the business and I will work every day in the week."

At 12:45 P.M. he spoke with Flora. "Are you making money?"

"Not bad. It is on account of the holidays."

"How was it Monday? Was it better than Tuesday? Does she like you? She is a nice woman? I hope this week will be a good week."

"I hope so."

"You will be good for two hundred or more."

"I hope so."

And the girls called him. "This is Helen."

"What Helen?"

"The tall girl."

"Is it a good date?"

"Yes."

"With who?"

"A man."

"Did you make money?"

"Yes."

"How long do you know the man?"

"Oh, I know him a long time. I met him yesterday."

"Is he a good sucker."

"Pretty good."

"Come out to the Island with him. I will give you a room so you can always be sure. Can you get at least 50 dollars out of him?"

Then Peggy checked in.

"Peggy, the little Italian girl?"

"Listen Louie, I had to beat it last night and so did Abie."

"That bastard! I will kill him yet. What happened?"

"Someone called up and tipped him off that the cops were going to pull a raid, and the madam was all excited and began to get dressed, and the two Abies went down to the superintendent, and Abie, with the glasses, he stayed and so did Mazie, but the other Abie ran away. The superintendent said that the bulls came in and asked him what floor 5D was on, and he told them that we moved out and so Abie wanted to get another apartment for the night."

"That bastard. Who told him in the first place to go back to that home?"

"Louie. How much do they make in Williamsburg?"

"About one hundred to one fifty."

"I want to go back to work soon as I am hard up."

"Did that no good son of a bitch pay you and how much?"

"I made forty-two dollars in two days and I am home safe and sound, thank God."

"Listen, honey, do you want to tell me who tipped off the cops?"

"Yes."

"That big fat bitch Lilly."

"Louie, I have to get to work soon."

In the late afternoon the whoremaster spoke with an angry madam named Billy.

"Louie, where is that bitch, Helen, the one you sent me last week, working now? The reason I ask you is that she stole a pair of silk pajamas belonging to Suzanne the French girl, and I know she paid 15 dollars for them, and that bitch stole them."

"How is business? Don't worry about the pajamas."

"Couldn't be better. I have about six now, waiting to be taken care of."

"Well, what the hell is the delay?"

"Virginia and Frenchie are coming in late again. I wish you would speak to them."

"I will, don't worry. I'll see you some night next week."

On September 3, Susan telephoned. "Hello, Louie dear, what's the matter?"

"Never mind that dear stuff," exploded Cockeyed Lou. "When you were sent over there you were told to be there at 12 noon not at 1:00 or 1:30 in the afternoon. Do you know this business starts at 12 and I don't give a God damn for that cocksucker of Joe, the bastard. I don't care whether he is your sweetheart or not. That son of a bitch don't know nothing about this business, and you can tell him I don't give a fuck for him or his six girls. I have more girls than he ever thought of."

"Now is that a nice way to talk to a lady. Maybe you don't want me to work for you anymore."

"Sue, you are a very nice girl, and I sure do like you, but I don't like trouble, such arguments and fights. It don't pay in this game."

"Well, I am not going to work for you anymore."

"I don't give a damn."

"No, honey, I am only fooling. Everything will be alright. Come and see us soon."

At 1:45 P.M. Weiner arranged a date for himself with Francis. "Listen, sweetheart, I want to go over and see a beautiful body tomorrow."

"That's just what I have and I will be waiting for you, but I think you are kidding me."

"I am not kidding you at all. I will be over and take care of that beautiful body tomorrow, and if I feel good I will give it to you both ways."

"Okay."

Officer Morris noted that Cockeyed Lou was concerned about his girls. "Hello, kid, what's the matter?"

"Louie, I have a severe pain in my left side over my right tube."

"You know the doctor said last week that you have pus on one of them tubes, so the best thing is for you to go home and take it easy and keep applying cold applications to your tube, and if you don't feel alright by Tuesday I will take you back to the doctor."

A week later, the wiretap dossier was spreading its net, with more results. "Hello, Doc Speilberg?"

"Doc Speilberg is not in."

"Did he go away? Where?"

"I think he went over to the Island?"

"He should get killed on his way over. Know what he does to Dixie? He hit her over the head. Why does the cocksucker fight for? The dirty fucken bastard, the cocksucker knows he is up against it. That dirty dog I could kill him for that."

Louie telephoned Rose with the news that one of her girls was getting out of prison. "She is coming home on parole. Take it easy, take your time. Attend to your business."

"My heart is a lot quieter she will be home soon."

If Lou couldn't book a girl into a house, she got the street. "Mazie, this is Louie. Go over to work at 1:00 next corner by Florence."

"Oh, I can't. I don't want to go on the street."

"You won't go on the street?" bellowed Cockeyed Lou.

Hung up in a very mad way, noted Officer Morris.

The record of the wiretaps was delivered to Brooklyn's Fourth Division. The district attorney prepared a case based on considerable evidence, but the charges against Cockeyed Lou were strangely dismissed by Magistrate Rudish. Weiner returned to flesh peddling.

Cockeyed Lou was but one of several major procurers. The others were Nick Montana, Dave Marcus, Pete Balitzer, and Jack Ellenstein. They sent women to numerous whorehouses in Manhattan, Brooklyn, the Bronx, and Queens. Usually, income was split between the madam and girls, but 10 percent of a girl's earnings went to the bookers. Hundreds of women offered themselves for money. The suppliers kept the girls busy, since the demand never ended.

The police began another investigation into Lou Weiner's illicit trade. On March 28, 1933, William Mack was assigned wiretap duty. The officer eavesdropped on a madam named Rose Cornfield.

"Hello, Miss Cornfield, this is Vincent from Yale. My brother was up there last night?"

"I don't remember."

"I mean Joe."

"Oh yes, he was here."

"Did anything happen? Did he have a black eye?"

"No, there was no trouble up here. You know me. If they start any trouble I just lead them to the door and out."

An hour later there was another call.

"This is Casey. Can I come up?"

"I'm sorry we are closing up."

"Don't you remember me? Look up your index cards and you will find my name there."

"I said I'm sorry. You can't come up."

At midnight the madam telephoned the Hotel Victorian, requesting room 1148. There was a conversation about elegant clothing. Rose asked for black evening gowns, size 18, and a male voice said he would deliver them.

The next day, the wiretap disclosed the madam was moving; most surprising, it revealed Rose's whorehouse was frequented by law officers.

"Hello, Barney, how are you?"

"I was not going to call you anymore because the last time I called at 2:30 in the morning you hung up on me."

"I never hung up on you. It must have been someone else."

"Well, it was you alright. I know your voice, and the next time you do it to me I am going to come up there and be like Jerry. I am going to kick that door right in."

"Don't you forget to have a warrant when you do. You know the D.A. and I talk the same language."

"How is Sammy?"

"They picked up Sammy last week, but they let him go. Do you still go down to the Richmond Club?"

"No, I haven't been down there in a long time."

"There is a detective up here every night that is sweet on Trixie. I think you know him, too."

"Gee, that is a good one."

"This is second headquarters. I have them all coming up here. Why don't you come up more often?"

"I only get about 30 dollars a week now."

"Stop kidding me. I know how much you get."

"After I get finished paying my alimony and everything else I wind up with about 20 dollars. Who is standing alongside of you right now?"

"Why there is no one here. I am in a room all by myself. What makes you think there is someone standing alongside of me?"

"Well, I can see. You are standing there in pajamas."

"No, I am in a brown cloth street dress now. You know I am taking it easy now, because Trixie is able to answer the door, and I don't have to be on the go so much. Why don't you come up here once in a while."

"I don't care to go up there. I'd rather call you up and take you out after you are through."

"Those fellows from Boston were here the other night for three and a half hours, and they left a hundred dollars. But they raised hell."

"Alright, you spick. I will call you up some night and we will step out."

In a conversation with Sammy she vented her wrath on extortionists.

"Buddy called for money. If Whitey comes up I won't let him in because if he knows us girls are alone he might beat us up and break my nose. I am sick of all those phony cocksuckers. If they were real men they would not bother women and bully them."

"Don't let them in, and listen Rose, be very careful."

"You don't have to tell me. I know what to do."

"Did you tell them to come up."

"Yes, I told them to come up Monday, but I won't have any money for them."

A revealing telephone call was placed from the madam's apartment to Cockeyed Lou. "Yeah, this is Louie."

"This is John and I don't want to mention any names over the wire. Now listen: I got your kid cousin shaking these joints down and I hit him over the head and let him go as soon as he said he was your cousin. Now he has to take that rap over the head and let it go at that."

"John, you should have kicked him around."

"I know, but because he said he was your cousin I let it go. The kid said to me, 'Oh, my head hurts.' And I said, 'What did you want me to do, kiss you?' So you tell him when you see him he has to take that rap on the head and let it go at that, and listen, Louie, you'll have to take him out of that, that is bad business."

"John, I appreciate that very much. When are you going to come up and see me?"

"Louie, this is a very serious offense and the D.A. assigned us to work on this. Now tell your cousin to get rid of that other guy. He is no good."

The dozens of telephone calls in April disclosed numerous assignations made by Rose for herself and her girls. Customers were Dickey the laundryman, Joe the florist, and Nick the tailor. Clients were all safe regular customers. Rose carefully screened her visitors.

"Hello, Rose, this is Frank."

"Frank who?"

"Frank. Don't you know me?"

"No, I don't know you."

"Why I am surprised."

"Well I'm not."

Frank never got in, nor did others.

"This is Lapeto, the barber from Fourteenth Street."

"Who?"

"Lapeto."

"Well I don't know you and don't be bothering me."

There was another surprising call when a prostitute named Ruth telephoned Washington, D.C. "Hello, mother, did you get the money?"

"No."

"Listen, mother, I sent a tracer from New York and Washington. I also spoke to the postmaster and he said somebody must know I am sending you the money through special delivery. I will send you some money tonight. How is Dad?"

Officer Mack discovered that not only was a lawman intimate with the madam, but he was shaking down the extortionists who demanded money from her. The crooked cop called Cockeyed Lou.

"Hello, Louie. This is Johnny's friend, Joe."

"Oh, you mean Johnny that called me up Saturday."

"Yes."

"What is doing?"

"Louie, we split that dough with the other guy. You know I don't go for that kind of stuff. I think more of friendship, but you know what cops are. They are a bunch of hoodlums and will always be hoodlums. We grabbed two kids last night. We thought they were from your bunch. They looked like wops, but they didn't know you and they didn't mention your name, so we bagged them."

"Who are they?"

"Two kids. One of them is an Irishman by the name of Wallace; the other kid was a spick. Tell Whitey and Buddy to come up for that dough but not to choke her. She might make a holler."

"Okay, Johnny. What is your name, Johnny or Joe?"

"Well, it is both. My name is John Joseph. I have a name for each gun I carry."

"Okay, Johnny, come up and drink some beer. I want to see you anyway."

Late in the evening Ruth placed a call. This time it wasn't to her mother.

"Well, what is the trouble?" asked Ruth.

"You know what it is."

"No, I don't."

"Well, you wouldn't stay away from the Alba and your chinky girlfriend, so they are going to give it to you. You better not go near the Alba at any time."

"Oh, hell, it can't be that. I didn't do anything wrong. If it is anything, it is because of you. They don't want me to be with you, so they are trying to break us up."

"Christ, if you ever did anything to me I would have you murdered."

"You know how I feel about you."

"Well, how is everything down there?"

"Okay. When can I come back?"

"I will write and let you know and tell you all about it."

"That don't sound so good for me. I was thinking about Sunday. Can I come back then?"

"Didn't I tell you not to mention time or date over the phone. The wire might be tapped." Officer Mack realized that crooked cops were tipping off the prostitutes about the investigation.

Matters were glum for Rose, as the extortionists bled her for money.

"Hello, Rose. How is everything?"

"Not so hot."

"What is doing?"

"Nothing much. There is a few men up here; that prick is making my whole life miserable."

Despite her worries, Madam Rose kept her mind on business.

"Hello, Rose, this is Jack. Are you busy?"

"Jack, there is a few waiting but you can come up. I will let you go first. The other boys will not mind waiting."

"Okay, Rose, I will be right up."

CHAPTER FOUR

Sex Underworld

Would you like to work in a house?

Each day a fresh crop of hopefuls arrived in New York City, eager to start a new life. Men with a single suitcase stood amidst the roar in Grand Central Station, undaunted, pursuing secret dreams. Women came, too, sharing similar hopes of success in the world's greatest metropolis. Suddenly, they were tiny insects staring agape at the skyscrapers looming above them, soon disappearing in a mass of humanity. Many newcomers fast discovered that life in the big city was tough. Disillusion and despair came fast, especially during the hard times of the 1930s. Whether desperate, or simply tempted by fast money, many women were lured into prostitution. Females were always in demand by the merchants of flesh, and the underworld harvested the willing. A woman's shame from selling her body was offset by the money: the *scarlet* for the *green*.

Lonely men gladly left their apartment sepulchres in search of sexual pleasure. There was the midday debauch, the evening whirl or the midnight frolic. Respectable society had ironclad rules of decorum and propriety. But many citizens simply asked, so what? The vice chain supplied all the decadence money could buy.

In 1933 Cockeyed Lou Weiner was at the top of the vice chain. But there were others. Dave Marcus, known in the sex underworld as Dave Miller, had arrived in New York in 1929. Marcus was tall and slim, with protruding ears and a glass eye. He had once been a constable in Pittsburgh, but too many shakedowns brought dismissal. Soon after, Marcus was arranging assignations at his own residence; a single whore worked for him; if she was unavailable, his plump young wife substituted. An undercover detective followed Ruth Marcus to a bedroom where two children slept. She agreed to sexually entertain him. The detective left immediately and police arrived. Marcus was convicted of operating a disorderly house, sentenced to serve 30 days in jail and forced to pay a two hundred dollar fine.

Marcus moved to New York, where he peddled dresses and jewelry but soon opened a house of prostitution, with Harry Chicago as a partner, and their wives as assistants. But after a month the place was raided. Both men went into the booking business. By August of 1933, Marcus supplied 40 women to 20 houses in Manhattan and Brooklyn. At age 40, he had attained the money he craved. Each week he stuffed his pockets with several hundred dollars. There were stylish clothes and shiny automobiles, and his wife no longer hustled strangers. Life was good for Dave Marcus. He never referred to himself as a whoremaster. The term in the sex business was *booker*. The bookers modeled themselves after theatrical agents, only they booked women into whorehouses for sexual entertainment. And the women were always referred to as *the girls*.

Pete Balitzer, known as Pete Harris, furnished women to dozens of madams. His assistant, Joseph "Jojo" Weintraub, handled the telephone in Pete's office at 110 West 70th Street. Jojo jotted down business messages and

relayed them to Pete. Jojo was quiet, squat and balding, with a hairy face and long nose, while Pete was friendly and tall. The team stayed busy, sending bright-lipped women to apartments in Manhattan and Brooklyn. Each Sunday night, Pete and Jojo made their rounds, collecting booking commissions from the girls.

Pete had learned the business as a brothel bartender in Chester Park, Pennsylvania, in 1928. After being arrested for bootlegging, he moved to Philadelphia. In 1930, at age 27, he came to New York, to work for his uncle as an electrician, but he fell in love with a rich prostitute named Billie and became her pimp. In early 1931, he began booking girls, charging them the standard 10 percent based on their gross earnings. Jojo was hired in the fall of 1933 and paid 35 dollars a week, plus expenses. Pete never sent a girl to

This call girl is believed to be Helen Kelly, circa 1936 (courtesy NYC Municipal Archives).

a house unless he first looked her over. Pete was proud of the women in his stable. He boasted his girls were attractive, dependable, and left customers satisfied. The girls he favored, he kept as mistresses, like Sally Osborne, a petite blonde from South Carolina. Though she was Pete's special girl, he booked her like the rest. When her shift was over, long after midnight, Pete would dutifully pick her up and drive her to his apartment. At least she didn't have to work steady, she told friends. Pete protected his girls. In the event of a *pinch,* bail money and a lawyer were available. Vice was a risky business, and arrests were inevitable, but bookers like Pete always did well. For the girls though, times could be tough.

Renee Gallo was 22. She had lived with her lover for five years, but when the relationship ended, she found herself broke and began soliciting men in the streets. After six months, Renee was hired by Molly Leonard, a prominent madam. On a Saturday afternoon, she overheard Molly talking to Pete, who stared at the new girl. Renee was attractive. Though rather tall, she had a pretty oval face with a pointed chin. Pete liked what he saw.

"Will you book me steady?" asked Renee.[1]

"What did you do before?"

"Worked the streets."

"Okay, but you have to get evening gowns."

Each week, Pete or Jojo telephoned Renee and gave her a precise schedule. She was usually sent to a four-dollar luxury penthouse or a two-dollar apart-

By 1936, Pete Balitzer was the major booker of prostitutes in New York City. Pete boasted the women he sent to bordellos were the best (courtesy NYC Municipal Archives).

ment. While at Grace Halls's house, during a slow week, Renee and another girl only earned $22. Renee complained to Jojo. He shrugged, then asked if she would complete the losing week by giving him a free lay. She told Jojo to put on a gown and go to work himself.

When Cockeyed Lou's eyesight began to fade, he introduced his son to the business. Pudgy Al Weiner wore glasses, walked with a limp, and made baskets as a hobby. Al had failed at running a candy store, so he went to work for his father in a bar at 146 Rivington Street. Lou worked the telephone from noon until late evening, supplying 50 girls to 30 houses. Al dutifully drove his father to collect commissions. Al was introduced to the madams and pimps, especially the top echelon: Nigger Ruth, Abie the Rabbi, Max the Barber, Hungarian Helen, and Cokey Flo. Lou told his son the lucrative trade would belong to him one day.

Nick Montana and his partner, Jack Ellenstein, were also doing well. Nick was Italian-born. He had been in the sex business for several years. Ellenstein was a war veteran, fat and bald; once a respectable real estate agent, he had abandoned his career for the fast money.

The minor bookers only serviced five or six houses. They had started in the sex underworld as pimps, but became *male madams*, progressing to bookers.

Danny Brooks juggled all three positions at once. His real name was Dominic Caputo. Born in Italy, he had been raised in Brooklyn and attended school until the eighth grade. At age 19, he was sentenced to ten months in jail for possession of a revolver. Arrests for narcotics and assault soon followed. Danny tried to make an honest living as a truck driver, pipe fitter, and machinist. But in 1920 he became a bootlegger, operating speakeasies and cheap night clubs. He owned a show called "Thrills and Frills of 1926," which toured Pennsylvania for several months, until it went bankrupt. He married prostitute Nancy Brooks, who neglected to tell him that she already had a husband and was committing bigamy.

At age 39, Danny launched his career in the sex underworld after meeting Jimmy Fredericks in the Stadium Club on 48th Street. They became partners in flesh peddling. Jimmy was known as "gorilla," and had a large head, topped with oiled black hair parted in the middle. Beneath a low brow were bushy eyebrows and piercing dark eyes. The fierce face rested on a stocky hulking body. Vincenzo Federico was a whoremaster, and a brutal one, running his own whorehouses. Jimmy's criminal rap sheet began in 1912 with truancy violations at age 11. At 15 he stole a piece of zinc valued at 50 cents. Jimmy told the judge he was a peddler and managed a suspended sentence. But a year later Jimmy was arrested for burglary and served two years in Elmira Reformatory, "the college on the hill." In 1921 he was arrested while

Jimmy "Gorilla" Federico demanded that prostitutes and bookers submit to demands by the Luciano mob (courtesy NYC Municipal Archives).

driving a new Oldsmobile Roadster, stolen from out of state. Convicted as a second offender, Jimmy was sentenced to five years in Sing Sing Prison. On November 23, 1925, Jimmy blew up a safe in the Warner movie theatre on Broadway and fled with eight hundred dollars. He was later arrested for parole violation and sentenced to Sing Sing, but at Grand Central Station, while the guard bought train tickets, Jimmy escaped. He was arrested several months later and served two years in the penitentiary. In 1927 he was arrested, hacksaw in hand, for trying to cut the lock of a grocery store on Eighth Avenue. Jimmy became a gunman. In June 1930, Fredericks was arrested for homicide. John Sciammette was at the Italian-American Tammany Democratic Club when two strangers walked inside. They spoke with Sciammette a few minutes, then drew revolvers and blew three holes in Sciammette's head. Nearby firemen witnessed the assassins run from the building and drive off in a Chrysler coupe. Police traced the vehicle to John Oddo. Jimmy was arrested, but the case ended when the firemen suspiciously failed to identify those charged. Jimmy had a wife he seldom saw. Most of his free time was spent in brothels.

After Jimmy and Danny Brooks became pals, they rented adjoining apartments at 350 West 30th Street. Danny began living with 18-year-old Ellen Grosso. At age 16 Ellen had been kidnapped and forced to submit to prostitution. Once free, Ellen had worked as a housemaid, but she found whoring more lucrative. A pimp introduced her to booker Sol Dichler in

Oscar's Luncheonette at 133 West 28th Street. She was sent to the loft buildings. She charged $1.25. A quarter went to the booker and a quarter to the elevator man. Ellen kept the remainder.

Then Ellen received a message that someone wanted to meet her. She went to the apartment. The door opened and she stared into an ugly face. "Would you like to work in a house?" asked Jimmy Fredericks. "I could book you."[2]

Ellen nodded.

But there was a minor catch. "You would have to be a 'three way girl,'" said Jimmy. He made a sexual request of Ellen, indicating that he wished to teach her then and there.

"You can do that to your sister," she snapped, "and if she likes it, then I might take a chance."

Jimmy then asked her to commit a different sex act. She refused. "I can't book you," he said, "unless I book you with another girl who would be a 'three-way' girl and she would make all the money, instead of you. You would make much more money this way."

Ellen said it made no difference. She refused to participate in *circuses.*

Ellen met Danny Brooks as a customer, but soon became Danny's steady girl, which meant he didn't have to pay. Danny set her up as his mistress and made her a madam. Jimmy Fredericks booked girls into the house, too. But she disliked him due to his vulgarity.

If arrests were made, the madams and girls called a bail bond company downtown. Office boy Michael Redmond answered the telephone. At 15 he had been hired by Abraham Karp, an attorney with an office at 113-117 West 10th Street. Karp had been the premier crooked lawyer in Manhattan until he was disbarred. Redmond was paid seven dollars a week to take telephone messages and run errands for Karp, whose clients were prostitutes, pickpockets and bookmakers. Meyer Berkman and Jesse Jacobs were partners in the office, and both were unlicensed bondsmen. After a girl was arrested for prostitution, Jesse Jacobs would appear in court, filing a writ of habeas corpus for his client, and the judge usually reduced the bail from a thousand to three hundred dollars. Meyer Berkman handled legal affidavits; after fabricating a defense, Berkman instructed Redmond to go before a notary. The office boy signed each affidavit with a false name. After the prostitute was released on bail she met with Abe Karp, who coached her. First, he advised, she had to use a fake name in court. Next, Karp posed questions: "Now what is your testimony going to be?" Of course, the truth had to be denied, so Karp simply fabricated defense alibis. And why *would* an innocent girl be in a madam's apartment? Karp would suggest a party invitation or maybe a charitable act, just visiting a sick friend who surprisingly turned out to be a whore. Just deny the truth, Karp insisted. The girls only showed up in court if the case was fixed or dismissal likely. If a girl was caught stark naked, servicing a client, then the case was hopeless. Karp ordered her to *go on the lam*. Unfortunately, such clients forfeited the bail money, but arrests were part of the business. After a few days, the *lamsters* returned to work with a different name.

There were hundreds of brothels in Manhattan and Brooklyn. The most prominent were operated by women. The madams were usually former prostitutes who booked girls to work 12-hour shifts. It was customary for the prostitutes to rotate from house to house, so the madams could offer variety for regular customers.

Molly Leonard, known as Molly Glick, had attended school in Brooklyn, but at 16 she became a prostitute; within three years she was a madam. Leonard operated a house in Albany for nine years but returned to Brooklyn. She was successful as a madam, clearing five hundred dollars a week, but opium smoking siphoned her income. She booked girls through Pete Balitzer because he had "a better selection."[3] Pete's girls were popular and usually earned $250 a week; Molly kept half. After Pete's commission and expenses the average girl kept about a hundred dollars a week.

Dorothy Arnold, nicknamed "Dixie," was raised in Virginia. In 1933 she traveled with a carnival and married a concessionaire. The couple moved to New York, where her husband, Slim, sold lingerie and evening gowns. He also smoked opium. After Slim's sales faltered, Dorothy decided to open a whorehouse. Mickey, a girl friend from Baltimore, serviced customers in Dorothy's apartment. Soon, other girls did the same. They paid Dorothy a dollar for every man entertained. Dorothy decided to run a house full time. She purchased numbered green cards to keep track of the greenbacks. If a customer paid two dollars, she punched the number *two;* if three dollars was paid, then *three.* Business was so profitable that Dorothy and Slim relocated to a plush penthouse. Though only 22, Dorothy ran one of the most successful and chic houses in New York City.

Jennie Benjamin, whose real name was Mary Glasenberg, was a madam in her late thirties. She had three children and was separated from her husband. She had been a sales clerk in a clothing store for nine years. In 1930 she opened a Roumanian restaurant on 3rd Street, but the venture failed. A madam named Levy taught Jennie the business. In August 1932, while Jennie was located at 104 Second Avenue, Mrs. Levy sent girls to her. The restaurant customers soon became sex clients. A booker, Charley Persana, known in the sex underworld as "Charley Spinach," knocked on her door, making a professional call. "You have heard Mrs. Levy speak of me," he began his sales pitch. "I will send a girl every week and come around every Sunday to get commissions."[4] Charley Spinach had won another house for his small chain.

Grace Hall was born in Steelton, Pennsylvania. At age 13 she left school and entered a brothel. She worked in carnivals for three years, then worked in burlesque with Sliding Billy Watson. Thereafter, she made a career in call houses and ran houses of prostitution in Buffalo, Cleveland, and Harrisburg, before age 30. In New York she opened a house at 117 West 58th Street.

Margaret Venti was known in the business as Peggy Wild. Raised in East Harlem, she married a musician at 16 and had a child at 17. After 15 years of marriage her husband said goodbye. Peggy's first house was frequented by gangsters: Vincent Coll, Legs Diamond, the Amberg brothers, and Charley Lucky Luciano. Afterward, Peggy catered to prominent businessmen with money to burn. Wild hid her cash in a cupboard at her daughter's home.

Roumanian-born Joan Martin wore glasses and resembled a well-fed housewife. She had been convicted of prostitution in 1913 and served three years in the Bedford Reformatory. She had a four-year-old daughter and a husband who had wandered off. In 1930 she lost her job as a waitress and began street hustling. She then opened a house and hired girls herself, but Cockeyed Lou paid her a visit. He could furnish all the girls she needed, he assured her. In September she discovered that Cockeyed Lou was sending stickup men to her place. After breaking a chair on Lou's head, she stopped doing business with him.

Polly Adler was a Russian-born immigrant who opened a house in 1920. She had been introduced to the fast crowd by Joan Smith, a gorgeous show-girl. Smith was a Broadway singer, tall and blonde, with sapphire-blue eyes. At Joan's nine-room apartment on Riverside Drive, Adler met Broadway entertainers. There were nightly *hop parties* where Joan and her friends smoked opium. A bootlegger named Tony asked Polly to find him a girl. Adler made 50 dollars and the girl a hundred. Before long, Joan Smith was addicted to cocaine and heroin and her stage career was destroyed. She sexually entertained men in Adler's house of prostitution. Her attractive mother came, too. Adler discovered there were clients who would pay "double and triple for the kick of having a mother and daughter in bed with them."[5]

Florence Brown was a newcomer, but she fast became a successful madam. After two years of high school, Flo left Pittsburgh for Youngstown, Ohio. At 14 she peddled cheap picture frames from house to house. At 15 she moved to Cleveland where she partnered a speakeasy with an older woman. Flo was seduced by a local businessman and was kept as a sexual mistress. At 18 she packed a suitcase for Chicago; in her purse was four thousand dollars. Flo became the mistress of several men. One lover, Butch, worked in gangster Jack Zuta's prostitution syndicate. Zuta was murdered by Al Capone, and Butch lost his job. Flo moved to Duluth, Minnesota, for three years, as the mistress of Joe Sussman, who gave her money.

In 1929 Flo and Sussman moved to New York. Sussman had a friend who ran a Brooklyn house of prostitution. Flo studied the business for two months; afterward, Sussman lent her money to open her own house in Yorkville, at 121 East 76th Street. She hired a Chicago girl named Dolly, but Flo herself solicited clients in cafés with a warm invitation, "Come on up, I'd like to introduce you to a girlfriend of mine."[6]

At the apartment, Flo would introduce Dolly then leave. A year later, Flo opened a classy five-dollar house on West End Avenue. In 1931 Flo lived with a new boyfriend, who wanted her to experience the dreamy sensation of opium smoking. On a fall night, after closing, they met in Flo's bedroom. On a long, thin rod resembling a crotchet needle, he placed an opium pill on a pipe. He extended the pipe over a small flame and inhaled. He told Flo to suck the smoke in short, jerky breaths. The fruity fumes just made her sleepy. A month later, Flo tried the pipe again. This time she experienced a feeling of relaxation. Flo began smoking every two weeks; then it was weekly. Business was good. Her girls entertained hundreds of clients and she was regarded as one of the sharpest madams in the business. There was never any trouble with police until the winter of 1933, when there was a raid, but Flo escaped arrest. She relocated and began booking girls through Cockeyed Lou.

After two years of opium smoking, Flo became addicted. She entered a treatment clinic. In 1933, at age 26, she was cured of opium addiction and returned to the vice world. She enjoyed the business and made hundreds of dollars a week.

Mildred Balitzer lived with Pete as his common law wife. She was a blonde from a respectable family in West Virginia. Mildred had studied nursing. After a failed marriage in Pittsburgh, which produced a daughter, she moved to New York. There was a brief marriage to a wealthy businessman, but the couple divorced in 1930. Mildred became the mistress of a prominent manufacturer. A month later, she met Pete Balitzer. Pete said he was a gambler. In May of 1931, when she was 27, they began living together. Pete introduced Mildred to his family, telling them she was his wife. On her deathbed his mother placed her wedding ring on Mildred's finger, but the couple never wed.

The following spring Mildred was invited to a party at the Century Hotel. She smoked opium to satisfy her curiosity, but after several pills she became nauseous. Despite the initial experience, Mildred grew to enjoy the soothing effect opium had on her nerves, but after three months she was addicted, puffing 12 to 15 pills a day. After an argument, Mildred and Pete separated. A month later, Mildred entered a house of prostitution, operated by Pearl Adams on 96th* Street, but only for a week because she wanted to

*West or east street orientation included when provided by archival source.

learn the business. Pearl's five-dollar house offered a selection of three girls. Mildred sexually entertained 30 to 40 men during her stay; she netted one hundred dollars and a business plan. A wealthy customer gave her money to start a sex penthouse on 55th Street. It was a five-dollar house, open from 2:00 P.M. until midnight. Drinking was forbidden. At cheaper houses, men were allowed 15 minutes behind closed doors, then they paid for more time. But Mildred set no time limit.

Mildred became friendly with Gus Franco, a convicted drug dealer and opium addict. Gus was in the numbers racket. Each day he bought an opium tin for two dollars. After the house closed, Mildred and Gus indulged their *pipe dreams* into the morning hours. She began living with Gus at the Victoria Hotel.

Mildred opened another house at 120 West 58th Street. The price was three dollars, and there were two girls always available. In a restaurant on Mott Street, Gus introduced her to a friend who sold narcotics. Little Davie was a boyish looking, hawk-nosed Italian with dark curly hair. Davie became a frequent guest at the hotel opium parties hosted by Mildred and Gus. Davie brought a companion to a drug party. The heavyset man with cold, gray eyes was known as "Tommy the Bull." But his real name was Tommy Pennochio. Mildred and Gus began buying opium from Tommy. In the winter of 1932, Little Davie accompanied Mildred to a restaurant on Mulberry Street. He introduced her to a dark complexioned man, "Meet my boss, Charley Lucky."[7] Mildred heard that Charley was a gangster.

On another occasion, while Davie was visiting, Tommy appeared in Mildred's room at the Hotel Victoria. Tommy was enthused over a new way to make money. A group of pimps had a plan to organize the bonding fees for whorehouses. "They take ten dollars a week from each girl for protection. It looks like a big thing that can be worked up into a big proposition for big dough. I think we ought to go into it." Davie said he didn't think there was enough money in it. Tommy insisted it was a good idea. Davie shrugged and said he would consider it.

Mildred was told her new friends were members of the *Unione Siciliana*. Murray Marks had been her friend, too, but he had become too powerful selling narcotics. Marks belonged to Waxey Gordon's gang. Mildred discovered he had been murdered on the orders of Lucky Luciano. In March of 1933, Mildred returned to Pete Balitzer. Pete and the sex bookers stayed busy arranging jobs for hundreds of women. The telephones rang all day, as the girls sought work. And who were they?

Mary Thomas was a widow, 27, a matronly, buxom blonde who wore glasses. She had two children to support. She was booked by Pete and became Jojo's mistress.

Jean Matthews was a brunette from Pennsylvania who married at 17. The marriage failed, and she became a prostitute in coal towns before drifting to New York.

Eleanor Jackson was a native of Los Angeles. She was 22, well-educated, and exuded an air of refinement. Eleanor had been in New York since 1930, working in a variety of jobs—telephone operator, clerk and model—but in the summer of 1933 she decided to call Nick Montana and become a whore.

Shirley Taylor was 20, an attractive auburn-haired girl from Pittsville, Maryland, born Mary Wilkerson. She began soliciting men at 16. After arriving in New York in 1933 she booked with Jack Ellenstein. While working in Danny Taylor's house, at 140 West 71st Street, he fell in love with her. Taylor gave her a house to run, but a few weeks later the place was raided. She escaped, but two girls were arrested. Shirley returned to the life of a common prostitute.

Helen Horvath, known as Helen Kelly, was 19. Helen was very attractive, five feet six inches tall, with dark blonde hair and brown eyes. Born in Kentucky, she had been adopted by a Hungarian couple. Her father was a plasterer, and her mother worked in a cigar factory; they saved enough money and returned to Hungary to purchase a home. Two years later, after a brief romance with a Hungarian medical student, 17-year-old Helen became pregnant. Her parents felt disgraced by the scandal and vowed to send her back to America. Her father arranged a hostess position at a beer garden at 314 74th Street. She was paid to sit and drink with customers. Not long after her arrival in New York, a drunken customer forced her inside a taxi and raped her. She was taken to the Florence Crittenden Home on 21st Street, and later transferred to a maternity home where a daughter was born six months after her return to America. Helen returned to the beer garden, where she met "Gypsy Tom" Petrovich, a sophisticated Austrian-born musician. With fine clothes, money, and the promise of marriage, he enticed her into prostitution. She briefly entered a house on 92nd Street. Gypsy Tom then took her to Jennie Schwartz's place at 262 West 21st Street. Tom stole her money. Helen found out Tom was the pimp-lover-partner of "Hungarian Helen" Frisch, the wealthy madam of a ten-dollar house at 1225 Park Avenue. During her first week at Hungarian Helen's, Horvath serviced two hundred men. Her share was $314. Tom demanded most of it. Helen was often confined in her room without clothes, so she wouldn't run away. She was beaten by Gypsy Tom and forced to become "a two way girl."[8] He even forced her to work while menstruating. After four weeks at Hungarian Helen's she became ill. Gypsy Tom said she was faking the illness and beat her. Finally, she managed to leave, returning to hostess work in taverns and tea rooms. For a year, Helen worked as a waitress at the Green Kitchen, where her income averaged 11 dollars a week. But after her boyfriend became ill, she needed money. She returned to Hungarian Helen's but refused to pay Gypsy Tom. After two weeks, the madam said she would be circulated. Pete Balitzer came to look her over. Horvath explained she was selling herself to pay her boyfriend's medical bills. Pete remarked she was too nice a girl to be in the business; if she wanted out, he would help. Helen was booked into several houses, including one at 224 East 87th Street, frequented mostly "by policemen from the 101st Street Station," who never paid for sex, but they never raided the house either. Whenever she needed money, Pete always had an address available.

Jeanette Lewis, whose real name was Margaret Bell, was born and raised in Florida. She was 18, five feet four inches tall with brown hair, brown eyes and olive skin. In the spring of 1931, the teenager ran away from home. In Atlantic City she worked in a whorehouse for five months. She married Tommy Menna, a Philadelphia narcotics dealer with mob connections. Husband and wife transported drugs between Philadelphia, New York, Baltimore and Washington. A few months after her marriage, she began smoking opium and became addicted to heroin and morphine. After her husband was sent to prison on a narcotics conviction, Jeanette worked in Washington, until arrested for operating a disorderly house. After her arrival in New York she was booked by Pete Balitzer, even though she was mentally unstable.

Anna Cohen, 25, was a former beautician. Her mother was Jewish and her father Irish. Anna was an attractive redhead who wore glasses, dressed stylishly and displayed an air of refinement. Her sister, Marilyn Summers, was also a prostitute.

Muriel Ryan was a lovely woman who spoke with a lisp. Tall and slender, she was often compared to a showgirl. At the age of 15, Muriel completed high school in Indiana but soon eloped. Her parents had the marriage annulled. Muriel left home at 17 and became a prostitute in Indianapolis and various western cities. She arrived in New York in 1932. Nick Montana sent her to houses operated by May Spiller, Sadie the Chink, Pearl Woods, Grace and Evelyn, Birdie, then Pops at the Hotel Normandie. While working at Dago Jean's there was a raid. Muriel gave her name as Babe Jones. She was referred to *a whorehouse lawyer* named Emmanuel Bush, who coached her to lie. She lied, and the case was dismissed. Muriel was soon back at work.

When police raided Jean Bradley's house, located at 1 West 56th Street, Renee Gallo was arrested and taken to the West 47th street precinct station. After bail was arranged, she was directed to a bonding office near the Women's Court. She met Abe Karp, who suggested a seamstress alibi, then suddenly changed his mind, since she had been caught far from the factory district. Karp invented the identity of a sales clerk in a department store; if asked why she was at the house, she was to say, "just visiting." As Karp predicted, the case was dismissed in magistrate's court. Renee Gallo returned to work, servicing 18 to 20 men a night.

Nancy Presser was from Auburn, born to immigrants from Poland. Nancy grew up amidst the picturesque hillsides, where prominent families traced their lineage to pre–Revolutionary times. Polish immigrants settled in the parish of St. Hyacinth, a Catholic Church, only a short distance from Auburn Prison. Josef, Nancy's father, found work in a shoe factory. In 1926, at age 16, she was sent to Newark for three months to live with family friends. Instead, she chose to "take the tubes" and find excitement in the city.[9] Nancy, a shapely blonde with dark brown eyes, became an artists' model in Greenwich Village. Nancy also modeled hats and dresses at Wilson Brothers. She began an affair with a married florist, who rented an apartment for her on 75th Street. Nancy dated other men who gave her money. She wore custom tailored outfits, since one of her lovers was a dressmaker. Nancy's life changed when she learned a girlfriend was "on call," ready to service men when the telephone rang. Nancy liked the idea of selling her body. She frequented hotels and slipped cards to male guests. She averaged three sexual encounters per night. Nancy met Charley Lucky Luciano in 1927. Nancy's friend, Betty Cook, was Charley Lucky's girl. Betty was petite and pretty. Lucky expressed his fondness for Betty, but he had several girls, and they all gave him money. If Betty didn't make enough money, Lucky would beat her. A week after meeting Lucky, Nancy went to the Tip Toe Restaurant at Broadway and 80th Street. Lucky was there. They conversed until Betty arrived, but she didn't have much money. Lucky complained about Betty's disappointing week.

"Leave the kid alone," said Nancy.

"Shut up and mind your own business," he shot back.

Nancy knew Joe Masseria; she made professional calls to his apartment at the Hotel Beresford. She saw Lucky and realized he was a bodyguard. Nancy went to Chicago where she was intimate with members of the Capone gang. Nancy liked mobsters because they were good customers and generous with money. In 1929, while visiting Hot Springs with a client, Nancy met Willie Weber, a member of Waxey Gordon's mob. Waxey, whose true name was Irving Wexler, was a wealthy bootleg beer baron and narcotics dealer. Waxey hid millions of dollars in real estate investments. Gordon owned the Piccadilly, Palace, and Belvedere hotels and invested in Broadway musicals, including *Strike Me Pink* and *Forward March*. On her return to New York, Nancy was introduced to Waxey. The mobster and his associates became regular customers. On one occasion, after a party, Nancy boarded a special bus for a trip to Great Meadows Prison. Nancy rode with Broadway chorus girls.

At the prison there was a performance for inmates; all expenses were paid by Waxey Gordon.

One evening Nancy went to a party at the Belvedere Hotel. At the event was Waxey, Hymie Pincus, Chick Sherman and Willie Weber. This was the first night she smoked opium, and it made her ill. Months later, she returned to the hotel and "hit the pipe" once more. She again became nauseous; nevertheless, Nancy grew to enjoy the dreamy sensation and began smoking opium regularly.

Although Nancy found clients on her own, she occasionally answered calls to a 20-dollar house operated by Mrs. Max. The money was good, life was exciting, and her conscience never bothered her. Nancy enjoyed riding in limousines and frequenting trendy nightspots. At the Cotton Club she saw Lucky. He sat at a table with Big Frenchie and Dutch Goldberg; the trio disappeared in a private office.

Nancy kept in touch with her family in Auburn, sending money to her parents, but she never revealed her profession. In 1931 she met Ralph Liguori and fell in love. Ralph was in his mid–20s and charming. Ralph was born in Rome but grew up in Brooklyn. As a teenager he left school to work in the family's meat market in Sheepshead Bay, but Ralph had a secret life. Ralph was involved in criminal activities with Frankie Yale's gang. Liguori sold illegal alcohol and drugs. Ralph kept a mistress in a Brooklyn apartment. She was Josephine Gardello, known as "Gashouse Lil Gordon." Ralph extorted protection money from 15 to 20 houses. He guaranteed the madams that they wouldn't be robbed but only if they paid protection money. Ralph enjoyed double-crossing the madams. He bragged that he made most of his money robbing whorehouses. One of Ralph's tricks was entering a house of prostitution as a customer; suddenly, a phony raid would occur. Two confidantes, pretending to be police officers, displayed fake badges. The fake cops demanded the madam pay a five hundred dollar bribe or face immediate arrest. Ralph would graciously make the payoff for the madam, but he demanded one thousand dollars in return. Ralph had his hand in other ventures, including restaurant extortion, a scheme directed by Vito Genovese and Jerry Bruno. The mobsters demanded cash to prevent labor disputes. Ralph passed Joe Bloom's counterfeit bills at race tracks. If anyone asked his profession, Ralph said he was a butcher. "Wild Bill" Ercolino, his cousin, was a pimp for Peggy Wild. Ralph forced his mistress, Josephine, to prostitute herself. Ralph kept a room at the Central Park West under the name of Ralph Martin.

Nancy and Ralph spent time together at the Hotel Brent, where she lived. They shared secret lives. On Sundays, Ralph drove Nancy to dinner at his family's home in Brooklyn. At first, Ralph was pleasant and bought clothes and gifts for her. But his exterior charm masked a sadistic personality. After Nancy

The nephew of a priest, Ralph Liguori led a dual life: He was a vicious thug and pimp while legally employed as a butcher. He threatened to cut Nancy Presser to pieces (courtesy NYC Municipal Archives).

tired of him, she tried to move away. Ralph found her and threatened that if she ever left him again he would kill her. As time passed, Ralph's dual life, as butcher and criminal, created an increasingly unstable personality. Nancy was terrified.

After a night of drinking Nancy was ill, unable to sleep. A girl offered her relief. She swallowed a morphine tablet. Soon, she was injecting morphine in her leg. Several months later, she entered a sanitarium for treatment. The treatment stopped the morphine addiction, but her life with Ralph was an ongoing nightmare.

A prostitute's life was simply the fast road to death, said reformers; sooner or later, dope or disease would snuff out a pitiful existence but, until then, many girls enjoyed the fast money.

Thelma Jordan was an attractive woman with brown hair and hazel eyes; she was in demand by bookers and clients. Thelma was known for her uninhibited sexual charms. After graduation from high school, she worked in a drug store and theatre. At age 21, she joined the Beckman-Gary Carnival when it passed through Hutchinson, Kansas, in 1931. At a concession stand she sold soft drinks, candy, and ice cream for five dollars a day. She later worked in the penny arcade, but the job ended in Beaumont, Texas. Thelma traveled through the South for several months, until her savings disappeared.

Rather than return to her family and a dull life in Kansas, she went to New York in November 1933.

At Ann's Beauty Parlor at Seventh Avenue and 52nd Street, Thelma became friendly with a girl being styled. They went to a show and later had dinner. Thelma said she was broke and needed a job. She was given the telephone number of Nick Montana. Thelma started in a three-dollar house. Nick took the standard 10 percent fee. In a week, after expenses, she had made a profit of one hundred dollars. Then she was sent to 310 Avenue A. The clients were "plain, honest workingmen," who usually paid two dollars a visit.[10] There were few preliminaries, no kissing or foreplay. The men waited in the parlor. As one donned his coat and hat, another entered the bedroom. Thelma wouldn't remove her clothes until cash was produced. She was adept at fellatio and anything else the customer desired. Of course, those things were extra, so more cash was expected. Thelma averaged a hundred men per week. Clients were charmed by her Midwest drawl and uninhibited bedroom technique. But Thelma left the business to work as a hair stylist. She returned to Kansas for five months, but the excitement of New York brought her back. She resumed her career as a prostitute and met men in hotels, including the Belvedere, where she lived. For a while, she booked through Betty Cook, Lucky's prostitute-mistress. Like many girls in the business, Thelma kept her true name a secret. While working at Betty Winter's house she met Pete Balitzer. "Anytime you want a job," he said, "let me know and I will book you." But she remained with Nick Montana and his assistant, Jack Ellenstein. While working in May Spiller's house Thelma learned how lucrative a business whoredom could be. May operated the house with her common-law husband, Benny Spiller, a professional criminal and loan shark. Benny came in each day and removed the cash, fearful of robberies. Each week Benny would tally the girl's earnings. Once Thelma heard him complain, "Well, the business was not so good this week. We are used to taking in from twelve hundred to seventeen hundred." Benny fell for Thelma, and she became his secret mistress. Jack Ellenstein described Thelma as "a good number." That's what counted most. Paid sex was hard work. The girls pretended to enjoy sex when men took their pleasure. But the madams shrugged and greeted clients, smiling warmly as the crisp money was placed in a cold palm. When a girl satisfied a customer, the *john* was happy. He returned to the house each week, and the madam was happy. The madam telephoned the booker for more girls, and the bookers stuffed their pockets with commissions, and they, too, were happy. The greenbacks passed along the vice chain. And everybody was happy. Lucky Luciano wanted to share in the joy.

CHAPTER FIVE

The Takeover

I'll knock your teeth down your throat

By early 1933 the repeal of Prohibition was imminent. The attempt to ban alcohol had failed. Prohibition brought wealth to many, but now the golden goose was dying. Breweries that had produced weak, legal beer suddenly became desired businesses. During Prohibition, Luciano had forced Waxey Gordon and his partners, Max Hassel and Max Greenberg, to turn over a brewery in Union City, New Jersey. Lucky shared it with Willie Moretti, Abner Zwillman, Kid Steech Bongiovani and Carmine Sarbino. After legalization, Max Greenberg secured permits for various breweries but failed to obtain a permit for the Union City Brewery. Luciano was furious. So was Kid Steech. He murdered Hassel and Greenberg at the Cateret Hotel in Elizabeth, New Jersey.

Lucky's gang was unfazed by the beer fiasco. Their illegal enterprises, especially narcotics, brought the mobsters lucrative profits. Davie and Tommy retrieved secret shipments of heroin, smuggled aboard freighters, which they packaged for sale. They also worked together as loan sharks; clients who failed to repay were beaten mercilessly. Davie and Tommy were eager to seize the prostitution rings, but their plans suddenly came to a halt. Jerry Bruno claimed the bonding racket for himself, since he had brought it to the mob's attention. A bitter dispute began in the Luciano gang over which underling would control prostitution. A group comprised of pimps and bookers was successfully demanding bond money from the girls, they told Lucky.

The fledgling vice entrepreneurs were making money, and the Luciano mob wanted it. The vice-entrepreneurs were Charley Berner, Diamond Tooth Eddie, Big Jack, Johnny Wahl, Jack Goldstein, Patsy Santora, Jack Gillespie, and Johnny Fisher. The pimps solidified their business venture at a board

Dave "Little Davie" Betillo enjoyed high mob status due to his reputation as a killer for Al Capone in Chicago (courtesy NYC Municipal Archives).

meeting in a cafeteria on 49th Street. The new *combination* would demand 10 dollars a week from each girl working in a house and 15 dollars from the madam. The money would be pooled, taken to a bail office, and kept in an account to cover arrests. The madams would be told that *bonding* meant a guarantee of no conviction, since money would grease the palms of crooked bondsmen, attorneys and policemen. The arrangement had long existed with individual madams; now it would be organized. Diamond Tooth Eddie had already suggested clearance from *downtown,* fearful intruders might *muscle in.* He told the group that Jerry "the Lug" Bruno was close to Lucky Luciano. Bruno ran a gambling club over Moore's Restaurant at 245 West 72nd Street. A meeting with Bruno was arranged at Alphonse's Restaurant on Broome Street, near Mulberry Street. The vice-entrepreneurs waited patiently in the back room until 7:00 P.M. when Bruno arrived and listened to their proposal. They wanted to eliminate all competition. Bruno said he would think it over. Bruno told Davie about the combination. The pimps received word that Bruno approved the plan; they could drive out all the competition, especially bondsmen, but they were to use Bruno's name only, if necessary. The group approached Hymie Toline, whose wife wrote bonds. He was told to close down or join them. Hymie Toline surrendered. A few days later, the group went to the big-time bookers, intimidating them. They were told to join the combination. Pete Balitzer, Nick Montana, and Cockeyed Lou Weiner gave them a few houses, just to keep the peace.

Thomas "Tommy the Bull" Pennochio was a thief, narcotics dealer, loan shark and murderer. Taking money from prostitutes was his idea: "It looks like a big thing." Lucky agreed (courtesy NYC Municipal Archives).

The New High Grade Restaurant at 401 Eighth Avenue was the hangout of bookers Jimmy Fredericks and Tony Pisanelli. Jack Gillespie and Big Jack sauntered inside. Fredericks and Pisanelli listened. The bookers not only refused to turn over any houses, but they also demanded a piece of the bonding scheme. Gillespie and Big Jack were taken aback. They played their ace card and revealed that Jerry Bruno was the power behind the pimps. But Jimmy Fredericks and Tony Pisanelli simply shrugged; they would talk to Bruno. As a result, Bruno included them in the venture, too.

Shortly afterward, the group held a meeting at the Chesterfield Hotel. Jimmy Fredericks and Pisanelli unexpectedly took control. Jimmy the Gorilla assigned duties. The little gang of pimps was being swallowed. The big shot bookers were next, said Jimmy. They would be forced to pay protection money. Meanwhile, Charley Berner and Hymie Toline collected bonding money from whorehouses in Manhattan, while others collected money in Brooklyn. Charley Spinach Persana was cornered in a speakeasy on 29th Street. Fredericks and Pisanelli demanded that his chain of whorehouses pay bonding fees. Charley Spinach shook his head. He was protected by Dave Betillo and didn't want to submit. "See Little Davie," he told them, "he will let you know whether I should give you the houses."[1] Tony went downtown to straighten things out. He reported the results. "Davie doesn't think we are entitled to have the bonding business as he was one of the first

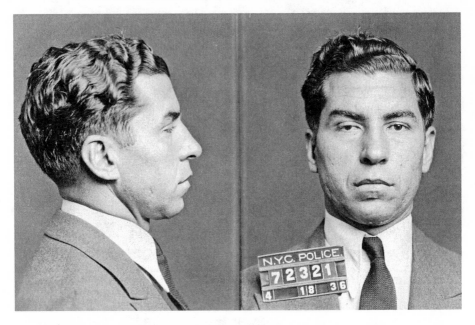

Salvatore Lucania, aka Lucky Luciano. An obsessive gambler and brutal gangster, "Charley Lucky" eventually saw his luck vanish (courtesy NYC Municipal Archives).

to be in the idea." The Luciano mob now claimed the bond scheme as its own project, but Bruno and Little Davie argued over control.

The pimps listened dumbfounded. Days later, Tony Pisanelli made an announcement: "Boys, there is going to be a meeting downtown and a decision given as to who is going to run this bonding business." Who was going to make the decision they asked.

"Lucky will be there," said Tony.

The next night the group met at Alphonse's. They assembled in a large room next to the kitchen. The fledgling vice-entrepreneurs sat at two tables, anxiously sipping espresso and anisette.

Lucky suddenly appeared. All the Italians stood, which surprised Charley Berner. Lucky shook hands with Betillo, Bruno and Fredericks and spoke to them in Italian. He surveyed the group sitting before him, and said, "You fellows are through. From now on Davie is taking over the bonding."

Berner and the others were afraid to say anything. Lucky walked out with Dave Betillo. The losers followed, stunned by Luciano's status and authority. "Just like he was a general," thought Berner, angered by the unexpected takeover.

The losers defied the edict and began collecting bond money. The news got back to Little Davie. He warned that heads would get broken if it didn't stop. The group realized they were no match for the Luciano mob.

A week later, Anthony Curcio, known as "Binge," was at the Hygrade Restaurant where he sold illegal booze. He overheard Jimmy Fredericks tell Danny Brooks: "I lost the decision downtown. Lucky told me to send my books over to Little Davie." Jimmy's new setup with the Luciano mob impressed Binge. Jimmy selected Binge as his assistant in the new operation.

Little Davie and Tommy the Bull had made a fast steal of the bonding scheme. Both were career criminals with violent personalities. Betillo lived with his attractive wife in a swanky apartment. His criminal career was a secret. Betillo's youthful appearance diverted police suspicion from his mob stature. Davie first served jail time in 1925, sentenced to 60 days in the workhouse for grand larceny; thereafter, he was arrested nine times with two convictions. Various robbery charges had been dismissed. In 1931 he was fined for drug possession. The next year he was arrested for possession of opium, which he had been smoking, but the charge was dropped. Davie was known as a narcotics dealer and gunman in the underworld.

Al Capone summoned Betillo to Chicago. This gave Little Davie high standing among mobsters. After Capone was sentenced to the federal penitentiary, Betillo returned to Little Italy with a deadly reputation. As a friendly gesture to Capone's former status, Little Davie was hired by Lucky and became the underworld's direct connection to the boss.

On the Lower East Side, where he grew up, Little Davie was regarded as "a benefactor."[2] Criminals approached Betillo for help. A loan shark unable to collect his debts would refer the matter to Little Davie, who would handle it, for a price. All decisions were approved by Lucky, who received financial tribute from his underlings.

In 1933, at the time of the takeover, Thomas Pennochio was 43. He resided at 89 Mulberry Street with his wife, Mary, and young son. Tommy had first been arrested at age 16 on a charge of disorderly conduct and sentenced to six months in a reformatory. Two years later, he was charged with grand larceny. He served 60 days in the city jail. In 1911 he was again arrested for grand larceny in Hoboken, under the name of "Thomas Nelson," one of his many aliases. He was sent to Elmira Reformatory for parole violation. In 1912 he was arrested for burglary and sentenced to a year and 10 months in Sing Sing. Tommy married in 1917; yet, rather than reform his life, he became further enmeshed in the underworld.

In January 1919, he was charged with narcotic sales and sentenced by Judge Hand to a year and a day in the federal penitentiary in Atlanta. In 1922 he ran the curbside alcohol exchange. In 1923, at the corner of Baxter and Canal Streets, Frank D'Avanzo was shot in the head during an altercation.

Tommy and two associates were arrested for homicide. But witnesses suddenly experienced memory lapses. In 1926 Tommy and George De Bello were arrested at Canal and Green Streets; they had offered to sell two pounds of opium to federal agents for $120. The charge was dismissed. Detective Milton Moffet arrested Tommy for selling narcotics in 1929. This time Tommy served 18 months in the Atlanta penitentiary. Once released, he was arrested for homicide but escaped prosecution.

As a front, Pennochio leased a soda fountain in a pharmacy at 230 Lafayette Street. He also pretended to be a barber. But his true profession was mobster. Like Davie, he had a reputation as a brutal killer and enforcer. Tommy the Bull struck terror in those who knew his real interests were narcotics, loan sharking, and murder.

Rose Lerner was hired by Tommy. She was a professional stenographer, 25, and married. When her position in an advertising agency ended, a pharmacist in Moe Ducore's Manhattan drug store telephoned her. The pharmacist introduced her to Tommy Pennochio. Did she know anything about bookkeeping? "A little," she answered. Lerner was hired to keep loan records.[3] Her salary would be 20 dollars a week. When she arrived at 72 Mott Street painters prepared the office. Tommy suddenly appeared. He handed her notecards and said if anyone came with money, just accept it. He introduced her to David Markowitz, an attorney whose name was painted on the window. Markowitz moved in a few weeks later. He informed Rose the office was a branch of his law firm, headquartered in Brooklyn. If anyone asked for him, simply take the message, and say she was his secretary. Rose Lerner organized Tommy's loan cards and performed minor typing for Markowitz. Tommy made five dollars on a 25 dollar loan and 10 dollars on a 50 dollar loan. All loan requests were referred to Tommy, and he alone decided if payment extensions would be made. Every month Tommy came in with an accountant named Tony. After a few weeks, Tommy brought Rose two new record books; one was for cash receipts, the other for payouts. At Tommy's request, she took the books home each night. Lerner also kept loan records for Benny and Willie Spiller, brothers who worked for Tommy. Benny Spiller was owed five thousand dollars in outstanding loans. "Cut Rate Gus" Koenig owed Tommy two thousand dollars. Gus sold dresses to prostitutes and loaned them money. After police made arrests in the loan shark business, Tommy instructed Rose to hide the loan records a few doors down, at Melnick's Glass Store. Each day she faithfully hid the books before going home. Markowitz paid the office rent, but it was Tommy who paid Lerner's weekly salary.

Abe Karp's bond office often telephoned for the attorney. On one occasion, Dave Betillo and Jimmy Fredericks came to see Markowitz. Jimmy told the attorney "a case was on." Lerner tried to be inconspicuous. She realized that Tommy was a loan shark, but she never asked questions.

The Bull kept several mistresses, including Mildred Curtis, a pretty 17-year-old from Akron, Ohio. Soon after her arrival in New York, a girlfriend introduced Mildred to heroin. Though married, she began living with a string of men and drifted into prostitution as a call girl. She met Tommy Bull at the Belvedere Hotel, introduced to him by Daniel Guidry, a racetrack bookie, and his wife Helen, a former model. Three months later, Mildred became Tommy's mistress. Tommy was her heroin supplier and visited her two or three times a week. Tommy introduced her to his friends, including Lucky. In a hotel lobby Tommy said, "Millie, meet Charles."[4] The men spoke privately. Mildred often saw them together. When Tommy took her to Foltis and Fischer's restaurant on 47th Street, he suggested they sit close to a window. "I'm waiting for somebody," said Tommy.[5] Soon after, Charles was on the sidewalk. Tommy went outside and spoke with him. When he returned she asked if something was wrong. "I seen the boss," he said. "Everything is okay."

Every week Tommy brought gifts and cash to Mildred; sums ranged from 50 to 150 dollars. Tommy told his mistress of secret narcotic shipments and occasionally asked favors. "I got about seven ounces of heroin. I want you to take it uptown."[6] At the Belvedere Hotel they enjoyed smoking opium together. During a *hop party*, Tommy, Daniel and Helen Guidry, and others passed around an opium pipe. Mildred was introduced to Dave Betillo. Later, a prostitute said Tommy was involved in the new bonding business. Mildred asked Tommy to explain it, which he did. Tommy Bull said Charley Lucky was the boss of the combination. She was curious how "Abie the Jew" got in the organization. "I thought the combination was only of Italians."

"We let Abie in because we needed the money and he had the money to give."

She asked Tommy who received most of the money.

"Well, Lucky is the boss, he gets the most. I get second, and the rest of the boys are even."

While walking on Broadway with Tommy, he suddenly said to her, "You want to meet a gorilla?" He introduced her to Jimmy Fredericks. When they walked away, she asked him what he did.

"If anybody needs taking care of he straightens them out."

Mildred answered professional calls at the Barbizon Plaza, where she sexually entertained Lucky. While the madams and girls were being coerced to join the combination, Lucky's enforcers went after the bookers.

In August 1933, Joe Levine and Harry Nichols accosted Pete Balitzer at Seventh Avenue and 54th Street. Pete was told a combination had been

Abraham Wahrman, "Abie the Jew," was a secret drug addict and a member of the Combination (courtesy NYC Municipal Archives).

formed and every booker would have to pay "for protection." Pete's bill was now $250 a week. Pete lied about his profits, claiming that he only made $125 a week for himself. He was ordered to a meeting the following day at Broadway and Marcy Avenue in Brooklyn.

On the corner was Abie the Jew, a blonde haired, blue eyed hoodlum with a violent streak. Abie Wahrman had seven thugs with him. Abie was angry with Pete's feeble attempt to fool the boys the day before. Abie told him told to pay $250 a week, which was cheap, since his weekly income was two thousand dollars. After more arguing, Pete said he would think it over and left.

A few days later, Joe Levine and Harry Nichols reappeared at 54th Street and Seventh. Levine said Pete had better settle or it would be "too bad."[7] Cockeyed Lou Weiner, Dave Marcus and Charley Persana paid, so Pete would have to reach in his pocket *fast*. The next day a meeting was held on 71st Street. Abie Wahrman came with his enforcers. Red Levine said the price was still $250.

"You take that money from me, I can't stay in business," Pete pleaded.

Levine lost his patience. "You will have to get out of town," he said angrily.

"Alright, I'll go home and pack."

"We'll take you home," said Levine.

Guns were pressed against Balitzer's stomach. The gunmen pushed him inside an automobile and they drove to Riverside Drive. The gangsters marched him to his front door. Pete's brother answered the buzzer. The men waved revolvers and demanded money. They began taunting Eddie Balitzer, until Pete protested. "What do you want from the kid, he is not in the racket."

"Eddie has to get out of town, too," said Joe Levine. Eddie begged his brother to settle with them. Pete saw the fear in Eddie's eyes and realized the enforcers might shoot them both. Pete reluctantly counted out a hundred dollars. Pete was ordered to be downtown the next night with more money. Pete agreed. After the thugs left, he told Eddie that the men wanted to control the town. Pete dutifully delivered the extortion payment to a candy store at 108 Norfolk Street each Monday. The money was sealed in an envelope for Abie Wahrman, as protection against "stickups and shakedowns."[8]

Soon after, Abie Wahrman accompanied Pete to a cafe at 121 Mulberry Street. He introduced Little Davie. He demanded that Pete turn over all of his houses. Pete didn't argue and gave Wahrman a list of addresses. Pete was ordered to explain the new setup to the madams.

After the meeting, Pete asked Abie who was behind the takeover. "Lucky," came the reply. Collectors soon swooped down on the madams. The mob discovered Pete was still hiding houses. Jimmy the Gorilla knocked on his door. "You know all those places got to be bonded," said Jimmy. "What are you holding out for? They are pretty sore downtown."

"That is a damn lie," answered Pete. "They can look over my list."

"You're holding out places and if you know what is good for you, you better go downtown and see Davie and Abie and get yourself straightened out or else you are going to get hurt."

Pete went downtown and tried to talk his way out of the trouble, but Wahrman was furious and slapped him repeatedly.

Eddie Balitzer pleaded with his brother to abandon booking, but it was hopeless. "Eddie, how could I give it up? I owe so much money. I can't get out of it. I wouldn't live ten minutes."

Mildred Balitzer went to see Little Davie at 121 Mulberry. "What is this I hear about this bonding and protection of bookies? Pete can't pay it."

Davie said there was nothing he could do.

"Who is behind this? Are you still working for Lucky?"

"Yes," he answered.

Jimmy Fredericks had become a major link in the bonding operation. Oscar Boim, the owner of Oscar's Luncheonette, discovered that Jimmy operated his own whorehouse, just a few doors away. When Tommy the Bull came to the restaurant, Jimmy told Oscar, "That is my combination man. Let him hang around."

Prostitutes came looking for Gorilla to pay commission fees. Boim told them to transact business outside. Jimmy met Fat and Skinny Rocci at the café, and the trio of pimps discussed procuring women from Pennsylvania, where they were eager to escape the mining regions. Finally, Oscar Boim became disgusted and wanted the entire gang out of his cafe. When Jimmy cursed and beat up a prostitute in the café, Boim called the police. When a mobster arrogantly tried to return a half-smoked cigar, Boim refused to accept it; the thug pulled out a gun. When the police started coming around regularly, Oscar told Jimmy and his friends to get out and stay out.

Frightened madams reluctantly deducted 10 dollars a week from the prostitute's money. When Muriel Ryan protested and refused to pay anything more, the madam didn't push the issue. Jimmy Fredericks began making visits. He spelled it out. "We are bonding all places now," he angrily told Molly Leonard. "The girls will be safe. If you don't bond, you won't be able to run. We will take the girls out on you."

Molly wanted to think it over. Molly complained to Pete Balitzer. Jimmy isn't the boss, said Pete. "There is good people behind the combination."

"What do you mean by good people?" she asked.

"Lucky is behind it," he replied.[9]

Gorilla heard of Pete's loose talk and warned him to shut up. Jimmy again came to Leonard's house of prostitution. With him was Dave Betillo. Thoroughly terrified, the madam acquiesced, paying 10 dollars a week for each girl. If the place was ever raided, assured Jimmy, she was to call the bonding office on 10th Street.

Jenny Benjamin balked at paying. "I never heard of a thing like this before."

"Everybody who wants to run is going to pay," said Jimmy. "You better make up your mind quickly unless you want your place broken up and your furniture thrown out the windows." Too frightened to resist, Benjamin submitted.

Charley Persana told Joan Martin she would have to join the bonding combination. She refused. Persana declined to book girls at her house. A week later, he returned with Abie Wahrman and three other men. Abie arrogantly flashed a ring with a pear-shaped cluster of diamonds and sapphires. A diamond studded platinum watch chain hung from his vest. "I came to collect 15 dollars," he said.[10]

The matronly woman with glasses shook her head. "I won't bond," replied Martin. "If I'm not arrested, I've still paid, and the money is thrown away." Abie the Jew turned to the enforcers. "Alright, go ahead and take the joint apart." Knives flashed. The thugs sliced the upholstery, then smashed chairs, tables and a sofa. Martin screamed, bringing the superintendent. "It's alright," said a henchman. "This is the police." Charlie Spinach begged them to stop, and the men left.

The next day there was a knock. Martin opened the door, secured by a chain. It was Charley Spinach and Jimmy the Gorilla. "This is a friend of mine," said Charley. "He wants to talk nicely to you." Martin agreed to pay Abie Wahrman 15 dollars a week. Instead, Joan Martin moved. But shortly afterward, there was a knock at her door. Through the peephole she saw Jimmy Fredericks. He had traced her, and he was mad. He kept banging on the door, until Lillian Gardello came to investigate. "Better open up before cops walk in on us," advised Lillian. Jimmy stormed inside.

"How come you did not call up the office and tell them that you moved?"

"I don't see why I should."

"You know you are still bonding."

"I don't want to bond anymore."

"I say you will."

"Jimmy, the best thing for you to do is get the hell out of here."

"I am going to knock you off your feet," threatened Jimmy.

"When you do it, you are going to have your hands full."

Jimmy bristled. "I'll knock your teeth down your throat."

He began slapping her. "You are going to take orders from me!" he shouted.

Martin fought back. Jimmy swung a blackjack but missed her. Martin's chow jumped on him. Jimmy pushed the dog away and pounded Martin twice on the head. Blood spurted from her scalp. Girls screamed and *johns* stared in fear. A girl rushed to the outer hall, shouting to the elevator boy to call a doctor. It took twelve stitches to stop the bleeding.

Martin moved again. There was a knock on the door. Through the peephole she saw Abie. She refused to let him inside. Then Ralph Liguori knocked on the door. He was alone. When Martin opened the door, two unseen thugs stepped into view. Ralph waved a gun and robbed her of a watch and 36 dollars. Before leaving he searched a prostitute's purse and removed a dollar, which he pocketed. Martin didn't argue. She made a few weekly payments to Abie, then moved. Months later, Martin was even angrier at Jimmy. He had sold one of her girls a fake driver's license for 15 dollars. The girl had been stopped while driving and was jailed. Martin made a telephone call and asked for "Jack Rose."

Binge answered.

Martin was given an address, which turned out to be the Hotel York. She sat with Jimmy and discussed the fake driver's license, but Jimmy wanted to know why she had again moved without telling him. Before she could answer, the phone rang. "When did it happen?" asked Binge. "Hold the wire." He turned to Jimmy. There had been a pinch.

"Check the list," ordered Jimmy.

Binge went to a light switch and removed the metal plate. He unscrewed it, and pulled out a piece of paper. He looked it over and handed it to Jimmy who nodded.

Binge returned to the phone. "They will be right down to get you out."

During the conversation Martin lost her nerve and slipped away. Not long afterward, she opened a house at 219 East 33rd Street after being out of business for a month. Abie Wahrman came for the 15 dollars. She protested that the collection date was the following Tuesday. In that case, said Wahrman, he just would have to remove the girl in the house.

"Go ahead," said Martin.

But the girl refused to leave. Thirty minutes later, Abie returned with Jimmy, who told the girl to get out. Martin asked for a break, saying that she had been closed and did not have the money. Jimmy said he was going to break her jaw. The girl refused to leave and Jimmy threatened her, too. Then he hit Martin in the face and beat the girl. Martin's chow jumped at Jimmy. He pulled a gun. Martin tossed the dog in the next room and grabbed a coat hanger. Jimmy hit her in the face. She had until the next day to raise 15 dollars.

Not long after, Martin had money trouble and asked the combination for a loan. She was sent to Jamison's Bar. Benny Spiller loaned her a hundred dollars and told her to make installment payments to his brother Willie. Benny bought her a beer. While they were drinking a group entered. "There is the boss, Charley Lucky," said Benny. Martin stared at the crime czar who forced the madams to pay. Everybody paid.

Greek-born Peter Tach ran a house of prostitution. He agreed to pay bonding fees. His booker, Nick Montana, was told to collect the bonding money and take it downtown. But when a raid occurred, the girls were stuck in jail. Their angry pimps came looking for Tach. He was abducted and driven to the Sunset Hotel on 45th Street. Jimmy Fredericks arrived with four enforcers. "Why didn't you bail the girls out?" he shouted.[11] Without waiting for an answer, Jimmy hit him. Tach was hustled to a hotel room upstairs as he tried to explain. In the hotel room was Nick Montana. Jimmy was furious, realizing that Montana had collected the bonding money for Tach's house but never turned it in. He pounded Montana, who feebly said, "The house was no good anyway and that's why I wouldn't turn it in." Tach was told to leave, as Jimmy and his enforcers began beating Montana.

After the takeover, Jimmy Fredericks became a familiar face in Abe Karp's bonding office. He often slept on a sofa during the day. Jimmy complained he was tired because he had been running around all night. When Jimmy offered Michael Redmonds a job as an assistant, the young man conferred with Jesse Jacobs. "Don't listen to him," warned Jacobs. "It's rather risky working for him."

Redmond was only a court runner and office boy, but little escaped his notice. He heard madams discuss business and exchange information about bookers. On one occasion he heard Pete Balitzer explode with anger: "What the hell does that madam mean, calling my girls dogs!"[12] The madams all agreed Pete had the best-looking girls. Spreading in the underworld was not only terror but also anger. Lucky's underlings were intimate with the madams and girls, and the boys were talking too much.

Benny Spiller and Thelma Jordan were out on the town several nights a week. Benny discussed business with her and admitted he was in the combination, allowed to join because the group needed bail money for the girls. If the madams refused to bond, said Spiller, their houses were robbed and wrecked. At Jamison's Bar he introduced Thelma to Jimmy Fredericks. "This is my partner. This is the guy I have to put up with all the time," he half-joked. Spiller was paid weekly, receiving a portion of the bond money. He told Thelma that Lucky was the boss of the combination. But Lucky was merely a phantom presence, since he was far removed from the sordid operations of the vice chain. Mob meetings were arranged in hotel rooms or in a building behind 121 Mulberry Street.

In July 1933, Antonio and Rosa Lucania moved from 10th Street to an apartment at 205 East 14th Street. Bartolo Lucania signed a lease for apartment 3A. Bart Lucania was secretary-treasurer of the Master Barbers Union in Brooklyn. Fanny Lucania had married a plumber and lived in White Plains. Lucky's sister Rosa had married and returned to Sicily. Joe was in the garment business. The building manager often observed Lucky visiting his parents late at night.

Lucky lived at the Essex House on Central Park West. Lucky invested $5,000 in the Helen Morgan Club on West 54th Street. He frequented expensive nightspots, meeting celebrities Harry Richman and George Raft. Lucky frequented the Jamaica Race Track and was a friend of Colonel Knebelkamp, whose *King Saxon* had established track records during the 1934 season and established a world record at the Jamaica track. Colonel Knebelcamp had been in the racing business for 35 years and gave tips to Lucky. After a day of betting at the track, the boss played high stakes poker. While Lucky lived the life of a playboy, his underlings brutally enforced the new laws in the sex underworld.

After Pete Balitzer was brought in line, Dave Marcus was next. In July a pimp called Crazy Moe visited Marcus at his home at 17 West 71st Street. Marcus supplied girls to Moe's whorehouse. Moe heard that a combination was being formed downtown, which would soon demand two hundred dollars a week from Marcus. For a fee, Moe would provide protection. Marcus said to forget it. He furnished women to 20 houses in New York and Brooklyn. He was making money and wasn't worried.

Ralph Liguori was asked if he wanted to join the combination. Ralph declined, The money wasn't enough, but he agreed to be a freelance enforcer. On a warm August evening Nancy rode with Ralph in his Cord automobile. They picked up Ralph's hoodlum friend "Johnny Roberts" Robilotto, Joe Levine, Jersey Ralph, Whitey and Little Dick. With the five passengers the Cord was crowded, so Nancy found a lap to sit on. Ralph drove to Eighth Avenue and 54th Street and parked. The men got out. Ralph ordered Nancy to remain in the car.

Near the Alba Hotel, as Dave Marcus and his wife crossed the street, they were surrounded by the enforcers. Marcus was shoved against a wall. Joe Levine pushed a knife against his stomach. "You have 24 hours to get out of town."[13] When Marcus begged for an explanation, he was punched in the face.

"We got orders," said Jersey Ralph, "that you get out of town or we give you the business." A second voice threatened, "Do you know Lepke and Gurrah?"

The gang returned to the car and drove off. Johnny Roberts accompanied Nancy and Ralph to their hotel room. Nancy asked Ralph what they had done. He told her. "I had orders from the combination downtown to tell him to get out of town and stay out, and that's what we did."[14]

When Marcus failed to leave, he got another message. As Marcus entered his automobile on 71st Street shots rang out, fired from a passing vehicle.

The following day, Moe called Dave Marcus. "I made a meet for you."

Marcus was terrified. "They shot at me yesterday. What are they trying to do, put me on the spot?" The same night he went to a saloon on Myrtle Avenue. Crazy Moe said the men present represented the combination. They demanded ten thousand dollars from him or he had to quit the business. Marcus called Abe Karp and signed a will. Crazy Moe telephoned again. Another meeting was arranged in a restaurant on Avenue C. Red Levine reduced the extortion payment to five thousand dollars. But Marcus put his furniture in storage and fled to California.

As the combination extended its tentacles, the bookers had more new women to supervise. Like livestock, the girls were kept healthy, so no complaints from clients could hinder business. To prevent venereal disease, some clients brought condoms to protect themselves; several madams sold them on the premises, but usually the girls and their clients took no precautions and disease was rampant. Danny Brooks introduced his "sweetheart" to Dr. Henry Seligman, to treat a vaginal discharge.[15] Seligman diagnosed sub-acute gonorrhea. The patient admitted that she was a prostitute. Danny began bringing in other sweethearts.

Dr. Seligman visited Pearl Gold's house in Brooklyn each week. The physician made a vaginal smear to determine if any girls were infected. The exam fee was three dollars. If test results were negative, Dr. Seligman issued a certificate stating the girl was in good physical condition. This was shown to clients.

Danny Brooks introduced the doctor to Jimmy Fredericks, who needed treatment. Jimmy was so pleased, he promised Dr. Seligman he would tell all the madams in the chain about the physician's services, assuring the doctor that lots of business would come his way. Relying on that promise, Dr. Seligman moved to 350 West 30th Street. Seligman demanded cash for his services and never kept records. The physician was contacted by Abe Karp. A city code stipulated that if a girl under arrest was infected or ill, the court had to place her in the custody of a doctor for treatment. It was simply another angle for quick release.

The physician observed the vice chain in operation. When Abie Wahrman came to Seligman's office each Monday night, the staff was told to leave. Jimmy handed over the weekly cash. Abie took the money to Dave Betillo. Jimmy booked girls from the medical office. Though Seligman complained about Jimmy's boorish behavior, he allowed the premises to be used as a combination hangout.

Everything seemed to running smoothly, but Danny Brooks was frightened. Jimmy advised him not to worry, just concentrate on their five houses: rotate the girls and at the end of the week, go out and collect the commission. Danny was leery of the business; too many people had their hands in the vice pie.

But Jimmy exuded confidence: "This is the toughest thing to convict anybody on."[16]

"I'm kind of scared," Danny admitted. He knew Jimmy the Gorilla wasn't the big shot. Caputo asked who was really behind the operation. Jimmy insisted that he was the head man.

"You haven't got no money; now I want to know the truth." Jimmy said that he wouldn't hold anything from Danny. "Davie, Abie, and Lucky were behind it," he revealed.

Dr. Seligman began receiving calls from other bookers, such as "Big John" in Brooklyn. He wanted Seligman to treat his black prostitutes "in the jungles." There were other vice physicians. Dr. Jacques Alper kept a plush office at 160 Park Avenue. Alper treated Nick Montana's girls and was New York's most prominent abortionist. He had been arrested in the death of a lovely 18-year-old girl. After Alper administered chloroform for an abortion, the teenager had died in his office. Alper had also been prosecuted for sexually assaulting a patient. A year earlier, he had been arrested for failure to notify police after he had treated a patient for a gunshot wound. All the charges had been dismissed. Dr. Myron Silberstein specialized in neurology and genital and urinary diseases. Each Monday he examined prostitutes at his 94th Street office. Silberstein diagnosed at least 16 cases of venereal disease a week from Pete's girls alone.

Physicians were required by law to report venereal infections to the Health Department, including the name and address of the patient, but the doctors who treated the vice underworld ignored the law.

When Shirley Mason was diagnosed with syphilis in Atlantic City, the physician reported her to the health office. Despite the untreated disease, Jack Ellenstein booked her into a house anyway, allowing her to copulate indiscriminately, scoffing that the law was "a lot of bunk."[17] Ellenstein eventually sent her to Dr. Ollswang for mercury injections; she developed an abscess on her hip, which required hospitalization, and Ellenstein refused to pay Mason's medical bill, so she was sent to a charity ward. Shirley didn't complain; it would be dangerous to do so. Ellenstein warned her that troublemakers were taken downtown for a beating. Ellenstein told her Dave Betillo "was a killer."

When booker Spike Green fell behind with his weekly payments, owing three hundred dollars, Jimmy summoned him to Dr. Seligman's office. "How about that money?"

"Charlie Spinach has it."

"You better come down to the corner and tell it to Davie himself. Davie thinks I'm taking the money."

After Spike left, Jimmy turned to Danny Brooks. "Take a walk to the corner, you will see some fun." Little Davie and Vito Genovese were waiting in front of the Mayfair Hotel when Spike approached.

"Where is that money?" Davie asked.[18]

"This week wasn't so hot," said Spike. Little Davie spat at him, then slapped Green with the back of his hand until his face was bloody.

Danny chauffeured Jimmy to 19 houses a week for collections. One morning Danny drove Jimmy to an elegant apartment building at 200 West 16th Street. After waiting for 90 minutes, Danny wanted to leave. The doorman escorted Danny to the elevator. He ascended to the top floor. When he rang the buzzer, a lovely woman, Madeline Betillo, opened the door of the plush apartment. When Dave Betillo saw who was asking for him, he became enraged and pushed Danny from the doorway.

Soon after the incident, Jimmy ordered Danny to a meeting at 121 Mulberry Street at seven in the evening. Pete Balitzer, Al Weiner, Charley Spinach and Nick Montana loitered at the cafe entrance when Danny joined them.

After Little Davie and Vito Genovese arrived, the bookers followed them through the café. They exited a rear door. Once outside, they walked through a courtyard to a brick building. They entered a hall and turned to the right. Inside a square room, ten feet wide, Little Davie sat at a large round table. "The reason I called this at such short notice," said Davie, "is so no cops would get wind of this." He threatened the bookers who were still hiding houses. The Luciano gang demanded that everyone in the sex trade pay tribute.

Danny often drove Jimmy to 121 Mulberry Street for conferences with Davie or Tommy. When a girl needed bail, Tommy Bull walked to his nearby apartment for the money. Danny was impressed by the power held by Davie and Tommy. Once, when girls were held on a bail fee of a thousand dollars each, they told Little Davie at the café. Judge Cotillo would not reduce the bail, said Jimmy. Little Davie disappeared for 20 minutes. An hour later, the bail was reduced.

On November 7, 1933, revelers across the country celebrated the death of Prohibition. Though alcohol was now legal, Lucky shrugged. Many bootleggers decided to open legitimate businesses, but not Luciano. Why go legit and pay taxes, just so the government can take the profit? Vito Genovese was cutting into Dutch Schultz's illegal lottery tickets, which brought more cash. Vito Genovese was a key *capo*. He had risen in the ranks of Joe Masseria's gang. His front was a junk and paper company at 184 Thompson Street in Greenwich Village. Vito was Lucky's age, born in Rosiglino, near Naples. His rap sheet was long, filled with charges ranging from assault to homicide. When his first wife died of tuberculosis in 1931, he fell in love with Anna Petillo, a married fourth cousin. Anna's husband was found strangled; 12 days later, Vito married Anna. Tony Bender Strollo was his best man. Though affiliated with Lucky's mob, Vito had his own enterprises. The prostitution takeover began while Vito and his wife were in Italy, where he presented a letter of introduction to Achille Pisani, an important fascist in Mussolini's government. On his return, Vito consolidated the illegal lottery in New York and New Jersey, and he shared the profits with Lucky. The money rolled in for the sultan of vice, but on the horizon was an approaching storm.

On January 1, 1934, Fiorello La Guardia became mayor of New York. La Guardia publicly denounced hoodlums and ordered the police to crack down on them. La Guardia's sincerity was manifest when he confiscated Frank Costello's slot machines from businesses. Mayor La Guardia proudly posed for newspaper photographs, sledgehammer in hand, smashing the slots, which were later dumped at sea. Costello arranged a deal with Governor Huey Long to transfer the slot machines to Louisiana. "Dandy Phil" Kastel, his partner, moved to New Orleans to supervise the new operation. Mayor La Guardia had personally told police to crack down on mobsters, especially Luciano. But Lucky wasn't worried. It was all part of the racket game; the cops and politicians make a little noise every now and then. But he disliked his name in the newspapers. In polite society he often called himself Charles Lane or Charles Ross, to avoid notoriety.

In Saratoga Springs, the racing season drew society aristocrats and millionaires. During the day racing enthusiasts placed bets on the thoroughbreds. At night the wealthy frequented the expensive nightclubs on the outskirts of town, the Arrowhead, Piping Rock, and Riley's. For five dollars there was dinner and cocktails. Helen Morgan, Harry Richman, and the Yacht Club Boys sang and danced. Professional prostitutes were available in many nightspots. At Jack's Hi De Ho, mulatto professionals mingled with the clients. Though gambling was illegal, the nightspots had casinos. There were rumors the swankier places had fixed roulette wheels and loaded dice.

Meyer Lansky and Frank Costello had major investments in the Piping Rock. It was known that Lucky owned the Chicago Club, with attorney Jim Leary as his front. There was talk he was part owner of the other casinos as well. Lucky and Fred Bachmann, his gambling partner, came to Saratoga each season. They openly ran the craps game at Smiths.

After dinner, patrons gambled at the six roulette wheels, and blackjack and craps tables. The games were designed to separate the rich from their money. Lucky supervised as attendants raked in the dice and a man named Cardoza handled the cash. Lucky gladly took the suckers' lost bets, paying 10 percent of the profits to manager William Bischoff. In the Saratoga casinos Lucky met wealthy gamblers and arranged high-stake card games with them in New York City.

Hot Springs, Arkansas, was also favored by the sporting crowd. The elite stayed at the fashionable Arlington, a magnificent, twin-towered hotel nestled above Central Avenue. Tourists came to Hot Springs to enjoy the thermal mineral baths and to frequent the races at Oaklawn Park. And there was nightly gambling.

Lucky was a frequent visitor to Hot Springs and owned property in the area. He was a friend and business associate of William S. Jacobs, the owner of the Belvedere Club, a spacious supper club and gambling casino. The Belvedere's lobby boasted crystal chandeliers high above sleek chrome furniture and a huge stone fireplace. The dining room could seat several hundred guests. Guards with loaded shotguns patrolled the parking lots. Jacobs, a dour, dark-eyed man with an artificial leg, limped along, leaning on a black cane with a gold handle. Jiggs, his pet dog, trailed at his heels, the only dog in town with a gold tooth. Jacobs was quite wealthy. He also operated the Southern Club, a horse racing parlor, and owned several smaller turf clubs in the area. Jacobs owned extensive property, including the Belvedere Dairy, a front for bootlegging; corn liquor was hidden in dairy trucks and hauled to northern cities. Jacobs was generous to his girlfriends, bestowing lavish gifts, cars, jewelry, and perfume. Though powerful, Old Man Jake was respected by many because he helped many poor families survive the hard times of the 1930s. He could afford such generosity. The tuxedoed gents and jewel-draped ladies lost high sums of money. The dollar bills won at the Belvedere each night were so plentiful that they weren't even counted but boxed for the bank tellers to handle.

W.S. Jacobs, the gambling king of Hot Springs, was Lucky's friend (courtesy Garland County Historical Association, Hot Springs, Arkansas).

Next to St. John's Catholic Church lived Owney Madden. The notorious killer had married Agnes Demby, the postmaster's daughter. The Maddens lived in a small house, hidden by rose trellises, with carrier pigeons in a shed in the rear. Owney Madden kept a low profile but exerted influence in private. Reports circulated that he was in secret partnership with Old Man Jake.

Al Capone, his brother Ralph Capone and their Chicago associates were frequent visitors to Hot Springs. Scarface Al passed out money and big tips. He once requested that a band play *After You've Gone,* then handed the musicians five hundred dollars.

Mobsters had hidden investments in Hot Springs or, as the locals termed it, "a bankroll interest."[19] The hidden operators would lease a building in a local person's name; that individual would sublease to a third party who received rent for a gambling saloon, restaurant, brothel or legitimate store. Mobsters, gamblers and even Oklahoma oilmen, dodging taxes, came to town. All took advantage of the clandestine business deals. After normal hours, restaurants became private social clubs, closed to the public, but open for high-stake gambling.

For decades Mayor Leo P. McLaughlin ran the city. He allowed the out-

Club Belvedere, circa 1935. Hot Springs offered classy gambling resorts long before Las Vegas did (courtesy Garland County Historical Association, Hot Springs, Arkansas).

of-state gangsters to transact business, as long as there was no violence and the mayor was rewarded. Casino gambling was illegal in Arkansas, but politicians and law officers in the capital ignored the clubs, even though church groups constantly complained about vice. Old Man Jake knew where to send the tribute envelope, and there was seldom serious trouble. Outlaws, thieves, and robbers could hide in Hot Springs. Mayor McLaughlin's administration was as crooked as a three dollar bill. Not only was gambling winked at, but also whorehouses were commonplace. Most days, blonde Grace Goldstein walked her Great Dane along Central Avenue. In winter, Goldstein's ample bosom was snuggled in a fur coat. She strutted past the Arlington, to the Hatterie Hotel next door. Grace daily walked past the lobby hat shops that gave the building its name. On the second level was a bar and dance floor. Young women poured drinks, enticingly dressed in sexy gowns and high heels. Nearby were gambling rooms. On the third floor was a brothel where Grace was the madam. Lovely women, between ages 17 and 24, were available.

Alfred Raso, known as "Mr. Gee," was a Sicilian-born saloon keeper from Chicago.[20] He had been an aide in the Capone circle and had worked as a bouncer and doorman at Texas Guinan's club in Manhattan. Raso became Frank Costello's assistant. Raso was introduced to many underworld figures, including Charley Lucky. In 1935 Raso went to Hot Springs with Bugsy Siegel. They stayed at the Arlington for two months, and invested 25 points in the White Front Club, at a thousand dollars a point. Dick Glattis, former operator of the club and a sports bookie, was in prison, serving time for harboring Frank Nash, a bank robber later killed in Kansas City.

"Mr. Gee" Raso looked after outside investments. He leased a resort residence on Lake Hamilton, which became an Italian restaurant. The resort had a bar, slot machines, and a card room. Al Capone, Frank Nitti and other mobsters were welcome guests. Hot Springs was paradise for the underworld. Frank Costello gave Raso $35,000 to start the Villa Nova Restaurant. Hot Springs impressed Bugsy Siegel, who eventually moved to Las Vegas.

Lucky always stayed at the Arlington Hotel. Across the street was the Southern Club, decorated with striped awnings over the windows. On the main level was a café. A winding marble staircase led to the racing room. Under a domed ceiling an ornate chandelier illuminated mahogany counters where sporting gentlemen studied racing forms. Results would come in from the major tracks, from Hialeah to Santa Anita. Lucky owned an interest in the racing wire service. Though Lucky spent August in Saratoga, winter was divided between Miami and Hot Springs. Life was good. Back in New York the vice chain grew as madams were forced to join the combination.

Charley Persana paid a business call to a brownstone residence at 225 West End Avenue. It was Flo Brown's place. Charlie had a friend with him.

"Meet the bondsman," said Persana.[21]

Flo recognized Ralph Liguori. She knew his reputation as a stickup man. "You ought to bond," said Ralph.

"But I'm broke," answered Flo, who was an opium and cocaine addict.

Soon after, Charley Spinach returned with Jimmy. She liked Jimmy, and the bonding operation seemed reasonable to her. Flo began dating Jimmy. He stayed at her brownstone three or four nights a week. Flo fell in love with Gorilla.

A few months later, Flo was living with Jimmy on 77th Street, as his mistress. He proudly told her how the bonding business had started, but anytime he had to bail anyone out he had to ask Tommy the Bull. He explained there were a dozen people receiving percentages. Among the group were Lucky, Dave Betillo, Jerry Bruno and Vito Genovese. The combination was making money, but a large portion was set aside for safekeeping in case of pinches. After payouts, Jimmy told her the weekly profit was usually five or six hundred dollars.

In the pre-dawn hours they borrowed Benny Spiller's car. Flo drove

Jimmy to a Chinese restaurant at Broadway and 130th Street. They arrived at 3:00 A.M.

At a large booth sat Lucky, Davie and Tommy.

"Meet a girlfriend of mine," said Jimmy the Gorilla.

Flo sat opposite Lucky. The men conversed in Italian, as Flo ate lobster and steamed rice. Afterward, she drove the men downtown. They discussed bonding. "I think some of the bookies are holding out joints on us," said Jimmy.[22]

"Can't you get them all together?" asked Lucky.

Davie answered it could be done, but he pleaded for time. Jimmy said the problem was the bookies holding out the addresses.

Lucky had a solution. "Well, I tell you what to do. Bring all the bookies downtown tomorrow, I will put them on the carpet, and we will see that doesn't happen again."

"Nick is the worst offender," said Jimmy. The conversation switched to Italian, then back to English when they discussed Jerry Bruno taking over a whorehouse on Long Island that was faring poorly and turning it into a gambling spot. They agreed that Long Island houses should be forced to pay bonding fees. Flo parked near 121 Mulberry Street, and the trio walked away. Days later, Jimmy told Flo that the bookies had come down and were "bawled out" by Little Davie. "Nick thought he would get away with it because he has a brother, a big shot in Harlem; they didn't care whether he had 50 brothers; he had to kick in just the same." Jimmy said the bookies would receive a five hundred dollar fine for every house not reported.

Nick Montana did as he was told. Nick warned Muriel Ryan, who always complained, that she had to pay bond fees. Thereafter, bond money was regularly deducted from Muriel's earnings.

Although Flo was the mistress of Jimmy Fredericks, she was also a prostitute, no longer a madam due to drug use. Flo worked at a house at 124 West 72nd Street for several months. In the fall, Flo drove Jimmy and Benny Spiller to a garage on the Lower East Side. She was left in the car, but she stepped out and walked near the garage. Flo heard loud voices echo in the garage. Benny was told to keep his mind on "shylocking, and not to be so much of a pimp." Spiller was also suspected of not turning in bond money and threatened. Flo saw Lucky, Davie, and Tommy Bull leave the building.

On another occasion, Flo again overheard the men arguing inside the garage, angry over recent police raids. Jimmy spoke: "We have got to get some pictures taken of the locks. That the doors were broken in without warrants and we have to get three or four lawyers to represent the madams and girls. If we just get one, people will realize it is a combination." Flo listened to Jimmy's complaints that he was poor, that all the money went downtown.

She began working at 333 West End Avenue, falling deeper into cocaine addiction.

Through her boyfriend Ralph, Nancy Presser also observed the inner workings of Lucky's gang. Ralph sold narcotics with Tommy the Bull and his brother Johnny Pennochio, who used the name Johnny DeLucca. Nancy drove with Ralph to piers along the North River, where smuggled narcotics were loaded and transported to Brooklyn. While driving on a drug pickup with Ralph, Tommy, and Johnny DeLucca, the men told her that if anything went wrong, she was expected to say the narcotics belonged to her. On the return trip, the automobile was guarded by a second car driven by Joe Bloom and enforcers with machineguns. They deposited the drug shipment at Frank Celano's Restaurant at 98 Kenmare Street.

Ralph continued robbing houses of prostitution. He kept three guns under the mattress of Nancy's bed at the Emerson Hotel. When Nancy accompanied him on the robberies, she was ordered to carry the pistols. After a robbery, Nancy wanted money for new clothes and asked him how much money he had taken. Not so much, Ralph revealed; after the combination was formed Jimmy or Tommy demanded most of his robbery loot.

During the time Nancy and Ralph had a relationship she continued to see other men. Nancy conducted a private business from which she supported herself. Nancy made dates with her regular clients and kept names and telephone numbers in a black memo book. Nancy was afraid of Ralph. When arguments erupted, he would threaten to kill her. He brandished a knife and jabbed her in the back or legs as a warning. Lillian Gardello telephoned Nancy, cursing her, saying she worked without rest for Ralph, but that he spent the money on Nancy. But Ralph took Nancy's money, too. She was averaging two hundred dollars a week. She paid for the hotel room and tried to hide money before Ralph snatched it. As time passed, Nancy became knowledgeable about "the downtown mob," as she called it. Each night Nancy and Ralph drove to Little Italy. Celano's was a regular meeting place for "the boys." Ralph delivered money extorted from restaurants to Vito Genovese and Jerry Bruno. Nancy usually remained in the car, but on one occasion she went inside Celano's, where Ralph introduced her to Tommy Bull. Another mob hangout was Godolfo's on Broome Street, where deals were made concerning dope and counterfeit currency. Like Flo Brown and Jimmy, she accompanied Ralph to the Sixth Ward Garage, next to 146 Mulberry Street. Nancy waited while meetings were held in the office upstairs. She saw Little Davie, Vito Genovese, Jerry Bruno, and Abie Wahrman enter.

One evening, while Nancy was seated in Ralph's car, parked in front of a cafe on Mulberry Street, she saw Tommy Pennochio and Jimmy Fredericks emerge. They stood on the sidewalk near the car. Nancy slumped in the front seat so they wouldn't see her, but the window was open and she overheard part of the conversation. Jimmy said the combination was going to go after all the independent houses; they would be forced to join the bonding operation. "We'll close them up if they don't," said Tommy.[23]

One night Nancy and her date walked into Kean's Tavern. She was introduced to Lucky. He winked at her, a hint that he remembered her from earlier days. Before leaving, she handed him a slip of paper with her telephone number.

In May Lucky appeared before Chester G. Wagar in Troy, New York, and requested a permit for a Colt pistol. He lied that he was a salesman and an American citizen. Surprisingly, Lucky had never been naturalized. Lucky swore in court he had never been convicted of a crime.

Everything was running smoothly. The takeover of the vice chain didn't bring in the money the mob expected, not yet, but it would pay eventually. Like Pete Balitzer, Cockeyed Lou was being forced to hand over extortion money. As the largest booker Cockeyed Lou's tribute was assessed at two hundred dollars a week. Al Weiner delivered the money to the candy store. Abie Wahrman's name was printed on the envelope. Dave Marcus was still in hiding in California.

The bookers, madams, and girls grumbled but did nothing. How could they? If they complained to the police, they might end up dead. Besides, the kingpins would never fall. Politicians and police officers were bribed to protect the mobsters. Honest citizens were disgusted, too. Corruption was rampant. New Yorkers believed the vice empire would never fall.

Chapter Six

Rotten to the Core

Tammany Hall represents all that is evil in government

By flaunting the Volstead Act, New Yorkers satisfied their thirst for illegal booze but at a high cost. Organized crime had subverted the electoral process. Payoffs to politicians and police had rotted the social fabric of society. No longer did the average citizen feel confident elected officials answered to the voters.

A half century earlier, William Marcy "Boss" Tweed bled the city dry. As the leader of Tammany Hall, which dominated the Democratic Party, Boss Tweed exerted control of New York from the beginning of the Civil War to 1876, when he was jailed. The New York County Court House, 70 feet from City Hall, was a money tree. Billpadding allowed Tweed to line his pockets; a chair that cost $15 was charged to the city for $300. Tweed also sold judicial and legislative protection. Tammany Hall, ostensibly a social organization, named after a chief of the Algonquin Indians, was in reality a nest of political intrigue, where payoffs abounded.[1]

With the arrival of Prohibition, political graft exploded. In the 1920s, James J. "Jimmy" Hines controlled political district leaders for the entire West Side of New York, including the Broadway district where nightclubs and speakeasies were numerous. The Tammany overlord supported city aldermen, state legislators, and congressional members. Wherever illegal alcohol was poured, influence was bought with payoffs to officials. In 1926, at a public political dinner, novice reporter Warren Moscow was shocked to see the mayor, the police commissioner, district attorney, and members of the judiciary drinking "the best alcohol bootleggers could provide."[2]

City jobs were for sale as Mayor James J. Walker turned a blind eye. Law-abiding citizens felt helpless. Even judicial positions were bought and sold. George Ewald paid $10,000 to a Tammany district leader. After he resigned from the bench, Ewald was indicted for using the mail to defraud stock investors in a mining deal.

Deaths proliferated as mobsters vied for territory and profits. Dutch Schultz, born Arthur Flegenheimer, controlled the Bronx beer trade, with his partner Joey Noe. On October 16, 1928, shots rang out and Joey Noe was murdered. Dutch continued his rise alone and seized control of the numbers game in Harlem. Schultz extorted money from restaurant owners, who were forced to join a phony trade association.

Vincent Coll, once a Schultz gang member, began encroaching on speakeasy trade and lotteries. Coll and his thugs ambushed members of Schultz's gang outside a social club in East Harlem. In the gun battle four children were wounded, and a baby in a carriage died. Later, Coll shot Joe Mullins, a member of Schultz's gang. Thereafter, the press dubbed him "Mad Dog" Coll. As retaliation, his brother, Peter Coll, was murdered by Schultz. Not long afterward, Vincent Coll stopped at the London Chemist Drugstore, at 314 West 23rd Street to make a telephone call. Machinegun bullets shattered the phone booth and ripped into Coll.

Some died, some prospered.

Before his retirement to Hot Springs, killer Owney Madden had hidden interests in nightspots like the Cotton Club. Big Frenchy De Mange, his partner, had been indicted for stabbing a man, but the case never went to trial. Frenchy was later arrested for safe cracking and mail robbery. With Prohibition he found easy money. De Mange entered the fight world and backed Italian boxer Primo Carnera in rigged bouts.

Lepke and Gurrah, nicknames for Louis Buchalter and Jacob Shapiro, had started as strikebreakers against unions. They worked for Little Augie Orgen until they murdered him in 1927. But by 1933, they hid behind a respectable facade and hired others to intimidate and kill.

While criminals raked in racket money, the Roaring Twenties ran out of steam with the Wall Street crash of 1929. Stock value vanished, along with millions of savings accounts. The Great Depression shocked the nation as banks and factories closed. Quipped Will Rogers: "You stand in line to get a window to jump out of."[3] Twenty-five percent of city workers were dismissed. Shantytowns sprung up in city parks. A crowd of 100,000 leftists staged a rally in Union Square, which ended in a riot.

Jimmy Walker, elected in 1926 after 14 years in the state legislature, enjoyed support as a popular mayor. Seen nightly on the town, charming and witty, Mayor Walker made good newspaper copy. The mayor thwarted a move to censor novels with a sharp retort: "I have never yet heard of a girl being ruined by a book."[4]

Though 18,000 men comprised the police department in the 1930s, and 40 percent of the city budget was for the protection of life, property, and health, crime spiraled; 350 people were slain in 1930. Graft was rampant, as well as outright police extortion, with framing of innocent girls and women. "Vice Fiends Prey Upon Mothers," headlined the *Daily Mirror*.[5] In a shocking story New Yorkers read how the respectable wife of a physician had been arrested for vagrancy. Booked at the West 100th Street station, she remained overnight. After release, she was told to contact a specific lawyer, and did so, at which time he asked for her diamond engagement ring. The woman later discovered her apartment had been looted.

Subsequent investigations exposed how Louis Taube, a criminal called "the Dove," confessed his partnership with vice squad detectives, known as "body snatchers."[6] The Dove lived in an expensive apartment on West 70th Street and even had a valet. He boasted how the ring had operated for 15 years and netted an average of $13,000 per month. Their techniques were similar to the story of Winifred Grayson and her cousin, both arrested in a seven-man raid, accused of being whores. A raider slapped Grayson's face and stole her purse, cash, and jewels. Then she was pushed down a flight of stairs. But the most notorious case was that of Rose Ricchebuono, a stout, convent-bred housewife, the sister of two priests and a nun, whose two uncles were monsignors. She stood at a window waving farewell to her husband when a stranger entered her home and made an indecent proposal.

"Get out or I'll scream for help!" she yelled.[7]

The intruder grabbed her wrist and pushed her against the wall. She was arrested for prostitution. In court she pointed: "This policeman handled me like a gorilla."

If terrified women had money to bail themselves out of jail, the name of a bondsman and attorney was provided, and they were released. The attorney to contact was Abe Karp. Angelina Coloneas, a young Greek waitress, was victimized. The policeman, bondsman, and lawyer took eight hundred dollars from her before the magistrate discharged her case. Two months later, the same policeman entered her room and sprinkled white powder in a closet, then arrested her for narcotics possession. She lost six months of savings defending herself.

Emanuel Lavine, a newspaper reporter, captured New Yorkers' anger. "Our present judicial system is a humorless farce," asserted Lavine in a shocking book published in 1931. He documented numerous cases of corruption by police, judges, city officials, and even school directors. But unlike the old days, when Boss Tweed ruled, unseen masters were pulling the puppet strings. As always, Tammany prevailed, ignoring reformers and their cry echoed by the press.

Political clubs in Manhattan and Brooklyn were places where elected officials met, but gamblers ran craps games in the clubs and paid the district leader a portion of profits. In 1930 Albert Marinelli announced his candidacy for the district leadership of the Lower East Side, a position held by Harry Perry, a member of Tammany Hall. Perry was Chief Clerk of the City Court. Two men entered Perry's office, located in the court house built by Boss Tweed: "Lucky has a message for you. You're through." They patted the guns in their pockets. A few days later, a reporter asked Perry if he intended to fight to keep his leadership. "Do you think I'm crazy? Do you think I want my people shot down in the streets? They can have it."[8] Lucky's thugs took over the polling places south of 14th Street. Gunmen rang up the votes as cops looked the other way. Marinelli promptly appointed Joseph "Socks" Lanza to a $3,600-a-year job as assistant clerk in the Second District Municipal Court. Socks Lanza controlled the Fulton Fish Market. Lanza had been arrested 17 times, including once for homicide. Socks Lanza, 32, was the business agent of the United Seafood Workers Union. Socks enforced violence against union members who spoke against him.[9] In June 1932, Lucky and Marinelli traveled to Chicago to attend the Democratic National Convention. They spent time at the race track and jointly entertained in Marinelli's room at the Drake Hotel. Marinelli became the leader of the Second Assembly District and a powerful politician.

New Yorkers were fed up with the rampant corruption. What finally triggered an investigation was the disappearance of Judge Joseph Crater. After saying goodbye to friends in front of a West 45th Street restaurant, Crater stepped into a taxi and was never seen again. There was strong suspicion that Judge Crater had bought his seat on the bench. Had Crater been murdered? Governor Franklin Roosevelt called for an official inquiry.

Justice Samuel Seabury was appointed to investigate the Magistrates Court.[10] Seabury, a former court of appeals judge, was a Republican but supported by honest citizens of both parties. Seabury examined court financial records. As a result, three judges resigned and two were removed, including Jean Norris, the city's first female judge. Seabury uncovered the police ring that trapped innocent women and prostitutes alike for the purpose of extortion. The ring operated in Women's Court. In one instance, a framed woman, charged with prostitution, was obviously innocent, but she had been sentenced to a hundred days in the workhouse. The investigation documented that Judge Jean Norris altered the official record to protect herself from accusations of violating the defendant's rights. It was apparent that innocent people were expected to pay bribes before release.

The nine deputy district attorneys assigned to various magistrates courts in Manhattan did little prosecution. Seabury discovered one of the nine had not even filed work reports to his superior, the District Attorney. But during seven years he had "helped to throw out six hundred cases and stowed away a tidy fortune in bribes."[11] Lawyers and bondsmen also were in the bribe system. And where was District Attorney Thomas C.T. Crain? Citizens and the City Club of New York called for an investigation. Governor Roosevelt relied on Seabury to investigate the Manhattan District Attorney's office. Seabury found no evidence that D.A. Crain was involved in criminal activities but regarded him as grossly incompetent. Seabury uncovered how Socks Lanza was engaged in racketeering. Every two years the United Sea Food Workers Union negotiated a contract with Carman and Company, seafood distributors. Lanza was paid $5,000 by the company to *prevent* union wage increases. Seabury reported that racketeers controlled dozens of industries. The state legislature passed a resolution calling for a committee to investigate the departments of government in New York City. On May 25, 1932, Judge Seabury questioned Mayor Walker. Walker had to explain a bus franchise he had awarded, despite lower bids by competitors. Most damaging was a joint brokerage account, to which he had contributed nothing but others contributed money for him. The account earned $246,692. It was obviously an account for payoffs. Mayor Walker later resigned in disgrace.

Mob control of unions was a lucrative source of money, especially in the garment and longshoreman unions. The mob even controlled movie theaters. In 1932 George Browne lost the presidency of the International Alliance of Theatrical Stage Employees. Two years later, Browne decided he wanted a return to leadership. In Riverdale, Illinois, he met with Chicago mobster Frank Nitti. Louis Buchalter arrived in Riverdale. Buchalter said he would return to New York, to discuss the situation with Charley Lucky and Harry Sherman, business manager of the local union in New York. Browne and labor racketeer Willie Bioff had been involved in extorting money from motion picture studios, to defeat strong unions. Browne and Bioff had evenly split the payoffs with the Chicago mob. The mob sanctioned Browne's return to leadership but demanded "two thirds" of the studio extortion money.[12]

Citizens who resisted mob decisions were murdered. Lepke and Gurrah directed a team of assassins. The death contracts were carried out by Albert Anastasia's team of killers. The initiators of the arrangement had been Lucky, Dutch Goldberg, Frank Nitti, and Joe Adonis. The execution squads were unknown to law enforcement. The scheme was a perfect arrangement; the murder directive was passed along through a hierarchy, so no evidence could ever touch the bosses.[13]

The government fought crime as best it could. The federal government prosecuted Dutch Schultz for tax evasion. Schultz fled, afraid to surface due to his tax troubles. But his gang continued paying Jimmy Hines, who made certain the police in Harlem avoided arrests; so the numbers games prospered. Restaurant extortion continued. Mob-controlled unions and a fraudulent restaurant association intimidated businessmen and collected thousands of dollars.[14]

In May 1933, Leo Linderman, the owner of Lindy's Restaurant at Broadway and 51st Street, was told he had to increase staff salary and unionize. He refused. Pickets appeared, then a stink bomb exploded; the stench remained in Lindy's for nearly two weeks. Linderman gave in. He paid $2,750 for labor peace, and $150 each month. The owner of the Metropole Bar and Grill was forced to pay $3,500 to join the Metropolitan Restaurant Association. Other restaurants capitulated; owners were forced to sign a contract that denied coercion. The owners were given a gold plaque designed and manufactured by Jules Martin, a member of the Schultz gang. Even boxing champion Jack Dempsey was afraid. To protect his restaurant, Dempsey paid extortion money. The mob controlled the Waiter's Union. Those who resisted paid dearly. When union official Abe Borson refused to remove a picket line from a restaurant that had just paid $7,500, he was forced in a car and driven to a lonely road in Westchester. He was told to say his prayers and executed. Almost daily, the city newspapers featured horrific murders.[15]

After a decade in New York City, Thomas E. Dewey was disgusted by the gangster mayhem and political corruption. A native of Owosso, Michigan, Dewey was the descendent of a staunch Republican family. As a young man, he had trained for a career in music. At the University of Michigan in Ann Arbor, Dewey studied literature but loved opera and hoped for a career as a stage singer. Dewey's rich baritone won the Michigan State Singing Contest. In 1923 he competed in the National Singing Contest in Ashville, North Carolina, and placed third. Dewey's superb voice led to a scholarship at the Chicago Musical College, where he became a student of Percy Rector Stephens, a renowned voice coach. Despite his love of music, the law became a passion. Dewey fell in love with Frances Hutt, a singer from Sapulpa, Oklahoma. When Frances went to New York to continue voice studies, Dewey followed. In the fall of 1923, Dewey joined the Episcopal Church of St. Matthew and St. Timothy, where he sang each Sunday. But Tom Dewey was more than a choir boy; at heart Dewey was a fighter.[16]

"Tammany represents all that is evil in government,"[17] said his father. The machine politics of Tammany Hall corrupted community values, believed Dewey. The Society of Tammany was founded in 1789 as an anti–British political club. Members dressed like American Indians and engaged in rituals. Over the decades, the club developed into an organization that controlled patronage and politics in New York City. In 1925 Dewey graduated from Columbia with a law degree. During a trip to Europe, he grew a moustache to add maturity to his youthful appearance. Tom and Frances married in 1928. While practicing law Dewey met George Z. Medalie, a prominent trial attorney who was highly impressed with the young lawyer. Medalie became United States Attorney for the Southern District of New York. On March 15, 1931, Dewey joined Medalie's team as Chief Assistant. Dewey's main task was the recruitment and supervision of 60 attorneys. Wealthy friends scoffed at a civil servant career; the real money was in private practice, they insisted. Medalie's yearly income as a trial lawyer was $400,000, reported newspapers. But Dewey found deep satisfaction prosecuting fraudulent stockbrokers, corrupt union officials, alien smugglers, corporate tax evaders, and mobsters. Among Dewey's recruits were Barent Ten Eyck, a law school classmate from a socially prominent family of Dutch heritage, and Murray Gurfein, the son of a diamond importer, a brilliant scholar, and a respected trial lawyer. Medalie's team soon impressed New Yorkers.

Dewey prosecuted Legs Diamond for making illegal alcohol. Diamond was fined $11,000 and sentenced to four years in prison. In his three years as chief assistant Dewey acquired legal expertise and was admired for his long hours and hard work. As a Republican, Dewey was a political outsider. Tammany Hall practically ran the city. But everything was about to change. The Seabury investigation revealed deep corruption.[18] Seabury pointed out that the district leaders of the political clubs were all rich men, whose wealth was unexplained. James A. McQuade, a Tammany leader of the Fifteenth District of Brooklyn, and the Registrar of Kings County, admitted that he had deposited a sum of $520,000 over a period of six years, on a total salary of less than $50,000. McQuade said he borrowed small sums, "here and there," to help poor relations but couldn't recall the source of the loans.[19] Thomas M. Farley, Sheriff of New York County and leader of the Fourteenth Assembly District, frequented a political club that boasted gambling. Sheriff Farley had deposited $396,000 in his bank account during a six-year period when his income totaled $90,000. Farley claimed it was from savings, kept in a tin box at home. Seabury wasn't convinced.

"Kind of a magic box, wasn't it, Sheriff?"

"It was a wonderful box."

Deputy City Clerk James J. McCormick, a Tammany district leader, was the director of the Marriage Bureau. McCormick was paid $8,500 a year to perform marriage ceremonies. His 34 bank accounts had accumulated $385,000, tips doled out by bridegrooms, claimed McCormick. Governor Roosevelt removed "Tin Box" Farley; James McCormick went to jail for income tax evasion, but James McQuade ran for Brooklyn Sheriff and won.

In 1932, George Medalie resigned his position to campaign for Republican senator. Dewey stepped in as Acting United States Attorney. Dewey planned the downfall of Waxey Gordon and Dutch Schultz. Dewey discovered that Schultz had secret bank accounts in various names; these amounted to $856,000. The investigators would follow the paper trail. Schultz's extortion network controlled restaurants, cafeterias, and nightclubs. Dewey's strategy was based on George Medalie's prosecution of Henry Miro, the Harlem king of *policy*. Miro made millions from bets gamblers made on the arrangement of numbers. Wilfred Brunder, another policy king, also made high sums without paying taxes. Brunder was convicted and sent to federal prison. Dewey gathered information that Jimmy Hines, a powerful Democrat, was bribed to keep the police away from a lucrative numbers racket.

Waxey Gordon had made the astronomical sum of four million dollars in two years, but paid income tax of only $2,010. Gordon was convicted, fined $80,000, and sentenced to 10 years in prison. The conviction brought Dewey into the national spotlight. But Dewey's days were numbered. The Democrats had been swept into office. Medalie lost his bid for senator. President Roosevelt had the opportunity to appoint the new United States Attorney. Roosevelt replaced Dewey with Martin Conboy on December 27, 1933. Conboy asked the rising prosecutor to remain in government service, but Dewey declined the offer. Dewey wanted to advance in the world, and private practice would produce a higher income. After the departure, the Deweys resided in an eight-room apartment at 1148 Fifth Avenue. They also bought a home in Tuxedo Park. Dewey's return to private practice occurred just as the city's houses of prostitution were being seized.

By January 1934, the bonding business was in operation, but Little Davie fumed over the bookers who were still hiding houses. Davie complained constantly to Abie Wahrman. As a result, Abie ordered the bookers to the secret headquarters behind 121 Mulberry Street. Pete Balitzer, Nick Montana and Charley Spinach Persana said nothing as Davie angrily demanded that all houses be turned over. Jimmy Fredericks, Vito Genovese, Tommy Bull and Abie Wahrman hovered menacingly. Afterward, Abie sadistically taunted Pete Balitzer and demanded that Pete buy him a birthday present. Pete bought an expensive watch, but Abie angrily sneered at it and raised Pete's weekly payments to $150. The bookers were terrified they would end up like Sam "Muddy" Kassoff, a narcotics dealer who had poached on Lucky's territory. A death contract had been arranged with Lepke and Gurrah. Assassins kidnapped Kassoff and offered release for five thousand dollars, but only $2,700 was raised. The executioners drove Kassoff to Island Park in Nassau County. On March 14, Kassoff was found dead, shot through the heart.

Every phase of Lucky's life was protected by mystery and duplicity. On April 4, a guest calling himself "Charles Ross of Miami Beach," registered at the Barbizon Plaza Hotel, located at 101 West 58th Street. Mr. Ross was assigned Room 3102, an expensive suite. The next day, the registration card was changed to "Charles Lucanio, Arlington Hotel, Hot Springs." On May 10, when Lucky arrived in person, he registered as "C. Lane, 232 W. 47th Street, New York."

Service personnel gossiped about the large tips from the guest in room 3102. The news came to the attention of George Grant, staff supervisor. Since Mr. Lane avoided public areas, hotel management became curious, especially after Lane requested that a table, dishes, and silverware be sent to his room but no food. Male companions brought dishes of spaghetti. Piero Rosalbo, room service director, personally delivered cocktails to room 3102. Rosalbo recognized Lucky from a newspaper photograph. Bugsy Siegel was present. Siegel had leased room 2651 the previous year, until he was recognized and asked to leave. Bellboy William McGrath observed men enter Lucky's room in the early morning hours. Lorenzo "Chappie" Brescio, a bodyguard, became a familiar face. A man known only as Dave often asked the bellboy to bring up the morning papers. On one occasion, just a few days after the robbery of the Rubel Ice Company, when $470,000 was stolen, the bellboy knocked on the door. When Dave opened it, the men in the room were startled and jumped to their feet, frightening the bellboy.

Nancy Presser answered professional calls to Lucky's room. On her first visit, Nancy asked Lucky how the bonding arrangement was coming along. Everything was fine, answered Lucky. They didn't engage in sexual relations but just talked. Later, after being paid, Nancy asked for more money. Lucky gave her 50 dollars, with an offer of more, if she needed it. Not long afterward, Lucky summoned her again. They chatted and drank champagne until two bottles were empty. Lucky, fully clothed, fell asleep on the bed.

Nancy dared not tell Ralph she was visiting the Boss. Ralph was pressuring Nancy to enter a common whorehouse; she never had enough money, he complained. Nancy feared losing her call girl status and independence. He had already telephoned Pete Balitzer and told him to book Lillian Gardello. Nancy was expected to do his bidding also.

While Lucky prospered, living life as a sportsman, Legs Diamond dodged bullets. While hosting a party at the Monticello Hotel on 64th Street, Legs entertained guests in Room 829, along with his mistress, former showgirl Marion "Kiki" Roberts. Three shots suddenly exploded. Legs survived but insisted he didn't know his assailants, he told police. Newspaper articles linked Diamond to an international drug ring. Legs had gone to Germany to arrange a narcotics transaction but had unexpectedly been deported. Financers demanded the return of $65,000 advanced for the deal, but Legs kept the money. After the shooting in the Monticello Hotel, he fled to Albany where his luck ran out. As he slept, unknown executioners fired two bullets in his head.

Though unaware of Lucky Luciano's seizure of the prostitution rings, the New York police prosecuted the criminals for other illegalities. On July 20, police arrested Dave Betillo in Tom's River, New Jersey. He was charged with operating a gambling boat near Point Pleasant. Lorenzo Brescio lost his investment of $2,500 on the gambling disaster.

In October, Ralph Liguori and Johnny Roberts Robilotto attempted to extort money from Dora Hearn, a madam who operated a house at 320 West 72nd Street. Johnny Roberts was a stocky thug, a loan shark, and a killer. Later, Deputy Inspector McDermott and two detectives attempted to arrest the pair. McDermott shot Johnny. Ralph was arrested and beaten at the 68th precinct station. Inspector McDermott had arranged a sting; marked money was in the envelope the madam gave to the extortionists. The shooting left Johnny Roberts hospitalized for months. Ralph was arraigned in the West 54th Street Magistrates Court. Nancy was present at the hearing. Al Marinelli suddenly appeared. He was furious over Ralph's beating. Marinelli vowed to "break the coppers involved."[20] Marinelli shouted at court clerks that he was going to have Ralph photographed downtown, to document the beating.

Ralph later told Nancy that Marinelli had summoned Inspector McDermott and the detectives involved. Marinelli ordered them to drop the case. After the warning, McDermott telephoned the Emerson Hotel, leaving a message for Ralph to call him. At the 68th Street precinct station, Nancy stayed in the car while Ralph went inside. According to Ralph, McDermott apologized. He offered to "do anything for the downtown mob." Ralph said Marinelli was going to fix the case. Though held for the Grand Jury, no indictment was ever returned against Ralph and Johnny Roberts. The charge was dismissed on April 2, 1935.

Despite his sudden departure to escape the mobsters, Dave Marcus had second thoughts. Seriously ill with heart trouble, he needed money and wanted to resume his booking career. After fleeing to California, Marcus had later opened a service station in Mineola, New York, which fared poorly, as did a second station in Glen Cove, Long Island. On a trip to the city, to buy supplies, he unexpectedly met Benny Spiller on Seventh Avenue. Spiller said he was operating a house on 54th Street but explained the new arrangement. The once mighty bookers were now paid servants. It didn't matter, responded Marcus. Spiller listened to Marcus' change of heart and advised that Jimmy Fredericks was the man to see.

Pete Balitzer was close to an emotional collapse. Abie Wahrman demanded a thousand dollars from Pete, as a loan. Pete pleaded that he was broke. There were no excuses, said Abie, and made arrangements with a loan shark. Pete was forced to borrow the thousand dollars and gave it to Abie. Later, Pete asked Abie to repay the money. It wasn't a loan, laughed Abie but a donation. Abie's brutal extortion was prompted by a secret: he was a drug addict.

After Jean Bradley's house was robbed, Pete Balitzer and Jimmy Fredericks drove to Brooklyn, and cornered two youths suspected of the robbery. Jimmy got out of the car and began questioning a boy; he slapped his face, pushed him in the car and drove back to the East Side. At a hangout, Jimmy questioned the youth about his accomplices, but the boy refused to talk. Jimmy hit him in the face and shouted, "Didn't I tell you to keep away from those bonded joints because they belong to Charley Lucky?"[21]

Pete Balitzer was playing a dangerous game. From remarks made by mob underlings, it was apparent to him who ran the combination; nevertheless, Pete kept several houses hidden. In fact, he bought Mildred a fur coat, but the mob payoffs were siphoning his money, and he was in deep financial trouble. Mildred pleaded with Pete to walk away from the booking business. The fear and pressure was damaging their relationship. She boldly confronted Little Davie at 121 Mulberry. "What is this I hear about this bonding and protection of bookies?"[22]

Davie admitted he was involved.

"Is Lucky behind this?" she asked.

"Yes."

Mildred asked Davie, as a favor, to go easy on Pete. Davie refused. Months later, Pete and Mildred decided to marry. She again went to Davie and told him of their plans and that she wanted Pete out of the business. "He can't get out," said Davie, "he owes too much money."

"He keeps getting more hopelessly in debt," said Mildred. Davie laughed at her. Mildred said she would talk to Charley Lucky. "It won't do you any good," said Davie, "because anything I do is alright with him." Not long afterward, Davie demanded that Pete buy tickets for the Al Marinelli Beefsteak Dinner. Davie was a major fundraiser. Pete and Mildred married. The bride was determined to remove Pete from the vice underworld. Each winter, Lucky went to Miami. Mildred would see the *capo di tutti capi* and beg for her husband's freedom.

CHAPTER SEVEN

Soulless Creatures

I will break their heads

In the winter of 1935 Lucky boarded a flight to Miami. In the Palm Island Casino he booked a table for the premiere of Earl Carroll's new revue. Lovely women in scanty costumes paraded in the spotlight; a honey blonde dancer caught his eye. Galena Orlova, known as Gay, was only 21, but was the latest Broadway sensation. Gay performed a specialty dance, stripping behind fans. Gay was the mistress of wealthy stockbroker J. Theus Munds, a widower who lavished gifts on her, including a luxury apartment on East 57th Street. Months earlier, Gay had dated newspaper cartoonist Peter Arno, but she liked big spenders. Lucky was entranced by her blue eyes and charming lisp. As a child, Gay and her mother had fled Russia to Turkey. Gay never wanted to be poor again. Lucky became her new boyfriend.

Mildred Balitzer registered at the Meridian Hotel in Miami, accompanied by Pete's young nephew. Mildred no longer smoked opium; she now injected morphine. To satisfy her addiction, she carried an ounce of dope. Mildred traced Lucky to the Hialeah Race Track where he had consulted with bookmakers, but he was gone. Gambler Joe Frank told her to try a bar called The Paddock.

After midnight she entered the bar. Lucky was seated with friends. When he was alone, she walked over. "Do you know I married Pete? I want him to get out of the business. He is in debt up to his neck and getting nowhere. He is not cut out for the racket and he will never amount to much in it. I spoke to Davie about it and Davie said there is no getting out. He told me you were the boss and whatever he did was okay with you."[1]

Why wouldn't Davie let him out, asked Lucky.

"Because he owes too much money," she told him.

Mildred Balitzer was Pete's common-law wife, and asked Lucky to let Pete leave the booking business, but Lucky refused (courtesy NYC Municipal Archives).

"As long as he owes the money, he can't get out, you know the racket." Lucky was firm and repeated, "There is no getting out." Mildred kept begging until Lucky softened. "See me in New York," he finally said. Mildred sent Pete's nephew home and went to Cuba for two weeks.

Lucky and Gay became constant companions. They were seen together in Broadway clubs, especially Dave's Blue Room on Seventh Avenue, the haunt of the theatre and sports crowd. Though stockbroker Munds paid for Gay's luxurious apartment, she slept with Lucky.

On a cold February night, Dave Marcus walked inside Joey Silver's cigar store at Seventh Avenue and 51st Street. Jimmy the Gorilla listened to his plea. Marcus wanted to be a sex booker once again. The next night, Jimmy introduced Little Davie. Marcus groveled for a job. He offered to start at the bottom. Davie agreed to let him back in. First, he would have to call downtown and tell Abie Wahrman. "I just okayed Dave Miller, the fellow that was shot up."[2] Little Davie explained the arrangement: For the first two weeks Marcus could keep the money he collected; from then on, he would receive a salary. Explained Davie: "Whatever is left over, you are to give it to Danny, who will give it to Jimmy, who will give it to Tommy Bull." Marcus thanked him. The next night Jimmy broke the news to Spike Green; Marcus was now taking over Spike's houses.

"What's the matter?" asked Spike.

"Nothing's the matter," answered Gorilla. "Those are the orders and that's what you got to do." Marcus was back in the vice business; five madams and several girls paid him on a weekly basis.

Danny Brooks was also ordered to turn over his houses to Marcus. Danny was in trouble. Detective Hugo Harris was looking for him. Marcus soon realized he had been accepted back in the vice fold to replace Danny. Dave Marcus asked Jimmy about more houses.

"Take it easy," said Jimmy, "and I will try to get all the houses I can possibly get you." Marcus was assigned more madams, but he refused to send Flo Brown any women, since she was always broke and "charged up" with drugs. Marcus began calling her "Cokey Flo."

In March, Cockeyed Lou complained to Abie Wahrman that he could no longer pay two hundred dollars a week to the combination. Abie said he had to pay. But Cockeyed Lou argued he would soon be out of business. "We'll come to terms. We'll let you know at the end of the week."[3] Three weeks later, the payment was dropped to $150.

Jimmy hated the bookers, because they were always hiding houses. Peter Tach and his partner, Vincent Giordano, had opened a secret house at 200 West 50th Street. Gorilla was furious they were not paying bonding fees. There was a meeting in the Crown Restaurant. "Do you think we are shit heels?" Jimmy asked Tach. "Do you know who is behind us?" Tach said he wasn't interested. "Little Davie will take care of everything," threatened Jimmy. Tach shrugged. He didn't know Little Davie. Jimmy told him that Little Davie used to work for Al Capone.

While Lucky evaded prosecution, Dutch Schultz was in deep trouble. He had surrendered to authorities on a tax evasion charge. Schultz was desperate; the millions he controlled had to remain hidden. Schultz demanded $21,000 from Jules Martin, the mob link to the phony Metropolitan Restaurant Association. Martin claimed no funds were available, but he secured a loan for $21,000. In the small town of Cohoes, Schultz accused Jules Martin of embezzling money from the restaurant association. In the heat of the dispute, Dutch whipped out a pistol, stuck it in Martin's mouth, and pulled the trigger. Schultz was forced to borrow money from gangster Max Silverman, a fatal mistake. In Troy, New York, the district attorney questioned him about the death of Jules Martin. Schultz denied involvement, but defense attorney Richard Davis knew the truth. As Dutch concentrated on his legal difficulty, word circulated in the underworld that Abe "Bo" Weinberg conspired with Lucky to carve up the Dutchman's territory. Bo Weinberg disappeared.[4]

While Dutch fought to stay out of prison, Lucky moved to more luxurious quarters, occupying Room 39D in the Waldorf-Astoria at 301 Park Avenue. He paid $375 a month for a Tower Apartment. Hedwig Scholtz, a German-born chambermaid, noticed the new tenant with the peculiar appearance, so different than the usual guests.[5] Lucky ate breakfast late and didn't leave the apartment until early afternoon. The maid patiently sat in the hallway. She watched the men who came and went; they were also out of place, she thought. The visitors spoke in low tones and referred to Mr. Ross as Charley or the boss. Lucky tipped the service large amounts, and word of his generosity spread.

Pauline Fletcher, the bathroom maid, also had to wait for Lucky to emerge. She waited in the doorway of 39C. The maid watched as Jimmy Fredericks and other "greasy men" came and went. On one occasion, while cleaning room 39C, she heard Jimmy's voice through the ventilator: "We cleaned up 90,000, but the boss says that we have got to clean up some more."

Elevator operators became accustomed to seeing Lorenzo Brescio, dressed in a riding outfit with jodhpurs, on his way to a daily trot in Central Park. Brescio pretended he was a beer salesman, but police detectives knew he was a gunman-bodyguard for the mob. Lorenzo slept in the apartment several nights a week.

Bugsy Siegel moved to the Waldorf in April. Siegel had purchased a house for his wife and children in Scarsdale. In his room on the 27th floor, he entertained Lucky, Longie Zwillman, and French actress Ketti Gallienne.

Police kept an eye on major gangsters of New York City. A trio of detectives was assigned to watch the Parvel Company on Marks Avenue. During a stakeout, a sleek Cadillac arrived. A chauffeur opened the door, and Max Silverman stepped out. Silverman was the frontman for Lepke and Gurrah. Like the angel of death, Silverman seemed to be around when murders occurred. In September 1934, William Schneider, president of Teamsters Local 138, was shot in Garfein's Restaurant during a labor conference with truck owners. Negotiations were underway to avoid a strike when a lone gunman stepped inside and shot Schneider. Max Silverman drove the victim to the hospital, but he died.

Detectives tailed the Cadillac to the Jamaica Race Track. On the clubhouse grounds, Max Silverman met Lucky, Frank Costello, Louis Buchalter, and Jake Shapiro. After conversing, Silverman went to a grandstand where bets were placed. He walked over to Max Courtney, a bookmaker, and handed him several hundred dollars. "This is for Charley Lucky" said Silverman. Detectives Stephen Di Rosa, James Cashman, and John Kennedy watched the mobsters the entire afternoon, certain that more than racing was being discussed. Police reports later documented that Silverman had purchased a Cadillac for Lucky; it was exchanged for a Lincoln worth $371.50 and $1,800 cash. Police noted Lucky's shrewdness in using underlings to cover his every move.

Lucky lived the sweet life while his gang spread terror. Mildred Balitzer approached Lucky in front of the Villanova Restaurant on 46th Street. She reminded him of the Florida meeting. Lucky's response was icy. "When Pete pays the dough, and not until then, can he get out."[6]

One summer night crates of silk stockings were stolen from a warehouse in Williamsburg, Brooklyn. The theft was orchestrated by Frank Davino and members of the Little Augie Pisano mob. The thieves normally did business with Vito Genovese and Tony Bender. When plans to hide the loot failed, the thieves were stranded on the streets with the stolen merchandise for twenty-four hours, until Vito and Tony agreed to find a safe location. The trucks were sent to a private garage on Bergen Street in Brooklyn. Lucky bought the silk stockings for $20,000. Nancy Presser heard about it. She patronized Kean's Tavern. Lucky's group usually invited her to join them for a drink. Once, she overheard Davie tell Lucky that a madam named "Dago Jean" Brill had refused to join the bonding association. "She and all the rest of the madams will have to bond," ordered Lucky, "and if they refuse, wreck their joints."[7]

After performing on sexual dates, Nancy returned to room 380 in the Hotel Emerson to find Ralph. Though she was a call girl, he was insanely jealous. Ralph taunted her. He demanded to know where she had been. If she refused to talk, Ralph beat her and threatened to kill her. Ralph once placed a gun to her temple. If she didn't stop running around with other men, he warned, he would blow her head off. Nancy dared not reveal that Lucky was a client.

"This is Charlie," said the caller.[8] She went to the Waldorf at night. Nancy made several business calls; they usually sat and talked, then engaged in sexual relations, except for the time Lucky admitted he had a venereal disease.

Lucky discussed the bonding business with her. He said Pete Balitzer had been trying to get out of the racket for some time, but he knew too much. Occasionally, as they conversed in the living room, Nancy became privy to telephone conversations. Once, Lucky grew furious, cursing, shouting he would have to get Al Marinelli to straighten things out. Afterward, he fumed and said the caller was Little Davie. If he wanted something done, he complained, "I'll have to do it myself." When there were knocks on the door, Nancy was sent into the bedroom or bathroom and instructed to turn on the sink faucet, so the flow of water would drown conversations. After the visitors left, Lucky told her who had been there but not what was discussed. The visitors included Al Marinelli, Dave Betillo, Tommy Bull, Jimmy Fredericks, Jerry Bruno, Vito Genovese, and Charley Prunes, a loan shark. Lucky told her of his big plans. "I'm going to take all the bitches' houses away from them."[9] The madams would be paid a salary. "We're going to raise the prices in all the houses," asserted Lucky. Little Davie would manage the business for him. But there was a shadow on Lucky's plans.

William Copeland Dodge, the new Manhattan District Attorney, was in trouble. A commissioner discovered a gambling syndicate, controlled by Dutch Schultz, was protected. Gambling bets were collected daily from hundreds of shops. If there were arrests by honest cops, bail was arranged, but the bail money actually came from the Schultz mob. Perjury had been committed "no less than 1,584 times," wrote reporter Martin Mooney.[10] The scandal surfaced and the public read about the corrupt bail bondsmen. Martin Mooney wrote that Schultz was protected by politician James J. Hines.

Lee Thompson Smith, the grand jury foreman, was disgusted by the weak cases brought by District Attorney Dodge. It appeared that Dodge had no interest in prosecuting the racketeers running rampant in New York. Jimmy Hines had backed Dodge in the 1933 election; Dutch Schultz had contributed money to the Dodge election campaign. Rumors circulated that Dutch Schultz had spies in Dodge's office. The six jurors, all businessmen, were fed up with gangsters running the city.

On May 13, 1935, the grand jury demonstrated its contempt for the entire process by excluding from a secret session Maurice Wahl, an Assistant District Attorney. The incident made the newspapers. The grand jury demanded an independent prosecutor, free from political control. A complaint against Dodge was filed with the New York Bar Association.

The Society for the Prevention of Crime, led by the Reverend George Egbert, called for Governor Herbert H. Lehman to appoint a Special Deputy District Attorney. The angry grand jurors agreed; they gave the governor a secret report about Dodge's office. The jurors conferred with the Bar Association and the names of distinguished attorneys were offered, including George Z. Medalie. In a bid to maintain control, Dodge tried to appoint his own man, attorney Harold H. Corbin, a lawyer with Tammany ties. The jurors objected and Corbin withdrew. Dodge then offered to select someone from the governor's list. If Dodge was involved, the prominent attorneys declined to serve. To resolve the impasse, the attorneys recommended Thomas E. Dewey. The New York Bar Association concurred in the decision and newspaper editorials echoed the solution. Governor Lehman hesitated. Lehman told colleagues that Dewey, only 33, was too young and inexperienced. But Dewey had impressed the Bar Association when he prepared a case against Judge Harold Kuntsler. The judge had failed to explain the large deposits to his bank account; before a formal investigation was underway, Judge Kuntsler resigned. Dewey's service as a federal attorney was admired by the public, and citizen organizations clamored for his appointment.[11]

Governor Lehman, a Democrat, reluctantly agreed to appoint Dewey as a special prosecutor. Also selected was Justice Philip J. McCook to preside in court proceedings, if indictments resulted. McCook, 62, was admired for his legal acumen and famous as a veteran of the Spanish American War and the Great War. Dewey pondered the arrangement; technically, he was just another Deputy Assistant District Attorney, legally answerable to District Attorney Dodge. Before accepting the appointment, Dewey demanded autonomy. Governor Lehman agreed. The Special Prosecutor earned the same as the D.A., $16,695 annually, a far cry from what Dewey could have made in private practice. Dewey wanted his own staff and personally selected 20 attorneys. Assistants would be paid from a single dollar to eight thousand dollars. At 121 Broadway he personally interviewed the applicants. Among those chosen were Barent Ten Eyck, Murray Gurfein, William B. Herlands, and Jacob Rosenblum, lawyers who had served with him in the U.S. Attorney's Office. As for the others, Sol Gelb had risen from a humble family; Harold Cole was from a wealthy New Jersey family; Eunice Carter was an African-American who had served on a committee to investigate riots in Harlem; Sewell T. Tyng had worked in Republican campaigns, while Frank Hogan was a staunch Democrat, and Paul Lockwood was a former reporter for the *Brooklyn Eagle.* One of the most crucial positions was handed to Allen J. "Goody" Goodrich, who was assigned to obtaining documents. There were political independents but party men as well; seven of the twenty were Republicans; six were Democrats. The Board of Estimate allowed Dewey a five-month budget of $121,000. Dewey and his legal staff withdrew from private practice; they all sacrificed income. Dewey could have earned a sum as high as $150,000 a year in private practice. The staff was comprised of ten investigators, ten accountants, four process servers, a chief clerk with three assistants, two grand jury reporters, twenty stenographers, and four messengers. Deputy Inspector John A. Lyons recruited 75 police officers for the investigation. For his office, Dewey chose the 14th floor of the Woolworth Building, located at 233 Broadway, near City Hall. The skyscraper was built by Frank Woolworth, famous for his five and ten cent stores. With 60 floors, the building had once been the world's tallest structure. On the 14th floor, a uniformed police officer stood guard at the entrance to the 35 offices. The cubicles had frosted glass and Venetian blinds to insure privacy. In July, Dewey was formally appointed a Special Deputy Assistant District Attorney. Dewey's job was to conduct an investigation of criminal racketeering in the city. Dewey immediately asked the state legislature to enact a law whereby the courts could link several individuals for a number of related offenses under the same indictment. He also wanted the deletion of witnesses' names in all indictments. Dewey asked to be called Chief. Staff members viewed Dewey as somewhat abrasive and cocky; yet, they came to admire the long hours Dewey spent in investigating the criminal stranglehold on New York City.

After Dewey's appointment, Lucky Luciano decided it was time to pay delinquent income taxes. Al Capone and Waxey Gordon were in prison for tax evasion. Dutch Schultz would likely meet the same fate. On July 18, citizen Luciano filed delinquent federal tax returns covering 1929 to 1934; net income for the previous four years was estimated at $20,000; the income was derived from gambling. He gave his brother Bart's address, 205 East 10th Street, as his own, even though he resided at the chic Waldorf Astoria. Lucky was confident authorities would never penetrate his criminal empire.

Shortly after Dewey's appointment, Cockeyed Lou Wiener was sent to prison; after decades of flaunting the law, Lou was finally convicted of compulsory prostitution.

Dave Marcus was suddenly worried. The Dewey investigation was gathering steam, and he was a salaried booker for mobsters. Marcus nervously chauffeured Jimmy around town. On one occasion, they stopped at the corner of Broadway and Canal streets. Little Davie and Jimmy jumped inside. Marcus drove them to the Lido Hotel. Afterward, Marcus asked, "Who is Tommy Bull?"

"He is the treasurer," said Jimmy.[12]

Dave Marcus blurted his fear, "Who is going to take care of me in case of trouble?"[13]

Jimmy became enraged. "Why, you son of a bitch, you're always hollering who's going to look after you. I told you once before it was me."

"I want to know who it is," repeated Marcus.

"Davie, Abie, and Charley Lucky," revealed Jimmy.

After Cockeyed Lou went to Sing Sing, the madams deserted his son until Al had only 15 houses; after expenses, he was left with a paltry one hundred dollars per week.

On July 30, the Special Prosecutor addressed New Yorkers in a radio broadcast. "The object of this investigation is to rid the city of racketeers," asserted Dewey. Prostitution was also a target. "We are concerned with those predatory vultures who traffic on a wholesale scale in the bodies of women and mere girls for profit." Dewey's promise to clean up the rackets elated citizens. Outraged citizens streamed to the Woolworth Building with complaints in over two dozen rackets. Indignant letters disclosed where vice haunts were located. There were calls for immediate action.

The mother and widow of executed union president William Schneider contacted Dewey. The unsolved Schneider murder had been forgotten. Barent Ten Eyck reopened the Schneider murder and reviewed other unsolved cases in police files. Barent Ten Eyck concluded mobsters had seized control of the flour truckers union and were extorting payoffs from the baking industry.

From his desk on the 14th floor, Dewey surveyed the beauty of New York.

The architectural wonders pointed heavenward. But far below was a sordid vice chain, a sex underworld. As he read the citizen complaints, he was shocked. A lengthy letter described the boardwalk of Coney Island as a marketplace "for operatives of the white slave syndicate in New York."[14] The writer S.A. Rush of Brooklyn had previously complained to public officials, and one letter reached Commissioner Lewis Valentine. The result was an immediate improvement, with arrests of prostitutes. But Rush was again upset. He had witnessed a girl in flight from pimps. "What a damnable thing it was, I started in pursuit of them, and finally to escape from him, she entered the Ninth Avenue Toilet Station. The spectacle of this man pursuing this young girl, evidently respectable, like a hound chasing a rabbit, was about the most contemptible performance I ever witnessed."

Rush was overjoyed after Dewey's appointment: "Not in seven months has the boardwalk been so free of prostitution habitues as it was on last Sunday and Monday." But the pimps returned. They were identified as "all Italians, a half dozen or more who practically live on the walk, cruising back and forth and spotting likely victims." Rush asked Governor Lehman to act in the interest of "your own people [...] On my way home on the subway at a mid-station I observed a well known procurer with a very beautiful Jewish young lady who possessed to a rare degree the madonna likeness of purity that characterizes so many young ladies of your race. If you witness what is going on in the work of destruction of young women in the flower of their youth you would have your indignation stirred as mine [...] prostitution is a terrible blight upon the city social life and it will take courageous and heroic action on your part to eradicate it." Rush's investigations had previously sent two men to the penitentiary for pedophile crimes. He urged both Governor Lehman and Dewey to prosecute: "For fifty years the same fiendish influence has fostered and fattened on the souls of innocent and hapless young womanhood in this city."

A letter arrived at Dewey's residence at 1148 Fifth Avenue. The writer complained of male prostitutes. Dewey was asked to break up "the meat market" hustlers, streetboys who congregated in Times Square and in "the little park behind the 42nd Street library." Homosexuals who picked up loiterers were subject to blackmail warned the writer. The Barrel was identified as a shady bar patronized by soldiers, sailors, and male prostitutes.[15]

For over a year, Brooklyn clergymen and residents had waged a campaign to close a café on King's Highway, believed to be a house of prostitution. A sign identified the café as the "Hot Nuts Club." Every night young boys emerged "reeling drunk."[16] Partially dressed girls were carried into waiting taxis. Children stood on the sidewalk and watched the proceedings, complained reformers.

Elderly John Romano was so fed up with vice that he made a trip to Dewey's office. Eunice Carter and Victor Herwitz dutifully took notes as the old man lashed out at politician Anthony Coppola. It was Coppola who rented a house to prostitutes on Navy Street, next to Romano's home. From early afternoon, until late at night, Jean and Christina offered teenage prostitutes. Romano told the women to stop soliciting, but they ignored him. Jean and Christina were madams; they had paid five hundred dollars to bring a teenage runaway to Brooklyn from Philadelphia. The girl had escaped, but no prosecution resulted. Jean bragged to Romano, "I got protection."[17] Romano was convinced the local police were bribed to do nothing. Romano wrote to Commissioner Valentine for relief. A raid occurred and the police threw a bed and table out a window. Though arrested and taken before a magistrate, the young madams were soon released. They strutted up and down the street again. Five months later, Romano seethed with anger, upset the arrogant madams were still in business. "That's how much they care for the police sitting in New York, 18,000 men. I am plain talking."

"Quite," remarked Eunice Carter.

The previous night Romano had argued with them again. "Mr. Romano," said Jean, "I respect you because you are an old man, and if you weren't I would have you beat up."

"You have got to kill me," Romano answered. He refused to be intimidated. "I am not tough," he told the investigators. "I am not a gangster. I told them in a nice way, when they were arrested. Let them come, let them come to see me, and then I'll know what to do. I will break their heads."

In another letter a mother in Schenectady blamed a pimp for making her daughter a whore. "I am so deeply grateful for the interest you are taking in the case of my daughter as expressed in your letter [...] it is evident that my daughter is enslaved to a life of prostitution [...] and has been for three years."[18]

Mayor La Guardia sent Dewey a letter he had received about prostitution in Harlem. The writer had visited a house "just for curiosity, and they had women and men of both race, black and white, liquor was sold, gambling going on very strong in one room, white slavery in another room, and dancing under very low dark lights in the main room."[19] To the writer's surprise, four policemen entered. The elderly woman who owned the house calmed the crowd: "Don't get excited," she admonished. The cops only wanted their regular payoff. In the kitchen each policeman was handed money. The citizen-informant disclosed the addresses of a dozen houses in Harlem: "They stand on their stoops and call the men, in the presence of these little children, now tell me what will your younger generation be, in the future to come? They won't be any good to their country or themselves, just will cause lots of trouble to the city with their various diseases from such a terrible life."

Other letters detailed hotel prostitution and documented where couples rented rooms by the hour, half hour and even by the minute. "You can get into No. 1131 for one dollar, you say 'the Edison man sent you.' You can also get into No. 1138 by saying 'Isn't Rooney living here anymore?'"[20] Mrs. Carter obtained letters about Harlem houses, sent to the Complaint Bureau: "All these girls are colored and attract white and colored trade."[21] The girls and their pimps operate in the Bella Restaurant on Lenox Avenue in the Empire Grill on Seventh Avenue. "A woman who lives above the Heat Wave Restaurant, called T.C., owns three or four Lincoln cars, is colored and is supposed to run a lot of joints, dealing in colored girls, around Twenty-Seventh Street and the West Side. She anticipates immediately leaving for Texas."

Another informant wrote that "Mrs. Gay" was operating three houses.[22] One of them, located on 134th Street, had four young boys as occupants. "They sit in the window dressed in girl's clothes. Only white men are catered to. Any kind of an affair with a man may be had here. Mrs. Gay's house on 127th Street caters to white and colored males and females. On Thursday nights there is a party given for lady lovers, both colored and white. On Saturday nights a party for feminine men, with an admission charge of 35 cents. Admission is obtained by ringing upstairs bell and asking for Marie."

If irate citizens were heartened by the investigation, Lucky wasn't worried. At the Villa Nova Restaurant he relaxed with friends and associates. He openly made decisions about the vice chain. Hotel thief Joe Bendix approached Jimmy the Gorilla about a job collecting bond money. Jimmy said to talk to Lucky. "You know, Joe, it doesn't pay a hell of a lot," explained the boss, "35 or 45 dollars a week."[23]

"I'm not doing anything right now," said Bendix. "I need the money." Lucky nodded. Davie would find him a job. Bendix returned for a second meeting in the same restaurant. Lucky had good news. "I put you on as a collector for 40 dollars a week. See Binge in the Hotel Walcott." Bendix would earn a little more since he was "high hat." Bendix missed meeting Binge at the hotel and continued as a hotel thief.

On a warm summer night, Flo accompanied Jimmy to a Chinese restaurant at 21 Mott Street, a former gambling den. They descended a flight of steps. Lucky, Davie, and Tommy sat at a table. There was a discussion about making the madams pay.

"I told you just talking won't do any good," Lucky said.[24]

"Things are a little tough now," answered Jimmy. "You want to go a little easy."

"Alright," said Lucky.

"We'll make a go of this thing," assured Dave Betillo. "It's bound to go because it's a good proposition. It's got to."

Peggy Wild's name came up. Peggy had tricked a collector. She peeped through a door secured by a chain lock, and insisted that she was closed, but the madam was in business across the hall. "She's trying to be a wise guy," said Lucky.

"We will take care of it. Don't worry," assured Davie.

"Being nice to them isn't any good," explained Charley.

"I thought if I could talk to them," answered Jimmy, "it might be better."

Lucky disagreed. "You can't talk to them. Step on them a little bit."

Alone in the car, Jimmy voiced his displeasure with Peggy and her pimp, "Wild Bill" Ercolino, who was constantly coming downtown, arguing about paying bond money, trying to contact people to get to Davie because everybody knew he was under Lucky. Then Jimmy told Flo about a drug shipment; Tommy had a large narcotics supply on hand but didn't want to unload it because prices would sink.

Tommy was Flo's supplier. He also furnished dope to Nancy Presser and Mildred Curtis. Whenever Flo need a fix, Jimmy sent Danny Brooks downtown for whatever was available — opium, cocaine, or morphine. But Danny was gone. He had been arrested in Westchester County. Ellen Grosso and a girl named Frenchy had gone to Somers, New York, to work in a house. Grosso was caught in the act and photographed naked by police. The women were fined and held as material witnesses against the house operators. Danny, accused of booking them, was in jail facing a charge of compulsory prostitution. His bigamist wife, Nancy Brooks, telephoned Binge at the Hotel Walcott. She begged Jimmy to get in touch with Danny's parents. Within an hour, Jimmy was at the Caputo's home, conversing with them in Italian. Jimmy telephoned Nancy and told her to pick up Danny's car, but before she went to White Plains, she was to meet him at a funeral home at 211 Mulberry.

Jimmy was mad: "Jesus Christ, Nancy, he's held for forcible prostitution. Danny was sent to do someone a favor and they picked him up. Don't ever say he's your husband."[25] Nancy wanted information, but Jimmy refused to answer any questions and sent her away. That evening, after she returned from White Plains, Jimmy met her at the Caputo residence. Nancy said the state police had questioned her at Hawthorne, but she denied that she was Danny's wife. She also denied knowing Jimmy Fredericks. "Why should the state police be interested in you?" she asked.

"I'm in it, too," said Jimmy. "I'm in the bail bonding."

Jimmy explained the bail bond operation and lamented Danny's arrest: "He was getting along so well with me." Nancy was frightened when state troopers questioned her and searched her apartment. When she told Jimmy, he bought her a bus ticket. Jimmy and Dave Marcus put her on a bus for Pennsylvania. She was advised to disappear. Jimmy was afraid she would become entangled in her own lies about Danny. Released on bail, Jimmy gave Danny money for legal fees, and he promised his pal if a conviction resulted, an appeal would be made.

Following reports that the Magistrate Court was corrupt, Eunice Carter and Murray Gurfein began a probe. They discovered that prostitutes were always provided with immediate bail money and seldom convicted. Eunice Carter uncovered the tragic story of 17-year-old Polly Sorrell. When the runaway teenager resided at the Girl's Service League, a female inmate had secretly introduced her to older men. One offered to marry her. Polly accompanied him to the Alexandria Hotel; unexpectedly, her clothes were taken and a string of men were led to her room. For nearly six weeks she was forced to sexually entertain men; if she complained, she would be turned over to the police as a whore, they threatened. Though Polly suffered severe physical trauma, she was afraid to flee. She finally returned to the Girl's Service League and to the custody of her guardian.

By August 1935, the combination worked effectively, squeezing every dollar possible from the bookers, madams, and prostitutes. In Saratoga, Lucky flashed his white teeth for another season. Lucky and his partner, Fred Bachmann, were running the craps table in the Saratoga Club.[26] Music publisher Robert Crawford rolled the dice. Crawford, a wealthy gambler, was a former partner of songwriter Irving Berlin. He and his wife shared a summer home in Saratoga with Bing Crosby. Crawford gambled alongside Sam Rosoff, a subway builder. When their cash vanished, Lucky extended five hundred dollars credit to both losers. Lucky was glad to accommodate the suckers; he knew the odds favored him. The teenage peddler of liquid morphine now socialized with the upper class, and he fleeced them. From his Waldorf suite he had a magnificent view of the city. Once a slum dweller, he had connived his way to the top.

After Lucky's mother died in August, he purchased a family vault for $25,000 in Queen's St. John's Cemetery. The mausoleum had Greek columns, bronze doors, a stained glass window, and sixteen crypts. At the funeral, Joe Valachi expressed his sympathy to the boss. The gunman seldom met with Lucky, so he took the opportunity to complain about his numbers racket. Lucky arranged for gangster Frank Livorsi to provide $10,000 for the business.

In early September, Dewey made his first move and indicted a teenage youth who threatened to smash store windows unless he was paid extortion money. "Jury Indicts Youth as A Little Shot," ridiculed the *Herald Tribune*. "After weeks he nabs a window breaker," jeered the *Mirror*. Other newspapers questioned Dewey's initial effort and speculated if he truly intended to prosecute major racketeers. But several mobsters were fearful.

At a meeting of the crime bosses, Albert Anastasia, a member of the Vincent Mangano gang, was angry. Anastasia wanted Dewey murdered.[27] He had already set up the hit. Dewey left his apartment each morning with two bodyguards and walked to a nearby pharmacy. Once inside, he entered a telephone booth and called his office. Dewey thoughtfully avoided waking his wife. A mob assassin had borrowed a child and casually strolled along behind Dewey. Anastasia said it would be easy to pump Dewey with a silencer in the phone booth, while his bodyguards waited outside. Lucky listened but said nothing. Joe Bonanno was shocked, as were other *padroni*. Lucky's silence indicated no objection to the idea. Dewey's death would be the bosses' death knell, argued Bonanno. The public outrage would assure federal prosecution of their rackets. Bonanno believed Lucky was influenced by "a largely Jewish coterie whose views of life and moneymaking were alien to ours."[28]

The prostitution racket was faltering. The bookers received a telephone summons from Jimmy. He ordered them to meet at the bonding office. At 9:00 P.M. the bookers sat nervously. Pete Balitzer, Jack Ellenstein, Dave Marcus, Al Weiner, and Jojo Weintraub waited. Also present were Jesse Jacobs, Meyer Berkman, and Jimmy Fredericks. A half hour later, Dave Betillo arrived with Vito Genovese. Davie glared and told the bookers to form a circle. The combination wasn't making enough money, said Davie. Through carelessness, too many places had been raided: "We have had so many pinches, and we are behind in money."[29] Davie said there would a five-hundred-dollar fine for every hidden house. His cold eyes surveyed the group. He stared at Jack Ellenstein. "If I hear of any places you are holding out, I will kick that big fat belly." He stared at Pete. "I am going to send you back to Philadelphia, but not the way you came." And Dave Marcus was told, "If I hear of any places you are holding out, you won't go to the cops; we will put the cops on you." Davie suspected possible treachery. "You're all a bunch of no-good louses, and we're doing you a favor letting you be in the business and handling it for you. You're all a bunch of rats and if you squeal, we'll get you."

Jesse Jacobs then spoke, calmly admonishing them to give up the hidden houses. Jacobs assured them that no girl would ever go to jail as long as he was the bondsman for the combination. Little Davie and Vito cursed them, threatening to run them out of town. Abie Wahrman then demanded a list of each booker's houses and addresses. Little Davie then concluded the meeting: "I've told you what is what. Goodnight, gentlemen." The holdout houses were operated by well-known madams. Marcus knew their names but said nothing.

In October, Flo Brown again observed Lucky's waning interest in prostitution. At the Chinese restaurant at 21 Mott Street, Jimmy and Davie argued for time, but Lucky was glum. He wanted the bonding stopped altogether.

There wasn't much money in it, he said sourly. He was angry that bookers and pimps were driving downtown begging Davie to talk to the boss, trying to avoid making bond payments. "I am tired of having my name mentioned like that. I don't like it."[30]

Davie pleaded for more time, but Lucky was worried: "I don't know. This Dewey investigation is coming on, and it may get tough, and I think we ought to fold up for a while." After the investigation they would try again. "We could even syndicate all the places like they do in Chicago, and instead of three or four combinations having the syndicates, as they do in Chicago, there would be only one in New York, us."

Davie kept at him: "Even if the Dewey investigation does start on us, they will only pick on phony bonding, that's all. They will probably grab two or three of the bondsmen and that is all there will be to it." Dave Betillo's persistence won the argument. The vice chain would continue.

"Well, all right, then let it go. I will let it go for a couple of more months, and if things are the same you will have to let it drop." But Lucky's instincts were right. The vice investigation was edging closer to the Luciano mob.

On October 8, Eunice Carter was handed a surveillance report. It dealt with a vice ring operated by Sadie Kaplan, a stout redhead, about 40, with headquarters at 157-159 Rivington Street. Red Sadie procured women for 15 houses on the East Side, Manhattan, and Brooklyn. On October 10, Detective Robert Goldstein was assigned to the prostitution investigation by Murray Gurfein. The detective spent a week talking with the staff and police officers, and he investigated Red Sadie. He discovered that if anyone attempted to open a house on the Lower East Side, the police swiftly raided it. Goldstein concluded that Sadie was being protected by officers at the Clinton Street Station. The protected brothels were quiet and profitable. On October 24, Detective Goldstein met with a secret informant, supplied by Dewey. Together they determined that the bonding office at 117 West 10th Street was the center of a ring that operated at the Women's Court. Stated the report: "Max Rachlin, attorney, Jesse Jacobs, front man, Meyer Berkman, bondsman, not licensed. James Frederick or Jimmy Fredericks, contact man between this man and their backers. The five men who control the ring are: Tommy Pinaccio [Pennochio], alias Tommy Bull, Dave Petillo [Betillo], Little Abie the Jew, Benny Spiller, and Willie Spiller [...] Jesse Jacobs attends to court fixing."[31] As the investigation explored secrets of the vice chain, a startling event rocked the underworld: the Dutchman took his last breath.

CHAPTER EIGHT

Lamster

Don't let Satan draw you too fast

Frank Costello and Louis Buchalter were waiting in 39D. There was a knock. Dutch Schultz stood hesitantly in the doorway. Costello apologized, explaining that Charley couldn't make the meeting. He offered the Dutchman a seat. But Dutch was angry that Lucky wasn't present. Schultz hovered in the doorway, then he made his point: Dewey had to be killed. Costello warned him to wait until he spoke to Charley.

On the evening of October 23, Dutch Schultz strode inside Newark's Palace Chop House at 12 East Park Street, accompanied by bodyguards Bernard "Lulu" Rosenkrantz and Abe Landau. As usual, the trio walked past the 75-foot bar and continued down a narrow corridor to a rear dining room, which was vacant. They sat at a corner table. Schultz resided at the nearby Robert Treat Hotel. He prepared for a third trial on charges of tax evasion. After Dutch surrendered to authorities on an outstanding fugitive warrant Max Silverman provided the $50,000 bail money. Silverman appeared at the Palace Chop House and sat with Dutch. He came to collect outstanding bills; Dutch owed him $3,500, and he owed $10,500 to attorneys. Dutch said he didn't have any cash, so Silverman left. Later, Otto "Abbadabba" Bierderman joined the group. Behind closed doors, beneath a lamp with an orange glow, Dutch and his lieutenants discussed business.

At 10:35 P.M. two men in overcoats ordered bartender Jack Friedman to lie on the floor. They strode to the back room; one raised a .38 caliber pistol, and the other aimed a sawed-off shotgun. They blasted the trio sitting at the table. Schultz opened the restroom door and a bullet ripped through his stomach, piercing his liver.[1] Despite their wounds Rosenkrantz and Landau managed to fire at the assassins, before collapsing. When police arrived Schultz

113

was slumped at a table, holding his right side. "I don't know nothing," he groaned.[2] Police found an adding machine and a tape with a sum totaling $827,253. The bleeding victims were rushed to Newark City Hospital.

A few hours later, Martin Krompier was shot in the Hollywood Barber Shop on Seventh Avenue. The same day, "Pretty Louis" Amberg was discovered in Brooklyn, hacked by an axe, and stuffed in a burning automobile parked near the Navy Yard. He was suspected by police of 18 murders. Louis and his brother, Joe, were former Schultz allies, but police knew a mob takeover was underway. A month earlier, Joe Amberg had been murdered in a Brooklyn garage. For several months there had been mob violence surrounding Schultz. Bo Weinberg had recently disappeared; informers said he had been murdered, for betraying Schultz.

Now the Dutchman was fading. "This is the journey's end," he muttered.[3]

A telegram from Madam Queen arrived at the hospital. Schultz had stolen her numbers business. "Don't be yellow. As ye sow, so shall ye reap," read the message. One by one the bullet-riddled quartet slipped away. Dutch asked to die a Catholic and was baptized. He lapsed into a drugged, delirious state; nevertheless, a police stenographer documented his rambling thoughts. "Don't let Satan draw you too fast.... He eats like a little sausage baloney maker." Finally, Dutch Schultz died.[4]

Police told reporters Schultz may have tried to regain control of his criminal empire, which had slipped from his grasp during the tax trials. Rumors swept the underworld that Charley Lucky ordered the executions. Deputy Chief Francis J. Kear ordered a city-wide search for "the most powerful gangster in Manhattan."[5]

On October 29, there were raids that netted 24 loan sharks. The same day, Henry Woelfle took the elevator to Room 39D. An employee of the Tower Apartments had recognized a photograph in the morning paper: Mr. Ross was Lucky Luciano. Henry Woelfle told Lucky to leave. Lucky was indignant. The rent was paid until the end of the month, he argued; in fact, he wanted to change rooms, but Woelfle insisted he immediately vacate the room. Lucky gave up and handed the manager a 20 dollar bill to cover outstanding expenses.

Frank Gregory, senior house detective, conferred with Woelfle in the lobby. Gregory had also seen Lucky's photograph in the newspapers but was unaware he was a guest in the Waldorf. Gregory was a former police detective who was familiar with Lucky's background. He asked Woelfle if he could return the change.

Lucky answered the buzzer in a lounge robe. He stared at the former detective, recognition in his eyes. Gregory told him he had better get out.

"How long have you been here?" asked Lucky.[6]

"I have been here since the house is opened. How long have you been here?"

"Well, now, I don't know."

"I never saw you before," said Gregory. "You had better get out." Thirty minutes later, Mr. Ross checked out. Lucky went to Atlantic City, socializing with his friend Doc Kootch, then he went to Miami.

By November 2, detectives had traced Lucky to the Waldorf, but he was long gone. During the next weeks, detectives John Gallagher and Leon Kaplan searched for *B72321*. Kenmare and Mulberry Streets were watched at various hours, without success. On the afternoon of November 20, a report came to the New York police that "subject is at this time in Hot Springs, Arkansas, and that he intends to remain there until the opening of the winter season in Miami."[7] An informant told police that Mike Coppola was in charge of Lucky's affairs in New York.

While detectives tried to put together a case against Lucky for the Schultz murder, Dewey's team, led by Captain Bernard Dowd, investigated all leads on houses of prostitution. Eunice Carter and Murray Gurfein investigated the bail bondsmen in Women's Court. Carter arranged a wiretap on the bonding office. The wiretap revealed that Abe Karp, though disbarred in March of 1934, still gave legal advice. Madams, prostitutes, and criminals daily called the office for help.

Michael Redmond was worried. The bonding office was involved in illegal activity. There was something called a *combination* directing everything, realized the office boy. On one occasion, Meyer Berkman went to court and bailed out three girls. "About time," one huffed.[8] "What the hell kind of *combination* was it?" The madam silenced the girl, but the office boy overheard the comment. Cokey Flo had also mentioned a *combination* one day at the office. Jesse Jacobs became angry and asked her what she knew about it. Abe Karp kept a diary but, after the new year began, he ordered Redmond to destroy it. The diary didn't matter. The mistress-prostitutes of Lucky's lieutenants knew everything and they were terrified.

Thelma Jordan and Benny Spiller danced nightly at the Bal Musette at 301 West 46th Street; the nightclub was owned by combination members. Yet, despite the surface glamour, Thelma felt trapped in a sordid life. Her roommate, Mary Morris, was the prostitute-mistress of killer Johnny Roberts Robilotto. Mary told Thelma about mob beatings and murders. Thelma discovered her boyfriend, Benny Spiller, participated in a gruesome execution, prompted by his brother. A gunman had robbed Willie Spiller's girl in a whorehouse. The robber was caught and driven to marshes in New Jersey. After being tortured, he was buried alive.

Late one evening there was a knock on Thelma's door. It was Benny. He had just left a regular Tuesday night meeting: "I have been called on the carpet quite a few times about taking money from you." The combination suspected him of being a secret booker who hid houses. "I was called on the carpet again tonight," said Benny. "I have to take you downtown."

They drove to Celano's Restaurant. Gathered in a back room was Dave Betillo, Tommy Pennochio, and Abie Wahrman. Little Davie ordered Wahrman outside. He glared at Thelma. "Benny can't take money from you and stay in the combination."[9] Tommy the Bull spoke next: "I know you have been making a lot of money here of late, and if you are not giving it to him, what are you doing with it?"

"Clothes, liquor, sending the rest home," Thelma answered. Little Davie issued a warning: "If we ever hear of Benny taking money from you, he will get kicked out of the combination, and if you are going to go with Benny, work as little as possible."

One evening, while she and Benny drank at Jamison's Bar, Benny had suddenly left for the Waldorf, to see Charley Lucky, the boss. Now the police were searching for Charley as the executioner who had wiped out the Dutch Schultz mob. Thelma was frightened; so was Nancy Presser. Months earlier, Nancy had gone to Kean's Tavern for a drink and was suddenly startled. Ralph sat with Lucky, Davie, and Wild Bill Ercolino. She left, afraid Ralph would learn she knew the boss.

The relationship between Nancy and Ralph had become increasingly violent. Ralph's brutal nature kept her in constant fear of beatings. Nancy tried to give Ralph at least $125 a week. She hid the rest, but Ralph would find the money, accuse her of holding out, and beat her. In July, Ralph moved in with Nancy. Ralph now ordered her to work in a common whorehouse. He complained constantly that he needed money. Nancy refused. During the heated argument, Ralph threatened to cut her face until her own mother wouldn't know her. He smashed her in the face and beat Nancy until she surrendered.

Only twice had Nancy booked herself to work in cheap whorehouses. As a call girl she was in charge and worked when she wished. Servicing men in a house was humiliating, and a big drop in the sex underworld social strata. In a house she was expected to lie on a bed and spread her legs for whoever walked through the door, but she was so terrified of Ralph she obeyed.

As instructed by Ralph, Pete Balitzer came to the Hotel Emerson. Ralph demanded that Pete book Nancy. Pete booked Nancy at Jennie Fox's house on Riverside Drive, but Nancy failed to show up. At the end of the week she had no money to turn over to Ralph. He cursed her, beat her, and tried to strangle her with a wire coat hanger. Nancy screamed until knocks on the door stopped the savage assault. Ralph telephoned Pete. He instructed Pete to book Nancy at the same place.

This time Nancy went. At Jennie's house Pete introduced himself to Nancy. Pete gave Nancy his telephone number. If he couldn't be reached, Jojo Weintraub would find her a job.

At the end of the week, Ralph took her money and ordered her to work in Joe Green's house in the Hotel Normandie on West 64th Street, near Broadway. The house was booked by Jack Ellenstein, but Ralph insisted that Nancy arrange the job herself because people were calling him "Ralph the Pimp." She obeyed.

When Pete booked her at Jimmy Russo's, Ralph drove her to work, but Russo wasn't impressed; he didn't want any more blondes. Russo escorted Nancy downstairs. Ralph got out of his car and confronted Russo: "This is my girl and you better put her to work, if you know what's good for you."[10] Russo took her back to the apartment. Nancy begged Russo not to tell Ralph how much she earned or he would steal it. Ralph summoned Pete to the Emerson Hotel. He had robbed Pete before and knew the booker was afraid of him. He threatened Pete and demanded all of Nancy's money.

Ralph drove Nancy to work every day and came for her every night. But Nancy still had her own clients and preferred their company. She kept client names in a black address book. Once again, she defied Ralph's orders to work in a house. Ralph slashed at her face with a knife. When she tried to protect herself her arm was severely cut.

Despite the order to stay out of New York, Nancy Brooks unexpectedly appeared at 87 Mulberry Street. In the café she asked for Jimmy Fredericks. A balding man with deep circles under his eyes emerged. "I'm Tommy Bull. You've heard of me."[11]

"No, I've never heard of you."

"I'm Jimmy's partner. What's the message?"

She asked about Danny Caputo, who was still in jail. Tommy nodded and she left. Later, Jimmy sent her a message that he was doing all he could to help, but the boys downtown didn't like Danny because he talked too much. Nancy finally located Jimmy. She was angry that Danny was still in jail. She would go to "the big boss myself."

"You'll go to the big boss?" asked Jimmy. "Well, he's out of town."

They met again at the Caputo's home. By now, Jimmy had grown weary of the entire situation, feeling the Caputo family was bothering him. Nancy pleaded for him to help. "Danny's taking a rap for you, Jimmy, and you ought to do something for him. If not, I'll go to Dewey myself, and see that you are put where Danny is."

"If you do anything like that I'll blow your brains out," he threatened, and stormed away. Fearing for her life, Nancy Brooks moved to Corona. Danny Caputo was convicted of compulsory prostitution and sentenced to Sing Sing. Danny grew despondent; no help came from the combination to appeal his conviction.

Pressure was building on Pete Balitzer. He argued with Little Davie about exorbitant payments. Pete and Mildred had separated, though he continued to support her. Mildred's little girl was sent to live with her uncle. Pete worked closely with Jimmy Fredericks; they spoke almost every day, discussing business, especially robberies, shakedowns, and raids.

Malcolm Bailey, a former sailor, worked as a collector for Pete. Bailey had been honorably discharged from the Navy. After he met Pete in a poolroom on 48th Street, Bailey was hired to answer the telephone at Pete's office. Bailey introduced Pete to Bonnie Connolly, a newcomer from Maryland. Pete looked her over at the Monterey Hotel. "Pinches you don't have to be afraid of; you got to take them, but it is a one hundred percent sure thing that you will get out. You can average for yourself about a hundred a week."[12] Connolly was arrested three weeks later. The next day she was released, just as Pete had promised.

After a prostitute was arrested in Brooklyn, Dave Marcus took bail money to Jesse Jacobs. When the case was dismissed, Marcus asked Jacobs for the refunded bail money. "How do you think we pay off the coppers and fix these cases?" snarled Jacobs.[13] If there were more complaints, warned Jacobs, "You'll get your head kicked off." Marcus went to Pittsburgh. When he returned Jimmy Fredericks cornered him at the bonding office, angry that he hadn't received the weekly payoff. Marcus said he wasn't making enough money. "You will give me 75 dollars a week," demanded Jimmy, "and you will like it, or I will kick you right in the belly." Marcus said to go ahead and kick. Jimmy picked up a chair and was about to hit him over the head, but someone in the office shouted at him. The stress aggravated Marcus' heart condition. After he was confined to his house for the next three months, his wife booked women.

In October 1935, Pete was the target of police surveillance. Officers noted that Pete booked a job for "Frisco Jean" Irwin, a slender blonde. She went to work at 10 West 86th Street, where Ruth Davis was the madam. Jean became Pete's new mistress and moved in with him.

Detectives began shadowing Jimmy Fredericks. They stopped him at the corner of Second Avenue and East 5th Street. When questioned, he said he was a laborer. Jimmy was in the company of known criminals, Jack Citron and Alex Glickson. Jimmy was arrested on a vagrancy charge, unable to demonstrate a visible means of support. Though the charge was dismissed, Jimmy was also under surveillance.

In November, Inspector Lyons led a morning raid that netted 30 loan sharks. They were brought to the Woolworth Building and placed in a holding room. During the day, witnesses peeked through blinds and identified the guilty. One woman had borrowed a hundred dollars, but by the time she was able to repay the loan, the interest amounted to 260 percent.

Ralph told Nancy to put two handguns in her purse. Ralph drove to a house known as Jean's Place on 71st Street. Nancy handed him the guns. She remained in the car while Ralph and Little Al went inside. Dave Betillo had given orders to rob the madam, since she had refused to pay bond money. Afterward, the trio drove to a restaurant on Mulberry Street and Ralph turned over the cash. But Ralph gave jewelry and a watch to Nancy. Nancy was afraid of Little Davie. While in Chicago she had heard of Davie's reputation as an executioner. Nancy was sinking lower each day. Either Ralph or an overdose would eventually kill her. Nancy stopped shooting heroin and underwent withdrawal in her hotel room. She was desperately sick. Ralph drove her to a sanitarium in Connecticut, where she recuperated for two weeks.

The vice investigation was unexpectedly exposed in December. "Two Million Dollar a Year Bond Racket," headlined the *Evening Journal*.[14] The article, citing "an authoritative source," disclosed that prostitutes paid ten dollars weekly to booking agents, who in turn paid the bond office, where the women rehearsed stories. Arrests were imminent, including "the head of the mob, a well known East Side gunman and racketeer."

Investigators decided it was time to organize a raid. Meanwhile, detectives carefully documented the vice chain's illegal operations. One night they followed a 1935 Packard registered to Pete Balitzer. Pete and Jojo exited and walked to Jamison's Bar and Grill at 148 West 54th Street, an underworld hangout, noted police. During the holidays, Katherine O' Connor arrived from Chicago. She was 24, just an inch over five feet, with red hair, gray eyes, and a perfect set of teeth. At the Knickerbocker Hotel she met her friend Patsy Day, who was also a prostitute. Pete and Jojo knocked on the hotel door; it was Christmas week and there was a shortage of girls, so Katherine could start work right away, said Pete. Katherine was driven to a house on the West Side and left with a madam named Hazel. Pete never stopped booking, fearful he would be murdered if he stopped.

On Christmas Day, Ralph drove Nancy to the Liguori home. Ralph's mother and sister were unaware Nancy was a prostitute. Nancy told them she sold cigarettes in a nightclub. Ralph tried to behave around his family, but his mother agonized over his dark life. A priest was often called to speak to Ralph and help him get out of trouble. Herman Liguori, his brother, was also a member of the underworld.

Lucky left Hot Springs for Miami; a detective was close behind. On December 28, he registered with the Miami police, as required by law for a convicted felon. The same day police listened to a wiretap on Jack Ellenstein's telephone line. "I am in Brooklyn. I use two girls. They can make from $85 to $95."

"Okay," said Ellenstein, "you'll have them Monday morning."

Then Moishe called. He ran a house and cursed a girl over a money dispute.

"She's not coming," said Ellenstein, "so I'm sending you a new one, who is better and prettier than the other one."

"That's a lucky thing for that cocksucker," fumed Moishe. "I'd punch her in the fucken mouth if she came back here."

"Listen, never do that to any girl because they talk too much, and if they ask for some money, give it to them."

Julia later called, complaining about Moishe.

"Julia, I want you to go back there."

"No, that man is drunk."

"Oh, it's nothing. He had one of his spasms."

"I won't go. Do you realize that man wanted to break a chair over my head? If it wasn't for a couple of guys there, he would have killed me."

"Okay, okay, don't go."

"Will you get my money for me?"

"Go and get it yourself."

"Okay then. If you get something decent, give me a ring."

As the days passed, the wiretaps linked the bookers. It was apparent the men knew each other and worked together.

Frank called, "mad as the devil," noted the wiretapper. Frank spoke with an Italian accent and wanted Jojo Weintraub's number.

"I don't know it," lied Jack.

"He promised to call me Monday between twelve and one, who the hell does he think he's kidding? Someone told me he has already collected the money. If I get hold of him I'll break his fucken nose."

On January 2, Pete Balitzer called. "Got anything, Jack?"

"I'm trying to get Patsy. Little Ruthie is supposed to call me."

"You can't get hold of her? I sent one to Max's. Then you got nothing?"

"I'm trying to think. I'll call you back."

Then the wiretappers caught a big fish.

"I just woke up, Jack."

"Who is this?"

"This is Jimmy. I want to talk to you but not over the telephone."

"Tomorrow," answered Ellenstein.

"This afternoon, any place you say."

"I spoke to Mary, she's not sure about the weekend."

"Did you get in touch with Grace and Evelyn? Get them down here."

"It's okay. I met Benny and gave him a bundle of those cards, you know just announcing like. It's a date for Forty-Sixth Street, Jimmy, between 12:30 A.M. and 1:00 A.M."

"Don't you forget," said Gorilla.

Shirley Mason, Jack's prostitute-mistress answered calls while Ellenstein was gone.

"Oh, hello, Melba, he'll be back sometime tonight."

"Will you ask him to give me something this week?"

"Yes, I will. Where are you now?"

"I'm home on Seventy-Second Street."

"Have you got an apartment?"

"No, I live in a hotel. I have just a room. I think I'll move the first but I don't know where."

"What are you doing today, working?"

"No, I have to go to Jackson Heights for dinner."

"I'm going out, too. I think I'll go to the Paramount and see Jack Oakie. I like him."

"That's good."

"How is your hair?"

"Oh, it's coming in fine."

"You know I found out something while I was in the hospital. They can't tell if you have anything while taking a blood test when you have typhoid, and I wouldn't tell them. You know I've had everything."

Women called Jack. They sought work and complained of slow houses. "What happened to that place? It's terrible. I'm not making enough to keep me in Kotex," complained a girl.

"I think it's because they're snowbound," answered Jack.

On January 14, Pearl called, and she was unhappy. "What kind of a place was that you sent me to, 3318?"

"I hear you were out late, who with?"

"Oh, I had a little fun."

"Oh, a little love and kisses, eh, what's the matter with Max?"

"Oh, he ain't got a good fuck left in him."

Thelma Jordan's name surfaced. She was Jack's best moneymaker. "I'll give her 35 percent," he said. His voice filled with joy.

All day Ellenstein handled calls about booking women, money pickups and, occasionally, personal matters. "Tell that butcher that the meat is good for a cat," complained Ellenstein. "I don't want shredded meat. I asked for veal steak. I'd like to have him deliver it so I could throw it in his face."

On January 13, the wiretap hit the jackpot. The police connected Tommy Bull to the vice ring.

"Did my brother get in touch with you last night?" asked Johnny Pennochio. "He wanted to get Pete Harris' address."

Jack Ellenstein was miffed. "Why mention names over the phone, can't you just say Pete?"

"That all right," replied Johnny. "Tell him to get in touch with Tommy Bull."

The wiretaps continued providing names and addresses. At 11:35 A.M. Officer Isidore Pinsker listened as Pete Balitzer telephoned a girl named Mickey.

"Take this, 244 W. Seventy-Second Street, penthouse. Take the elevator."

"Whose place is it?"

"Dixie's. A very good place."

"Okay."

Around noon a "Jewish voice," telephoned. It was Jennie.

"Hello, Pete?"

"Yes."

"Who is that girl who answered the wire?"

"One of the girls, why?"

"Let her get killed, she was asleep yet."

"Yes, you woke her up."

"What's new? Why don't I hear from you? Are you getting rich, you pimp?"

"Yes, very rich."

"You know, three days ago I'm walking along; I spot two fellows in a car near the house. I didn't like their looks. When I walked in the hall they walk over to me and say, 'Hello, Jennie, how are you doing? You remember us?' So I got sore and said, 'I don't know you. This is my daughter's house, so beat it.' I got the license number of their car and had it verified in the license bureau. I found out they are two vice cops. One lives in Long Island.... You know Kramer, the vice cop. He is a wiretapper."

In the afternoon Jojo dialed out, calling home.

"Hello, mamma, how are you doing? Anything new?"

"Nothing new."

"Is papa working?"

"A little bit."

"I'll be home tomorrow at five, positively. I am working now. Don't worry."

During the Christmas holidays Jimmy and Flo argued. She had given Jimmy a hundred dollars as a Christmas gift, but Jimmy gave her nothing at all. Then Flo discovered Jimmy had given a mink coat to a woman he had been keeping for six years. But worse trouble was ahead for Flo Brown.

At Flo's house on 86th Street Joan Young argued she was underpaid by ten dollars. Angry, Joan went to the police. On January 19, a raid closed Flo's house. Flo was charged with a misdemeanor, maintaining a house of prostitution. Flo confessed to police that Pete Balitzer had sent the girls. Police raided Pete's office, but he was gone. While being escorted to a police van police saw Flo drop a hypodermic needle in the snow. It was for insulin injections, which she was taking to gain weight, she explained. Officers discovered a cube of morphine in her purse; it had been planted, she argued. Flo paid $2,900 to the bonding office to cover her bail and that of the girls arrested.

A madam named Daisy called Pete with the news.

"Did you hear?" asked Pete.

"Yes," said Daisy. "I read it in the paper. You know, Pete, this would be a good business if you could get rid of the rats."

Pete blamed himself for Flo's arrest. "I just talked to downtown. It takes time in court, you know. I'm on pins and needles," he fretted. "But in this racket, you've got to take chances."

"Who was the girl?"

"A Joan Young. She worked for you on 71st Street. She used to room with that Norma who committed suicide. You know her?"

"Well, maybe if I seen her, I'd know her."

"She's about 5' 7", platinum blonde."

"Who booked her before you?"

"Well, Dave Miller a little bit, and somebody else. I don't know who had her before me. Oh! It's the madam's fault."

"It's enough to make you nervous."

"I'm nearly crazy."

"You know, Pete, you'll always have this trouble unless you have an organization of the madams."

"You can't do that. There's too many independents, and too much jealousy among the madams."

"I mean the ones under you and Jack Eller, you know? Otherwise the combination will be ruined. Things will be wiped out."

"I guess we ought to try it."

"It's a racket like all the rest."

The next day, at 3:20 P.M., Al Weiner telephoned Jojo. Flo's arrest was still a hot subject. The police were searching for Pete.

"It's on account of that madam Flo Brown."

"That son of a bitch, that skinny one?"

"Yes, she insulted a girl and didn't pay her off, so she went to the station house."

"Looks bad for him."

"No, he'll be alright; he has no record."

A few days later, Pete asked Malcolm Bailey to drive him to 10th Street. In front of the bonding office they sounded the horn. Jesse Jacobs came out.

"How does it look?" asked Pete.

"What the hell are you doing here?" shouted Jacobs. "You have to look out for those girls. If one of them squawks it is going to look bad for all of us." Pete asked about Kitty O'Connor. Jacobs said he had her sitting in a candy store all afternoon. He had advised Flo to skip bail, since she was facing a charge of compulsory prostitution and maintaining a disorderly house. Jacobs told Pete not to book Flo any longer. "If she gets caught once more, it's going to be everybody's ass. I am going to give you a little advice, Pete. Get out of town."

Pete went to Philadelphia.

Al Weiner called Jack Ellenstein. He had just returned from Sing Sing where he saw his father and Nick Montana. "They cook together," reported Al. "I brought him up some groceries."

"It's nice up there," remarked Ellenstein. "The sun is warm."

The conversation turned to Pete, who was in hiding. Al Weiner said Pete had created his own problems by allowing Flo to mismanage the girls. "Do it by yourself. That's what I say."

"Oh, he'll be back in a couple of days," said Jack.

Then came business. "Joe Green took the blonde upstairs."

"What's her name?" asked Jack.

"You know that Jean Harlow blonde."

"Oh, that's okay."

"And I sent to Betty one by the name of Jerry, a little one; I don't think you know her."

"I know her. She's a dark one, and a cute one. I sent her to a good place and she never showed up."

"She's a little bum, that dark one. She is so uncertain. Joe Green took the blonde upstairs; now I have to find another one to take her place."

The entire vice operation poured in through the tapped telephone lines. Dewey gathered his staff. It was time to strike.

CHAPTER NINE

The Big Pinch

How much did you give that girl?

At the Bal Musette nightclub Tommy Bull stopped Mildred Balitzer. He wanted to know where Pete had gone.

"Out of town," she told him.

"Yes, I know he is out of town, but where is he?"

"I really don't know. Why?"

"You tell him to come back, that everything is fixed up; it won't cost him a penny."

Mildred said if Pete called she would deliver the message. Mildred knew the police were searching for Pete; now the combination was trying to lure him back. Pete was in deep trouble. But unknown to the vice underworld, the combination's reign was about to end. On January 31, just hours before the planned raid, the wiretap on the bonding office hammered another nail in the prosecution's case.

"This is Tommy Bull, let me speak to Meyer."

"He just stepped out. I'll have him call you."

David J. McAuliffe, deputy chief inspector, assembled 56 police officers at the West 68th Street Precinct Station.[1] McAuliffe was the police liaison with Murray Gurfein and Eunice Carter. The plan was to raid 32 houses of prostitution. Those arrested would be driven to 19 Barclay Street, the delivery entrance to the Woolworth Building. Staff members would question those brought in. Special arrangements had carefully been made to convert the 13th floor into a temporary detention area. The raiders were divided into teams and handed a sealed envelope. On the single sheet of paper was a typed address and instructions: "Hit the house at 9:00 P.M. tonight on a jump raid. Make every effort to make a complete case which will stand up in court." The officers were told to act quickly in order "to catch some of the inmates in the act of prostitution." They were to seize records, memoranda, diaries, and phone numbers. Customers were to be questioned in the presence of the women regarding payment of money; the men were to be released but the women held. At the Woolworth Building tension was high. Dewey had carefully planned the raid. The officers had a special telephone number to call regarding where to take suspects. Dewey knew the precinct stations were riddled with informers who could tip off whorehouses and bookers, so the assault crew had been hand-picked. Two policemen hovered before 233 East 12th Street; at precisely 9:00 P.M. they stormed the building. Officer William Duggan pushed open a front door as Betty Connors was saying goodbye to two clients. Eight clients sat nearby. Duggan rushed down the hall, past the kitchen, and forced open the bedroom door. Inside was Ann Moore, hastily putting on her coat. A man stood, dressed only in his shorts; he pulled up his trousers. He told the police officer his name was Milton; he and his friend Morrie had come for a good time.

"How much did you give that girl?" asked Officer Duggan.

"I was to give her a dollar fifty."

Ann Moore spoke up. She had received nothing. Milton explained he was supposed to pay when he was finished. The girl was asked who booked her. A girlfriend named Eleanor had brought her, she answered. She had been at the house for three weeks. Officer Duggan ordered her to come along with him. She removed clothes from a closet and dressed. Officer John Finley also had suspects. In an adjacent apartment he had pushed open a bedroom door. Eleanor Jackson sat on the bed, dressed in a white evening gown. A man stood without his trousers. He admitted that it was his second visit and that he was about to have intercourse with Jackson for $1.50. The girl pleaded with the officer to let her go. She had arrived from California only a few months earlier and hadn't been in the business long. She had been brought there by her friend, Ann Moore, and had never been arrested before. On a dresser, scribbled on napkins, were customer calculations, tallied for several days. She acknowledged the calculations were hers. She slipped on her underwear and exchanged the evening gown for street clothes.

A trio of officers stood before 261 West 21st Street. They were about to raid the house of "Polack Frances" Blackman. Nancy Presser had been working in the apartment all week. Ralph had booked her through his crime associate, Johnny DeLucca. Johnny pimped for Frances and claimed most of her money. At 9:10 P.M. the officers entered the building. As they approached the apartment, a woman was escorting a man out; both were arrested. The officers hurriedly located the bedrooms. Officer Le Castro observed a man standing near the bed; his pants rolled down and his genitals were exposed. Nancy lay on the bed with her dress pulled up. She jumped from the bed. The customer admitted he had come to "get laid" and intended to pay Nancy three dollars, once he had finished. On Third Avenue a woman handed him a slip of paper with the address. A man who nearly made it out the door was brought before Nancy. "I paid her three dollars in return for a lay," he said. He identified himself as a lawyer. Nancy was silent. During the interrogation, the door bell rang. Another customer came inside. He had a slip of paper in his hand with the address. The three men were released. The officers hailed a taxi and took the women away.

At 219 East 40th Street Marie Dubin and Joan Martin were fully clothed but alone when officers entered. As they were led away, the group encountered two men on their way up to the apartment. Questioned, the men admitted they were frequent clients. Joan Martin said she would find a girl for them.

At 315 West 57th Street Gussie Silvers opened the door. The officers pushed her aside. Hearing the commotion, Muriel Ryan ran out of a bedroom, leaving a customer behind. He "hadn't laid her" but was about to do so for two dollars, he told the policemen. Muriel said nothing. There was a douche syringe and condoms in the room, noted police. Sitting with a man in the living room was Helen Thomas. Her bedroom also had a syringe. Officer John Cox recognized her as a woman he had arrested on 103rd Street the year before; at the time, she gave her name was Jean Ware.

At 1 West 68th Street the apartment had no women, but three clients awaited their arrival. At 244 West 72nd Street officers took the elevator to the penthouse. Dorothy Arnold paid $300 a month for the suites; it was the most expensive house on the police list. In the plush penthouse were Betty Anderson and Mary Thomas, dressed in negligees; five men sat in the apartment. The maid told the police all they wanted to hear. She worked in "a sporting house" where girls led men into bedrooms and closed the doors. The maid told police there was a black address book on the premises and prophylactics. Dorothy Arnold sat quietly. Police confiscated punch tickets and receipt slips, but the address book could not be located. When Dorothy was forced to stand, police smiled. She had been sitting on the address book which contained an alphabetical list of customers.

Later, Charles "Slim" Mosby admitted his wife, known in the trade as "Dixie," ran two whorehouses. The prostitutes were supplied by Pete Balitzer. Slim insisted his wife, Calvert Mosby, was not a whore.

At 110 West 96th Street officers went to Room 9A. They forced the door to get inside. Sally Osborne was in a bedroom, pulling a dress over head. A man confessed he was going to pay two dollars for sexual intercourse, which had not yet taken place. "It's a raid!" shouted Marie Rolands from another room. Marie rushed to the bathroom to dress. The girls were arrested along with the madam, Lucy Sterne.

In Brooklyn, above a restaurant on Neptune Avenue, officers found Helen Hayes removing her dress. She was about to get in bed with a client. The policemen questioned a physician and a lawyer, who both acknowledged they had come for sex. Helen Hayes admitted she been had intimate with five customers, for two dollars each. Earlier in the day, she had been examined by Dr. Lavine. Celia Newman, the madam, was 24 and an unemployed waitress.

Officer Richard Tilson approached an apartment at 167 West 71st Street. His partner, patrolman Cornelius Walter, stood guard in the hall. The door opened slightly and a girl peered out. The officer identified himself, but the door was slammed in his face. He conferred with his partner, then returned a few minutes later and knocked again. When the door reopened the officers pushed inside. They checked out the apartment which consisted of one bedroom, a sitting room, and bathroom. Jean Rogers claimed the apartment had just been rented for 15 dollars a week. Edna Russell said she was just a guest. Both said they were unemployed showgirls. The officers were perplexed until a man arrived. He had come to be "fixed up with a woman for two dollars." The girls were arrested. Rogers informed the police she was 21, a native of Wilkes-Barre, Pennsylvania, where she had studied dancing and toured with The Millette Troupe. Rogers was her stage name; she refused to give her real name. She had arrived in New York four years earlier and performed with the Brick Top Orchestra, led by female bandleader Bobby Aron. Rogers traveled with the orchestra for two years and earned a salary of 25 dollars a week. For the past six months her parents sent her money. She lived on 83rd Street. A friend, Marian Taylor, also a showgirl, had rented the room that afternoon but had left the apartment about a half hour earlier, just before the officers came, to go "night clubbing." Taylor's personal belongings were at the Hotel Victoria and were being held by the management due to unpaid bills. She admitted that several men had been searching for Taylor, but none were allowed in the room. Officers found the names of several men written on slips of paper. Rogers said the men were just friends. Rogers insisted she was a professional tap dancer and had never been a prostitute. She was convincing, and the officers didn't know what to do with her.

Edna Russell asked for permission to dress. Officer Tilson agreed but did not allow her to leave his sight. When Russell removed her dress, he observed that she wore no underclothes. Russell said she was 25, an acrobat dancer with the Miller Brothers; an agent in the Hotel Marquardt would verify her story. When asked why she was not fully dressed, she said she had removed her slip and pants due to "hot flashes," the result of an appendix operation. She denied ever being a prostitute. Despite protests, the officers finally arrested both women.

Officers Ehenfeld and Katz were reluctantly admitted into an apartment at 127 West 82nd Street by Helen Wilson, the madam. Betty Baker was inside, fully clothed, and so were 13 men. All the men said they had come for sex, ready to pay the two-dollar fee. Betty was 23, a native of Utica. She had left home four years earlier. She worked as a waitress and dishwasher for ten dollars a week. The previous month she became a prostitute, she explained. Ellen Day referred her to Helen Wilson's house. When Betty had arrived at 7:00 P.M. the madam greeted her and told the maid to prepare a meal. After she ate, she read a while, and had a brief conversation with Helen Wilson, who complained that business was poor. The officers determined Baker had been a prostitute for quite some time. Helen Wilson said she was a manicurist and the 13 men in her apartment were there "to play cards." She denied being a prostitute or madam. Police found a client notebook, paper napkins, a jar of Vaseline and "some sort of medical instrument." Wilson finally admitted operating a house of prostitution, but asked the officers to give her a break. Despite the plea, both women were driven to the Woolworth Building.

Dressed in a kimono, Marilyn Summers had been arrested at 338 Lincoln Place in a house run by Molly Leonard. She admitted she was guilty of prostitution but denied using a booker. However, Summers said that when she did work at a house controlled by bookers she was forced to pay the booking percentage, even though she made independent arrangements with the various madams.

At 1 West 68th Street, madam Sally Bender was taken in custody, along with 60 rubber contraceptives as evidence, noted officers.

The following day Thelma Jordan was arrested as she walked toward 310 West 106th Street, the apartment where Pete Balitzer lived. She had arrived around 3:00 A.M. to help Jeanette Lewis pack a trunk, and stayed overnight. As Thelma left for her apartment at 214 West 96th Street, she was arrested. She was taken upstairs, where Jojo Weintraub and Jeanette Lewis were already in custody. They remained in the apartment several hours until all were driven downtown.

In Jean Bradley's black book, found at 127 W. 82nd Street, was the name of Harry Cohn, head of Columbia Pictures, and Ben Fox, a studio executive.

Mildred Balitzer was arrested at the George Washington Hotel, where she shared a room with Phil Ryan, a homosexual producer of cabaret shows.

Detectives waited outside 125 West 12th Street; they were in search of the big catch. At 2:15 A.M. they arrested Dave Betillo, Tommy Pennochio,

Benny Spiller, and Patsy Ragel. A detective removed a notebook from Tommy's pocket. Among the telephone numbers in the notebook were those of Pete and Mildred Balitzer and Jesse Jacobs. On the reverse of a business card police found the telephone numbers of Jimmy Fredericks and Benny Spiller. Detectives also found written notes about the murder of a drug informant who had turned state's evidence. Business papers were taken from Dave Betillo, who initialed the documents as his property. Among the items were business cards from Kean's Tavern, Celano's Restaurant, and the Red Devil Inn. On one card Betillo had written the telephone numbers of Jimmy Fredericks and Benny Spiller. In Philadelphia detectives went to the Walnut Park Plaza Hotel and arrested Pete Balitzer.

Justice Philip McCook conducted a court session in the Woolworth Building; 87 suspects were ordered held on $10,000 bail each. Binge Curcio gave the investigators a list of houses. Eunice Carter carefully examined all the confiscated items. The women were transported to the Women's House of Detention at Greenwich Avenue and 10th Street.

On February 2, detectives arrested Jimmy Fredericks. In his possession was an address book listing 20 houses. He was charged with being an accessory to the crime of compulsory prostitution. The next day he was questioned by Milton Schilback. He denied knowing any of the bookers. "Ever been in a whorehouse in your life?" asked Schilback. "No, sir," responded Jimmy. He claimed he was a wastepaper buyer for a Brooklyn company, but the firm denied Jimmy's story. Flo Brown read of Jimmy's arrest in the newspapers. They exchanged letters. She was still in love with Jimmy and decided to help him.

Tommy Bull was questioned at the Raymond Street Jail in Brooklyn. He answered questions but claimed to operate a soda fountain. He denied knowing Lucky or Jimmy Fredericks. Dewey carefully studied the notes found in Tommy's pocket. He concluded that Tommy the Bull had murdered a narcotics dealer who had turned state's evidence. Tommy kept an account of the victim's date of arrest, release, assault, hospital stay, death, and date of burial. A week after Tommy's arrest, Rose Lerner handed over the loan records in the Mott Street office; an unknown man walked off with the books.

Jerry Bruno was arrested at 807 Riverside Drive. He denied any knowledge or contact with the combination. Bruno fought the police. While being questioned at the Woolworth Building, he kicked an officer. He was arraigned at Justice McCook's home on 57th Street. In default of $25,000 bail, he was jailed in the Tombs. Defense attorney Caesar Barra asserted in court, before Justice Asron Levy, that Bruno had been beaten, bled profusely, and was held incommunicado for three days. Dewey indignantly denied the claim.

Those arrested were tight-lipped except for Dave Marcus. He confessed his guilt and gave details of the combination: Lucky Luciano controlled the prostitution syndicate, though he could only confirm the information by hearsay. Marcus became ill from his heart condition while in custody. After arraignment before Justice McCook, he was taken to a Brooklyn hospital.

By Sunday morning only a handful of the prostitutes and madams had confessed. Dewey realized the women had been "schooled in perjury," by Abe Karp and Max Rachlin. They protested that they were innocent business girls, manicurists, waitresses, or visitors. A few women were released as innocent victims of the raids. Dewey's lightning strike was the talk of the city. In the privacy of his office Dewey expressed pleasure over the criminals caught in the police raid. The police identified the men arrested as Lucky's subordinates, but the boss had cleverly concealed his participation in the numerous illegal activities he directed.

On February 4, federal agents stormed a building at 77 Park Avenue. Mae "Billie" Scheible, an attractive blonde, was arrested as "a million dollar vice queen." She was charged with violating the Mann Act in a conspiracy to transfer a minor, "Boots" Carter, from Pittsburgh to New York for immoral purposes. Billie was Pete Balitzer's former girlfriend. Dressed in a mink coat and tiger skin hat, Scheible heard herself described as a menace to society. Federal attorney John Dowling estimated her net profit to be at $100,000. She interrupted his comments with denials. "Sir, I made that money selling liquor."[2] But Dowling countered that she was an associate of an imprisoned counterfeiter and her net worth was a million dollars. "She never earned an honest penny in her life," the prosecutor told the court, "and her actions have menaced the life and health of a great number of girls."

Already on bail, charged with car theft, the judge set bail at $6,500, which Scheible failed to provide. She was locked in the House of Detention with Dewey's girls. Investigators informed reporters that Scheible's appointment book was filled with prominent clients, including the owner of a baseball league, a bank president, business executives, and politicians. These men paid as high as a thousand dollars a night, but the girls were handed a paltry $15. Mae Scheible had been so well protected that the combination avoided her plush house, just as it had avoided Polly Adler's house.

Barent Ten Eyck had been investigating extortion in the bakery industry but was transferred to the prostitution case and appointed Chief Assistant. Ten Eyck assigned staff members to interrogate the women. Frank Hogan spent from 14 to 16 hours a day inducing each of the witnesses to confess. Hogan told the madams they faced two to ten years in jail, but if they agreed to tell the truth they would be offered immunity. Many of the women had been dependent on alcohol and drugs for years, so the effect of their physical condition was apparent. Physicians treated those showing withdrawal symptoms.

Barent Ten Eyck's interrogations produced scant information because the women wouldn't talk. Patsy Day told him they were afraid, since the entire ring had not been rounded up. Patsy secretly spoke of a "higher up" who was the real power; she gave the name of Lucky Luciano. Ten Eyck told Dewey what he had discovered. Dewey was pleased. Ten Eyck learned, for the first time, what Dave Marcus had revealed on February 1: Charley Lucky Luciano was the head of organized vice in the city. As the days passed, more evidence corroborated Lucky's involvement. A report stated: "Informant told Mrs. Carter, Tommy Bull had obtained permission to conduct the business of prostitution with Charley Luciano."[3] Also: "Detectives attached to Inspector Seery's staff believe Luciano to be actually in charge of the mob operating the combination. One detective gives the hangout of the group as a candy store at the corner of Essex and Rivington Streets.... Lieutenant of police tells Mr. Rosenblum that Betillo was triggerman for Charley Luciano for several years, to be pursued further.... Informant stated that Jimmy Fredericks told him that Charley Luciano was the man behind the combination and the mob controlling it.... Certain madams mention Luciano, also, as the boss."[4]

Officer Anthony E. Mancuso filed a report on Dave Betillo. In conversations with East Side informants Mancuso had discovered that Little Davie was of greater importance than assumed: "He is in reality the real leader of the syndicate."[5] During the years of Al Capone's supremacy in Chicago, Betillo had been summoned to Al's side; to other mobsters, this was a high honor. When Capone went to prison for tax evasion, Betillo had returned to New York with an established reputation. Continued Mancuso: "As a friendly gesture to Capone's former status, Betillo was taken under the wing of Luciano, and since this organization had a hand in most every racket in the city, Betillo, because of this direct connection with Luciano, was the most important man in the vice racket." The reaction on the East Side to Betillo's arrest made it clear that Little Davie was a top lieutenant. Mobsters were surprised that "one of his importance should have been apprehended so easily."

Pink subpoenas were handed to witnesses: "You are hereby commanded to appear before the Grand Jury, Room 222, in the second story of the County Court House, Pearl and Centre Streets." Failure to appear brought a $250 fine and 30 days in jail. Witnesses were told to report any persons who attempted to discuss the subpoena or testimony.

Dewey was surprised when Helen Horvath telephoned and arranged a meeting. Without coercion, she offered to testify. Dewey briefly questioned her. She wanted to recover her self-respect, she said, and make a break with the past. Horvath had not been arrested during the raids because she was a fugitive from justice. She had earlier been arrested at the house of Hungarian Helen Frisch. Jesse Jacobs told her the arrest was a "straight case" and could not be fixed. Jacobs advised her to drop from sight, so she never appeared in court. She read newspaper accounts of the raids and was worried about being a fugitive. She spoke freely about her experiences with Gypsy Tom and Hungarian Helen. Dewey referred her to a team investigator. But the other prostitutes were tight-lipped. Mildred Balitzer was questioned in the prosecutor's office. She denied knowing any of the defendants or anything about prostitution.

Paul Lockwood questioned Jenny White. She had been arrested in Betty Winters' house on 79th Street. Lockwood noted she was only 24 but a seasoned prostitute.

"How long were you in there?"[6]

"Just a week."

"How many men did you have that week?"

"Just 21."

"Are you a two-way girl?"

"No, straight."

Despite Lockwood's persistence, Jenny was reluctant to talk. She was booked at the house by an unknown girl, a stranger she had met in a beauty salon. As for previous madams, she had forgotten their names, and she had no idea what a pimp did.

"Now you don't mean to tell me you don't know what a pimp is?"

"I hear girls have sweethearts; that's their business."

"Does your father know you are in this business?"

"No, sir."

"What's he think you are doing?"

"He thinks I am working."

"Had you just finished with a man?"

"No, we were just starting."

"On an average, how much did you make a week?"

"About fifty dollars."

"Wear kimonos in there?"

"What I have on me."

"Wear underwear?"

"Yes."

"While you were working?"

"I did. I wore what I have on now. Wear underwear, little panties."

"I don't want to see them. Did you wash your panties yourself?"

"Yes, sir."

On February 6, William Herlands interviewed Nick Montana at Auburn Prison. Montana was serving a 25-year sentence for compulsory prostitution. He claimed four policemen had framed him, including Hugo Paris, who extorted money from him and madam Billie Scheible. Montana protested that he was merely a sports bookie. He disclosed that Abe Karp and Max Rachlin paid detective Hugo Paris to fix prostitution cases, and then Hugo Paris instructed the arresting officers how to sabotage convictions. Montana said that most of the magistrates in the Women's Court could be bribed, especially Magistrate Burke. But Goldstein and Murphy "cannot be reached." Montana denied knowing most of the combination, except Balitzer and Marcus. He said in late 1934 Jimmy Fredericks had paid someone in the District Attorney's office to fix a case, after a madam complained about a shakedown. On February 8, Jean Irwin was arrested after it was discovered she was the mistress of Pete Balitzer. She had been missed in the raid. When officers searched her, they found a memorandum book that belonged to Jojo Weintraub. She had previously lived with Danny Brooks and Jimmy O' Brien, who were both serving time for compulsory prostitution. Sol Gelb questioned her, but she was uncooperative. From time to time, Barent Ten Eyck also spoke with her. During an interrogation session, Irwin admitted smoking opium with Lucky and Dave Betillo. But she refused to testify. Even when Pete Balitzer urged her to tell the truth, she always refused, finally admitting she feared for her life.

Harold Cole stayed busy. Cole investigated the restaurant extortion cases and interviewed prostitutes and madams. He surprised Shirley Mason with wiretap transcripts from Jack Ellenstein's telephone. At first, she denied being a prostitute or knowing anything about the business, but finally she gave a statement.

David Markowitz answered a subpoena. Questioned by Sol Gelb before the grand jury, the attorney brazenly lied. He said Rose Lerner had come to him and asked for a job. Investigators discovered the lawyer had never filed an income tax return. Markowitz claimed he was exempt, since he had never earned five thousand dollars in a single year. He admitted knowing Tommy Pennochio "from an accident case."[7] And he knew Dave Betillo because he represented Betillo's sister-in-law in a divorce case. And the Spiller brothers? He had defended Willie Spiller on a charge of bookmaking. Benny Spiller was his client in the prostitution investigation, he acknowledged. He denied distributing loan shark money on behalf of Tommy Pennochio.

On the evening of February 10, Milton Schilback questioned Thelma Jordan as a stenographer took notes. Thelma was afraid and did her best to avoid the truth. When shown photographs of Dave Betillo and others, she denied knowing them.

"Do you know anything about any combination?" asked Schilback.

"No," she lied. Thelma was taken to a large room where witnesses roamed or napped. The women hoped to be released soon. They all had an alibi, like

Margaret Martino, who said she was "an unemployed tango dancer" who was visiting a friend when arrested. Thelma Jordan was escorted to the House of Detention, where she was placed in a cell with Molly Leonard. As time passed, the women began to talk.

Edna Russell admitted that she had given the police a fictitious name and address when arrested. She confessed that her real name was Emma Grilli. She lived with her family in New Jersey. Although she was an entertainer, she admitted she had been convicted of fornication in Newark. She had been sentenced to a year's probation; the period had just expired. Emma became hysterical during the interrogation and screamed that she was innocent.

Frank Hogan recalled Thelma Jordan. He accused her of lying during the first interview. Cooperative prostitutes revealed that Thelma did indeed know members of the combination. At her next interview with Harold Cole, Thelma decided to tell the truth.

A week after being arrested Nancy Presser was taken from the House of Detention and driven to the Woolworth Building. Nancy passed through the granite and marble polished lobby. When the elevator stopped at the 14th floor, Harold Cole led her to Dewey's office. Detective Stephen Di Rosa was also present. Nancy was questioned about being booked and about knowing Dave Betillo and Tommy Pennochio. Frightened, she denied living with Ralph Liguori. Harold Cole knew she and Ralph had indeed lived together.

The following day, as Ralph left a hotel, Detective Di Rosa stopped him. "You are wanted up in Mr. Dewey's office," he told Ralph. Harold Cole questioned Ralph for two hours. Ralph acknowledged he knew Nancy, and that they had lived together, but claimed he was unaware of her profession. Ralph asked for permission to speak to her. He would encourage her to tell the truth. When Cole told Nancy that Ralph was in the office, she expressed a wish to see him. She promised to talk if they would release Ralph. The couple spoke in the presence of Harold Cole and police officers.

Nancy, Ralph, a police matron, and a male officer all went to the Emerson Hotel. Nancy was allowed to remove clothing. While in the bedroom, with the door slightly closed, she slipped Ralph her client address book.

On February 12, Harold Cole heard that Nancy Presser was afraid to talk, since Ralph Liguori had threatened her life on numerous occasions. The next day, Cole questioned Nancy in his office. She now admitted Ralph lived with her at the Hotel Emerson but expressed ignorance about Ralph's livelihood.

By the middle of March, Nancy Presser had become thoroughly terrified. She had become upset after seeing men from "the downtown Italian mob" standing on the elevated train platform outside the prison.[8] They shook their fists at the women who were visible in the windows. She was sure the men had recognized her. She told Frank Hogan she knew a great deal more about the leaders of the prostitution racket than she had disclosed. Nancy insisted on seeing Dewey before revealing anything significant. She complained to Cole that her stay in the House of Detention was terrible, since the madams accused her of being Ralph's accomplice in robbing their houses. Nancy was taken to Dewey's office. With Cole and Hogan listening, Nancy confessed that she knew "all the big shots" in the prostitution racket. She was in fear of her life and wanted protection. Dewey assured her that protection would be granted. Nancy said she was nervous, unable to eat and needed medical attention. She begged to leave the House of Detention. Soon after, Nancy was transferred to a hotel with other witnesses, who were constantly guarded by officers and a police matron. Nancy told Cole that Thelma Jordan had indicated to her that she knew a great deal about the persons connected with the prostitution ring, though Jordan had yet to disclose anything. Nancy was acquainted with Thelma before the raids. She was sure Thelma did know the defendants. Thelma Jordan was brought to Cole's office. Thelma agreed to disclose information if she were allowed to leave the House of Detention. Dewey arranged for Cole to transfer Thelma and Nancy to an apartment in Jackson Heights, together with Peggy Wild, Jenny Fisher, and Mildred Balitzer.

Nancy made a full confession. Harold Cole listened attentively as Nancy discussed her relationships with racketeers in New York. Nancy said that after the death of Joe Masseria, Lucky had become the real boss of the rackets "not only in New York City but throughout the country and he had succeeded Al Capone as head of the Union Siciliano."[9] Because she knew Lucky previously, he had occasionally discussed the prostitution racket with her, but she was afraid to testify against him. If she or any other witness ever did so "they would be murdered." When Ralph had seen her, he warned that if she discussed him or any of the other members of the combination, "that it will be just too bad for her."

She showed Cole a stolen wristwatch Ralph had given her after robbing a house of prostitution. Nancy was nervous and complained of severe abdomen pain. Though drug free, she still had a craving for morphine, she admitted. Nancy was allowed a shot of whiskey and given medical treatment. As Nancy disclosed more and more information, Harold Cole believed Nancy was a key witness. Cole corroborated facts with different madams. Dora Hearn identified the watch Nancy wore; it was hers, and Ralph had stolen it from her. Early on the morning of April 4 police arrived at the Hotel President. A manager gave investigators a passkey. They entered a room where Ralph Liguori slept. Ralph and his brother, Herman, were both arrested.

While Thelma Jordan sat in Cole's office with Nancy Presser, a detective nearby, Ralph Liguori was escorted inside the office. Ralph warned Nancy not to talk. If she did, Ralph would make certain her photograph would appear in Auburn newspapers for her parents to see. "You remember reading about that Titterton case?" he asked.[10] Confused, Nancy didn't understand. Ralph made it clearer. "She was found murdered in the bathtub. Don't forget that."

Ralph's sister appeared. Anna Liguori conferred with Harold Cole. Nancy was a prostitute, said Cole, and Ralph was involved in prostitution. "If Ralph doesn't give us what we want we are going to send him away for 25 years."[11] Cole said there was a piece missing in the puzzle, and Ralph had the answer. Anna spoke to Ralph alone. Cole wanted him to identify Lucky as the head of the combination and verify Lucky had paid him. Ralph told his sister it was all a lie. Anna confronted Nancy Presser. "You told me that you were working as a cigarette girl."

"You really weren't so dumb were you?" asked Nancy.

When Ruth Marcus was brought to the prosecutor's office, she was afraid. When shown a photograph of Ralph Liguori, in the presence of Nancy, Thelma Jordan, and a police matron, she refused to identify Ralph as one of the assailants who had threatened her husband. She told Nancy that she was very embarrassed over the situation. She cautioned Nancy and Thelma against giving information against "that certain party."[12] That party was obviously Lucky. Nancy was not only frightened, but also sick. She had been diagnosed with a venereal abscess in her left fallopian tube.

Eighty-one women, identified as prostitutes, were administered mandatory health tests. Twenty-three women tested positive for gonorrhea; 15 tested positive for syphilis; 11 had syphilis and gonorrhea, and 32 were free of any diseases. One prostitute refused any tests. Celia Newman was diagnosed with breast cancer.

Mildred Balitzer was questioned by Charles Breitel. She now admitted knowing Little Davie, Tommy Bull, and Jimmy Fredericks, but admitted "fear of these people."[13] Even if witnesses fled, the mob would follow, she said. Finally, Mildred disclosed information: "It's a general rumor. This I can't truthfully tell you, but it was general information that Charles Lucky was the head of it, that he was Little Davie's boss." Breitel continued: "And by Charley Lucky do you refer to the Unione Sicilione?" Mildred admitted Lucky was in charge.

On April 24, Mildred Curtis came to the office, answering a subpoena. A gun had been found in a safe deposit box in Mildred's hotel room. Mildred faced a charge of illegal possession of a weapon, though she claimed the pistol belonged to the Guidrys. Mildred told Harold Cole she knew Lucky, Davie, Tommy, Jimmy, and Abie. As she spoke about Tommy Bull, she grew frightened. She did not want to testify against Tommy in court. Sol Gelb warned that if she didn't tell the truth, she faced prison for illegal possession of a handgun. As a heroin addict, Mildred took seven or eight injections each day; after five hours of questioning, she experienced withdrawal symptoms. She was sick and admitted being an addict; she pleaded for an injection.

"You wouldn't like to take cold turkey would you?" asked Cole.

Mildred was afraid to testify; she would rather accept the gun charge, she argued, but soon she changed her mind. A police matron telephoned a doctor. After Mildred was given an injection she was taken to an apartment on 101 First Street where three witnesses lived. Unable to sleep, she sat by her window and wept. Mildred Balitzer comforted her. Mildred understood what it was like to be an addict without drugs. The next morning, the young woman was taken to a police station but again became ill. An ambulance arrived and transported Mildred to Dewey's office. She begged not to undergo an immediate withdrawal cure. Mildred faced the standard treatment: over five days the morphine was gradually weakened; on the sixth day there would be excruciating withdrawal pain. A doctor administered a shot to calm her, and Curtis was taken to court, where she fainted. She was terrified of the painful ordeal of narcotics withdrawal. Dewey agreed to lengthen the treatment time in her case. Mildred was sent to the House of Detention. Over several days, the shots were reduced to three daily injections, and if any were delayed, Mildred screamed for an ambulance.

In April, Thelma Jordan left the House of Detention for an apartment at 2635 Jackson Heights. She roomed with Nancy Presser, Mildred Balitzer, Margaret Venti, and Jennie Fisher. Later, she and Nancy were allowed to share an apartment at 1093 Jerome in the Bronx, supervised by a police matron and two officers. After two weeks they were transferred to 33 Washington Place. After Thelma and Nancy became friendly, Nancy divulged details about her sad life. The women in the vice underworld had tragic lives, as did their families.

Paul Lockwood interviewed the son of Hungarian Helen. Born in Hungary, the young man had been raised in Germany but had come to America in 1933 at age 17. For a time his great-aunt looked after him. She had revealed his mother was a madam. Helen Frisch was 37, attractive and wealthy. She operated several whorehouses and invested the profits in various restaurants. When Paul visited his mother he noticed that she received mail under several names. The young man wanted his mother to quit the sex business. Helen told her son that Gypsy Tom Petrovitch loved her and wanted to marry her. Tom was her partner, so she couldn't quit. Paul visited his mother at various apartments, which she admitted were for prostitution. She discouraged him from associating with the girls. His mother kept a fashionable apartment on Park Avenue, where she was known as Helen Bennett. He visited the Park

Avenue address only twice, the second time to celebrate her birthday. But Gypsy Tom hated him. He warned Helen that if Paul "mingled in" he would cut him to pieces. The boy witnessed bitter arguments over money. Once, Paul told Tom to leave his mother alone. Gypsy Tom threatened to beat Paul for interfering. Helen lectured her son. She defended Gypsy Tom. He had done had a great deal for her. Paul begged his mother to leave but she refused. Paul heard that Tom beat his mother but never witnessed physical mistreatment. Helen and Tom had been arrested in Miami. At first, Petrovich claimed to be an orchestra leader but surprised investigators by suddenly making a confession that he was a pimp. Hungarian Helen Frisch remained silent and refused to cooperate with Dewey's staff. But many women were talking.

Sol Gelb spent hours encouraging Mildred Balitzer to reveal everything, but she was afraid that her daughter in West Virginia would be murdered. Mildred also feared Gus Franco. Gus had shot a man she knew. Only after Dewey gave her unconditional assurances of police protection for herself and her daughter was Mildred satisfied. Davie and Tommy sold her narcotics, she revealed, and Lucky had ordered the murder of her friend Murray Marks, another drug supplier. She expressed deep hatred toward Lucky over the murder and was angry the boss prevented Pete from leaving the business. Later, Gelb told Dewey that, according to a witness, Mildred had once briefly been a prostitute, but when Gelb questioned her, she denied the story. Dewey met with Mildred. During the two-hour interrogation, Mildred was confronted with the report. She finally admitted that for a short time she had been a prostitute, just to learn the business; afterward, she became a madam. Mildred adamantly refused to admit being a whore in court, not wishing to disgrace her respectable family. But Dewey explained she could not withhold any facts before the jury. Mildred finally agreed to tell the entire truth.

One night Margaret Bell had a long and bitter argument with Jean Irwin in the House of Detention. Though once friendly, both women complained to Ten Eyck. When he tried to question Irwin she became hysterical and constantly repeated that she was afraid. Though Margaret Bell had intricate tales of drugs and meetings with the combination, her testimony was deemed to be unreliable. Paul Lockwood determined Bell was mentally unbalanced.

Antoinetta Napolitano came to the Woolworth Building. She was Tommy Pennochio's cousin. Raymond Ariola spoke with her. She and her husband owned a restaurant at 60 Mulberry Street and had been in business 28 years. Tommy had become a regular client at the restaurant only three years earlier, she insisted. Tommy and his friends came three or four times a week. Tommy, Dave Betillo, Jimmy Fredericks, and Abie Wahrman dined together in a private upstairs room. She identified the men in photographs; they met Tuesday, Wednesday, and Friday evenings. Each Tuesday night Tommy usually carried loose papers under his arm. Tommy asked her not to disturb him. She said that Lucky never ate in her restaurant but did eat at the Red Devil Inn, at 173 Mott Street and in the Red Devil Restaurant at 111 West 48th Street.

After Dewey's staff interviewed madams, prostitutes, bookers, pimps, and assistants, they were all held as material witnesses. Dewey carefully assembled evidence for a prosecution against the boss and his henchmen. Dewey's team had credible witnesses ready to testify before a grand jury to obtain an indictment. But Lucky was unconcerned. Detective John J. Brennan of the New York police department kept Lucky under personal surveillance. He had followed Lucky from Miami to Hot Springs, where Lucky took a room at the lavish Arlington Hotel. Lucky played the sportsman and enjoyed the crisp mountain air and gambling in the resort town. Each day he placed bets on the thoroughbred races at Oaklawn Park; at night he gambled in the supper clubs.

Dewey made his move. A warrant was sent to Hot Springs, issued by a city magistrate for the arrest of Charles Luciano. He was accused of extortion accompanied by threats of violence and flight from New York to avoid prosecution pursuant to Section 2408 and title 18 of the U.S. Code. While Lucky made racing bets at the Southern Club he was handed a message; a detective at the hotel desk wanted to see him. Lucky walked across Central Avenue to the Arlington, but the detective was gone.

The next morning, April 1, Lucky played golf at the Hot Springs Country Club. Around noon, a hotel bellboy found him. There was a detective and sheriff waiting in his hotel room. "That's all right," said Lucky, and immediately left. The desk clerk at the Arlington told him the lawmen were gone but had intended to arrest him. Around noon, Lucky descended the steps of the hotel, dapper in sports clothes, on his way to the race track, but Lucky Luciano had placed his last track bet. He walked alone along Central Avenue. As he approached the tree shaded promenade of Bath House Row he was spotted by Sheriff Marion Anderson and Detective John J. Brennan. They quietly took him into custody. After three hours in the county jail, Lucky was desperate to get out. Defense attorney Richard Ryan filed a petition for a writ of habeas corpus. Chancellor Sam Garratt agreed to release the suspect and bail was set at five thousand dollars. Lucky walked away.

When Dewey heard of the low bail, he was furious. He described Lucky Luciano as the most dangerous racketeer in New York. In Hot Springs Chancellor Garratt responded that he was unaware of the seriousness of the charges and revoked the bail. Lucky was rearrested in his hotel room. Lucky was locked in the county jail. From his cell he requested a local reporter, a friend of several years, to write a statement for him. Chief Deputy Roy Ermey read

The Southern Club; Lucky placed his last bet here (courtesy Garland County Historical Association, Hot Springs, Arkansas).

it to the gathered newsmen: "I may not be the most moral and upright man that ever lived, but I have not stooped so low as to become involved in aiding prostitution."[14] Lucky vowed to fight extradition to New York. Sheriff Jim Anderson permitted the prisoner to use his office for phone calls and legal conferences. Lucky telephoned New York. He instructed his family to hire attorney Moses Polakoff.

Dewey wrote to Edward McLean, his legal representative in Little Rock. He described Arkansas as "a rotten state." He related how a district attorney from Westchester County in New York had just returned from the resort city and achieved the rare extradition of a robbery fugitive. "The whole crowd are a complete ring, the chief of police, the chief of detectives, the mayor and the city attorney," warned Dewey. The detectives slept all day, wrote Dewey, and donned tuxedoes in the evenings to guard the casino gamblers. On the weekends the city firemen did the same. Only one man in the police department was trustworthy, Cecil Brock. And Attorney General Carl Bailey was dependable, described by Dewey as a "two-fisted, honest man, and has everybody afraid of him.... The Governor appears to be weak and definitely helpful to the prize collection of criminals they have in Hot Springs."

Dewey prompted McLean to act fast, since he had 110 witnesses in prison whose presence cost the State of New York five hundred dollars a day. "The only way you will succeed is by fighting like the devil," he emphasized. On April 2, Dewey obtained an indictment of Charles Luciano on four counts of compulsory prostitution. The next day, Detective Stephen Di Rosa departed New York with a warrant issued by the governor for extradition.

Carl Bailey and Edward McLean arrived in Hot Springs with a state warrant issued in Little Rock; it called for Lucky's arrest under a recent extradition law. At the hearing to remove the prisoner, Chancellor Garratt listened to both sides as Lucky sat expressionless. A.T. Sonny Davies, city attorney, joined James R. Campbell and Richard Ryan in permitting release. Campbell described Lucky as "a citizen of Garland county, an owner of property here and entitled to a hearing in his home country." Davies had signed a municipal warrant and charged Lucky with being a fugitive. The city warrant was a desperate attempt to keep Lucky in Hot Springs, where his subsequent release would undoubtedly occur. Carl Bailey was unimpressed: "I am amply trying to demonstrate to the outside world that Arkansas is not an asylum for criminals."[15] Davies insisted his warrant had prior status. Chancellor Garratt denied custody to local authorities. Little Rock deputies arrested Lucky on Bailey's warrant. As he was escorted to the courtroom door, A.T. Davies motioned to Deputy Ermey, who suddenly took charge of the prisoner. Carl Bailey was astounded by the maneuver.

Site of Lucky's last walk as a free man. The path before the Arlington Hotel where Lucky was arrested.

Lucky was taken to a jail cell in the courthouse basement. A local photographer attempted to get a photograph of Lucky but suddenly confronted two of Lucky's friends: "Charley would not like to have his picture taken," cautioned one. The photographer left without taking a picture. Carl Bailey announced he would obtain a contempt citation against A.T. Davies and Roy Ermey. Little Rock deputies were posted at the courthouse. They were instructed to arrest Lucky if he was released.

The following morning at 3:00 A.M., a dozen state rangers and two deputy sheriffs arrived at the courthouse. They had contempt citations and a circuit court order from the Attorney General for prisoner Charles Luciano. Bewildered, Chief Deputy Ermey telephoned defense attorneys, but there was nothing to be done. At 5:00 A.M. the state rangers left with Lucky. The prisoner was taken to the Pulaski County Prison in Little Rock. Lucky declined to speak with reporters until he could shave. When he emerged in the anteroom he observed bright lights and newsreel cameramen. He became enraged and demanded that deputies return him to his cell, which was done. Ed Dillon, a state senator, was added to Lucky's defense team.

Governor Marion Futrell presided at a hearing. State rangers armed with machineguns stood guard at the door of the capital reception room. The governor decided the extradition warrant to New York was valid. Lucky's team of lawyers demanded a habeas corpus hearing. Bailey scoffed that the delay was only a ploy so the attorneys could get "more of his filthy money."[16] While the drama played in Little Rock, the case against Lucky was becoming stronger in New York. Several employees of the Waldorf vividly recalled Lucky and his henchmen. Pauline Fletcher, the Waldorf bathroom maid, recognized Willie Spiller, because he was better looking than the group of "greasy men."[17] She also identified Jimmy Fredericks as a visitor. Dewey obtained Waldorf telephone records. Among those Lucky had telephoned was entertainer and nightclub owner Harry Richman; he also telephoned Myron Selznick, a prominent theatrical agent and gambler. The gangsters on the list were Ciro Terranova, Louis Buchalter, Vito Genovese, Dave Betillo, and Leo Byk. Lucky contacted Joseph Discioscia's pastry shop on Kenmare Street, Joe Salise's smoke shop on Cleveland, and Ruth Stevens' brothel on 77th Street. There were calls to several restaurants, including the Villanova, the Versailles, and Celanos. The latter was telephoned 20 times.

The last-ditch legal maneuvers to thwart extradition failed. On April 17, at 12:01 A.M., Lucky was unexpectedly handcuffed and removed from his jail cell. He shouted he was being kidnapped. Surrounded by three detectives, he was taken to an express train en route to New York City.

The following day, he was arraigned before Justice McCook in room 139 of the County Court House, even though it was Saturday. Defense attorney Moses Polakoff sat with his client. Dewey rose and asked that bail be set at $350,000. "He is reputed to be, and I believe it to be true, one of the individuals who derives the largest source of revenue from the policy racket in New

York City. His henchmen are, beyond question, actually operating a number of industrial rackets in New York City," said the special prosecutor. Dewey listed Lucky's criminal activities as drug peddling, bookmaking, and lottery tickets. Moses Polakoff spoke against the high bail, but Justice McCook agreed with Dewey. The hearing was the beginning of the legal duel between Dewey and Moses Polakoff. Dewey was a novice compared to the veteran defense lawyer, a member of the New York bar since 1920. Polakoff had served as a Federal Assistant Attorney for the Southern District of New York; from 1921 until 1925 he was Chief of the Criminal Division. For several years, he investigated election fraud for the State Attorney General's Office. George Morton Wolf, another prominent attorney, assisted Polakoff.

On April 20, Dewey sent a letter of thanks to Carl Bailey: "Without your help I am sure this prisoner would not have been removed, and the people of the State of New York owe you a great debt of gratitude." According to Dewey's sources, a bribe of 50,000 dollars had been offered to Bailey for Lucky's release.

After the sensational arrest, Gay Orlova was summoned to the Woolworth Building. Late one evening she arrived clad in a four-thousand-dollar fox fur coat. She was featured in newspaper stories and defended her boyfriend: "Lucky's a perfect gentleman. I don't know why they say such mean things about him."[18] Although a gentleman, said Gay, "He didn't give me anything too wonderful." Investigators furnished a confidential report that Orlova "slept with Lucky about four nights a week."[19] Reporters revealed that the exotic dancer lived in an expensive apartment at 17 West 64th Street.

A month before the trial, attorney Raymond Ariola was dismissed from Dewey's staff, after his indictment for legal malfeasance while in private practice. The attorney was charged with sharing the fees with his brother, a physician, in an automobile accident case.

Flo Brown received a pitiful letter written in jail. Jimmy Fredericks didn't understand the indictment and wanted to talk to his lawyer. Flo responded on April 14: "Dear Cousin: Well, it is the day after Easter, and everything is still the same. There is nothing new. I feel very melancholy tonight, very blue. I am disgusted with the whole world. There is no justice at all. I wish Uncle D. had died of cancer, the louse. He should have died from leprosy when he was a baby. I think it is terrible to make a person do time before they are even convicted. It is not fair. They let lousy murderers go free, and a person that never did anyone any harm in their life has to lie in jail. Look at that Vera Stretz case, a confessed murderess. She even admitted doing it on the witness stand, yet she is free, but a person that hasn't even been convicted yet has to stay in jail until some louse gets good and ready to bring them to trial. Look at the money that was spent on Hauptman, the Governor intervening for a filthy foreigner of a baby killer, the worst kind of killer there is. That is why I say there is no justice in this world. Gee, I am so blue and lonesome for you, I don't know what to do. Believe me, if I had about five minutes with a few certain people alone, I would know just what to say and do. There would be just five rats left to bother people. Well, it is no use wishing. I am going to see Siegel Wednesday, I guess. I want to know what he intends to do, what defense has he worked out. I want him to get busy and try to get his head to working, not to think he is going to get money for nothing. He should never mind Bull, and the rest is rather plain, so much, but get something done. I can't stand this suspense and inactivity much longer.... All my love, your faithful cousin."[20]

Flo went to Sam Siegel's office, hoping to find out what was being done for Jimmy. Though Siegel said he was too busy to talk to her, he did allow her to read the indictment. Flo sat in the law library and made notes. Later, she visited Jimmy's sister and left a gift pipe for him.

On April 23, Joe Bendix entered Sing Sing. Bendix had been arrested at the Madison Hotel on 58th Street. Detectives caught him stealing jewelry in the assistant manager's office. Bendix was so poor his attorney was from the Volunteer Defender's League. While awaiting trial, Bendix learned the district attorney's office was investigating bond thefts. Bendix supplied information. At his trial Bendix pleaded guilty to burglary and faced a mandatory sentence of 15 years to life, but there was an understanding that the district attorney would recommend release, after he served two and a half years, since he had cooperated. As a career criminal, Bendix had already spent 14 years behind bars. After the prostitute raids, Bendix sent word to Dewey's staff that he had information and wanted out of jail immediately. So did Danny Caputo. Jimmy and the combination had left him to rot in prison, despite the promise of legal appeals. He confirmed to Dewey's investigators that Bendix knew about Lucky. Joe Bendix began talking to Dewey's investigators.

Cockeyed Lou Weiner also made a deal. Lou stood before the grand jury but lost his nerve. In Sing Sing he had given indications that he would talk, but when Dewey asked how long he had been a booker of prostitutes, Cockeyed Lou refused to answer. Dewey tried again, but Weiner was silent. Dewey lost his patience, "I am going to advise the parole commission that you have refused to answer questions in the grand jury and that in my opinion you have shown no signs of rehabilitation or reform and are not a fit subject for parole at any time during your term. Do you understand that?"[21]

"You are going to recommend the parole board to keep me there the full ten years because I can't turn state's evidence?"

"You are excused."

Nancy Presser went before the grand jury. She told what she knew. Nancy identified mob hangouts; the most prominent was the Sixth Ward Garage on the east side of Mulberry Street. Nancy had been there on several occasions. She disclosed a secret entrance from the upper level of the garage into another building, where a room was used to intimidate and punish enemies.

Police began surveillance of mob hangouts. Marie Chavici's cafe at 176 Mulberry was a target, as was the Cafe Toledo on the southwest corner of Kenmare and Mulberry. Regular patrons in these cafes were Vito Genovese, Mike Miranda and Tony Bender.

On April 29, Nancy Presser again went before the grand jury. She answered questions about Lucky, Ralph Liguori and the takeover. Nancy discussed how Ralph had threatened to kill her, that she had accompanied him on drug pick-ups and that he had sold narcotics to Mildred Balitzer. She discussed meeting Lucky at the Waldorf. Dewey asked if she had consumed brandy in the prosecutor's office. Yes, she answered, due to nervousness.

"Have any threats been made by the district attorney, myself, or any of my assistants of prosecution of you?"

"No."

"Have any promises of money or anything else been made to you if you testify?"

"No."

"You merely testify to the truth because you are under oath?"

"That is right."

On April 22, Charles Berner, under the name of Sam Warner, stood before the jurors. He told of the night Lucky had made the decision against the pimps, telling the group, "You fellows are through."[22]

Dewey realized that witnesses could be bribed or intimidated to change their testimony. False witnesses could even be planted, secretly sent by the defense to provide grand jury information, then unexpectedly change their testimony and exonerate Luciano in court. Dewey had to prepare against a host of tricks. He steeled himself for the trial. He would have to outfox Moses Polakoff and even his own witnesses. The trial would rest squarely on his shoulders.

CHAPTER TEN

The Trial

You had three thousand customers?

Dewey was pleased when Governor Lehman signed the Joinder Law; defendants charged with conspiracy in the operation of a criminal enterprise could now be tried as a unit, instead of individually. The law was unconstitutional, protested criminal defense attorneys who vowed to challenge it. The Luciano trial would be a test case, but Dewey was certain the law was legal and fair, since federal law already permitted the merger of indictments.

The Grand Jury of the County of New York brought an indictment against members of the combination. The defendants were charged with the crime of compulsory prostitution, a violation of Section 2460 of the penal law. Indicted were Charles Lucania, David Betillo, Thomas Pennochio, James Frederico, Ralph Liguori, Abraham Wahrman, Benny Spiller, Jesse Jacobs, Meyer Berkman, Pete Balitzer, Dave Marcus, Jack Ellenstein, and Al Wiener. The bail for the defendants reached $535,000.

Vito Genovese escaped prosecution due to contradictory evidence. There had been a shadowy bonding collector named Vito who vanished; the uncertainty over identities created doubt, which provided Genovese with a strong defense, so prosecutors declined to indict him. Jerry Bruno also escaped the indictment. Ironically, after being pushed aside by Little Davie, Bruno had kept his distance from the vice chain.

On May 4, jury selection began. The legal process was barely underway when Pete Balitzer, Dave Marcus, and Al Weiner pleaded guilty. The bookers faced 20 to 25 years in prison for each girl they sent to a whorehouse. They were marched out of the courtroom to await sentencing. The bookers immediately turned state's evidence and agreed to testify against the accused defendants. During jury selection, Dewey explained his policy of granting immunity to prostitutes and pimps. He told prospective juror Witherbee Black, a Park Avenue businessman, that "in order to get the big fellow, I have given immunity to the little fellow."[1] George Morton Levy asked a prospective juror, an investment banker, whether he would view Luciano unfavorably if he did not take the stand. Indeed he would, responded the banker. Levy excused him. The selected jurors were diverse in occupations: consulting engineer, dental gold manufacturer, accountant, art importer, and several salesmen. Their names and addresses were published in city newspapers. Among the jurors was Robert Center, a book editor. Center had known Nancy Titterton. The attractive young woman had approached the editor about a book-of-the-month-club idea. She wanted to feature crime publications. Not long afterward, in a brutal murder, Titterton had been raped and drowned in a bathtub.

According to press reports, George Morton Levy's legal fee was $50,000, with another $50,000 to be paid for an acquittal. The defense team was paid a weekly sum of $5,000 for expenses. The trial was scheduled to start on May 11. Dewey told reporters he had 121 witnesses ready to testify, though it was unlikely all would be called. Dewey's assistants prepared prospective witnesses for the trial. But there were setbacks. When Antoinette Napolitano came to the prosecutor's office she suffered a memory lapse. Sol Gelb showed her a photograph of Tommy Pennochio. She acknowledged Tommy was her cousin but, when shown other photographs, her memory faded: "I don't know the boys, there were lots of them that come. I can't tell you if they were them and them."[2] Gelb suspected she was afraid to testify.

Dewey's investigators spoke with staff employees of the Barbizon Plaza and the Waldorf Hotel. Lucky and his associates were distinctly remembered in both places, since they were so different than the usual guests. At the Barbizon Plaza the switchboard operator said Lucky had received numerous calls. The records showed he telephoned underworld criminals Ciro Terranova and Phil Kastel.

Unexpectedly, a key witness was dropped in the prosecution's lap. On May 8, Flo Brown was arrested for solicitation. She had been living with an elderly invalid who wrote stories and music. Flo was paid 25 dollars per week for nursing and typing duties. After three months, Flo decided she needed more space and freedom. She moved to 140 West 75th Street and rented a basement room with a small yard for her dog. Flo was soon arrested in front of her new residence. An undercover officer said she had offered to commit an act of prostitution for five dollars. She was taken to the Women's House of Detention and locked in the ward for drug addicts. Dr. Anna Nimmelman started Flo on the five-day reduction cure. Isolated and ill, Flo grew angry over Jimmy Frederick's indifference to her situation. She was upset that

Jimmy simply ignored her. Grace Hall gave Flo the names of Dewey's staff attorneys in case she decided to assist the prosecution. On May 12, Flo was convicted of solicitation. Still pending were charges of being a fugitive from justice and narcotics possession. She was scheduled to be sentenced. Flo asked to see Sol Gelb.

Barent Ten Eyck was daily in the House of Detention, questioning witnesses and preparing trial briefs; he was surprised to learn that Florence Brown was a prisoner. For weeks, the witnesses had told him that a madam named Cokey Flo knew a great deal about the prostitution rings. One evening Frank Hogan handed Ten Eyck an envelope. Inside was a note. "Dear Sir: I would like to see you on a matter of great importance in the Dewey vice case. I am, and was, for three years, James Frederico's sweetheart. I can help you a great deal. Some of the witnesses saw me today. I know they will tell you anyway. I might just as well tell you myself. Please excuse writing. Respectfully, Flo. P.S. Here under name of Fay Marston, fourth floor." Ten Eyck went to see her. When he arrived, Sol Gelb's interrogation was underway. Ten Eyck asked her a few questions, which she avoided answering. She complained she felt sick. Flo was unable to sleep in her cell on the addict's corridor of the fourth floor. Noise from the Sixth Avenue L trains kept her awake. She begged to be moved to a quieter section. Ten Eyck offered to help, but she was not a material witness, so the police matrons would have to approve the transfer.

Gelb told his colleague that Flo was evasive. She admitted knowing Lucky and the other defendants but refused to give details. Ten Eyck spoke to the chief matron about transferring Flo to a quieter floor. The same evening, around midnight, Flo sent Ten Eyck another note. "Must see you. Have decided to tell you the truth. I lied to you, and Mr. Gelb. Have thought and thought, and now I feel stronger and better able to think." Though it was late, Ten Eyck was still at the House of Detention and arranged a meeting in the psychologist's office, where Ten Eyck usually interviewed witnesses. She complained that Sol Gelb had upset her with his aggressive cross-examination. Flo discussed her life with Jimmy. Ten Eyck took notes on a yellow legal pad. He asked which of the defendants she knew. As she recited their names, the attorney wrote them down. Lucky came first. Flo gave a detailed account that filled four sheets of paper. She was definite in her recollections. The documentation was astounding, believed Ten Eyck. The next day the effects of the last injection faded and Flo experienced severe pain in her stomach. One evening Flo heatedly argued with Joan Martin and called her a rat. Ten Eyck was sent a note about the dispute. "She had me locked in solitary. I said nothing, she sure has a good imagination. Am very sick, please see what made her angry with me."

The trial began amidst police concern that gang members would storm the courthouse to liberate Lucky. To thwart a riot or escape attempt, police had gas bombs and machineguns close at hand, concealed in corridor closets. Tension and excitement permeated the courthouse when the trial opened. Surrounded by five detectives, Lucky was the first defendant to enter the courtroom. Dressed in a blue suit, white shirt, and black tie, he sat on a long bench. The other defendants trailed behind him.

Dewey stood and addressed the court. "*Compulsory* has nothing to do with most of the charges in this case." Dewey explained that the defendants had violated the law by placing a woman in a house of prostitution; the same law made it illegal to receive money for such acts. "They were going to organize prostitution into a great industry in this city, and they did so." Dewey acknowledged the difficulty of eliminating prostitution and described the profession as "an age-old institution. I certainly should be insane if I thought I was going to interfere with or stop." Formerly, it had been an individual matter, he went on. The vice combination controlled a chain of houses and operated "a kind of Orpheum circuit in the business of booking women." Dewey outlined the vice chain. "The bookers had assistants and lobbyguys, the latter being hangers-on for meals; then there were pimps. We sought their testimony against the big men." Dewey said the major bookers in 1933 were Louis Weiner, Nick Montana, Dave Marcus, and Pete Balitzer. When Nick Montana was jailed, Jack Ellenstein took his place, as did Al Weiner when his father was convicted. "All we can give you is a fragmentary picture of any great criminal enterprise, practically nobody in the underworld is known by his right name," said Dewey. "Charley Lucky is the customary, in fact, uniform name by which the defendant is known." He mentioned the aliases: Tommy the Bull, Little Davie, Abie the Jew, Pete Harris, and Dave Miller. Several vice chain members, such as Teddy, Yoke, and Vito were never found, but they were all the servants of Salvatore Lucania, said Dewey.

In his opening statement, George Morton Levy said his client was merely a gambler who was innocent. In fact, he only knew a single defendant, Dave Betillo. Like Lucky, the other defendants had expensive criminal lawyers. Samuel J. Siegel, a veteran attorney with 34 years' experience, represented Jimmy Fredericks; counsel for Betillo and Pennochio was Caesar Barra; Abie Wahrman hired David P. Siegel; Lorenzo Carlino represented Ralph Liguori; Benny Spiller retained David Marcowitz, Tommy Bull's office partner on Mott Street.

Dewey's first witness was a state insurance examiner. He testified that Jesse Jacobs and Meyer Berkman were unlicensed bondsmen.

Renee Gallo was called next. She wore a blue hat and dress, a red scarf at her neck. For two hours she told of her life; she admitted the name Rose

Cohen was an alias. She had started as a streetwalker and was later booked into houses by Pete Balitzer. When arrested, Abe Karp had coached her to lie. Sam Siegel began the cross-examination and sought to humiliate her. Siegel demanded to know how many men she slept with each night.

"I didn't sleep with them," she shot back.

"Well, use your own term. How many men did you lie down with?

"That depended, sometimes 18 to 20."

"Did you ever stay with a colored man?" asked Siegel.

"No," she answered.

Muriel Ryan followed. A wide brim hat covered her dark hair, lowered over an eye. She spoke in a thin, child-like voice. Muriel announced her profession without shame. "I am a prostitute." She gave her age as 24 and said she had a boyfriend. She explained how she had first booked with Nick Montana but switched to Pete Balitzer, hoping to make more money.

Black haired and plump, Betty Winters was dressed in a blue silk suit with a frilly white collar. She admitted she had been convicted of prostitution and had served a hundred days in the workhouse. Betty sobbed as she testified. As the days passed, the prostitutes furnished the names of bookers, pimps, and madams. Dozens of reporters swarmed the courthouse corridors searching for stories. Dewey prohibited cameras in the courtroom, so those who testified eluded photographers by entering through courtroom doors. Despite the sordid publicity, the wives of the defendants dutifully came to court. When Madeline Betillo and Martha Wahrman arrived, flashbulbs popped; both women were slim, attractive, and stylishly dressed. Jimmy's wife, Lillian Fredericks, and Tommy's wife, Mary Pennochio, smiled for photographers.

Dorothy Arnold was described as stylishly attired in a brown suit and felt hat with a green feather. Barent Ten Eyck questioned her. Arnold explained how she punched cards to keep track of payments. She identified Jack Ellenstein, Nick Montana, and Pete Balitzer as bookers who sent girls to her penthouse. On cross-examination by Sam Siegel, Arnold admitted she had lied when arrested. When Siegel asked if a prostitute had been her husband's girlfriend, Dorothy leaned forward. "I'm my husband's wife and girlfriend," she replied indignantly. She emphatically denied ever being a whore.

Joan Martin tearfully recounted how Jimmy Fredericks had forced her to submit, knocking her unconscious with a blackjack and threatening to kill her dog. She sobbed as she told of the takeover. Sam Siegel tried to discredit her testimony: "Despite the fact, as you say, that Fredericks had hit you with a lead pipe and fists, and tried to kill your dog, didn't you run to him for bail for the girl?"

"He put up bail," she cried, "because he had to. He was the one who sold her that forged license. He was scared to death the girl would turn him in to the cops." She sobbed, and rose up in a half crouch, staring at Jimmy. "Stand up and deny it, you, like you'll deny everything else. I wasn't going to tell that on you, Jimmy. Honest, I wasn't, but you asked for it. Your counselor asked for it. So you got it. So there."

Al Weiner confessed that he was a booker who had been trained by his father. Al avoided visits to his father in Sing Sing. Al's visits would only draw attention to himself. During the testimony Al said he was afraid of being murdered. Samuel Siegel asked him if he had ever filed a tax return. "Never heard of it," he answered.

On the sixth day of the trial, Spike Green took the witness stand. Green explained he had become a collector after Charley Spinach fled to Philadelphia. He was a booker for only a few weeks, until Dave Marcus was given the houses. David Siegel faced him squarely. "You're a pimp, aren't you?" "No," he answered, then turned to Justice McCook. "Your Honor, if you'll give me the definition of a pimp, I'll try to answer the gentleman." Spectators laughed and McCook banged his gavel. "I'll tell you," said Siegel, "it's a man who lives off the earnings of prostitution." Siegel forcefully probed, Green acknowledged that at one time he had five women working for him, including Bedroom Fanny. "You didn't tell Mr. Dewey that, did you?"

"No," he mumbled.

Dave Marcus followed and told of his life as a booker, how he had been threatened and shot at but returned and begged for a job. Marcus asked Jimmy who was behind the combination: "Davie, Abie, and me," answered Jimmy, "and Charley." The spectators murmured. This was the first trial reference to Luciano. When questioned by David Siegel, Marcus denied he had ever operated a house in Pittsburgh or been arrested for prostitution. He reluctantly admitted an arrest but claimed it was for overcharging a man on a warrant while he was constable. He understood he faced long years in prison for every girl he booked in a whorehouse and that his wife was liable for the same sentence. Marcus admitted he decided to cooperate to avoid prison.

Molly Leonard took the stand dressed in a faded blue flowered dress. The questions centered on Jimmy Fredericks. While operating a house on Midwood Boulevard in Brooklyn, Jimmy appeared. She would have to join the combination, if not, she wouldn't get any girls. She spoke to Pete Balitzer, who also told her everyone had to bond. "Big people behind the combination," said Pete. After she probed again, Pete revealed a name: "Lucky." George Morton Levy ripped into her testimony. Molly acknowledged she had been arrested for opium possession but added she had taken a cure two years earlier. Like the other madams, she had lied after her arrest, falsely telling officers she was the hostess of a card party.

"Did you ever hear of Lucky before?" Levy asked.

"Not before Pete told me about him," she replied.

Levy tried to get her to admit she had been coaxed to mention Lucky's name in exchange for immunity, but she strongly denied it. Levy asked Lucky to stand. "Ever see that man in your life?" Molly stared at him. "No," she answered.

Jean Matthews told her story. Pete was her booker. On New Year's Day she earned $29 in a Manhattan house. Justice McCook asked how long had she had worked for the money. From 11 in the morning until 10 at night, she responded. Siegel asked what was the most she had ever earned in a week.

"About $235 as near as I can remember."

"Was that in a two dollar house?"

"Yes."

"Did you get more than two dollars from some of the customers?"

"Yes."

"What was the most?"

"Ten dollars."

"How many men do you think there were in that week?"

"Oh, about 50, I'd say."

Eleanor Jackson approached the stand. Reporters noted she was stylishly dressed in a brown suit with dark gloves and a matching hat. The reporters were struck by her refined demeanor and educated voice. She could have been a church secretary, but she was a prostitute, she confessed.

Shirley Taylor explained how she was briefly a madam, after her boyfriend gave her a house; unfortunately, it was raided, so she booked with Jack Eller as a common prostitute. Maurice Cantor asked, what was so important about the house?

"Why, customers, of course." Cantor asked how many customers.

"Must I answer that?" she laughed. She turned to Justice McCook who smiled.

Cantor withdrew the question, incensed that Taylor had made him appear ridiculous.

"Jack Eller is a booker?" asked the attorney. Taylor put her hand on her lip, leaned forward in the chair, and imitated Cantor's voice and expression. "Why certainly he booked me. He gave me addresses. He sent me to houses."

Sol Gelb queried Margaret Martino about her life. Martino was 23, an attractive woman with reddish blonde hair. After she completed high school she had worked for two years. "I was engaged to be married on February 22, 1932," she said wistfully. A few days before the wedding, her fiancé died. To survive, she began a life of prostitution. Martino found jobs through Dave Marcus.

As New Yorkers read the lurid accounts, it was clear that Dewey was building a solid case, linking the bookers, madams, and prostitutes. Next, he would directly tie in the mobsters. Dewey told reporters he was pleased with the information disclosed during the first week of the trial. Editorials praised the prosecutor and compared Dewey to Charles E. Hughes, a famous prosecutor who became governor, Republican nominee for president, and secretary of state under President Harding. But the trial was far from over.

Danny Caputo was released from Clinton Prison in Dannemora to testify. Danny was on the witness stand nearly six hours. He explained how he had assisted Jimmy as a chauffeur and booker. George Morton Levy emphasized that Danny Caputo had never seen Lucky at any of the business meetings of the combination.

"Didn't you have any moral scruples about going into the booking business?" he demanded.

Danny stared at him. "Any more what?" The stenographer read the question. Danny shrugged his shoulders. "I don't know what that means," he said.

Danny told how he had visited Little Davie's home. Betillo suddenly straightened up in his chair and pointed. "You're lying! You couldn't get up into my house!" he screamed in a high-pitched voice. Caesar Barra tried to calm him. McCook banged his gavel, and the courtroom quieted.

Sam Siegel stood before the witness. The defense lawyer accused Dewey of signaling to Caputo. Dewey jumped to his feet, visibly angry, and objected to the comment.

Siegel glared. "There are no wings on your shoulders even if you have been given a title," he snapped.

Dewey addressed Justice McCook: "Since when does a prosecutor have to stand for such vilification from counsel for a criminal defendant?" Siegel demanded a mistrial, which Justice McCook refused.

Danny acknowledged he had lied at his trial for compulsory prostitution in White Plains. At the trial he had denied being Danny Brooks, an alias he used. Danny told the court Dewey had promised nothing specific, only to bring his case to the governor's attention, but added: "He said he would put me in a different jail to keep me from getting killed by these men."

"You weren't afraid of being murdered, were you?" asked attorney Sam Siegel.

"Yes, I was," answered Caputo.

Helen Hayes, Gussie Silver, and Helen Walsh gave more damning evidence about the vice combination's activities.

Helen Horvath was elegantly dressed in a white flowered gown. She wore a purple hat trimmed with white flowers. In a low and bitter voice she described how Tom Petrovich had offered affection and promises of marriage, only to betray her. Reporters found her articulate, with a hint of haughtiness in her voice: "I was held in the house by force, so that I couldn't get out." Horvath earned $314 for her first week in the sex business, but Gypsy Tom took the money. She had gone to Dewey's office voluntarily: "I went to get back some of the self-respect I lost during my life as a prostitute." Reporters were impressed by Horvath's testimony, sympathetic over her tragic life, since she was only 19. James Murray, attorney for Meyer Berkman, questioned her. Horvath acknowledged she was being paid one dollar and fifty cents per day as a witness.

"You're living pretty well now aren't you?"

"If you call 40 cents for lunch and 75 cents for dinner living pretty well, then I am." David Siegel stepped forward. "Why did you move so frequently?"

"Landlords have a way of being insistent that you pay the rent," she said.

Maurice Cantor asked where she was living.

"I am much safer if I do not tell you."

Cantor changed the subject. "Were you arrested in this case?"

"No," she answered. "I came to Mr. Dewey's office as a volunteer witness." She admitted that she had skipped bail and was still a fugitive from justice, but Dewey had promised her nothing.

"Didn't your conscience bother you when you were working as a prostitute?"

"Yes, it did, but it seemed necessary."

Cantor asked the identity of her new sweetheart. She refused to give his name and insisted he was a respectable man. Cantor apologized.

Joe Bendix came next, neatly dressed in a dark business suit. His brown hair was combed back from his high forehead. His narrow eyes and mustache gave him a suspicious look, wrote a journalist. Bendix acknowledged a lifetime as a hotel thief. He was first arrested at age 18, caught with a stolen bicycle, and sentenced to 30 days in jail. Bendix verified that he had written to Dewey's office the previous month, while facing a life sentence. Before going to Dewey he had tried to make a deal with District Attorney Morris Panger, who prosecuted him for grand larceny. He offered Panger information about a gang of bond thieves who had stolen a half million dollars in securities from the Bank of Manhattan, but Panger refused to negotiate. As for Lucky, they had been acquainted for several years. Bendix discussed the meeting with Lucky in the Villanova Restaurant, when he tried to become a collector. George Levy challenged Bendix to state where he first met Lucky. "In the Club Richman," he answered. It was 1928, during a party for his wife, at another table sat Captain Dutton, the person who introduced him to Luciano.

The next day, Dewey received information from Morris Panger. Bendix had written a letter to his wife wherein he suggested that she should think up "a clever story" that would prove of interest to the prosecutor. After the receipt of Panger's letter, Dewey refused to call Bendix's wife, Muriel Weiss, as a witness, even though she was present in the courthouse. Dewey feared a trap.

During the trial the *New York Post* analyzed repeated press claims that the vice racket in New York was a 12-million-dollar-per-year enterprise. The *Post* calculated that four hundred prostitutes, paying bond fees of ten dollars per week, would total $400,000 per year. But the calculation was arbitrary. Exactly how many prostitutes operated in New York? The 1912 investigation had placed the number of prostitutes at 14,926.

Nine days after the trial began, Pete Balitzer took the stand. Pete recounted how he had been threatened: "I was afraid they were going to dump me on the road to make an example of me." When the bonding started, Pete feared the combination could not afford to bail out several women a day, but "Little Abie says, 'Don't worry about this, Charley Lucky's behind it.'" In lengthy testimony Balitzer related the extortion demands by Abie Wahrman. His testimony implicated Ralph Liguori in the vice chain. Ralph had called about a job for Lillian Gardello. Pete was afraid of Liguori because wherever Gashouse Lil worked, the houses were robbed. Pete reluctantly agreed to book her, afraid of Ralph. Besides, Pete also disliked Lillian's attitude. "She was too fresh, and I couldn't book her in the good places." In 1935 Ralph asked Pete to come to the Hotel Emerson to see "a nice blonde." Pete booked Nancy Presser, but it was a disaster. "Ralph loved her and she was his sweetheart. He wanted to put her in the good places, but she wasn't reliable enough." Pete's flunkey, Jojo Weintraub, discussed his duties as Pete's assistant. Jojo agreed with everything Pete told the court.

On May 20, Dewey interrogated Mildred Curtis in his office. Mildred was hesitant to discuss intimate details, ashamed of being a call girl. Sol Gelb and a stenographer were present.

"Now you also visited Lucky privately, did you not?"

"Must we put it that way?" she asked.

"If anybody asks you about these matters, you must testify to the truth, but I'm merely asking you that for my own information now." Dewey knew what frightened her: "You don't want to testify that you slept with Lucky, is that it?"

"Yes."

"How many times did you sleep with Lucky?"

"Quite a few times."

"Did anybody connected with my office or the police force or anybody else ever suggest any testimony to you of any kind?"

"No."

Asked Gelb: "Did anybody in this office at any time say to you that if you would tell anything about any person that we will give you drugs?"

"No."

"You have been radically reduced in your drugs, have you not?"

"Yes."

"Is your memory affected when you take drugs?"

"No."

In the evening, Flo Brown was summoned to Dewey's office from the House of Detention. Flo was scheduled to testify the next day. Dewey had read Flo's interviews with Barent Ten Eyck and was generally satisfied, but there was a lingering suspicion. Flo had been Jimmy's mistress; perhaps she harbored a secret desire to take the witness stand simply to exonerate him. Dewey addressed her: "Now as I understand it, you have told Mr. Ten Eyck a number of things about your acquaintance with Lucky Luciano and Jimmy Fredericks, Dave Betillo, and Tommy Bull?"[3]

"Yes."

"It has been the policy of my office, like all prosecutors, to recommend consideration for anybody who helps the People, provided they tell the truth, you understand that?"

"Yes, I understand that," answered Flo.

Dewey listened to her admission of drug use and prostitution, then asked: "Has anybody connected with my office, or anybody else in the world, given you any promise or assurance whatsoever?"

"No, no one has."

Dewey issued a threat. "If I catch you in any lies, then I will make no recommendation for consideration of any kind and I will assist in your prosecution, that alright?"

"Very clear."

Dewey hammered at the point. "Now, has any assistant in my office suggested any testimony to you?"

"No."

"Has anybody connected with my office, or elsewhere, told you that you would be helped if you named any particular person?"

"No."

"Has anybody given you anything, or any indication as to anything in particular they wanted you to say?"

"None at all."

"Has anybody connected with my office, or elsewhere, made any threats against you?"

"No one has."

Barent Ten Eyck then began the formal questioning. Flo told of her first meeting with the prosecutor's staff. Dewey showed her photographs. Flo identified all the men but one, whose name escaped her. After two hours the interview ended. Dewey was impressed by Flo's mental clarity and directness. However, if Flo attempted to double-cross him in court the following day, Dewey had a sworn affidavit to contradict her.

The next day, Flo was handed the statements she had made. She read and initialed each page. She made minor changes in her own handwriting. Flo signed the document and swore it was true. At half past six, Flo Brown walked to the witness stand. Flo wore a hat with a face veil. She was chalky white and thin. She was still weak after narcotics withdrawal. Dewey conducted the questioning. Flo discussed her life in a low voice.

David Siegel cross-examined her and immediately asked about drug use. "While you just had the recess did you take anything, liquid of any kind?"

"Yes, I had coffee."

"Was there anything in the coffee?"

"Yes, sugar and cream."

"Did you use the hypodermic?"

"No I did not; there weren't any," sneered Flo.

"When you use the needle, where do you shoot the stuff, into your arm?"

"In the muscle of the leg."

Dewey objected, protesting that she was no longer on drugs. McCook overruled him and allowed the drug questioning to continue. How long had she been injecting narcotics? For a year and a half, three times a day, answered Flo. Siegel asked if she felt drowsy. "There's no reason why I should feel drowsy. I was just trying to think, so I can give correct answers." Siegel dramatically asked Justice McCook to summon a physician for a drug test. The implication was Flo had injected narcotics during the recess. Dewey said he had no objections. Flo continued her testimony. She admitted that when arrested she faced three serious charges: maintaining a disorderly house, soliciting, and drug possession. Although Flo had been convicted of soliciting men for sex, the prosecution had obtained a delay in sentencing. Siegel began a grueling interrogation. Flo was asked to pick out Jimmy Fredericks and did so. She admitted having seen photographs of Lucky.

"Do you see Luciano in the courtroom now?"

"Yes," she replied. "He is sitting down there, the third man from the front, second from the aisle." Defense lawyers leaned toward Lucky, as if to shield him. Again Siegel asked who she meant. Flo jabbed the air, pointing: "That man right there with the yellow pencil in his hand." Lucky tossed the pencil down with a look of disgust. Siegel hammered at Flo and tried to confuse her, but she answered each question. At mid-day two physicians arrived and a recess was called. Eunice Carter was present when the doctors examined Flo.

Attorney Kopp began the re-examination, continuing with more questions about drug use. Flo said she took three quarters of a grain daily; the narcotic soothed her nerves. She explained that morphine was purchased in cubes, with three to five grains in a cube. She cut the cubes for shots; a doctor had told her the tablets she bought were "three grain tablets."

"What was the name of this doctor?" asked Kopp.

"E.E. Gardiner. He died last Tuesday."

"How convenient," remarked George Levy.

Flo said she had last injected morphine two months earlier, then had switched to heroin because it was cheaper, using an ounce a week. "That is an apothecary weight," she noted. Kopp asked if she now cried for the drug. No, she answered. At 6:52 P.M. an adjournment was taken until the following morning. It had been a grueling day.

At 9:56 A.M. the day's session began. Samuel Siegel strode before Flo. He noted that in court she claimed to be Jimmy's sweetheart for two years, but in a letter she wrote it was three years. Siegel tried to undermine Flo's credibility. Flo discussed two visits to Siegel's office to help Jimmy. Siegel corrected her—it was three visits, he snapped. "You haven't got a very good memory have you?" smirked Siegel. "Yes, I do," she said defensively. As for Jimmy, she admitted she once had a soft spot in her heart for him.

"And what has eliminated that soft spot?"

"Time," said Flo. "I am disgusted with everything. I am quitting all this."

Siegel taunted her about her sweetheart. "Don't you think it would have been nice for you, if Jimmy Frederico, as you say, was your sweetheart for two years, to have said to Mr. Dewey's assistants, 'I will tell you everything about all the defendants, but in God's name turn Jimmy Frederico out.'"

Dewey stood. "I object."

Justice McCook ordered the remark stricken from the record. Siegel asked about photographs of the defendants. "Did any of Mr. Dewey's assistants say, 'We are not going to show you any pictures of the defendants, because we want to see if you are really telling the truth, and we are going to let you pick them out in court without seeing any of the pictures. Did they tell you that?"

Dewey stood again. "I object to the question, for the reason that no sane prosecutor would do such a thing."

Flo laughed at Siegel, who lost his composure. When Siegel began probing about the maiden name of Flo's landlady, Dewey addressed the court. "I think we have gone so far afield, your Honor, as to be utterly useless in this cross-examination." Dewey went to the water cooler.

Siegel was flustered. "It is terribly disconcerting when he walks up and down there."

"You may always do that," said McCook.

"What a lot of silly nonsense," scoffed Dewey. "If he cannot examine when I get a drink of water, then counsel ought not to be at the Bar."

Siegel stated Flo's only motive for cooperation was because she was about to be sentenced and had two charges pending. "As long as I was going to be punished, I might as well be punished and clear my conscience," she answered. "And then when I had left the House of Detention, be free." At 3:02 in the afternoon, Attorney Levy questioned Flo. At age 18, Flo admitted she was involved with three men at the same time, each believing he was her sole lover.

"And you let each one of the three think he was taking care of you alone, did you now?"

"I let them draw their own conclusions."

"So you learned to lie pretty well at the age of 18, did you not?"

"If a man wasn't satisfied, I would leave him." She began laughing. "They always thought I was home." Levy asked her to speak louder. Flo said she could not, since she was ill and her body was weak. Flo spoke of her early days. Levy opposed a recess and hinted he didn't trust Flo to be alone, as if she would seek drugs. Dewey objected, stating that a physician for the defense had already examined her. "Mr. Dewey," said Levy. "I do not know why you always imply something evil. It seems to be part of you."

"I never heard of such an insinuation," responded the prosecutor.

During the recess Flo was allowed a shot of brandy in a paper cup. Dewey disclosed Flo's sip of alcohol to the defense lawyers. During afternoon testimony Flo recounted how she began smoking opium. She said she found the pipe *fascinating*.

"You had a pretty good mind at that time, did you not?"

"Yes, I did."

"Didn't you find any change in your memory at all?"

"None at all."

"When you awakened in the morning you would have a clean-cut recollection of what took place the night before, would you?"

"I had to; I had to remember over three thousand customers by name and face."

"You had three thousand customers?"

"Yes."

"In your house of prostitution?"

"Yes."

"And when they called up you had to remember their voices?"

"Their voice, name, and face."

"I see."

Levy questioned Flo about Jimmy Fredericks. Flo expressed sympathy for Jimmy and described him as poor. Jimmy thought the bonding was legal. His bonding salary was only 35 dollars a week. Flo admitted she had fallen in love with Jimmy. He never mistreated her.

"Miss Brown, you love Jimmy Fredericks right now, don't you?"

"I am not sure." She expressed doubts that Jimmy had ever booked women in houses. When Flo discussed her encounters with Lucky, Levy said her voice had become stronger. He asked if she spoke in a low voice deliberately.

"I am not an actress," said Flo angrily.

"I object to counsel badgering the witness," interjected Dewey. During the ensuing examination, Levy implied that Flo implicated Lucky only to protect Jimmy. He noticed her smiling at someone and stopped. "Have you given Jimmy Fredericks a smile today?"

"I shall."

At 6:56 P.M. the trial adjourned. The next day, Levy asked Flo about her arrest for solicitation. The officer had perjured himself, she claimed; she had refused his offer to earn five dollars. The attorney returned to Jimmy. "Isn't it true, as a matter of fact, Miss Brown, that the sole purpose of your testimony is to help your former sweetheart Frederico?"

"No, it is not true." Flo was excused after nearly 11 hours of questioning.

When the trial commenced on Monday, Thelma Jordan was the first witness. She was questioned by Dewey and Cole for nearly an hour. Afterward, she was cross-examined by David Siegel. Thelma admitted that when an investigator had first asked her about the defendants, she denied knowing them. Why? asked Siegel.

"I was afraid to tell. I was afraid to talk, because I knew what happens to people that talk and who tell things about members of the combination, about racket people. I know times girls have had their feet burned and their stomach burned with cigar butts because they talked, and their tongues cut, and things like that, and I was afraid of it, and that is why I didn't talk."

"Is that why you are talking now?"

"No, that is not why I am talking now."

"Why are you talking now?"

"Because I have confidence in the people that are behind me."

"Who are the people that are behind you?"

"It must be Mr. Dewey and his district attorneys that are on my side."

The relentless questioning continued with Siegel trying to discredit Thelma Jordan's testimony.

"Did you make up any story that you would tell?"

"No."

"Did anybody coach you what to say?"

"No."

"Did anybody drill you what to say?"

"No."

"Did anybody tell you what meetings you should say these various defendants were at?"

"No."

"Did anybody tell you what you should say in case you were asked why you didn't tell the truth before?"

"No."

At 12:45 a recess was declared until 2:00 P.M. During the afternoon session Attorney Paley asked about her life in the sex underworld. A friend, prostitute Betty Cook, had lined up houses for both of them through Jojo, she explained.

As the relentless questioning continued, Jordan made a face.

"Are you suffering?" asked Paley.

"Your yelling makes me have a headache."

Only a few minutes had passed before Paley again began browbeating Jordan. Dewey objected to the bullying.

Judge McCook spoke. "I do not think it is abuse, but he should not lecture her."

"I am sorry. I did not intend to lecture her. I just wanted to see if we can get a little bit of cooperation from this witness, who is, it seems to me, definitely resisting."

"All that is stricken from the record," interjected McCook, "and if you keep on, that will be stricken, too, because it is nothing but a statement of your own views."

After a few minutes, Paley demanded to know her real name. "Buddy is good enough," she answered. The judge told her to give her first name. She answered that it was Mildred. She refused to give her hometown.

Samuel Siegel rose, asking the court to make her reply. Siegel turned to Dewey: "I ask that if the District Attorney has anything to say he make a legal objection."

"I am making one," answered Dewey. "The witness has advised me that her parents are decent, hard working, honest citizens."

Judge McCook ruled for the defense. "She is directed to answer."

Still, Thelma refused to give her last name. After much wrangling, Judge McCook relented: "I will not require her to give any more than she has under the circumstances." The defense attorneys did not press the point. Samuel Siegel returned to question her. He humiliated her mercilessly. When asking about her first week in a house, he sneered, "That must have impressed your memory, your first experience as a whore, eh?"

"I don't remember," replied Jordan.

Siegel kept at it. "And for two dollars you would take all your clothes off and go to bed with the men?"

"Maybe."

"Well, didn't you? Wasn't that required?"

"No."

"You didn't take your clothes off, did you, eh?"

"Sometimes."

"Oh, that is, if you had customers that you wanted to rush in and out, you wouldn't take your clothes off, is that the idea?"

"Maybe."

"And how much did you earn over at 310 Avenue A with these honest working people for customers?"

"A little over a hundred dollars, I believe."

"During all that period did you ever go to church?"

"No, I hate hypocrites."

Paley did his best to impugn Jordan's credibility and morals.

"Did you ever have illicit relations with her, with Nancy Presser, any time, before incarceration or after incarceration?"

"I should say not."

Thelma said no promises had been made to her by Dewey's staff.

At 3:53 Lorenzo Carlino continued the attack. "Didn't Mrs. Foley discover you with Nancy Presser in a compromising position?"

"She did not."

The attorney began baiting her. "This Margaret Venti that you said lived at that address, with you, is in reality Peggy Wild, isn't that so?"

"That is right."

"You didn't tell us that, did you, on your direct examination?"

"You didn't ask me."

"Why did you conceal that?"

"You didn't ask me."

Dewey was irritated. "I object to that. That is a very offensive question, when the witness wasn't asked."

"Counsel," reprimanded Judge McCook, "if you want a ruling on it, let me proceed. Do you want me to express my opinion of it? It is a very bad practice, sir. I advise against it."

Carlino was apologetic. "I respectfully except to your Honor's remark. I think if there is any expression of any kind, judge, it should be to both counsel, and not to one counsel singled out."

"No," answered McCook.

"I respectfully except. Now I ask your Honor to declare a mistrial on the basis of the remark the Court has made with reference to the conduct of counsel." Justice McCook refused.

"I respectfully except."

"But don't do it again," warned McCook.

"Pardon me, Judge."

"Don't do it again."

Carlino asked about her life in police custody, cocktails in restaurants, and brandy in Dewey's office. She drank because she was nervous, said Thelma. Carlino began baiting her again. "You only remember what you want to remember?"

"No, my memory isn't so bad."

Dewey rose. "Objection, as to argumentative."

Carlino tried to confuse her, "Now, then, you moved from Jackson Heights to 535 West 111th Street, didn't you?"

"No."

Carlino's sarcasm returned when he questioned her about visits to the Woolworth Building. "What would you do down there, drink brandy?"

"I was taken down there because they wanted to question Nancy Presser, and I had to go along."

"You had to go along?"

"Why, certainly. There was only one police matron, so if they took one of us down, they took the other one down."

"Please don't volunteer any information I don't ask."

After a ten minute recess, Carlino began again at 4:48.

"Did you have a little brandy during the recess?"

"No, I didn't."

Carlino asked how many times she had been interrogated by Dewey's staff in recent months. Then he asked about Ralph Liguori: "Did you hear Nancy Presser tell him that they wanted her to testify to a lot of lies?"

"No."

"Did you hear the conversation between Nancy Presser and Ralph Liguori?"

"Yes."

Carlino veered from the conversation.

"Did anybody tell you that something might happen to you if you didn't say something that they wanted you to say?"

"No."

Carlino's honed his words with a sharper knife. "You testified that as an inmate of a whorehouse you charged two dollars and up for giving your body to men that came there, is that right?"

"Yes."

"It was not necessary for you to be a prostitute, was it? Your mother and father sent you money when you needed it, isn't that true?"

"They used to."

"So that it was not necessary for you to be a prostitute, was it?"

"Yes. I couldn't live off my mother and father forever. After all, they are old."

"Now tell the court and jury what you mean by two dollars and up?"

"Well, what do you want me to tell?"

"What does the *up* mean?"

"Naturally, it means more."

"Yes."

"I don't know what you mean."

"You don't know what I mean? Was the two dollars for having intercourse with a man in a natural manner?"

"Why, of course."

"And the *up* was for unnatural acts of intercourse, isn't that so?"

"No."

"Well, all right, then tell us what the *up* meant."

"The *up* meant that some people just spent more money. Whether they wanted to or not. I don't know what they did."

"You were known as a French girl, weren't you. Come on, tell us."

"I was not."

"Weren't you told by the district attorney's office that they knew you were a French girl, and performed acts of degeneracy, and that is what they held over your head in this trial?"

"No."

"Didn't the district attorney tell you that the girls in the House of Detention had squealed on you, that you had indulged in those practices?"

"No."

"Were you told that the penalty for sodomy was 20 years in prison?"

"For what?"

"The crime of sodomy is performing unnatural acts of sexual intercourse."

"So?"

"Did you know that the penalty for that was 20 years in jail?"

"No."

"Didn't anyone in Mr. Dewey's office tell you that?"

"No."

"You were operated upon, were you not, and all of your sexual organs were removed? By that I mean the ovaries and the tubes, your fallopian tubes?"

Dewey's rose. "I object to that as too disgustingly irrelevant, your Honor."

Judge McCook: "Do you see some relevancy in that, Mr. Carlino?"

"I am leading up to something, if your Honor please." Carlino asked again about her operation, then made his point. "Since your operation, Miss Jordan, you have had no normal sexual desires, isn't that so?" Dewey rose. "I think I should object to that, too, as quite irrelevant."

"Sustained," said Judge McCook.

"I respectfully except. As related to a house of prostitution, do you know what a circus is?"

"What?"

"A circus."

"Certainly I have heard of such things."

"Tell the court and jury what that is."

"I refuse. You tell it."

"No, you are the witness, you tell. You are the inmate of the prostitution house."

Dewey spoke up. "I object to it as irrelevant."

"Sustained," agreed McCook.

Attorney Levy came forward and asked about Jimmy Fredericks and "the boss."

"You didn't know him at that time, did you?"

"No, I knew of him."

"You don't even claim now that you have ever seen him before, that you ever talked with Charley Lucky before?"

"I have never talked to him."

Dewey began a redirect examination. "My assistants did not make any threats of prosecution against you, did they? Did anybody ever tell you they had any evidence by which you might be sent to prison?"

"They never did."

"You were just walking along the street?"

"Yes."

"You weren't even anywhere near a house of prostitution. How much money have you been sending home every week?"

"Twenty-five dollars a week."

Nancy Presser took the stand. Harold Cole conducted the direct examination. Nancy recounted her early life in New York. Lorenzo Carlino came forward. He posed questions about her early romances, her involvement with three men at once. Nancy could not recall when the affairs ended. "There are so many exciting things in my life, that I really couldn't tell you."

"This call life, as a matter of fact, when you began it was rather distasteful to you, was it not Miss Presser?"

"I never liked it, if that is what you mean."

"It was obnoxious to you, was it not?"

"Sort of, yes."

"And you tried to drown your sorrows in the beginning by drugs, did you not?"

"Yes."

"That is the truth, isn't it?"

"Yes."

"And when you started this call business your conscience bothered you, did it not?"

"No, it didn't bother me."

"Well, I mean, coming from a nice family, you knew that it was a pretty low way of making a living, did you not?"

"Yes."

"You would give your body many times in one night, would you not?"

"Sometimes, yes."

She explained how she had met Lucky and visited him at the Barbizon and Waldorf. She spoke of her life with Ralph Liguori. At 8:15 the next morning Lorenzo Carlino continued the cross-examination.

Nancy admitted she had not told the truth when first arrested. She had denied knowing Ralph. The next day, David Siegel questioned her. The lawyer said she was diseased: "You didn't want it to come out, did you, that you had syphilis?"

"It doesn't matter."

Siegel accused her of being "a circus girl." Next were questions about opium smoking, drug addiction and visits to Lucky at the Barbizon. Siegel was incredulous on hearing that Lucky gave her money, though she did nothing for it. Nancy explained how she was often simply a hired escort. Men wanted her as a dinner or theatre companion; such outings netted 50 to 75 dollars. Siegel was surprised.

"I am not talking about no intercourse now."

"I know."

Nancy's visits to Lucky were discussed. On her second visit to Lucky's room at the Barbizon they each drank several glasses of champagne, but nothing sexual occurred. "We was going to, but we didn't," said Nancy. "I don't think he could have done anything." Lucky had fallen asleep on the bed, fully clothed, she said.

"You did not even call up to find out whether he fell out of the bed or not, did you, the last time you left him?"

"No, I didn't."

Siegel returned to her drug use. "In reference to the time you were trying to take a cure, when did you start heroin?"

"When Ralph couldn't get me any morphine, then he brought me heroin." Nancy suddenly became ill and a recess was called. At 8:03 P.M. Nancy returned to the stand. Questioned by Lorenzo Carlino, she said the discussion of drugs had made her ill. Dewey conducted the redirect examination. He asked Nancy why she didn't have relations with Lucky in his room at the Barbizon.

"I think there was something wrong with Lucky."

Dewey continued but defense objections ended the matter. The implication was that Lucky had a venereal disease. Carlino returned and accused Nancy of faking her illness the previous day. Nancy said she had a cyst in her ovaries.

"You are diseased there, aren't you?"

"Not that I know of, no."

"Aren't you suffering from syphilis?"

"Yes, I believe I got that from Ralph."

"How many men have you stayed with in your lifetime?"

"I can't answer that question. Could you answer me how many people you have seen in your lifetime?"

"I am asking you the questions, Miss. Don't you ask me questions."

Carlino was angry. "And you worked in a two dollar house, didn't you?"

"Certainly, because Ralph sent me there."

"And you did not get sick when you were handling those filthy penises of men, did you?"

"Don't be so vulgar."

"You did not get sick when you stayed with these hundreds of men or thousands of men?"

"I had my blood taken, and when it came back it was always negative, not positive, and the first I knew I had that was when I was arrested."

"Did you get sick to your stomach when you were staying with these men?"

"No."

"Very pleasurable to you, wasn't it?"

"No, I wouldn't say that."

"You enjoyed it, didn't you?"

"No."

"You enjoyed your depravity, didn't you?"

"No."

Carlino asked why she entered a house when Lucky had offered to give her money.

"I had to," she answered.

At 5:28 P.M. on May 28, Mildred Balitzer stood in the courtroom and took the oath. Her hair was dyed red. She was described by reporters as matronly with a "dulcet toned" Southern voice. Mildred was dressed in a black and white dress, a matching straw hat and white kid gloves. Dewey started the direct examination and asked about her life, especially the relationship with Pete Balitzer. The cross-examination by George Levy began rather mildly, compared to the scathing interrogations of Thelma Jordan and Nancy Presser. Levy asked about her training week as a prostitute. "You probably had affairs with 30 or 40 men?"

"Approximately."

"This prostitution business kind of shocked your conscience when you started it, did it not?"

"Somewhat."

"You were doing it to earn a living? Is that true?"

"Yes."

"And your husband was not doing so well himself in his own line of business, was he, or the man you were living with rather, at that time?"

"No."

Then Levy casually asked: "You know what a lesbian is, do you not?"

"Yes."

"And have you enjoyed that distinction in your business?"

"Never."

"You know what circuses are, too, do you not?"

"Yes."

"There are some customers who like it, is that true?"

"Yes."

Mildred denied ever operating a circus; she only allowed normal relations in her house. She went into detail about her drug use. At one time she smoked 15 opium pills a day but eventually switched to morphine. She first saw Lucky in a restaurant in Little Italy.

"Was your mind perfectly clear?" asked Levy.

"Yes."

"And the first thing Little Davie said is, 'Meet my boss, Charley Lucky,' did he not?"

"Yes."

"And when the word boss was used to you at that particular time, was there any clarification, such as boss of what particular line of business?"

"Well, I knew the business Little Davie —"

"Just a moment, I ask that my question be answered."

"I think that is her answer. Counsel asked her," said Dewey.

Levy asked the court if he could rephrase the question. "You remember the expression after three and a half years, 'Meet my boss'?"

"Yes."

Could she recall any conversation with a customer two and a half months after meeting Lucky. She said she could not.

"But you do remember distinctly, without any question, this fall talk with Charley Lucky in 1932, is that right?"

"Yes."

Mildred's testimony directly linked Lucky to the combination.

On May 29, Lorenzo Carlino questioned John J. Ryan, manager of the Emerson Hotel. Ryan said that Ralph was known at the hotel under the name of Presser. It was a humiliating revelation. Ralph Liguori took the stand. He wore glasses to confuse the witnesses. Carlino began the questioning. Ralph said he was a butcher and worked in his brother's restaurant. Thereafter, Ralph began a litany of denials. He had never placed women in houses of prostitution, received money from prostitutes, or robbed houses. Ralph admitted living with Nancy Presser but denied knowing she was a prostitute. He never gave her drugs, beat her, or accepted money from her.

"Did Nancy tell you she was in Mr. Dewey's office?"

"She did."

"I object to that," snapped Dewey. "Counsel ought to know that."

"Sustained," said Judge McCook.

Carlino glared at Dewey. "There are a lot of things that you ought to know that you do not."

"At least I do not ask questions like that."

McCook issued a reprimand: "I suggest, Mr. Dewey, I have commented on this before, that your advice to counsel is not proper here in the form of comment like that. I have heard attorneys making mistakes."

When McCook called a recess for lunch, the throng of reporters rushed to the telephones to file stories for the afternoon newspapers. Each day brought lurid testimony and new disclosures. As New Yorkers closely followed the trial, citizen admiration for Dewey grew. Citizens felt prosecutors were finally attacking the corrupt system that allowed racketeering. Dewey brilliantly outwitted the defense lawyers, despite dependence on unsavory witnesses. Occasionally, the witnesses injured their own credibility. Though Dave Marcus was repeatedly asked if he had been arrested for prostitution in Pittsburgh, he denied any such arrest, but the defense discovered a witness who would refute Marcus. While Ralph testified word came that Marcus had lied on the stand.

When the court convened in the afternoon, Ralph insisted Harold Cole had pressured him to lie. Cole said he was the only one who could help Nancy; if not, he faced a prison sentence of 25 years. Ralph was offered protection. Cole warned that Dewey was a busy man who was going to be governor. "So then he started to threaten me. He told me that, he showed me four pictures. It was Davie Betillo, Charley Lucky, and Tommy Bull. He wanted me to say that Davie Betillo was the strong arm man." At 3:40 P.M. Dewey began the cross-examination. Dewey began slowly and asked seemingly insignificant questions about Ralph's background. Ralph talked freely, unaware he was cornering himself. Ralph admitted that after 1932 he didn't have a job but lived at the Park West Hotel under the name of Martin. His roommate, who died, was a plasterer, also named Martin. Ralph had no idea where the man worked.

"He was not in the numbers or narcotics business?"

"He was not."

Dewey forced him to admit he paid no income taxes, that his family cared for his ten-year-old child and, though he claimed he worked five months for his brother in 1934, there was no such record.

David Siegel dramatically called a halt to the questioning of Ralph Liguori.

Detective Thomas Calig took the oath and testified that Dave Marcus had indeed been arrested for operating a house of prostitution in Pittsburgh. On June 11, 1927, Calig had pretended to be a customer who had gone to the home of Dave Marcus and asked if he had any girls.

"No, but my wife will do the work," Marcus answered.

The detective gave Marcus two dollars and followed a woman into a bedroom where two children slept. "Is this where you do business?" he asked. Ruth Marcus replied yes, but not to worry because the children were asleep and "wouldn't know anything anyway."

Marcus had tried to protect his wife's conviction.

Ralph returned to the stand and was asked the source of his income. "I was gambling on the side." Ralph gave the winnings to his mother, who kept it in a safe. Dewey got him to admit that there was no safe. Nor did his mother have a bank account. Then he asked about Nancy. He only knew she was a model, claimed Ralph.

"You mean you were not curious about her private affairs?"

"I was not."

"You did not have the slightest notion she was a prostitute?"

"I did not."

Ralph admitted he had lived with Gas House Lil but never asked her what she did for a living either.

"You signed yourself as 'Mr. Josephine Cardella.'"

"I did not."

He had met Josephine in a Coney Island cabaret. A friend named Tommy, whose last name he did not recall, introduced him.

"Did she tell you she was working for a living?"

"She didn't tell me anything."

"You thought she was just a nice girl overcome with your charm?"

"I object to that question," said Carlino.

Ralph admitted Josephine had been his mistress for two years. It was true he paid for the apartment in Brooklyn, but he denied knowing she was a prostitute.

"You heard these people testify that you booked her?"

"They are liable to testify to anything from your office."

Dewey showed him a signature. "You gave your date of birth there, March 17, 1904. Do you remember that?"

"Maybe I got my age mixed up."

Ralph removed his glasses to read.

"Do you have any difficulty in reading?" queried Dewey.

The birth date was false, he acknowledged, so he could obtain his chauffeur's license.

"Oh, you mean you deliberately signed this, knowing it was false? Is that it?"

"I had to make a living. That is not lying."

"That is the time you were a butcher boy over in Brooklyn, isn't it?" Dewey demonstrated that in 1933 Ralph had renewed the license with the false birth date. Ralph said he drove a truck that year. "In addition to shooting craps and getting a little money from your mother, you were driving a truck that year were you?" Liguori admitted he had bought a Cadillac, even though he wasn't working.

"Now you testified that you had no business transactions with Josephine Cardella, is that right."

"I did not." Dewey produced documents and showed them to Ralph. "Do you now remember that you had a little business transaction with Josephine and her father?"

"I wouldn't call it business."

"Well, you remember that Josephine had a life insurance policy, don't you?"

"I do."

"And you remember that sometime last year you went up to her father and had a talk with him about it, is that right?"

"She told me to go."

"Did you tell her father she was sick in the hospital?"

"That is what I was told to say."

"She was not in the hospital at all, was she?"

Ralph admitted he had received a check and forged her name on it. "She loaned it to me," said Ralph.

"Did you hear Pete's testimony that you asked him to book Nancy in houses?"

"I did not."

"You heard Thelma Jordan testify that you told Nancy that you would kill her if she testified against you? You heard Jimmy Russo testify that he had better put Nancy to work in his house if he knew what was good for him? You heard Joan Martin tell about the time you stuck up her house. She told about having your girl Lillian in the apartment at the time?"

Ralph denied everything.

At 6:33 P.M. George Levy questioned Ralph. He denied knowing Lucky or engaging in any activities with him. Dewey returned. He asked Ralph to indicate which of his assistants asked him to commit perjury. He pointed out Cole, Ariola, Grimes, and Hogan. Dewey had Hogan stand.

"He scared you, didn't he?"

"He told me I was going to get 25 years."

"And he told you to go and commit perjury?"

"He didn't tell me nothing about perjury."

"You told him it would be perjury if you told about the people in the case?"

"I did."

"And he said you ought to go right in and do it just the same?"

"He did."

Ralph acknowledged that his mother and sister paid his legal fees. Ralph said he didn't know where his family got the money; finally, he admitted Lucky gave the money.

Ralph's sister, Anna Liguori, took the stand. Anna was 26, a bookkeeper who earned 25 dollars a week. She told Lorenzo Carlino that she had known Nancy Presser and believed her to be a cigarette girl. Harold Cole had summoned her for a visit with Ralph, and said, "If Ralph doesn't give us what we want, we are going to send him away for 25 years." There was a missing link in the puzzle, said Cole, and Ralph had the answer. She met with Ralph in private. Ralph told his sister they wanted him to lie. Anna and her mother begged Ralph to cooperate, but he refused.

Dewey began the cross-examination. Anna Liguori knew Ralph kept both Josephine and Nancy as mistresses. She doubted Ralph booked Nancy because "he wasn't that sort." She doubted the women were prostitutes. When Anna testified that Ralph worked as a butcher in 1933, Dewey indicated that Ralph's own testimony proved otherwise. The trial proved to be sensational testimony. Dewey was prepared to question Lucky Luciano but was unsure if he would take the stand.

The defense summoned witnesses to establish Lucky was simply a gambler. Bookmaker Max Kalik said Lucky often placed bets with him. Kalik had been in the business 30 years. Dewey ripped into him; he pointed out that bookmaking was a crime. Kalik insisted he did business with only respectable people.

"And you never saw any well-known gangsters attending the race track?"

"Gangsters?"

Dewey recited the names of Louis Buchalter, Jacob Shapiro, Dutch Goldberg, Legs Diamond, and Leo Byk. Kalik admitted knowing Byk, described by Dewey as "the well-known fixer of Brooklyn."

"As far as I knew, he was all right with me."

"Do you know his record?"

"No, sir."

Levy sought to correct the damage. "Do the Vanderbilts do any betting with you?"

"I said that I wouldn't care to mention any names, that as long as you are at it, I say yes."

Captain George Dutton, supervisor of the state police, denied he was the Dutton who had identified Joe Bendix to Lucky. Henry Goldstone, Kalik's associate, testified he daily saw Lucky at the tracks. Thomas Francis owned thoroughbred stables. He had accompanied Lucky to the race track nearly every day for several years. After a day at the races, they would dine together at the Villanova. Lucky's bets averaged about three hundred dollars, said Francis. He went to the Waldorf to discuss races with Lucky. In the suite he saw trainer Sammy Smith, Lorenzo Brescio, and Joe Forgione, Lucky's betting commissioner. When pressed for details, the witness balked.

"My memory is very bad," remarked Francis.

"And yet you can tell us who you saw around Charley Lucky's room last August?"

"Yes, I do remember."

In five years of dining with Lucky, Francis could not recall anyone ever coming up to speak with him, or Lucky talking to anyone. Dewey was incredulous. "Did people come over and talk to him?"

"Yes, they would say, 'How was it today, Charley?'"

"That is all?"

"That is all I ever heard."

Fred Bachmann came to the stand. He related how he and Lucky had been partners in craps games since 1927, including the Chicago Club in Saratoga. He recounted his many years in the gambling business. "You ran craps games during the War, is that it?"

"I ran craps games."

"Is that all you did for your country during the war?"

"That is all."

He knew nothing about Lucky's life. "Didn't you ever say to him, Charley Lucky, what is your business?"

"No, I didn't."

Bachmann refused to identify the town where he did business. "Positively, no."

"You don't know the address of your place of business?"

"It is two doors from the corner. I don't know the address."

On redirect examination Levy was brief. "Have you ever run a whorehouse in your life?"

"No."

Colonel Knebelcamp testified to seeing Lucky around the tracks for the last four years; he gave tips to Lucky and anyone who asked. Lorenzo Brescio testified he stayed three of four nights a week with Lucky at the Barbizon but left when Gay Orlova spent the night. He also spent nights with Lucky at the Waldorf but had never seen Nancy Presser. When it came to his work history he had a difficult time. "Twelve years is a long way to remember," he pleaded.

"Give him a chance," said Levy. "He is a little dull."

"Mr. Levy wants the record to show that in his opinion the witness is a little dull-witted," said Dewey.

"I just tell you, give him a chance. He will answer finally."

"I can't recall so far back." Brescio obviously didn't want to remember.

Sidney Walker testified that he and Lou Frank were partners in Kean's Tavern. He admitted it was originally a speakeasy. Walker knew all the defendants except Lucky and Nancy Presser. Dewey took over the questioning. Where did he buy the illegal alcohol?

"I can't remember now," replied Walker.

On June 4, Samuel J. Siegel, Jimmy Frederick's attorney, took the stand as a witness. He gave his home address as 1160 Park Avenue. He recounted how Flo Brown had visited his office on 40th Street. Siegel showed her the indictment, which included Lucky's name. Lucky had not been included in the first indictments and Siegel wanted to know why. Flo said she didn't know the reason. The attorney allowed her to read the indictment in his law library. According to Siegel, at the time Flo denied knowing Lucky. She claimed that Jimmy was only involved in bonding. When Flo was arrested she had telephoned his office.

The long parade of witnesses grew longer.

William McGrath, a bellboy at the Barbizon-Plaza, testified he was on duty from midnight until seven. He knew "Charles Lane" and recognized Dave Betillo as a visitor. At one point, after Dewey successfully stopped Carlino's line of questioning, Carlino turned to Judge McCook. "May I ask the court to prevent Mr. Dewey from injecting his personality into this case?"

McCook smiled. "That would be impossible."

The witness testimony was so damning that Jack Ellenstein pleaded guilty and turned state's evidence like the other bookers.

William Bischoff, owner of the Saratoga Club, acknowledged Lucky and Fred Bachmann had rented the craps game concession from him in 1935. They had paid him $2,500, which amounted to 10 percent of their winnings.

When Gus Franco came to the stand, he denied he had introduced Mildred Balitzer to Dave Betillo. Only recently Mildred had telephoned him and said: "Dewey would not give her husband any consideration unless she positively identified Charley Lucky." Franco said he was shocked. Mildred had asked him to identify "an innocent man." When cross-examined by Dewey, Franco admitted being arrested for selling an ounce of dope. He was in the numbers racket, he admitted. Yes, he replied, he and Mildred smoked opium together. As for his income, Gus said his mother gave him "hundreds of dollars" anytime he needed it. He denied threatening Mildred.

The testimony of the Waldorf Astoria employees proved devastating to the defendants. Pauline Fletcher was allowed to use the fictitious name of Marjorie Brown. She identified herself as a bathmaid. Lucky's room was the last she would clean; she sat in a corner by his door, until he left. She waited and watched the visitors. She recognized "Charles Ross" from 39D. She pointed at Betillo and Wahrman. Jimmy Fredericks was not singled out, so Samuel Siegel spoke up. "You didn't see this man, did you?" She looked again. "Oh, yes, he was there oftener than anybody else."

The defense wondered how she could recall particular faces when there were so many hotel guests. "They were so different from the other Waldorf guests I couldn't forget them." The remark was so damaging that, during a brief recess, defense attorneys devised a plan to confuse Fletcher. The defendants changed neckties and seats. Brown was asked twice to place her hands on the shoulders of those she recognized and did so.

Joseph Weinman, a waiter, testified he had served a meal to Lucky on a summer evening when Jimmy Fredericks was present. He recalled the dessert he served was French pastry.

Henry Woelfle, manager of the Tower Apartments, identified Lucky as a guest, but when asked to pick out Abie Wahrman, he chose Moses Polakoff instead.

Hedwig Scholz recalled that during the summer months she saw Lucky almost every day. The chambermaid always finished the first apartment by noon, but Mr. Ross had his breakfast between twelve and one, so that she and the bathmaid had to wait every day, until they could enter 39D. She sat beside the guest elevator in the hallway. Lucky and his friends were peculiar look-ing, so they made a vivid impression. She heard the visitors address him as "the boss." She identified Lucky; she pointed to Dave Betillo, a frequent vis-itor in the apartment who came at least three or four times a week. She also recognized Jesse Jacobs and Meyer Berkman.

William Salach, the bell captain for the Tower Apartments, recognized Little Davie. He recalled the time when Abie Wahrman arrived with a flat package under his arm, wrapped with brown paper and tied with string. Jesse Jacobs, Al Weiner, and Willie Spiller were all remembered as guests.

Elevator operator Fred Seidel recognized Nancy Presser "as a young woman whom I have seen on three or four occasions entering or leaving the Tower elevators." Residents and guests were unaware there was a night record book. Mr. Rodrigues, the all-night elevator operator, kept entries of those who came and went between one and six.

William McGrath, bellboy at the Barbizon Plaza, testified he recognized Dave Betillo, Tommy Pennochio, and Benny Spiller as men he had seen in Lucky's room.

Newspapers reported the testimony of the hotel employees was damag-ing to Luciano.

During the trial, Jacob Rosenblum sent a letter to the New York Depart-ment of Taxation. George Levy had made the statement that his client, Charles Luciano, had paid income tax for a number of years. Rosenblum asked officials about recent years. The answer arrived four days later; there was no record Luciano had filed state tax returns for the last four years.

Morris Panger was called by defense attorneys. George Levy read from a letter that Joe Bendix had written to his wife but inadvertently mailed to Panger. It stated: "Try to think up some real clever story that will prove of interest." Panger testified Bendix wanted to avoid prison, and when police declined to use his information in the bond theft case, he told Panger, "Take me to see Dewey."

The trial had reached a crucial phase. Would Luciano be allowed to tes-tify? Allowing the accused to take the stand would be a major risk. But reporters were told Lucky wanted to testify.

An anonymous letter arrived at Dewey's office: "You will no doubt be surprised at the number of reputable people that testified for Charley Lucky, head of the Mafia society in the U.S." There were accusations that Thomas Francis was a racetrack front for racketeers. Max Kalik and Al Levy had been threatened by Lucky, and paid him extortion money to avoid being kidnapped and to prevent robberies at their gambling houses. "Bobby Crawford the songwriter has also been threatened with kidnapping and Lucky protects him. The same goes for actor Harry Richman, although he did not testify, also a world of other people." The gambling houses in Saratoga were all owned or controlled by racketeers, as were the illegal dog tracks in the state. Commissioner Valentine was regarded as honest but the vice squads "are all the rankest kind of extortioners and thieves." The author of the letter identified himself as a war veteran. "Dare not sign my name as the dagos are all too strong as yet — lots of luck to you Mr. Dewey, we need a few hundred like you in this poor racket ridden U.S."

A.J. Gutreich was told by an anonymous caller that Max Kalik was a former pickpocket known as "Kid Rex." He had not been a bookmaker until the last few years. At one time Kalik and his wife, Ida, operated a house of prostitution.

Victor Herwitz also received an anonymous telephone call. Kalik had not been a bookmaker for 30 years as he claimed, but only for five years, and that he obtained his current position at the track through political connections. Kalik was very friendly with George Morton Levy. They played golf together at the Lakeville Country Club along with Al Levy "and a man named Costello, a slot machine racketeer." Luciano and Little Augie were Kalik's guests at the Lakeville Country Club in Long Island, and an examination of the guest book of that club would show that to be fact. Max Kalik was known as "Rags" and used to run a house of prostitution. Investigators realized Luciano's tentacles and criminal contacts were vast. The link between Luciano and Frank Costello was evident, at least socially.

Lucky spoke to reporters. After more than a hundred prosecution witnesses, he said he was eager to take the stand. "I'm ready for Mr. Dewey, bring him on. Now the truth is coming out."[4] Dewey was ready for the challenge.

CHAPTER ELEVEN

The Verdict

Sing Sing is just an hour up the river

On June 3, at 2:13 P.M., Charles Luciano strode to the stand, poised and confident.[1] George Levy questioned his client. Lucky spoke of his early life and admitted he had served time in a reformatory for selling narcotics. But those days were behind him. He was now a sportsman. For the last ten years, his income derived from booking bets on horse races and operating craps games. Lucky denied being acquainted with any of the defendants except Dave Betillo, someone he had known for ten years. Betillo had visited him at the Waldorf to discuss a gambling boat, but "I told him I would not go into it." Beyond the hotel staff, "there has not been a witness that got on this stand of Mr. Dewey's that I ever saw in my life." Why did he oppose extradition to New York? "When I was in jail my lawyer told me that Mr. Dewey wanted to put me on trial within 48 hours, and I thought it was best to give my lawyer a chance to see what it is all about." Lucky admitted he had paid a fine in Florida for operating a gambling house. After only 24 minutes of questioning, George Levy turned to Dewey: "Your witness." Dewey walked to the stand and stood before Salvatore Lucania.

"Have you told us the whole truth about that little incident in Miami in 1930?"

"The whole truth?"

"Yes, sir."

"How about the gun?"

"Mr. Levy didn't mention no gun."

George Levy objected, but withdrew his comment, to allow an explanation. He had a weapon, explained Lucky, because he carried money. Dewey displayed a newspaper clipping that quoted Lucky as saying he thought he would take a little hunting trip to the Everglades. The witness was taken aback: "I don't remember saying that at all."

Lucky answered questions about his early life. He said that he was born in America. He admitted he had sold morphine to "a dope fiend" but didn't know the street dealer who sold him the narcotics. He had a customer in mind, so he bought the morphine.

"You could tell by looking at them?"

"That is right."

"You were an expert at that time, weren't you?"

"I was no expert."

Levy objected. It was unfair to question Lucky about something that had occurred 20 years before. Justice McCook overruled him. Lucky said he had been operating craps games his entire life.

"Do you remember whether you had any pretense of an occupation?"

"Maybe I did."

"Tell us what it was, please."

"I don't remember."

Dewey persisted, trying to get information about Lucky's career, to no avail. After dozens of questions, there was finally a response.

"Well, I was bootlegging for a while ... and I pretended I had a real estate business."

"Now where did the liquor come from?"

"I was not active in the business."

And who was the supplier?

"I am trying to think of his name."

"Was it Dutch Schultz?"

"No, sir."

"Now what legitimate front did you have fixed up, so you could look as if you were in a real business if you got caught?"

"I told you that I had a real estate business."

"You haven't had a piece in any restaurant, manufacturing company, bar, grill, drug store, or anything else?"

"Yes, I did, now come to think of it ... a restaurant."

Lucky said it was at Broadway and 52nd Street but he couldn't recall his partner's name. It was open for six months.

"Why did you lie about it for ten minutes, while I asked you about that period of your life?"

"I didn't lie about it. I didn't remember it."

"The only legitimate occupation you had in 18 years you couldn't remember?"

"That's right."

"Your false answers were just because you forgot it?"

"That is right."

"Are you married?"

"No, sir."

"Now do you remember on August 28, 1922, telling Patrolman Clay that you were married?" Lucky denied making the statement. Dewey handed him several documents that detailed his lengthy arrest record. He still denied telling the policeman he was married.

"All right. Now look at the next one, June 25, 1923. Do you remember telling W.J. Mellon, Secret Service Agent, that you were a chauffeur?" Dewey had laid a steel trap. Levy recognized that Dewey was doing. He jumped to his feet: "Now if it please the Court, I object to this indirect effort to submit something before the attention of the jury on the pretext that something was said in regard to employment, back in the year 1922, as having no significance, and purely an indirect effort to get prejudicial matter before this jury."

"Overruled," said Justice McCook.

"I respectfully except," responded Levy.

Lucky admitted that he said he was a chauffeur.

"If you told him you were a chauffeur, it was a lie, wasn't it?"

"No ... I have got a chauffeur's license."

Who did he drive around, Joe Masseria?

"I know him, yes."

"You drove him around a good deal, didn't you?"

"No."

"You were a bodyguard for him, weren't you, for some time?"

"Oh, no."

"Can you now remember whether you told Patrolman Harris that you were a salesman?"

"I might have said it."

"You deny that you told Patrolman Harris, of the New York Police force, shield 9879, of the 39th Precinct, on May 25, 1924, that you were a married man?"

"I didn't say it."

"You told him that you were born in Italy?"

"No."

"So in summary, you deny that you told him you were married, you deny you told him you were born in Italy, and you don't know whether you told him you were a chauffeur or a salesman?"

"That is right."

"Now on December 9, 1924, did you tell Patrolman Hunt of the New York Police force, that you were a fruit dealer?" Levy was angry: "This is

objected to as irrelevant, immaterial, and incompetent, in no way a denial
of any of the present testimony, and an abuse of the art of cross examination." Levy asked for a mistrial.

"The motion is denied," ruled Justice McCook.

Lucky said he had no recollection of meeting Patrolman Hunt.

Then came Patrolman Carter's statement in 1925 that Lucky was a salesman. He didn't recall making that statement either. And what about Patrolman O'Connor? This officer had been told by Lucky in 1926 that he was a
salesman. Lucky was stunned and realized he looked like a fool: "I am trying
to think where this record comes from."

"Now on February 7, 1926, did you tell Mr. Lo Frisco that you were a
chauffeur?"

"Maybe I did say I was a chauffeur."

"And you were not a chauffeur then?"

"I guess not."

And what about Detective Kane, did he tell him he was a salesman? He
acknowledged he might have said that. "You were not under oath then, is that
right?"

"That is right."

"And that is the reason you did not care whether you told the truth or not?"

"I guess so."

"You do not tell anything but the truth when you are under oath?"

"I am trying to tell the truth here."

"You would not perjure yourself?"

"No."

"You would not lie for anybody?"

"No."

"You would not ever tell an untruth under any circumstances, if you were
under oath?"

"That is right."

"Now if you are under oath, you always tell the truth under every cir-
cumstance, is that it?"

"I didn't say I told the truth all the time, but now I am telling the truth."

"Under what circumstances have you lied when you have been placed
under oath?"

"Maybe if I am looking to get something."

"Have you ever lied under oath or haven't you?"

"Not under oath like this, no."

"You lied about things, didn't you?"

"Yes, trying to get a pistol permit.... I probably told them that I had an
occupation, and I didn't have it."

"And the only thing you would lie about under oath is to get a pistol permit so you could carry it around the streets of New York?"

"That is right."

Dewey asked him about being with Joe Scalise, carrying two guns, a shotgun, and 45 rounds of ammunition. Lucky said he had been shooting *peasants*, as he mispronounced the fowl. The courtroom burst into laughter.

"Shooting pheasants in the middle of July."

"That is right."

"Do you shoot pheasants with a pistol?"

"No."

Lucky said they passed the shotgun to each other and explained there was a second shotgun "up the country."

"On August 8, 1926, did you tell Mr. Witskowski that you were a chauffeur?"

"I might have said that, yes."

More arrest records were probed until finally, Lucky acknowledged, "I generally say that I am a salesman."

"That was a falsehood, wasn't it?"

"Yes."

"Were you ever a material witness in a stolen goods case?"

"No, sir."

At 4:09 P.M. there was a recess. Lucky left the stand, battered by Dewey after two hours of unrelenting questions. Lucky returned to the witness stand at 4:43. Dewey began by asking about his bootlegging partner, Joe Manfredi. "Do you know of any other crimes he committed besides being a bootlegger?"

"No, sir."

"Wasn't Manfredi convicted as being engaged in the business of receiving stolen goods?"

"Yes, I remember him being arrested for it."

"He was convicted of being a fence, wasn't he?"

"That is right."

"You have been receiving stolen goods for ten years, haven't you?"

"I have not." Lucky said his partnership with Manfredi ended after his arrest.

Dewey suddenly asked if he owned half of Ducor's Drug Store. He answered he did not. He denied calling the drug store. Dewey showed him telephone records from the Waldorf Hotel. Lucky said he was probably calling the drugstore for Georgie Burns, a friend he had known for ten years.

"What is his business?"

"I don't know."

"He has been a dope peddler for 20 years, hasn't he?"

"I don't know."

"Isn't it a fact that he dishes out the dope for you?"

"For me?"

"Yes."

Levy raised an objection but was overruled.

"I don't handle dope," answered Lucky.

"You know that is what he has been convicted for, don't you?"

"I don't know that."

Dewey asked about selling a two ounce box of narcotics to John Lyons on June 2, 1923.

"I was arrested, but I never sold anything like that." He denied drugs had been found in his apartment.

"And isn't it a fact that thereafter a whole trunk of narcotics was found by the Secret Service at 163 Mulberry Street?"

"Yes, sir."

"Were you a stool pigeon?"

"I told him what I knew."

"I want to know how you knew about that trunkful of narcotics, if you were not dealing in them and owning them."

"I knew the fellow who was dealing in them."

Who? asked Dewey.

"I don't remember."

Dewey asked if Dave Betillo worked for Al Capone. Attorney Barra asked for a mistrial.

"In all seriousness I deny it," said Justice McCook.

Dewey continued. "You mean to tell me that you were not a good friend of Al Capone?"

"No, sir."

"You knew a great many people down in Kenmare, Mott, and Mulberry Streets, didn't you?"

"Quite a few."

Lucky denied knowing the defendants. He was asked about Marjorie Brown's testimony, that she had seen Dave Betillo in his apartment at least 20 times, as well as Jimmy Fredericks.

"And you say that there is not a word of truth in that?"

"No, there ain't."

"You heard the testimony about how the defendants in this case used your name in this business?"

"I heard it, yes."

"Do you know of any reason why your name would be so useful in this business?"

"I don't know why."

Lucky denied knowing Joseph Discioscia, owner of a pastry shop at 86 Kenmare Street.

"Isn't it a fact that on April 19, at 2:40 P.M., you telephoned to that place out of the Waldorf?"

"No, sir."

He acknowledged dining at Celano's Restaurant because the owner was a friend. He denied seeing the defendants there. "I go down there maybe, last year. I have not been down there an average of about twice a month."

Dewey indicated several calls to Celano's in a month. Dewey showed him the Waldorf statement. Lucky was stunned. "I never saw those slips until now." On May 14, the records indicated that a call had been placed to Celano's at 2:44 A.M. Lucky suggested that perhaps Chappie Brescio made the calls. As Dewey provided dates and times, Lucky finally gave in. "Mr. Dewey, I made a lot of calls to Celano's, but I cannot tell you just what dates." Dewey pointed out that he left New York on October 29; an hour before doing so, he called Celano's. Dewey asked about calls to Dave's Blue Room. Lucky denied making such calls. Dewey indicated the date and time. "What business did you have with the Standard Garage?"

"I have no business at all with any Standard Garage."

"Isn't it a fact that on May 22, 1935, you telephoned the Standard Garage out of your room at 4:54 P.M.?"

"Not me, I don't remember that."

Three days later, there had been another call to the garage, located at 251 Delancey Street. "I never made it." There were other calls to the garage as well.

Levy demanded to see the slips. Flo Brown, Thelma Jordan, and Nancy Presser had testified about garage meetings. The telephone documents offered corroboration of their testimony. "Do you know a Vito?"

"Vito Genovese."

"Yes, what is his business?"

"I think he has got a paper business."

"You are pretty well acquainted with Lepke, aren't you?"

"I wouldn't say I am pretty well acquainted; I know him."

"That is Louis Buchalter, is his right name?"

"Yes."

"Doesn't he have to pay tribute to you to operate his businesses?"

Levy rose. "I object to it as irrelevant, immaterial, and incompetent, highly improper cross-examination."

"Overruled," said Justice McCook.

Lucky denied he had ever been out to the race track with Buchalter, only that he had seen him there. Lucky said he had no business deals with him.

"Why do you call him on the telephone from the Waldorf?"

"From the Waldorf, call who? I never called Lepke at his home in my life. I wouldn't know where he is."

"Isn't it a fact that on April 10, 1935, you called Lou Buchalter at 11:48 A.M." Dewey handed him the telephone slip with the private number.

"I don't remember calling that. Maybe somebody else at my home called it."

Dewey recounted Lucky's daily routine, that he seldom left the apartment before one in the afternoon. And all the telephone calls? "Chappie again, I suppose?"

Levy objected. Responded Dewey: "Will counsel stipulate that Lou Buchalter's number at 25 Central Park West is Columbus 5-4220?" Levy refused to concede anything. Lucky said the call was probably made by someone other than him.

"Although it was made before noon, in the morning?"

"That is right."

"Jacob Shapiro?"

"I know him."

"What is his business?"

"I don't know his business either."

"You do not know that he is the biggest racketeer in the clothing industry in the city?"

"Just a moment," said Levy. "That is objected to, if it pleases the court."

"Sustained," agreed Justice McCook. "Disregard the question."

"Now can't you give us any idea as to what Lepke and Gurrah's business is?"

"I don't go into their business."

"Did you think maybe they were dope peddlers?"

"I don't know."

"How about Max Silverman?"

Lucky admitted he knew Silverman pretty well, that he was a former beer runner.

"How about Bugsy Siegel?"

"I knew Bug Siegel."

"A pretty good friend of yours?"

"He is a friend of mine, yes."

He knew Siegel as a fellow resident at the Waldorf, that his business was "putting on a couple of shows."

"You do not mean to tell us that you think Bugsy Siegel is just in the show business?"

"I know Bug Siegel having, putting on a couple of shows, and he was interested in a dog track in Atlantic City.... That is as far as I know.... He used to come up to my room, and I went down to his room, yes, a couple of times."

"Is Cyril Terranova a pretty good friend of yours?"

"I don't remember knowing Cyril."

"Why did you call his house on his private unlisted number?"

"I don't know him."

He showed Lucky the telephone slip. "Somebody else made that one?" Lucky glanced at it. "Maybe so." He acknowledged seeing Lepke and Gurrah in Miami and Max Silverman in Hot Springs.

"How long have you been living under phony names when you registered in hotels?"

"That is objected to," said Levy.

"Sustained," said Justice McCook.

"Let us see, you lived at the Barbizon under the name of Lane, didn't you?"

"Yes."

"Then it was Luciano for one week, wasn't it?"

"I just don't remember how long it was for."

"And then you changed it to Charles Ross?"

"I don't think so, not at the Barbizon." Dewey showed him the records, and he conceded he was in error. How many years had he been living under a false name. "Not many," he answered. He admitted he had lived in an apartment with a girl under an assumed name. "Do you know any other bookmakers who go around and reside in hotels under false names?"

"I never go into that."

Dewey asked about his two pistol permits.

"Is that all you ever had?"

"That is all I can remember." He said the regular permit went back so far back he couldn't remember where he got it. Dewey described a permit he had gotten in 1933.

"That is another one, yes."

"Did you deliberately lie, or has that just slipped your mind?"

"It just slipped my mind."

"You just did not think I had this one, did you?"

"No, it don't make any difference to me whether it is two or three."

"Let's see what you said on that pistol permit. You said your occupation was salesman. You swore to that. And it was false?

"Yes."

"On that occasion also you denied that you had ever been convicted of a crime, didn't you?"

"Naturally, that is the only way, maybe, you can get a permit."

"You needed it badly enough to commit six kinds of perjury, didn't you?"

"I wouldn't say that."

"How many times in your life have you been taken for a ride?"

"Just once."

Dewey had studied District Attorney Fach's grand jury interrogation of Luciano in 1929; it was apparent Lucky had lied numerous times to police officers. Dewey informed the court Lucky had testified before a grand jury about his abduction, and in court, under oath, Lucky said he was a chauffeur.

"It was a lie, wasn't it?"

"They wasn't false.... I made a couple of funeral jobs."

Dewey forced him to admit he had merely lent his car to an undertaker. "And therefore you called yourself a chauffeur?"

"That is right."

He admitted that he had not paid income tax until two weeks after Governor Lehman authorized the special prosecutor, then he paid for the six previous years.

"Was that a sudden rush of conscience?"

"For what?"

"Cheating the government all those years?"

"No."

"You suddenly decided you ought to become an honest man, is that it?"

"Yes."

"You were not at all afraid of criminal prosecution?"

"I wasn't afraid of you."

"Nobody told you that the statute of limitations expired at six years?"

"I knew that, too."

Lucky admitted he kept no records, so his income was "just an idea."

"You have not paid a dime to the state government in income taxes, have you?"

"That is right."

"And that is because the Federal Government prosecutes big gangsters, and the state does not, by income tax, isn't that so?"

"I don't know."

Dewey trapped Lucky in a web of lies. The reluctance to acknowledge telephone calls to known racketeers was especially damning. George Levy tried to reestablish the credibility of the witness. Why had he used aliases? Lucky responded that he didn't want people to know where he lived, but he used his correct name in Hot Springs. Why did he lie to police he was a salesman? Because he didn't want them to know he was a gambler. When Lucky discussed the infamous abduction of 1929, he revealed he was released because he had promised to pay ten thousand dollars but "I never saw anybody again."

"Mr. Lucania," said Levy, "did you ever accept, receive, levy, or appropriate any moneys which were the earnings of prostitution of any of the women mentioned in the indictment or who testified in this case?"

"Never."

"Did you ever authorize anyone of these defendants or any other persons to use your name or to state that you were behind them in the organization of a prostitution or bonding racket or to collect, receive, accept, or levy or appropriate any of the earnings of prostitutes or any of the women set forth in this indictment or who testified in this case?"

"No, sir."

Dewey strode before Lucky. "You did not tell the grand jury about that ten thousand dollar business, did you?"

"No."

"You lied about that, didn't you?"

"Yes."

Levy had the last word, questioning his client about the damaging telephone calls to Celano's and elsewhere. "As to telephone calls, they may have been made by either you or someone else in your room; isn't that true?"

"Absolutely." At 6:42 P.M. Lucky was dismissed, a thoroughly discredited witness. The headlines said it all: "Lucky Says He's A Liar and A Stoolie" proclaimed the *Mirror*. The sensational trial was approaching an end.

Office George Heidt had claimed that the women he guarded were often intoxicated. Heidt's accusations had reached newspapers. Dewey suspected Heidt had been bought by the defense. In fact, an investigation revealed that Heidt and his wife lived in a six-room penthouse on Fifth Avenue on a $2,800-dollar-a-year salary. And how did they achieve such luxury? The lavish lifestyle was possible due to Mrs. Heidt's penny pinching, insisted the couple. Heidt recalled a conversation he overheard concerning Lucky, when Mildred Balitzer asked Margaret Venti about Lucky. "I heard her ask her, I don't know whether she was kidding or not, about how tall he was, that is all." He never heard any reply. He said Mildred had wanted to go out to a nightclub for a drink because she felt nervous. Heidt admitted Sol Gelb had bawled him out for allowing Mildred to drink too much.

Joseph Wilmer, an elevator operator at the Waldorf Towers, came next. The defense had argued that Nancy Presser could not have reached Lucky's room at the Waldorf. Wilmer refuted the assertion. He testified that there were no restrictions on the 39th floor, nor was it necessary to announce a person going to that floor.

The vast array of witnesses finally came to an end. Summation began. Caesar Barra said Dewey was motivated by a desire to be governor.

"How preposterous," objected Dewey.

Barra gave his summation: "I never would believe Mr. Dewey is so dumb as to swallow hook, line, and sinker the propositions that these procurers made to him." Lorenzo Carlino called Dewey "a boy scout" and a "David in khaki shorts, trying to slay Goliath." George Morton Levy compared Dewey to a stage producer and the witnesses to actors. He blamed Dewey's assistants for constructing a drama that Dewey accepted as true.

After 13 hours of summation by defense attorneys, Dewey spoke, saying that it was an old adage, that when a case is bad on facts and law, attack the prosecutor. Dewey leaned against a table edge and spoke in low tones. But his voice became indignant: "Smear, smear, that's all you've heard for four weeks." Dewey defended his staff of attorneys. "They are all young men of fine character, graduates of the best universities in the country. They are the kind of men you would be glad to have at the dinner table in your home." He said that George Heidt "overplayed his hand."

"Smear everyone and everything in trying to save the rotten, stinking hides of these men. Smear me, smear my office, smear every witness that got on that stand. Think of the men and women who broke the first and only commandment of the underworld — Thou shalt not squeal." He acknowledged his witnesses were society's outcasts. Then he struck a vital chord. "I wonder if any of you has ever dealt with sheer, stark terror? Have you ever been faced by complete and paralyzing terror? Have you ever had to sit down to attempt to alleviate terror? We had to."

He called Ralph Liguori a human sacrifice for his master. He sarcastically described how Ralph removed his glasses on the witness stand to examine handwriting. As for the charge that witnesses were coached, Dewey seethed: "Does anyone think I would place my professional future in the hands of professional criminals? All they were told is that we wanted to get the big shots in this business and were not interested in the small fry. We wanted to break up the professional racketeering that had been going on." Dewey reviewed the testimony and spoke for six hours. Then he made his final point: "Unless you're willing to convict the top man you might as well acquit every one."

At 7:00 P.M. Justice McCook addressed the jury. He explained the 62 counts of the indictment: "Luciano cannot escape the fate that may befall his eight less notorious co-defendants if the evidence showed the group shared a common plan for dominating and exploiting the city's network of disorderly houses. The state has put on prostitutes and madams, panderers, and persons of shady reputation as witnesses. A prostitute is at once a victim of an enticer, and her life is full of lies, but I say she is not unworthy of belief because she is a prostitute. None of those persons fails solely because of low social standards. You must give to her story the same weight you would to a reputable person. Remember, gentlemen of the jury, your recollection of the testimony is to be a true guide. I have taken copious notes, but in the last analysis it is up to you." At 8:30 P.M. Justice McCook finished his instructions. The jury departed for dinner. Reporters noted that a look of relief swept the faces of the nine defendants. The men brimmed with confidence, observed reporters. As a prank, Ralph Liguori lit a box of matches on the toe of Jimmy Fredericks' shoe. The defendants were taken to a waiting room, where they played cards or stretched on cots. Justice McCook retired to his chambers on the sixth floor. Dewey was on the floor below. The wives of the defendants waited in the corridors. Police guarded the building entrance. In nearby Foley Park hundreds milled about waiting for a verdict. Thousands of curious spectators wandered through Mulberry Park. At 10:50 P.M. the jury returned and was sequestered in the courthouse. Fifty uniformed policemen guarded the courtroom, where lawyers, reporters, and relatives waited in suspense. As the rays of dawn lit the morning sky, the bailiff roused Justice McCook. A decision had been reached. On June 8, at 5:20 A.M., the jury returned to the courtroom. Dewey took his place as the defendants and attorneys were counted. The court clerk stood: "Gentlemen of the jury, have you agreed upon a verdict?"

"We have," answered foreman Edwin Aderer.

"How say you, gentlemen of the jury, do you find the defendant Luciano guilty or not guilty on Count Number One?" There was silence as Aderer fumbled with papers in his hand. "Guilty," he boomed. The foreman announced that Lucky Luciano was found guilty on all counts, as were the other defendants. Sam Siegel appeared stunned. He put a hand on Luciano's shoulder. Lucky was led from his seat to face the court. A clerk asked for personal information: "Where do you live?" Lucky's reply was inaudible.[2] "The Waldorf-Astoria," answered the bailiff, bringing a shout of laughter from the courtroom. Justice McCook addressed the jurors: "I congratulate you on the service that you have rendered the People and upon the righteousness of your verdict," said McCook. "And now run along."

Dewey thanked the jury but left without comment. After five hours sleep at his apartment, Dewey addressed a crowd of reporters. He thanked the detectives and his legal staff for their service: "This, of course, was not a vice trial. It was a racket prosecution. The control of all organized prostitution in New York by the convicted defendants was one of the lesser rackets of the defendants. It is my understanding that certain of the top-ranking defendants in this case, together with other criminals under Luciano, have gradually absorbed control of the narcotic, loan shark, policy numbers racket, Italian lottery syndicate, and other industrial rackets."[3]

The verdict was a great victory. The witnesses would soon be released.

Dewey knew that once free, it was unlikely he could ever find them again. Dewey harbored a lingering fear that witnesses might change their testimony, so he wanted a statement under oath that their testimony had been truthful. Justice McCook wanted to speak with the witnesses himself, to make certain that no coercion had been involved to make them testify. He also wanted them to speak with social workers from religious groups, so they would not return to their sordid lives.

On June 8, McCook and a stenographer arrived at the House of Detention. Barent Ten Eyck was also present. In a fatherly, casual manner, each person was questioned under oath. The first, Anna Cohen, had not testified. But like many others, she admitted she had lied when first arrested. Cohen said no one had threatened, intimidated her, or made improper advances. She hoped to once again become a beautician.

Muriel Ryan was next and took the oath to tell the truth. If called again, she would give the same court testimony. She planned to marry a man she had known for a while. "As for you telling him what you have done, that is up to you," offered McCook.[4] "Sometimes those things are good to tell, and sometimes they are not.... Some men are natural darned fools, and others have got sense, and some take a thing like that harder than others. Some are broad minded. So you will just have to do what you think is best. Good-bye, good luck. And after that, come in and tell me whether there is anything more I can do for you, and we will shake hands again." Muriel agreed to return.

Flo Brown was next. "May I congratulate you on looking so much better than you did in court?"

"Thank you."

"And I congratulate you on the way that you seemed to be able to stand the strain of the court. I heard you testify. Did you tell the truth?"

"Yes," answered Flo.

"And you have no criticism of the District Attorney's office either?"

"None at all."

After Ruth Marcus took the oath she begged for leniency for her husband. "He lied on the stand," responded McCook. "However, I will give him consideration to the fact that he helped the State."

Jean Bradley was enthused by the kindness of Mrs. McCarthy of Catholic Charities. Bradley called her "a very lovely woman." McCook told Bradley he was a member of the Friendly Sons of St. Patrick, "and I hate to see anybody with Irish blood in them in the situation you are."

McCook suspected Jean Attardi had not spoken the entire truth in her grand jury testimony. Attardi was 28, an educated woman who had become a prostitute. She was the common law wife of Andy LeCocco. They had lived together four years and had children. She strongly denied Andy ever booked women. McCook was skeptical: "What did you think he was doing, running a church?"

"He used to gamble, play horses," she answered defensively, but "I lived with him and I know he never did." Andy was just a driver for Jack Ellenstein, she insisted. Jean was a Catholic and wanted to get back to her religion but found it hard after neglecting it for so long. "The Catholic Church doesn't make it easy," said McCook," but you have got to behave." McCook asked for Father Hickey to join them. The priest listened, then said: "I would like you to marry this man, if you love him so much."

"I do," said Jean.

Jean had declined to marry Andy until he returned to his former job as a truck driver. Father Hickey was enthusiastic and eager for a wedding. But McCook was bothered by Andy's past. "He was once held for murder." Barent Ten Eyck added that Andy had a number of arrests. Jean responded that Andy was good natured but easily led astray.

Later, Justice McCook spoke with Andy LeCocco. McCook probed his criminal past. Andy admitted he had been a thief, operated speakeasies and, due to parole violation, had served time in Sing Sing. Andy explained the murder charge. When he and his friend Benny Benito had stopped at a cigar store, an unknown gunman shot Benny. Andy drove the victim to a hospital, but he died.

"To look at you, you are the kind of fellow that I would trust. I want to talk to you as man to man because I think you have a pretty good girl there."

"She is a swell kid," said Andy.

"And it would be awful if you were to break her heart again."

"She suffered enough with me."

Like the other women, Peggy Wild said she had been treated well. Her roommates, Nancy Presser and Thelma Jordan, were heavy drinkers, she related.

"Is Nancy's story true?" asked Justice McCook.

"I never knew the girl before, your Honor. I spoke to Mildred one day, and she told me she knew Luciano from Florida. She asked me if I knew him. No, I only knew him as a customer." Wild was a grandmother. Her oldest daughter knew her profession. Her career as a madam was over. She had received communion from Father Hickey and would return to St. Ann's Church in the Bronx.

Katherine Warren was going to live with her aunt.

"Are you going to tell her the truth?" asked McCook.

"I suppose I will have to tell her the truth, where I was all these months."

McCook agreed. "Unless you are frank with people, sooner or later they find out."

"They find out," echoed Warren.

Justice McCook listened to Malcolm Bailey. While in the Navy he had worked in a tuberculosis lab; the exposure damaged his lung. After he was honorably discharged, he became a Pennsylvania state trooper. However, when his medical records arrived, Bailey was dismissed. He confessed his guilt: "I thought I was a wiseguy by knowing some shady characters." He had suffered a lung hemorrhage and had applied to enter a sanitarium. Bailey was from a respectable family in Maryland: "I have got a family name that runs quite aways back. That is the only thing that hurts me out of this whole thing. My Dad didn't write to me for about a month." Bailey spoke favorably of Pete Balitzer because Pete supported relatives in Philadelphia. Bailey agreed to see an Episcopal clergyman. McCook asked Bailey to write to him: "The minute I saw you I knew there was hope for you."

Eddie Balitzer was returning to Philadelphia. He would continue as an electrician. Eddie said he was Jewish. "My secretary is a Jewish man," said McCook, "he will talk with you."

Red Healey, a bond collector, had shared a cell with Abie Wahrman. Abie said that Pete owed him $2,000 as "shylock money." Healey wanted to return to his former job at a power station in Brooklyn. He was back in the Catholic faith. McCook was encouraged. "I have got Protestants here too, and we have got Jews, but every fellow had better follow his own religion."

"That's right," said Red.

Daniel Guidry was questioned about Mildred Curtis. He admitted he had introduced her to Tommy Bull. "It is one of those things that happens among our element."

After Phil Ryan took the oath, McCook came to the point: "Mr. Ryan, I heard a good deal of testimony about you in the case. I am going to ask you an embarrassing question. I am sorry, I can't help it. Is it true that you are a homosexual?"

"Well, that is a question I prefer not to answer. If I say yes, it is not believed, and I place myself in an embarrassing position. If I say no, it is not believed."

"I am not going to press you any further then." Ryan insisted he was a cabaret host and manager. The shows he produced were decent and under constant inspection. He was proud of being a graduate of Holy Cross. McCook was satisfied. "I am assuming that you have the education and tastes of a gentleman, and I don't want to go beyond that."

"Thank you."

On June 17, Nancy Presser met with McCook. She said Ralph Liguori had initially told her not to talk, but Harold Cole said if she didn't tell the truth, she would "go away for six months." Nancy said she had told the truth before the grand jury and in court.

"Did anybody treat you badly, any of the district attorneys or any of the cops?"

"No, they didn't. They were very nice."

Nancy had attended Catholic services while in the House of Detention. She agreed to talk to Father Hickey. She told Justice McCook that she was afraid. "Is there any hope for Lucky?"

"No," she responded.

"How about Ralph? Is there any good in him?"

"No, there isn't."

"What do you think is the trouble with him? I have been trying to get him through my head. He puzzles me."

"He is just no good; that is all."

"You consider him a dangerous person?"

"I certainly do." Nancy said that Ralph had put a gun to her head. She showed McCook the scars on her arm. McCook read a letter from a priest. Nancy identified the priest as a friend of the Liguori family. She said Al Marinelli had fixed Ralph's extortion case. Ralph had told her that Little Davie was a killer.

"Did you ever see Liguori in the company of Charley Lucky?"

"Yes, I did. Ralph knows Charley very well."

And Tommy?

"Any man that will sell dope to people the way he did, and give them such terrible stuff on top of it, is no good."

Thelma Jordan followed Nancy.

"I remember you very well," said McCook. "Did Schilback say you would get time if you did not tell the truth?"

"No."

"What made you tell the truth?"

"So many people knew who I was and everything, and I didn't want to perjure myself." Thelma admitted drinking at dinner. She said police officer George Heidt had been paid off by the combination "for a long time." Both Jimmy Fredericks and Benny Spiller had told her the facts. Was there any hope of reforming them?

"That is really hard to say, but I know Benny has been, well, a pimp ever since he was old enough to know what it was all about."

"Is he dangerous?"

"Well, I couldn't say that. You know he is very brave among women. I know that he has beat up a few people. The combination used to grab somebody, take them in the cellar or some place, and beat them up." Little Davie was called "a trigger man." Davie had become a gunman for Lucky, said Thelma.

"Where did this story come from that somebody told me, that he is supposed to have buried a man alive in the New Jersey marshes?"

"That was over in Jersey, yes."

"You can explain it?"

"It is merely some fellow that they took out and tortured, and he was in on that, and they did a lot of things to him."

"Did they kill him?"

"Well, they buried him alive. He died, naturally. They cut his legs, your Honor, and another portion of his anatomy while he was alive, and then buried him."

"Wasn't that rather rough treatment for just doing what he did?"

"It would be for anybody else, but I mean, the combination thinks nothing of that."

Was there any hope for Ralph Liguori?

"Never."

"Has he any brains at all?"

"If he does, I don't know where he keeps them."

Thelma was frightened. She revealed what Mary Morris had told her. The day after the trial ended she had telephoned Mary. The women had shared an apartment at 214 West 96th Street. Thelma was trying to locate her clothes and personal belongings. Mary was angry Thelma had testified. Morris and her boyfriend, Johnny Roberts, hid in Schenectady after the raids, but Lucky's legal team brought them to New York City. Morris had agreed to testify for the defense, providing they would not harm her friend, Thelma Jordan. But the defendants were furious over Thelma's testimony. Willie Spiller was going to kidnap her, said Mary.

"They were going to snatch me and take me out and torture me and kill me because I testified to that torture on the stand," she told Justice McCook. "She told me that Lucky was positively after Nancy.... I had better get out of town as quick as I could and to be very careful because Willie wanted to snatch me, and he wouldn't stop until he did." Thelma was thankful for police protection.

Mildred Balitzer told McCook she would not change her court testimony.

Was there any hope for the defendants?

"My husband."

"You know Davie Betillo very well, don't you?"

"Yes, very well."

Mildred said she had smoked opium with him, that he was dangerous and deserved no consideration in sentencing. Mildred had overheard conversations between Davie and Tommy Bull. She was aware that Davie had "knocked off" people, to use their expression. She admitted buying drugs from Tommy.

"Have you ever heard it said that Tommy Bull controls the wholesale drug market in New York City?"

"No, I understood Lucky controlled it, and that Tommy took care of it for him."

Helen Nemeth, who testified under the name Horvath, said under oath she had never told anything but the truth in all proceedings. Gypsy Tom had placed her in two houses of prostitution against her will.

"Were they run on a basis of ordinary practices or abnormal practices?"

"Normal and abnormal."

"Did the girls mind? Did you mind, for example?"

"Oh, I minded it at first, but you eventually get used to it." Helen was trying to get back to the church and had performed her Easter duties.

Mildred Curtis, the youngest witness came forward. She had not been called to court, since she was sick. McCook observed that she appeared ill. "Pull up a chair over here, will you, please? How are you feeling?"

"I feel all right."

Mildred stood and was sworn in. She confirmed she had told the truth before the grand jury. She recounted how she had initially balked at going before the grand jury, then Harold Cole had threatened her with "a cold turkey."

"What did he mean?"

"They wouldn't give me any drugs; they would just make me suffer it out."

Ten Eyck offered to leave the room.

McCook agreed and Ten Eyck walked out. "Now tell me, what is on your mind?"

"Nothing."

"You needn't be afraid. I am here to help you." It was obvious Curtis wanted to discuss something.

"What is it?"

"The way they treat the drug addicts up there." Curtis complained about the five-day reduction treatment. "When these pains come up there, you have got to yell, and the matron comes at night. You can't help from screaming, the way you get those pains, and the matron comes at night and tells you to keep quiet. You ask her to do something for you. She says, 'Oh, I can't do anything for you. Leave me alone.'"

"You know, there are some people think that that is the only way to do, to suffer it out, but I don't know if that is necessary or not."

"No, that is not."

Mildred said the first thing addicts would seek on release is drugs. If the cure were administered properly, maybe more girls would stay off. She had been an addict for three years.

"Are you getting over it now?"

"I started the cure Saturday."

"Are you beginning to feel a little better?"

"No."

"Not yet?"

"The worst is yet to come."

"Well, I hope the Lord will see you through it."

Mildred said she was a Catholic, but she had not seen the priest. "They don't let you go to church here, not if you are a drug addict." She reluctantly agreed to see Father Hickey.

"When am I going to get out of here?"

"I am going to do it just as soon as I can. I am the one that has the power to do it, but I don't want to do it until it is for your best physical welfare to get out."

"Do you mean if I don't want to take the cure, they are going to make me take it, after they gave me immunity, on drugs?"

"My dear girl, I think that is the only fair thing, so that you complete your cure, before they turn you loose, don't you?"

"They told me down in Mr. Dewey's office that I didn't have to take a cure if I went to the grand jury and got immunity on it. Now isn't that fair?"

"I will talk to Mr. Dewey about it."

"If they do give me the cure, I am going to every paper in New York City and tell them how they promised me, because when I am treated nice, I can be nice, too."

"Do you think that the papers would consider that it was so terrible to keep a girl and try to cure her of a bad habit?"

"I don't care what they think."

Justice McCook said there were social workers who could get her a job.

"I don't want no job."

"I am not here to make trouble for you, Miss Mildred, I am here to help you."

"The only thing, I will stay off it when I am on a cure myself and I really want it."

Mildred told him that another addict, on drugs for 18 years, had encouraged her to take the cure, but now she regretted the decision. Mildred's mother was sick. When she returned to Akron, Ohio, for a visit, she wanted to be drug free. On her last trip she managed to hide her addiction. Mildred had celebrated her 21st birthday in jail. McCook offered sympathy. His family was from Ohio, too. "I am awfully interested in anybody from Ohio. How did you get into this way of life?"

"Oh, it is a very long story."

"You are pretty, that is one thing. That is one way you got into it, I know."

"No, it isn't that. It was because I needed money and I didn't want to go home, and because my dad is too mean, and once I ran away from home and I would come back, well, he would probably kill me,' so I stayed here a year, and then I went home."

"Do you have any schooling?"

"No, not much."

"When was it that you began to live with Tommy Bull? Is he a nice fellow to live with?"

"Yes, he was very nice to me."

"I have got to sentence him next week. Anything nice you can tell me about him?"

"He didn't put me in any house and make me work. If he found out that I went out with another man, he almost killed me for it."

"And you liked that, did you?"

"No, I didn't like to be killed, but I liked the way he treated me, and he didn't put me in any house of prostitution to work. He gave me all the money, and everything I wanted I got, just so I wouldn't go out."

"Do you know that he put other girls into houses of prostitution? Don't you know that?"

"He didn't."

"He did not?"

"No, he was in with a bunch, but he didn't put them; it was bookers that put the girls in."

Justice McCook said defendants like Jimmy Fredericks actually booked women. Mildred refused to see the social workers. "All right, you run along. I am not going to grill you. I want to help you, you know; that is what I'm here for. I was working awfully hard on that trial. I am very tired, but I have been up for two days, just to give you girls a break if I could. But you are an awful obstinate girl, Mildred, aren't you?"

"I don't know."

"I would awfully well like to see you cured. You don't think the game is worth the candle? Well, never mind, my child."

"When do I go home then?"

"I will have to think it over and talk to Mr. Dewey about it."

He escorted her outside. On his return, McCook addressed the stenographer. "She has just told me outside, 'Oh, your Honor, I forgot to tell you. Please be easy on Tommy. He was very good to me.' And then I said to her,

'Well, was Lucky so nice?' And she said, 'No, what do you mean?' And I said, 'Would he let Tommy go? Would he hold Tommy in it?' She said, 'Why, Tommy never had a chance with anybody else. If they didn't keep in, they would be shot.' I said, 'How?' She said, 'By Lucky's orders.'"

The women about to be released had plans also. Most were returning to their family homes. Nancy Brooks, Rose Cohen, Jean Matthews, Marie Williams, Shirley Mason, Bonnie Connolly, and Helen Thomas were all going back to Pennsylvania. Jean Bradley would open a small tea shop in Pittsburgh, and Eleanor Jackson would help her. Betty Anderson was also going to Pittsburgh. Marilyn Summers was returning to her parents in Florida. Edna Russell was returning to New Jersey to continue Catholic religious instructions. Katherine O'Connor was going back to Chicago, where Catholic Charities would help her. Margaret Martino would live with her parents in Brooklyn. Helen Hayes was returning to her parents in Massachusetts, as was Helen Walsh. Jean Demare was a mental case. Mary Thomas would live with her two children in New Jersey. Mary Dubin would reside with her sister in Brooklyn. Helen Williams would also return to Brooklyn, living with her parents, pursuing a career in secretarial work. Betty Baker would live with her parents in upstate New York, as Louise Dawson planned to do. Mary Leonard was going to Washington to live with her husband. Anna Cohen had been helped by Jewish Charities and had a salon in mind. Sally Osborne also planned be a hair stylist. Lou Kane promised to return to Detroit, to the home of her parents, for a reunion with her husband and son. Renee Gallo was going to Philadelphia to be a seamstress. Grace Hall would stay in New York. Molly Leonard would return to Brooklyn and live with her young son. Ruth Davis was going to New Jersey. Nancy Richter was returning to her parents in New Jersey, as was Fay Brooks. Helen Kessler would live with her husband and children. Jennie Benjamin planned to open a restaurant. Carol Lewis was going to California. Betty Connors was leaving for Ohio. Betty Winters planned to open a millinery shop. Florence Stern hoped to open a small beauty salon in New York. Jean Irwin was going to Philadelphia to live with Pete Balitzer's sister. Ann Moore would work in her father's stores in Philadelphia. Jeanette Lewis, also known as Margaret Bell, said she would marry Jojo Weintraub, after she divorced her imprisoned husband. The couple planned to move to Washington, to live with her brother. Jeanette would enroll in secretarial school. Jeanette promised to talk to Father Hickey about marriage to a person of a different religion. Muriel Ryan wanted to marry her longtime sweetheart. Lillian Gordon would marry a government contractor. Jean Attardi would marry Andy LeCocco and become a seamstress. Dorothy Arnold and her husband were returning to Virginia. Frances Blackman, Jane Williams, Jean Fox, Flo Brown, and Mildred Balitzer had no plans.

Nancy Presser and Thelma Jordan hoped to avoid being murdered. The cooperative witnesses would receive payment of three dollars per day. Those who didn't cooperate would receive nothing. The witnesses were to be released but not the convicted.

Lucky came to court surrounded by detectives. Policemen packed the courtroom, the halls and corridors, as well as the streets outside. Lucky dressed in a bluish gray suit, white shirt, and black tie. Justice McCook read from a prepared statement. "The crimes of which you stand convicted are those of placing females in houses of prostitution, receiving money for such placing, and knowingly accepting money for their earnings without consideration. An intelligent, courageous, and discriminating jury has found you guilty of heading a conspiracy or combination to commit these crimes." Not once did Lucky raise his eyes. Before sentencing Judge McCook asked if he wanted to make a statement.

"Your Honor, I have nothing to say outside the fact that I am innocent." Lucky was sentenced from 30 to 50 years. An officer took him by the arm and led from the courtroom.

Tommy Pennochio stood, dressed in a blue suit with a red necktie. He admitted his past record. He received 25 years as a third offender.

Dave Betillo's name was called. He wore a light green suit and a look of indifference. "As Luciano's chief and most ruthless aide, you deserve no consideration from this court. You are an unprincipled and aggressive egotist. There are four years unaccounted for in your report to the probation officer. These years correspond roughly with your time in Chicago." He would serve 24 to 40 years. Jimmy Fredericks, chewing gum, was next. He was described by the judge as "an incorrigible criminal, and a low and brutal character." Like Tommy, he got 25 years as a third offender.

Abie Wahrman was only 22, with no record, and was the support of his family, pleaded Davis Siegel. The attorney asked leniency for his client. But Justice McCook sentenced him to serve 15 to 20 years.

Ralph Liguori was sentenced to serve 7 to 15 years.

Benny Spiller, Jesse Jacobs, and Meyer Berkman would be sentenced at a later date, after Dewey sought their cooperation in prosecuting other cases.

The bookers came next. Jack Ellenstein got four to eight years. Pete Balitzer and Al Weiner received light sentences, two to four years. Dave Marcus had been caught in perjurious testimony, so it affected his sentence: three to six years.

A storm brought rain. Lucky was chained to Jimmy Federico, and they were led to a police van. The six combination members were driven to the Tombs Prison for processing.

"Sing Sing is just an hour up the river," Dewey smiled to reporters. Mayor

La Guardia led a ceremony at city hall honoring 16 police officers who had worked with Dewey in the prosecution. The officers received raises and commendations. The Mayor praised Dewey, who was present, and described Lucky as "a super pimp."[5] Dewey paid tribute to Detective Brennan of the Bronx. Brennan had kept Lucky under surveillance in Hot Springs and made the arrest.

Over a thousand spectators gathered at Grand Central Station. The gray prison van arrived. At 4:15 P.M. the prisoners boarded a train for Ossining, guarded by ten deputy sheriffs, five detectives, and three railroad policemen. Just before six in the evening a caravan of taxi cabs arrived at Sing Sing Prison. Lucky emptied his pockets of $199.40 and was handed a gray prison uniform. He gave the Waldorf as his address. Prison officials locked the seven men in solitary confinement. Lucky was soon transferred to Clinton Prison in Dannemora, located in the northern Adirondacks. The prison was isolated and nicknamed "Siberia." Also sent to Dannemora were Dave Betillo and Ralph Liguori. Tommy Pennochio and Jack Ellenstein went to Attica. Jimmy Frederico and Abie Wahrman were sent to the penitentiary in Auburn.

Thomas E. Dewey was praised throughout the country. Warner Bros. approached him about a motion picture based on the trial, but Dewey adamantly opposed a film dramatization. Trials were not public entertainment. Dewey reluctantly agreed to studio interviews with witnesses, since a film company could offer honest employment in the presentation of factual material. However, Dewey rejected repeated requests by studios to feature him as the hero. He disliked the sensationalism of "gangster movies."

Dewey believed Flo Brown and Mildred Balitzer were the most intelligent women in the witness group; each had intimate knowledge of the criminal underworld. He met with Flo and Mildred. They expressed a desire to make a decent living. Their sincerity impressed Dewey.

Edward Doherty of *Liberty Magazine* came to Dewey's office. The magazine had a working relationship with Warner Bros. and wanted a story by the key witnesses. The story would be a first step toward a film based on the experiences of Flo and Mildred. Dewey asked Barent Ten Eyck to handle the matter. Dewey later spoke with Fulton Oursler, editor of *Liberty,* and established strict guidelines. Dewey also met with Anthony "Binge" Curcio and Michael Redmond. Both were from respectable families. They assured him they were going straight. Dewey arranged for both to obtain work.

New Yorkers admired Dewey's prosecution of the Luciano gang. However, not everyone was impressed. Magistrate Anna Kross said the trial "proved nothing and got nowhere."[6] She denounced the financial cost and damned the trial as politically inspired. The money could have gone to hospitals or programs for the prostitutes. Kross blamed the Women's Court for permitting crooked bondsmen to exploit women. She ridiculed the statement of Police Commissioner Lewis Valentine that prostitution had been abolished in New York. "It cannot ever be abolished in a society like ours," said the magistrate. The director of the Women's City Club agreed with Judge Kross. Although prostitution was a social ill, it should be removed from the criminal code. Only public health was a major concern.

After the trial, Dewey announced that he would seek the disbarment of two unnamed attorneys. An assistant had been offered a Supreme Court judgeship as a bribe, just weeks after Lucky's arrest. The offer included $250,000, promised as a guarantee that the pledge would be fulfilled. During the trial, Charles Berner had been bribed with money and a position in a gambling house in the Adirondacks, said Dewey. The witness was in jail, but the money was paid "through a relative," reported newspapers.[7] During the trial, on the morning he was to testify, Berner balked. Two months earlier, he had gone before the grand jury, under the name of Sam Warner, and explained the takeover by Lucky's mob. On June 24, he gave a formal statement to Sol Gelb and Jacob Rosenblum. Berner had been held as a material witness, questioned by investigators, and was considered a key figure in explaining how the pimp-mob combination developed. Rosenblum asked Berner about the critical meeting: "You testified, also, at the grand jury, that at that meeting Charley Lucky came in and decided that Little Davie was to have the business instead of your group; you remember that you so testified?"

"Yes," acknowledged Berner.

"That was untrue?"

"That is not true."

"That was a story which you made up because you thought it would be of help to you?"

"Not only that, I done it for the simple reason that I was—was more of revenge in my own way, of trying to get back at them."

"Do you recall that you told me a day or two ago that you were sorry that you made up that story?"

"Right."

Berner acknowledged the truth of the bonding formation, and that he had heard Little Davie and Jerry Bruno were "with Lucky." Sol Gelb asked: "Did any one of us tell you what to say when you went before the grand jury?"

"No, nobody told me nothing."

"Your wife, Lillian Berner," said Rosenblum, "told me that she went to a lawyer's office on Fifth Avenue, at the request of some man by the name of Fisher, she made the statement to the effect that you told her, your wife, that Mr. Dewey had promised you $2,500 and to send you on a trip to California?"

"I did not tell her nothing, since the time I am in jail I didn't tell her nothing."

"Aside from whether you told that to her, did Mr. Dewey tell you that?" asked Sol Gelb.

"Nobody told me anything like that; that was drummed up from the other side in order to make her sign." Berner's final words were revealing. Dewey and his staff were certain Berner's account was accurate. Danny Caputo and Binge Curcio had heard Jimmy Fredericks discuss it. However, believed Dewey, Berner had been bribed to exclude Luciano from the takeover.

The cheering had barely died when the police raided a "swanky vice den" in the fashionable Central Park West neighborhood.[8] An undercover detective made his third visit to the Danish American Health Institute. A woman asked him to remove his clothes; instead, he blew a police whistle. On the second floor, a detective entered a room, to find a man with a whip beating a pretty blonde. She was a resident of the Institute. The man said he was a student of art and music. The female director was arrested for operating a house of prostitution.

Though the witnesses were released to pursue their destinies, some still made news. Margaret Bell made news in July in Washington, D.C. A month earlier, Bell had told Justice McCook she was planning to marry Jojo Weintraub; now she claimed she had been attacked and left to die. Dewey received a letter from a man who had lived with Margaret Bell. It was established that she was mentally unbalanced and subject to delusions, just as Dewey's staff had suspected. The police investigated and the story about an attack was found to be "absolutely groundless."[9]

Vice stories still made news. Witnesses testified Mae Scheible had kept girls virtual prisoners in the luxury apartment on Park Avenue where they were forced to entertain wealthy customers. She had been released on $10,000 bail but fled. The brutal madam was arrested in Stockton, California. Scheible was sentenced to four years in prison.

After Lucky's trial, Gay Orlova's life disintegrated. Her former husband telephoned reporters to blast his ex-wife. While dancing in *Murder at the Vanities* at the Majestic Theatre she had married an usher in 1934. Orlova had entered America on a Turkish passport and needed help to remain in America. The new husband overheard Gay tell a dancer in the show: "I just married him so I could go to Europe and get back in the country without argument."[10] Due to Lucky and her "passport husband" the notoriety was such that Orlova dyed her hair dark and changed her name to Dolores Delmar. She sailed on the *Rex* to Cannes with a troupe of chorus girls.

While Lucky was imprisoned, his childhood friend, Dominic Didato, was shot to death in front of a restaurant at 30 Elizabeth Street. They were the same age and from the same neighborhood. Didato had been a book-maker. Police said he had failed to pay a gambling debt. Over the next decades, several of Lucky's friends would meet a similar fate.

In August, James Noonan of Albany filed a writ of habeas corpus that challenged the constitutionality of the Joinder Law. Noonan had represented Dutch Schultz in the first tax evasion trial and won. Lucky's defense team sought a way to win his release. Lucky was escorted from Clinton Prison to file an appeal in Plattsburgh. State troopers were in the room; all visitors were searched. On the surrounding rooftops officials were posted with machine-guns. If the court eventually decided in Lucky's favor, Dewey was prepared to file additional criminal charges for compulsory prostitution and tax evasion.

Lucky Luciano, the sultan of vice, was now Prisoner No. 92168.

CHAPTER TWELVE

Betrayal

I am worried to death

Nancy and Thelma were terrified; both believed they were marked for death. Lucky's mob could find them anywhere in America, they told Harold Cole. Only in Europe would they be safe. Cole discussed the situation with Dewey. The women believed they were in immediate danger, so funds were obtained from private sources to send them abroad. Dewey's office obtained passports and booked passage for England. Before departure, they were each given two hundred dollars in cash, for which they signed a receipt. They boarded the *Samaria* for Liverpool. In London they stayed at the Sands Crescent Hotel in Knightsbridge. Later, they moved to the Regents Palace Hotel in Piccadilly.

Once Nancy and Thelma were in hiding, Dewey assisted other witnesses. He authorized Barent Ten Eyck to recommend to the Court of Special Sessions that Flo Brown receive a suspended sentence. She pleaded guilty to all charges and was released from jail. Ten Eyck told Dewey that Flo Brown and Mildred Balitzer should live away from New York, where they could start a new life. The pair moved to a small apartment in New Rochelle, in Westchester County. On July 17, Mildred walked into the prosecutor's office, overwrought and frightened. Jacob Rosenblum listened to her story. When she left the Paramount Theatre in Times Square, Bartolo Lucania suddenly appeared. Lucky's brother asked to speak with her. Too afraid to flee, she accompanied him inside a bar. Bartolo asked her to deny the truth of her trial testimony. She would be taken care of, he assured her. As she told Rosenblum, "I got up, jumped into a taxi, and I must have run around half New York looking behind me."[1] On the witness stand Mildred had testified that Gus Franco had threatened her. Now she was being coerced to change her story.

Moses Polakoff was determined to win an appeal. After the trial Jojo Weintraub found himself without money. Jojo went to Polakoff's office. Jojo became a shadowy intermediary for Lucky's defense team. Jojo approached prosecution witnesses and asked them to recant their testimony.

In late July, Flo wrote a letter to Barent Ten Eyck. Mildred had been hinting of an affair with Sol Gelb, but Flo knew the truth: "I'm pretty sure that Mildred was full of baloney. She is not as intimate with Mr. Gelb as she was pretending to be. She sure has no conscience. She is having an affair with Bill Grant, the cop that went home with her, when she went to West Virginia for the Fourth of July. I'm not sure why she wanted to give me the impression it was Gelb, unless she figured it would be a cover-up for her affair with Grant."

Nancy Presser's passport photograph, April 1937. Nancy's clients included Waxey Gordon and Lucky. After the trial, Nancy and Thelma Jordan fled to England, fearful they would be murdered (courtesy NYC Municipal Archives).

The magazine project with McFadden Publications was underway. Edward Doherty worked with Mildred and Flo for a series of stories about their lives and the trial. Once completed, the women would receive $500 each. Dewey's office had final approval of all stories. Dewey did not want the trial sensationalized. Although the trial's aftermath still generated news articles, Dewey kept the press away from his office, and staff members were forbidden to give interviews.

Mildred was enthused by the writing project. She came up with a title and opening line: "What It Feels Like To Testify Against A Big Shot Gangster: "I have violated the underworld code — thou shalt not squeal." Flo wrote about her trial testimony: "When I took the stand I felt it wasn't me at all. It seemed to me that I was someone else. I was in a daze. I was numb. I couldn't feel.... I answered mechanically whatever was asked me. It was a good thing I had told the truth, for if I had been lying, as they were trying to say I was, they would have trapped me, caught me, hundreds of times."

The women were excited when film studios expressed interest in their project. Flo wrote to Barent Ten Eyck that Doherty was bringing a representative of Warner Bros. to their home that very evening, but she added an ominous comment: "I had a little talk with Mr. Hogan this afternoon. He told me there was a rumor around that Mil and I were back on 'stuff' again. He didn't tell me who told him that. I didn't say much to Mr. Hogan, except to deny it. Somebody must be jealous of me, just because I'm getting along O.K. It must hurt them to see me doing well and looking good.... I'm sure you have faith in me and would never believe such rumors."

The women worked with Doherty during the summer. After the stories were finished, they moved to the Park Crescent Hotel, where they lived under the names of Gloria Moore and Norma Gordon. By early fall, Nancy and Thelma wanted to return home, though still afraid. For weeks, Dewey's office had wired money to support them. Cole sent them $100 for return tickets. On September 29, they docked in New York and being "dead broke," they took a taxi to the Woolworth Building. Nancy ascended in the elevator to the 14th floor, while Thelma waited in the cab. Cole reached into his own pocket and gave them ten dollars for taxi fare and a hotel room. Each day they went to Harold Cole for a handout. They assured him they were searching for legitimate work but were unsuccessful. In early September, Jojo Weintraub visited Sing Sing Prison. Jojo asked to see Pete Balitzer, but prison authorities denied permission. A month later, Mildred visited her husband to say goodbye. Flo and Mildred told most friends they were going to New Orleans, but this was simply a ruse, since they planned a trip to the West Coast. Word of Jojo's visits spread. Thelma and Nancy observed gang members loitering near their hotel and feared abduction. Dewey and his staff believed witness intimidation was underway.

Nancy, Thelma, and Harold Cole sat with Justice McCook in his private chambers. McCook questioned them under oath, with a stenographer present. "Your Honor," said Harold Cole, "there is a serious problem confronting all these former witnesses in the Luciano case. We are getting daily rumors in the office that various members of that particular group of defendants and their agents are endeavoring to contact many of the witnesses and through fear and intimidation, violence in some cases, bribes in others, they are attempting to get some of the witnesses to recant their former testimony." Thelma and Nancy were terrified.

"Miss Jordan, has there been any attempt to reach you in any such way or to threaten you or anything of that kind?"

"Yes," Thelma told McCook.[2]

"Since you got back from Europe?"

"Yes."

"How about you?"

"The same," said Nancy. "We were both together at the time the thing happened. There was no bribe."

"Miss Presser. Have you anything to change in your testimony at all that you gave on the trial?"

"None."

"You still insist that each and every word you said was the truth, in substance?"

"Yes."

They were anxious to "go straight." McCook suggested that Harold Cole contact The Church Mission of Help. Dewey personally telephoned and arranged an appointment. The following day, a case supervisor met with Thelma and Nancy. They told her they had seen gang members near their hotel; both believed they would be kidnapped, tortured, and murdered. If they were abducted, they stated, they would recant their trial testimony. They were sent to Kingston, New York, then to Cincinnati, but after ten days both returned. They decided they would be in jeopardy wherever they went. Police could give them protection.

On October 9, the *Daily News* headlined a story that "100 Grand At Work To Free Lucky." Narcotics were being used to entice witnesses to recant, revealed an unidentified informant. Important witnesses were again using drugs, reported the article: "For a month or two after the Luciano trial they left dope alone. At present they are receiving liberal supplies of dope from their *friends* and shortly will *sign anything* if necessary, to get fresh rations of narcotics." There was no mistaking who was being discussed.

Barent Ten Eyck met with Flo. She agreed to provide a sworn statement: "I have been asked to make this affidavit in view of material appearing in said story which might be construed as an accusation that I have been provided with narcotics from friends of the defendants in order to induce or compel me to sign a false affidavit of recantation of my testimony. I hereby make this affidavit of my own free will with no inducements, promises or hope of reward. The testimony given by me at the trial for compulsory prostitution of Charles Luciano and the co-defendants tried with him at the Extraordinary Trial Term was wholly true and correct. My testimony was induced by no promises or threats and was voluntarily given."

A week later Jojo made contact with Pete. He used the name "Simon Balitzer" as a cover. Pete soon wrote a letter to Moses Polakoff. Pete claimed the prosecution had tried to bribe him with money to lie.

At the end of October, Flo and Mildred were paid by McFadden Publications. Flo was eager to leave New York. She wanted to open a small shop on the West Coast. The moment had come to flee New York. Flo bought an automobile for $385. She and Mildred packed their suitcases and left town, accompanied by Fifi, Flo's cat. Soon after, Barent Ten Eyck received a letter from Hot Springs. In a neat, even hand Flo wrote: "I am sorry we didn't get a chance to say goodbye, but we sneaked out of N.Y. like thieves in the night. We've been on the road ever since. Hot Springs is on our route, so we figured we would stop over for a day or two and look over the place that put up such a good battle for our friend Charlie, this was the place, that was the beginning of the end for him. Ha! Ha! on him, eh?"

They sent a photograph taken at Happy Hollow, an amusement park. They grinned and pretended to swig moonshine liquor in a fake saloon. In Arizona, they stopped along the road and dug up a cactus plant, which Mildred sent to her mother. On November 24 Ten Eyck received a telegram:

WE ARE PLANNING TO LEASE A GAS STATION. THEY MAY ASK FOR A REFERENCE. HAVE GIVEN YOU AS MY LAWYER AND MANAGER OF MY MONEY. TOLD THEM WE ARE WRITERS

By the time they arrived in Los Angeles anxiety was growing. Mildred was broke. They found a room at the Stowell Hotel. A letter arrived, addressed to "Miss Gloria Moore." The news was disappointing. Warner Bros. had rejected the film deal. But Ten Eyck tried to keep their spirits up. Flo's maid was trying to locate her. The maid wanted to return Flo's fur coat.

The women leased a gasoline station at 985 E. Holt in Pomona. The new venture was financed by Flo's dwindling funds. On December 17, Flo wrote Ten Eyck an enthusiastic letter about the gasoline station. Nearby was a building shaped like a hen, so "we call ours The Rooster. See? Cute? I put my last nickel into the place.... I wouldn't give it up and go back to the old way of living. No sir! Never!" Flo woke up at 5:00 A.M. and worked with Mildred late into the night. Flo had seen the stories in *Liberty* and wasn't impressed: "I think Doherty wrote them up terrible, don't you? They don't make sense to me." Flo wrote Ten Eyck that her maid was not to be trusted, since "*they* tried to contact me through her once before." Flo included a business card. "I had them printed, as I go around soliciting business. But I solicit legit business now!" Flo sent "special regards to Mr. Dewey. I thank him for giving me a chance. And as far as you are concerned, Mr. Ten Eyck, I can never thank you enough for what you have done for me. I'll probably never be in a position to repay you, but I'll always think of you, and pray for all good things to come to you and yours. That's all I can say, and it comes from the bottom of my heart. Some day you'll feel real proud of us.... yours as ever, F.B."

Despite the glowing optimism, the venture was tottering. Mildred Balitzer was on the verge of giving up. On December 21, Mildred sent a collect telegram to Barent Ten Eyck.

On their way west, Mildred Balitzer and Flo Brown sent this photograph to Dewey's office; it was taken at an amusement park in Hot Springs. They were already back on drugs (courtesy NYC Municipal Archives).

AM COMPLETELY WITHOUT FUNDS. HAD NO MONEY TO INVEST WITH FLO SO THE ARRANGEMENT IS NOT WORKING OUT WELL. TRY TO GET MONEY FROM MOVIE COMPANY AT ONCE. MUST HAVE HELP AT ONCE. LETTER FOLLOWS.

Barent Ten Eyck received an alarming letter from Flo. The women were arguing and money was low. His response was just as disappointing; unfortunately, he knew of no source of funds to assist them, and the studios had abandoned their story. Though Ten Eyck tried to cheer Flo's sagging spirits with ideas of future hope, the turning point had come. In the early hours of December 22, just three hours after her telegram to Barent Ten Eyck, Mildred wired Jojo, obviously in a panic:

WIRE DUNNS ADDRESS AT ONCE. ANXIOUS TO GET IN TOUCH WITH HIM. ALSO JEAN IRWINS ADDRESS. LETTER FOLLOWS.

On December 23, Flo wrote a letter filled with fear. A customer reported that men were asking about two girls running a service station. "One goes by the name of Gloria Moore," said the stranger. "They are trying to *go straight* and I was sent out here to check up on them. I'm on my way to the police station now." Flo believed they had been traced by the letters she sent to Ten Eyck: "They know where we are, and they must be here for no good. I'm going to write a letter, seal it up, and if anything happens to us, I'll leave instructions to mail it to you. In it will be the names of the people that have approached me, while I was in New York."

The day after Christmas, Ten Eyck responded and assured Flo that two women running a gas station would draw curiosity, especially if their auto had New York license plates. He advised them not to worry for "you are of no use to them or to anyone else in the world only if you are alive and healthy. You have nothing to be concerned about short of a direct approach made with the purpose of negotiating some kind of a deal. I know you both too well to fear that you will be interested in anything of the sort." He was certain no leaks had come from Dewey's office but stated he would send future correspondence in plain envelopes with his secretary's address listed. As for Flo's fear of death, Dewey's office would investigate immediately.

Despite Ten Eyck's confidence, both women were about to defect to Lucky's team. Unwittingly, Ten Eyck had opened a door. They were worth more *alive* than dead. Ten Eyck received a pitiful letter from Mildred. She was out of money, and Flo was tired of supporting her: "I ran out of funds three weeks ago. Of course I have worked every day since we got the station. I was so happy. While I had no financial interest in it still I was willing just to make enough for room and board. It meant a new life living right, having the respect of people. Then the other day Flo come down to the station and she says I can't support you any longer.... I went to the bathroom and cried my heart out. I sure don't want any part of a racket anymore if I could get by with it which of course I can't as you know. Jobs are at a premium out here. I have tried several places. And on top of everything else yesterday those people found out where we were at as Flo wrote to you about. I am just about ready to go off the deep end.... I am up against a stone wall. There is no way to turn. I am a stranger in a strange land.... I wish you would write to her. She takes your advice. I am worried to death about these people to. You are allowed to have a gun out here in your home and your place of business. So today she said she was going to buy one.... I will be very grateful for any advice you can give me. Or any help. Sincerely, Mildred."

This was the last correspondence Barent Ten Eyck was to receive from either Flo or Mildred. They were about to engage in a shocking betrayal. Polakoff's web was spun even before their departure from New York City. While staying at the Park Crescent, Jojo had telephoned Mildred to arrange a meeting. Moses Polakoff and a hired investigator wanted to see her. In the fall, before their departure, Mildred had been asked to recant her testimony. On October 29, Mildred sat in the lobby of the Biltmore Hotel. Jojo arrived with Joseph

Dunn, a former special agent with the Department of Justice. Dunn had been in charge of federal offices in Seattle, Chicago, New York City, San Francisco, and Los Angeles. Dunn had resigned the previous year to become a private investigator. He kept an office in the Rowan Building in Los Angeles. In the hotel coffee shop Dunn said he was interested in "learning the truth."[3] There was a discussion of recanting her testimony. Mildred spoke with Dunn by telephone over the following days but did not commit to anything. As Flo and Mildred motored toward Los Angeles, Dunn patiently waited. On December 23, Dunn received a telephone call from his associate, Joseph McCarthy, in New York. Jojo Weintraub had received a telegram. Mildred Balitzer was at White's Auto Camp in Pomona, living there under the name of Norma Gordon. She was ready to talk. Dunn immediately drove the 30 miles to Pomona. Mildred agreed to recant. She went to his office in Los Angeles. Dunn showed her a transcript of her trial testimony. She told Dunn that her testimony "in the main, was correct and that only erroneous inferences were drawn from her testimony because she had not been permitted to give complete answers, and that she would be willing to correct her testimony to that extent."[4]

Flo had also weakened. On January 18, 1937, Flo and Mildred abandoned the gas station and drove to Los Angeles. Three days later, Joseph McCarthy arrived. McCarthy told them that he was authorized to represent Moses Polakoff. Dunn arranged for a notary to take their recantations. The women were advised to return to New York, so they could testify before the court, under oath, if necessary to do so. They were to remain in the custody of Joseph McCarthy, an attorney and private investigator. Like Dunne, McCarthy was a former agent for the Department of Justice. With Flo and Mildred snared, Moses Polakoff had a net filled with recanting witnesses.

Joseph McCarthy had already *turned* Nancy Presser. This was done with the assistance of Mary Morris, Thelma Jordan's former friend. Three weeks after returning from Cincinnati, Nancy and Thelma were contacted by Mary Morris at the Hotel Belleclaire, where they lived. Morris introduced them to "Mr. McArthur," a liquor salesman, who was actually Joseph McCarthy. The women were invited to visit McCarthy's lavish suite. Thelma paid several visits to Morris and McCarthy. Unknown to her, McCarthy had a hidden Dictaphone installed in a bedroom. On November 30, Thelma spoke with Mary Morris about the trial. As McCarthy later claimed: "While Thelma Jordan was visiting at my suite, she and Mary Morris engaged in a conversation that was overheard by me on the Dictaphone. They discussed the Luciano case. Thelma Jordan stated that she did not know Charley Lucky; that Danny told her that he was the boss of the gambling, but never mentioned him in connection with the combination; that she never saw the man and knows that he had nothing to do with the combination."[5]

Nancy told McCarthy that her trial testimony was false. In attorney Martin Conboy's office on Broadway she was questioned under oath; a stenographer took her statement. In February, Joseph McCarthy escorted Flo and Mildred to the same law office where they made recanting affidavits. Stated Mildred: "I was told that I had better admit knowing these defendants, because if I didn't, I had seven and a half to twenty years facing me for compulsory prostitution. I was confronted with a bunch of wiretaps on my phone in connection with conversations with Little Davie and Tommy Bull. I denied having these conversations." When shown Lucky's picture, she claimed she had said, "I don't think a man of his sort would bother with a racket of that kind.... Mr. Gelb told me that Charley Luciano was the boss, and that he had plenty of evidence to prove it. I said I didn't believe it." Mildred said that she had "made up" stories about meeting Lucky. This was done to protect Pete. On the witness stand she had lied about immunity. Mr. Gelb had given her a letter promising that she would not be prosecuted. Mildred said she now spoke freely and voluntarily and was not threatened or coerced into making the affidavit. She expected to receive no money or any other consideration, and no promises had been made by anyone to induce her to make the affidavit.

Flo claimed in her recantation affidavit that, while in the House of Detention, Mildred Curtis and other witnesses suggested she cooperate with Dewey's staff, that an argument had led to her being placed in "solitary confinement," that she was weak from narcotics withdrawal and that she faced jail time. She admitted telling Barent Ten Eyck that she knew most of the defendants, including Lucky. As the defendants "didn't stand a chance," she agreed to help. Her trial testimony was false, designed to protect herself. Now, the only reason for her to recant was "to right a wrong, and not because I am afraid of anybody."

Helen Horvath also filed a recanting affidavit. She had lied in court about assisting the investigation to regain her self-respect, she now claimed. She asserted she had been concerned about not being prosecuted for skipping bail. She said Harold Cole had rehearsed her before she testified, saying, "Put it on thick." At the House of Detention her only privilege was seeing her boyfriend.[6] She was forbidden to leave. "I never went outside of Mr. Dewey's office with any of the assistants.... I was never taken on any parties like some of the girls." She had written a letter of protest to Paul Lockwood, angry about her treatment, after she had come forward voluntarily. In April, Nancy Presser was assigned to live with her for a week, and the women were taken to Dewey's office every day. Most evenings, claimed Horvath, Nancy was taken to dinner and was usually drunk when she returned. Detective Bill Cunningham and a police officer helped carry Nancy inside. Horvath also claimed she saw Nancy studying a newspaper photograph of Lucky so she could memorize

Lucky's features. After Nancy testified, the other witnesses heard she would be rewarded: "Mildred told me that Thelma Jordan and Nancy Presser were being given a cruise to the West Indies." According to Horvath, the only witness who knew Lucky was Peggy Wild, as he was a customer and "a very good one." As for Mildred Balitzer, after her court testimony she had returned drunk. After the trial, Horvath told Paul Lockwood that "Luciano was convicted on a pack of lies." Horvath said she had no personal knowledge of Mildred and Lucky. In July, Horvath had gone to George Levy's office to tell "the absolute truth."

In Nancy Presser's affidavit of recantation, she claimed that since the trial her conscience had bothered her. She renounced all previous statements: "I was furnished with liquor on all occasions," she said.[7] She feared prosecution for check forgery and narcotics possession. "I was told I had better testify that I knew Charles Luciano, for they had enough to send me away for 10 to 20 years, both because of the check charge, and also because I was in the racket." If she refused to talk she would be turned over to federal agents on a drug charge. Her testimony in court was false, she stated in the affidavit. She now denied knowing Lucky, visiting his hotel rooms, or overhearing conversations. She had received no money for making the affidavit, nor had she been threatened, she swore.

Muriel Weiss, the wife of Joe Bendix, also made an affidavit. Weiss, whose theatrical name was Joy Dixon, said she knew Lucky, having met him when she performed in a show at the Park Central Hotel. "He seemed to be a perfect gentleman," Weiss stated.[8] Weiss also knew Moses Polakoff. She had previously met with the attorney concerning legal defense for her jailed husband. At the Woolworth Building Bendix had asked his wife to corroborate a statement he gave investigators, that she had been present at the Villanova Restaurant when he met Lucky. Though Weiss told Sol Gelb of the incident and affirmed her husband's version, the restaurant meeting was untrue, since she was in South America at the time. And after the trial: "I asked my husband whether his testimony was true, and he never gave me a direct answer."

Dewey wasn't surprised by the recantations. The women were morally weak and terrified of being murdered. Flo, Mildred, and Nancy were also addicts and were likely back on drugs. The trio had been the most important witnesses in the trial. Their testimony directly linked Lucky with members of the combination. The defense lawyers believed they now had enough recanting affidavits to overturn Lucky's conviction, but, unknown to the defense, Dewey had obtained affidavits that were made following the trial.

Dewey was suspicious of the involvement of Dunn and McCarthy. What prompted Polakoff to hire Dunn, whose office was in California? Most significant, why was it necessary to wait for McCarthy to arrive in Los Angeles, "unless it was because McCarthy brought something more than a letter of introduction to convince the girls they were dealing with Polakoff and would be taken care of."[9] Did he bring narcotics or money? Perhaps it was both. Dewey would now confront a sinister legal challenge to the conviction of Luciano and the other defendants.

CHAPTER THIRTEEN

Poisonously False

This fraud was discovered

In February 1937, Jacob Rosenblum hurried to Sing Sing Prison. Joe Bendix had sent a warning that the prisoners were unhappy. They were being called "Dewey rats" by the inmates and guards alike. Joe Bendix, Pete Balitzer, Danny Caputo, Dave Marcus, and Al Weiner lived separate from the prison population, ostensibly to protect them, but they felt they were being mistreated. After their trial cooperation, the men had expected more. Danny Caputo was angry that Governor Lehman had denied his appeal for clemency. Dave Marcus was bitter, upset that he was forced to communicate with his children through a screen. Joe Bendix told Rosenblum the inmates were easy prey for advances being made by the defendants' attorneys. Pete Balitzer had already sold out. Lucky Luciano was back in the news. Would his conviction be overturned?

After Lucky's attorneys filed the recanting affidavits in court, Dewey assembled the press: "I have known for many months of extensive effort to bribe and intimidate the witnesses in the Luciano trial."[1] Those who reported such to his office were none other than Mildred Balitzer, Flo Brown, and Nancy Presser. Their affidavits reeked of perjury, he blasted. They were now criminal conspirators. Dewey showed his cards; he had 128 witness affidavits, safely stored in the Irving Trust Company. The affidavits would be filed in court to refute the defense claims. Dewey told the press the women had been credible witnesses during the trial. However, from the beginning, defense lawyers had hurled every type of question at them, but, despite sordid details and insinuations, the jury still convicted the defendants. He revealed that Justice McCook had questioned the witnesses before dismissing them. Under oath, Nancy Presser swore she had told the truth. McCook asked her about liquor. She admitted she drank when she went out to dinner. She had been given a few drinks in Harold Cole's office because she was nervous. "But you did not get intoxicated any of those times?"[2]

"No."

When asked about her plans, Nancy expressed fear.

"And the reason that you don't seek immediate discharge is that before you get discharged, you want some arrangements made that will protect your safety?"

"That is it."

"All right, then I will say goodbye to you, Nancy, and one of these days I will be signing your discharge. You have been of great service to the State, and if you have nothing on your conscience, I hope you can get back into a decent way of life. Do you want to?"

"I certainly do. I want to get out of it."

The same day, McCook had asked Mildred Balitzer the following question: "Did you tell the same story substantially before the Grand Jury that you told before me and my jury?"

"Yes, sir," answered Mildred. She said that she had been properly treated while at the House of Detention. No indecent suggestions were made to her, nor did she have any complaints about the treatment for addiction. She informed the judge that her police guard, Officer Heidt, said he had been the payoff man for Owney Madden during Prohibition. Mildred expressed hope that her husband, Pete, could be reformed and that she felt sorry for Jack Ellenstein.

Flo Brown had stated in her recantation affidavit that her entire trial testimony was false. But when she had been questioned by Justice McCook, it was different.

"I heard you testify. Did you tell the truth?"[3]

"I did. I told the truth from the beginning."

Dewey also had Flo's affidavit, which he took before she testified in court. The testimony differed in no way whatsoever from the testimony Flo gave on the witness stand. Despite long hours of exhaustive examination, Flo's recollections never failed, asserted Dewey.

After reading news stories about the recanting witnesses, Edward Doherty contacted Barent Ten Eyck. He turned over the manuscripts that Flo and Mildred had written themselves; neither manuscript had been used. Flo had written about her decision to testify: "You are sure you will get a job for me, and help me get started on the road to living decently, if I talk? He assured me again, that he wouldn't let me down. So I decided to give him my statement. I had decided to be a squealer, and take my chances. I said to him, 'If I open up, I'll probably not live long afterwards anyway. They'll kill me.'"

Thelma Jordan did not recant. She had also made a formal statement under oath. While she and Nancy were in London, they had engaged in conversations about their testimony. After reading about Lucky's appeal in a London newspaper, Nancy remarked: "All we would have to do would be to change our story and say that we lied on the stand and we would get plenty of money, and after Lucky went free, we could always get anything from him we wanted." [4] At no time, during or after the trial, swore Thelma, did Nancy ever say that her trial testimony was false. In fact, Nancy had undisclosed information about Lucky, Ralph Liguori and others. But Nancy began to change. She wanted to locate Ralph's brother, Herman, to offer help. "The racket people were always much nicer to me than the legitimate people," she told Thelma.

Thelma had accompanied Nancy on all visits to Dewey's office. Nancy told Cole of the forged check incident in which Ralph Liguori and Lillian Gardello were involved. Nancy offered information about the narcotics trade. Added Thelma: "She also volunteered that she had known Charles Luciano when he was a pimp; that she had known him when he was a bodyguard for Joe Masseria." Thelma denied any testimony had been rehearsed. Trial briefs were scrutinized by Dewey's staff for accuracy. Nancy Presser told her many times that her testimony was true. As for alcohol, they were allowed to buy a dinner cocktail from their own funds; Dewey's office would not pay for drinks. Thelma stated she had never seen Nancy intoxicated.

Emma Brogan had been assigned to guard several women. While the witnesses were in her custody there were frequent discussions about the Luciano case. The policewoman refuted Helen Horvath's claim that Mildred did not know Lucky. Brogan recalled specific conversations when Horvath challenged Mildred. Horvath "was very argumentative for some unexplained reason and would instigate discussions of this kind with Mildred," stated Brogan. But Mildred forcefully replied that Helen "was a liar." [5] Brogan never heard a conversation that anyone was being forced to testify to false facts, nor did the women discuss lying on the stand. Brogan had never seen Mildred drunk, as Horvath claimed. As for an afternoon excursion, when Mildred supposedly confessed in Brogan's presence that she did not know Lucky, the policewoman said Mildred wasn't even on the ride, for she had remained at Dewey's office. In summation, Emma Brogan declared, "On many occasions I heard Mildred say to the other witnesses that, but for Charles Luciano, whom she described as a rat, she and her husband, Pete, would have left town and would have been finished with the prostitution racket."

William Cunningham, a veteran police officer, cited for meritorious service, had been in charge of Nancy Presser and Helen Horvath. Cunningham testified "they were unfriendly to each other, and rarely spoke to one another."[6] At no time did he observe Nancy Presser in an intoxicated condition under which she was unable to walk or conduct herself with normal facility. Robert J. Quinn, a detective, also confirmed the women disliked each other. He denied seeing Nancy intoxicated or in any condition "which required me or anybody else to assist them in walking."[7]

Harold Cole gave a lengthy statement detailing his interviews with Nancy Presser. Point by point, he refuted her affidavit: "At no time did I suggest to her to say anything but the truth. I never suggested any specific facts to her which she was to testify. The testimony that she gave on the witness stand was in substance exactly what she had related to me of her own free will prior to the time of the trial."[8] A great deal of the testimony not relevant to the prostitution trial had to be eliminated before her testimony, such as her knowledge of drug trafficking, since it could prejudice the jurors. Cole acknowledged Nancy had been given alcohol, though a moderate amount, as she was a former drug addict and was nervous. In addition, she suffered from a painful abdominal abscess. Lucky never ordered Dago Jean's house wrecked, Nancy now claimed. But Cole confirmed the incident. "Acting upon the information obtained from Miss Presser I ordered Dago Jean arrested. Jean admitted to me the damage done to her house of prostitution and related to me the troubles she had with the combination."

Nancy now denied visits to the Waldorf, but Fred Seidel, an elevator operator of the Tower Apartments, while being questioned in Dewey's office, recognized her. Though out of uniform, Nancy also recognized Seidel, and told him: "If you are trying to protect me, forget it. Others have recognized me. You may as well tell the truth."

Dewey had uncovered evidence that exposed the duplicity of the recanting witnesses. Jojo Weintraub gained access to Pete by using a false name. Pete boasted he was going to switch his story. He would receive 50 dollars a week "from the Luciano people." Jojo would collect the money for him. Pete said Flo and Mildred had received $500 for a drug cure in a sanitarium across from Central Park. The money came from Moses Polakoff. Pete urged Caputo and Joe Bendix to recant. There was money waiting. Instead, Caputo contacted Dewey's office and told Charles Breitel what was underway.

At the Town Hospital, 293 Central Park West, Ann Kenneth, admission secretary, was questioned by police. The secretary identified Flo and Mildred as patients from February 25 to March 8, 1937. They were being treated for heroin addiction. They had given false names and listed their home address as 104 Union Street in Buffalo. They had rented a room at 10 West 87th Street in New York. Flo and Mildred were accompanied by a relative who paid their hospital fee in advance. The "relative" was Jojo Weintraub. He returned during their treatment and pretended to be Flo's husband. On their admittance, the director reviewed previous records, noting that "Miss Wilson" had been a patient previously, treated for opium and morphine addiction. "Miss Wilson" was Mildred Balitzer.[9] On March 8, Jojo had unexpectedly appeared, before the treatment was complete. He showed them newspaper articles, and the women suddenly left in the early afternoon.

Dewey studied the police report. On February 19, 1937, Flo and Mildred had sworn in their recanting affidavits that they were drug free. But Dewey now had proof the statements were false. They had been addicted to heroin when they took their oaths. Less than a week later, they entered Town Hospital. How did they obtain narcotics? Dunn and McCarthy guarded the women. They must have been aware of narcotic use, surmised Dewey. Despite their impressive credentials, Dunn and McCarthy were tangled in a web of deceit, just as Moses Polakoff.

While preparing a motion against a new trial, Dewey led the prosecution of the restaurant extortionists in the Schultz gang; seven defendants were found guilty. Detective Stephen Di Rosa had been demoted during the trial. Di Rosa had leaked information to the defendants, asserted Commissioner Valentine. Di Rosa was stripped of his detective badge and returned to a regular uniform. On the train from Little Rock, Lucky was guarded by Di Rosa and John J. Brennan. Detective Di Rosa had conversed with Lucky in Italian. Brennan became suspicious and told them to stop. When they ignored him, Brennan took out his blackjack. "Lay off that stuff," he ordered Di Rosa.[10] After Dewey was told of the incident, high-risk assignments for Stephen Di Rosa ended. During the restaurant trial, false information was given to Di Rosa alone, to test the detective's honesty. Soon after, a man appeared at the special prosecutor's office and demanded to know why he was going to be indicted. Di Rosa, honored with five meritorious citations, was the source. "I guess my reputation is gone," he lamented. As for the conversation in Italian, Lucky had merely asked him where in Italy he was born, claimed Di Rosa. Dewey declined to comment on the detective's fall.

On April 19, Dewey filed 65 affidavits. He asserted the motions to overturn Lucky's conviction were based on perjured evidence, with the knowledge of defense attorneys. Dewey denied the defense claim that he had been out to frame Lucky: "Prior to the arrests and the testimony given by these witnesses, we had no evidence of Luciano's direct connection with this racket; we made no effort to locate him and did not even know where he was. Towards the end of March, however, the evidence was such that I felt it was my duty to present the case to the grand jury and attempt to locate Luciano. This was done."

Yet by October 1935, Dewey's office had an unknown informant who knew a great deal about the fraudulent bond office. Although there was no *direct connection* to Lucky, there were indeed whispers that he ran the combination. And while Dewey's office did not keep track of Lucky, the New York Police kept him under surveillance in Miami and Hot Springs, since he was suspected of murdering Dutch Schultz.

Dewey addressed Mildred's letter of immunity, given to her by Sol Gelb and witnessed by Frank Hogan. The defense trumpeted the fact that Mildred had denied such a letter on the witness stand and attempted to draw an inference that the jury was deliberately misled. But Dewey made it clear in his opening and closing remarks that the women knew they would not be prosecuted if they gave truthful testimony. Only after Mildred's testimony did Dewey learn that she had signed an immunity agreement, contrary to the general instructions to his assistants. Gelb's action was inadvertent, he said, as he simply wished to "keep faith with her." Dewey told reporters he would have approved of it had he known Mildred requested it.

On April 20, Moses Polakoff and Lorenzo Carlino were called to a special hearing. Justice McCook was angry over the recanting affidavits: "The district attorney has produced evidence these applications for a new trial are a fraud upon the court."[11]

"I think your Honor's very conduct shows bias," Polakoff answered. "These sensational charges by the district attorney are a mere camouflage to hide the real issues." But McCook disagreed. Dewey called Polakoff to the stand. The attorney was stunned: "I regard these proceedings as highly irregular, in the nature of a star chamber proceeding. I regard the court as biased and prejudiced."[12] Polakoff reluctantly took the oath and sat as a witness. Dewey demanded to know the whereabouts of Flo Brown and Mildred Balitzer.

"None of your business," he answered.

Justice McCook directed him to answer. Polakoff began arguing, but McCook silenced him. "You are here as a witness, sir."

"I am also here as counsel for myself, your Honor."

McCook again ordered him to answer. Polakoff relented: "The last I know of the witnesses they were in Hartford, Connecticut." They were in the custody of Joseph McCarthy. "We have an agreement that I am not to know where the witnesses are because we suspected this trick on your behalf, with the aid of the Court." Joseph Dunn was in New York and had been asked by the court to appear but failed to do so. Polakoff told Justice McCook that if Dunn was wanted, "You subpoena him." Polakoff had last seen Flo and Mildred on March 8, when he asked them to reaffirm their testimony in the office of Martin Conboy. Dewey had cornered Polakoff. "You knew at that time that the affidavits contained the statements they were not drug addicts?"

"No, I didn't," responded Polakoff. "I didn't read the entire testimony at that time, and if that statement was made, it was a slip or an error." Polakoff had been thoroughly humiliated. To avoid knowledge of perjured statements, he had claimed incompetence, in essence, that he had not read important affidavits. It was clear to Dewey exactly why Polakoff did not want to know where the women were kept: Flo and Mildred were being supplied with narcotics. Polakoff seethed with anger. He demanded to question Dewey. But McCook denied the request. Polakoff announced he would ask Governor Lehman for an impartial investigation concerning the issue of fraud.

Lorenzo Carlino was summoned to the stand but refused to answer any questions by citing "constitutional grounds." Carlino had claimed in an affidavit that juror Edward Blake told him the jury had received threats. Yet, Edward Blake denied ever making such a statement. When Carlino asked the juror to sign an affidavit about threats, Blake had refused. "Your Honor," said Dewey. "I have submitted complete proof that the affidavit filed by Mr. Carlino was perjurious from the beginning to the end."

The following week, McCook spent an entire day listening to legal arguments for a new trial based on the recanting affidavits. Polakoff said the turnabout began with Helen Horvath. She wrote him a letter. The girls wanted to recant their testimony. He had hired Dunn and McCarthy as investigators. Joseph McCarthy had Dictaphone conversations but "I did not include that in the motion papers. Some of it was scandalous, your Honor.... One day Mary Roberts, at McCarthy's direction, said to Nancy Presser, 'How about this Lucky trial and all that?' And she said, 'Oh, where can I get Liguori's brother Herman? I have done a terrible thing. I would like to correct my testimony.'" Polakoff's decision not to use the Dictaphone conversations was a surprising retreat. What exactly had been on the Dictaphone recordings, if anything? Was he hiding something? The Dictaphone trap gave the impression the truth had been secretly documented, but it was all smoke without a spark of evidence, for nothing was submitted to the court. Polakoff now gave a reason why Flo and Mildred were removed from Town Hospital so suddenly: "A reporter called up and told me about the motion I was about to make, and I realized that some leak had occurred somewhere, and the girls were taken out." But Justice McCook pointed out that Polakoff never told the court the women were undergoing a cure, while signing an affidavit they were not on drugs. Dewey discovered it. "Well, we were going to disclose all that," Polakoff lamely responded. "Every lawyer who opposes Mr. Dewey in litigation is not crooked." Polakoff knew his actions were transparent. The acclaimed defense attorney did appear *crooked*, enmeshed in a scheme to subvert justice.

Dewey addressed the court. The witnesses were intensely examined on the stand, he stated, especially Flo Brown. She had been subjected to hours of merciless cross-examination, all designed to confuse her. The defense had even implied in court that Flo was injecting drugs but, after a physical examination, the defense was rendered silent. No one could have withstood such examination had it been concocted, insisted Dewey. He acknowledged that after the vice raids the women had lied. They were afraid to talk, but slowly they told the truth. Dewey's disgust with the defense motion for a new trial was based on fraud: "Every single affidavit and statement submitted in support of this application for a new trial reeks with perjury."

Dewey cited a passage in Flo's manuscript which she had written in her own hand: "It was a good thing I had told the truth, for if I had been lying, as they were trying to say I was, they would have trapped me." Dewey regretted that Flo "has slipped back to the underworld." As for Mildred Balitzer, Dewey scoffed at her claim she did not have an opportunity to provide details. She was on the stand for nine hours. He outlined her terror after the trial. Then he presented the frantic messages to his office, desperate and pleading, since Mildred was out of funds.

Lorenzo Carlino stood before McCook. In a lengthy statement he struck back. "Mr. Dewey poses as God," he began, angry his retrial motion had been denounced as perjurious. "It reminds me of the Salem witch burners. When the sinner was caught, immediately they looked for a victim to burn at the stake to hide their own sins. He hates me, but I am not afraid." Dewey eased back in his chair as Carlino ranted. "When he pulled that Hitleristic coup on me last Tuesday or attempted to do it, he tried it against the wrong man."

Justice McCook denied motions for a retrial. "After reading both sets of papers any impartial person must, I feel sure, conclude that the information used was fairly and honestly elicited by proper means and accurately recorded, and that any contrary version now put forward is untrue. The hypothesis of a victimized, *framed* Luciano is utterly destroyed. The information about him came too late in the case for that, from the reluctant lips of too many frightened men and women, and too much internal evidence of truth. Flo Brown, Mildred Balitzer, and Nancy Presser were all interviewed under oath by the court, after the trial, in circumstances which would naturally inspire confidence and eliminate motive for falsehood, as well as supply the court with another opportunity for observing their demeanor. In my opinion, their trial testimony was substantially true and their present statements were, in my opinion, induced by fear, financial pressure, craving for drugs, and are poisonously false." The decision was a sweet triumph for Dewey.

Moses Polakoff submitted an appeal. Dewey answered each allegation in the *People's Brief*, a document that denied motions for a new trial. He attacked the affidavit of Muriel Weiss. Joe Bendix had testified that his wife was present in the restaurant but never asserted she heard the conversation. On the witness stand Bendix stated the meeting had occurred in May, June, or July. Weiss said she was not in New York until July. "Assuming that she is telling the truth, it is of no consequence. Bendix may have been mistaken in this irrelevant respect."

As for Mildred Balitzer, it was shown that her statement of January 26, 1937, did not refute her trial testimony, although she had been in the custody of the defense for a month. She said her testimony about the defendants in the case was substantially truthful but that there were certain things she was "not permitted to tell." After her arrival in New York, a new story was born, said Dewey. In February, she recanted her testimony about Lucky, but still maintained that she knew him, and had spoken with him in Florida. Mildred had been in direct communication with the prosecutor's office for months but *never* recanted in any way.

Flo Brown constructed a strange story, asserted Dewey, reweaving the notes she had sent to Barent Ten Eyck, to indicate she had been placed in solitary confinement to force her to talk. Flo's first note to Ten Eyck refuted her claim. The note exploded her concocted tale and demonstrated she sought out Barent Ten Eyck and offered testimony, all before she argued with Joan Martin. There was no "solitary confinement," scoffed Dewey. Ten Eyck's original notes were in essence the testimony she had given in court. They had only met a few times later, so Flo could straighten out the early chronology of her life. Flo claimed she was handed a typewritten sheet and "just glanced it over. I didn't read it. I didn't care what was in it or anything. I was too weak to care one way or the other." But Flo had not only signed the 37-page interview, conducted by Dewey in the presence of a stenographer, secretary, and five assistant district attorneys, but she was asked to read every page, and initial it, which she did, making minor changes in her own handwriting. In court Flo had been questioned "in the most grueling, nauseating, and detailed fashion by a battery of defense lawyers.... No witness could have invented a story in two hours, repeated it five days later in a formal statement of 37 pages, and then testified to it on the witness stand for 11 hours, 9 of which were consumed in cross-examination." And writing from Hot Springs, Flo was hardly a conscience-stricken witness, remarked Dewey, for she had ridiculed Luciano. Soon after, Flo was afraid and wanted to buy a gun.

As for the affidavit of Helen Horvath, Dewey sliced it to ribbons. Horvath claimed Mildred Balitzer was always asking about Lucky's appearance, but even in Mildred's recanting affidavit she admitted seeing Lucky many times. Horvath named police guards. Dewey questioned them and they all contradicted her affidavit. The truth was apparent: Horvath was jealous and felt overlooked. "Someone made a bad mistake in having Helen Horvath go to such lengths," stated Dewey.

The *People's Brief* was a forceful legal document that supported Justice McCook's decision that denied the motion for a new trial. The prosecutor argued that the case failed to present a situation in which the appeals court should substitute its judgment for that of the jury and the trial judge. No legal ground for granting a new trial was presented. The recanting affidavits were all "demonstrably false and in every respect a vicious fraud," Dewey summarized.

In the midst of the battle for a new trial, the Department of Labor ordered that Charles Luciano, on the completion of his sentence, be deported to Italy as an undesirable alien. It was established that Lucky had been born in Italy but never applied for American citizenship. In Dannemora Prison Lucky received a warrant from the state tax department. The state charged him with income tax evasion. The once-powerful boss had toppled from his throne.

Gay Orlova had fallen with him. In the spring she had returned from Europe aboard the *Normandie*. When photographers asked her to pose, immigration authorities recognized her. She was taken to Ellis Island and denied entry. Her "passport husband," as he was dubbed by the press, had filed for an annulment. Gay had entered into a fraudulent marriage, asserted the bitter ex-spouse, simply to remain in America. The glamorous showgirl was deported to France aboard the *Normandie*. She married a young count, identified as a former sweetheart, but divorced him three weeks later.

Moviegoers flocked to see *Marked Woman*, a Warner Bros. drama that featured Humphrey Bogart as a prosecutor after a gangster. The *Daily News* reviewer wrote: "The picture hasn't unreeled very far before you realize that it is modeled after the sensational expose and trial in New York."[13] The women in a nightclub, led by Bette Davis, were not portrayed as prostitutes but "hostesses." Across the nation, the image of Lucky Luciano, mobster and vice lord, became ingrained in the public consciousness, so had the image of gangbuster Thomas E. Dewey, the highly respected prosecutor. Ray Le Strange, a former publicity man for Tammany Hall and Jimmy Walker, announced that a major studio was willing to pay Dewey $150,000 to play the role of a hero in a gangster picture. Dewey wasn't interested, even though the press and films depicted him as America's gangbuster.

In July 1937, the Appeals Court upheld the conviction of Charles Luciano and the other defendants, though two of the five justices believed the sentences were excessive. The same court reversed the conviction of booker Nick Montana on the grounds Montana did not receive a fair trial; the judge had asked 1,350 questions, many of which had been prejudicial. The same month, Dewey won convictions against conspirators in the bakery industry, for competition and price-control violations. Dewey brought indictments against attorney J. Richard "Dixie" Davis and 11 defendants who operated the lucrative policy racket, inherited from their boss, Dutch Schultz. Although once an attorney for Dutch Schultz and other underworld figures, Davis was a fugitive. Stories circulated that the fugitive lawyer had hidden millions from the Schultz crime empire.

Dewey's triumphs made him the man of the hour. John Foster Dulles offered Dewey a $150,000 position with the law firm of Sullivan and Cromwell.[14] There was talk that Dewey should be governor. Samuel Seabury encouraged Dewey to run for district attorney. For the moment, Dewey savored the legal victories. But criminal arrogance was still rampant. One night police heard cries for help and pursued a speeding automobile. Near 10th Street and the East River, a body was thrown out. The corpse was identified as gambler John Masseria, brother of Joe the Boss. He had been shot through the heart, for refusing to pay a losing bet.[15]

In September, Dewey accepted the Republican nomination for New York County District Attorney. The position paid $20,000 per year. Dewey's friends were surprised by his decision to accept a low-paying job for four years, when he could become wealthy as a private attorney. Political glory, observed friends, rather than high income, is what motivated Dewey, at least for the moment. Samuel Seabury publicly endorsed Dewey, a significant expression of belief in Dewey's honesty and integrity. Dewey's candidacy was risky. The registered voters were comprised of 563,000 Democrats and 122,000 Republicans. In the midst of the political campaign, fugitive Max Silverman was arrested in Los Angeles. Silverman was immediately included in an extortion indictment filed against Louis Buchalter and Jacob Shapiro. Max Rubin, a potential witness against the indicted criminals, was the victim of a gunshot. Though seriously wounded, Rubin survived. During a radio broadcast Dewey said the attempted murder of Max Rubin was the frightened act of a desperate criminal underworld. He attacked Buchalter and Shapiro for rampant industrial racketeering. District Attorney Dodge was a man who "would not, dare not, and could not lift a finger" to stop the rackets.

In another radio address Dewey targeted Lucky's corrupt pal: "I am going to tell you about a politician, a political ally of thieves, pickpockets, thugs, dope peddlers, and big shot racketeers— Albert Marinelli, County Clerk of New York."[16] Dewey recounted how gangsters James Plumeri and Dominick Didato had made themselves dictators of the Truckmen's Association and intimidated independent drivers. Those who resisted membership became the victims of beatings and truck vandalism. If there were complaints, Plumeri boasted, "All we got to do is call up Marinelli and the rap is killed." The Truckmen's Association headquarters was at 225 Lafayette Street, the same building where Marinelli kept his office. Dewey had prosecuted extortionists Plumeri and Didato. They pleaded guilty and were sent to prison. But Al

Marinelli was still in office, mainly due to election fraud. In Marinelli's Second Assembly District "they had added 4,534 votes to their own set of candidates and stolen 3,535 from the others," said Dewey. And what about Marinelli's life style, maintained on a salary of $15,000 a year? "He has a luxurious estate surrounded by an iron fence on Lake Ronkonkoma, way out on Long Island. From his several motor cars he chooses to drive a Lincoln limousine. His Japanese butler, Togo, serves him well." Dewey referred to shady county committeemen and election inspectors in Marinelli's Second Assembly District who had police records and convictions. Most significant, Al Marinelli was a friend of Charley Lucky Luciano.

Dewey astounded the nation. The Republican candidate defeated Harold Hastings, 326,000 to 217,000. The triumph was the first time in 20 years that Tammany Hall had lost control of the District Attorney's Office in New York County. In January 1938, brimming with confidence, the new D.A. moved from the Woolworth Building to 137 Centre Street. More legal victories soon followed: Morrie Goldis and his brother pleaded guilty to manslaughter in the death of William Schneider; Max Silverman was sentenced to 30 years as an accessory. Vito Genovese fled to Italy, to avoid arrest for murder. He would remain abroad for eight years.

When citizen groups complained to Governor Lehman about Albert Marinelli, the county clerk was forced to respond: "They are trying to crucify me. If it's a crime to help the underdog, then I'm guilty." When Governor Lehman asked Dewey for proof of Marinelli's malfeasance, Dewey sent out three hundred subpoenas and gave indications that formal charges would soon follow. Marinelli resigned.

Dewey merged his special prosecutor's staff with the district attorney's department. Dewey issued a directive: staff members were forbidden night club visits. As for the racetrack, he suggested discretion. Dewey asked the bar association for a program of voluntary attorneys, competent lawyers who would provide legal defense for the indigent. Most important, Dewey unfolded plans to prosecute the most powerful Democratic politician in the state: James J. Hines.

Less than a year after being elected the new district attorney, Dewey accepted the Republican nomination for governor. Dewey supported President Roosevelt's relief programs, though they were denounced by many in his party. But Dewey detested Roosevelt's attempt to add another Supreme Court justice, simply to endorse the legality of New Deal programs. During the campaign, Dewey was a strong law-and-order candidate and called for the expansion of police wiretaps. He criticized Governor Lehman for failing to repudiate the corrupt elements in the Democratic ranks. The race was so close that President Roosevelt came to Lehman's aid. Roosevelt said Dewey was inexperienced. On December 9, 1938, despite a vigorous campaign, Dewey lost. Five million voters cast ballots and the incumbent won by 68,000 votes. Seeking peace and quiet, Tom and Frances Dewey bought Dapplemere Farm near the village of Pawling for $30,000. The down payment of $3,000 was borrowed from Leonard Reid, Dewey's cousin in Chicago. Dapplemere Farm carried a substantial mortgage that was slowly repaid over the next decades.[17] Dewey's relentless prosecution of mobsters attained national respect and fame. Thus far, Dewey's biggest prize was prisoner No. 92168 — Lucky Luciano.

CHAPTER FOURTEEN

No. 92168

Charley Lucky was a big guy

Dewey had fearlessly prosecuted embezzlers and gangsters; nevertheless, New Yorkers were astounded when politician James J. Hines was indicted for corruption. George Weinberg and Dixie Davis testified against the powerful politician in court. Dutch Schultz and his gang had paid Hines $750 a week, as bribe money, to make certain the police didn't touch the lucrative numbers operation. Unexpectedly, there was a mistrial. Dewey asked a question that linked Hines to extortion in the poultry industry. The question was ruled by the judge to be a prejudicial comment. Hines was retried, but in the middle of the second trial, prosecution witness George Weinberg shot himself. Despite the setback, the Tammany kingpin was exposed as a bribe taker. On February 24, 1939, Jimmy Hines was convicted and sentenced to four years in prison.

While No. 92168 washed clothes in the prison laundry, Moses Polkaoff continued to work for his release. The defense team filed a 184-page motion that challenged the legality of the Joinder Law and alleged court errors that favored the prosecution; despite the effort, the Court of Appeals upheld the conviction. Polakoff hired Martin Conboy to submit a re-argument. Conboy sneered to reporters that Dewey's methods were "reprehensible." Dewey responded that a personal attack on him was not the issue. In June, the Court of Appeals denied Conboy's motion. Polakoff then filed papers with the Supreme Court that contested the constitutionality of the Joinder Law. The Supreme Court declined to review Lucky's appeal. The legal process had come to an end. Dewey had won every court challenge.

Reporter Leo Katcher telephoned Polakoff and arranged an interview with his client. Prisoner No. 92168 was described as unshaven, with black

230

stubble on his face. Dressed in a drab prison uniform, Lucky faced the reporter in the visitor's room. An assistant warden and guard sat nearby; both listened to every word. Lucky showed the reporter the calluses on his hands. As for the lost appeals, "My lawyers told me not to expect too much, just to hope."[1] All he thought of was freedom. Lucky complained he was in prison because the witnesses lied. "I never had a thing to do with the prostitution racket. Charley Lucky was a big guy. His name was in newspapers. Anytime anybody pulled a hot job, they used my name." He didn't blame Dewey, just the witnesses. Lucky passed the time by listening to the radio through headphones. Radio laughter upset him. Lucky confessed he wanted to smash the headphones into pieces, he told the reporter, but he was hopeful of release. He would spend the remainder of his life following the horses and watching women. There were estimates that Lucky had spent in excess of $250,000 for legal fees. It was unknown how Polakoff was paid. Did mob associates deliver cash? During the trial, Dewey had searched for any hidden Luciano bank accounts, but without success.

Reports surfaced that Lucky lived in fear of prison violence. As a reserve colonel, Justice McCook was engaged in military maneuvers in the area. McCook felt it was his duty to investigate Lucky's welfare. But the deputy warden would not let him inside Dannemora Prison. After McCook telephoned the governor's office in Albany, a meeting was arranged. Lucky said he had no complaints.

After Louis Buchalter and Jacob Shapiro were accused by federal agents of violating anti-trust laws in the fur trade, they were released on bail but fled. Shapiro later surrendered and was sentenced to serve three years and pay a fine of $15,000. Louis Buchalter remained a fugitive.

Three years after the trial, Nancy Presser unexpectedly appeared at the Woolworth Building. Nancy gave a statement to Frank Hogan and Sewell Tyng that filled in pieces of the dark puzzle. She revealed what had taken place in the Hotel Belleclaire in the fall of 1937. Mary Morris had introduced her to a man named McArthur. They had become friendly. While out on the town they met Johnny Roberts and Herman Liguori. But nothing was said about changing her testimony. Nancy accompanied them to the Half Moon Hotel on Coney Island, where Mary Morris and Johnny Roberts had a room. Later, as she walked to dinner with Herman Liguori, he threatened her. Nancy was told to deny the truthfulness of her court testimony: "If I didn't they would blow up my whole family and me with it."[2] Herman Liguori was a member of "the Italian underworld." At the restaurant they were joined by Mr. McArthur. He was actually Joe McCarthy. The same night McCarthy dictated a letter addressed to Moses Polakoff. The letter stated Nancy had been troubled by the testimony and would like to see him. Nancy signed it. The group drove her to the Pennsylvania Hotel, where she began drinking. In the bathroom Herman Liguori told her not to be afraid, that everything would be alright but not to forget what he had told her. Nancy rode in a taxi with Mary Morris, Joe McCarthy, and his associate named Maxwell. But only Nancy and Joe McCarthy entered Conboy's law office. Nancy signed an affidavit that renounced her trial testimony. Nancy regretted what had occurred three years earlier: "Everything I said in that affidavit was all lies," she told Hogan and Tyng. Was there any truth that Harold Cole and other investigators invented stories for her to recite? "No, not true at all," she replied. Nancy was then driven to the Hotel Howard where Moses Polkaoff had set up a trap. Joe McCarthy and two assistants hid Dictaphone machines. Polakoff told her to get Cole to the hotel: "They wanted me to say I had inter-course with Mr. Cole and I wouldn't do it." Polakoff tried to intimidate her, 'You did, it is true.'" Nancy said it wasn't true. The men told her to telephone Cole, to entice him to the hotel. She telephoned Harold Cole and intended to alert him, to warn him a frame-up was underway. Nancy left a message, but Cole never came. That night Nancy was allowed to leave the hotel to visit her family for two days. On her return, McCarthy and an associate transferred her to Washington; thereafter, the trio constantly traveled. In Hartford, McCarthy ordered Nancy to darken her blonde hair. After a stay in Springfield, they left for Boston, where they met Flo and Mildred, who were watched by a man named White. They were sick from drug withdrawal. They said the stay at Town Hospital was a failure; they had entered the hospital with "an ounce of the stuff." Nurses assisted Flo and Mildred. After three weeks, everyone boarded a plane to Newark. Although McCarthy paid the bills, the money came from Polakoff, with cash picked up at Western Union offices. Telephone calls were forbidden. In May, while in Dallas, Nancy wanted to send a card home on Mother's Day, but McCarthy wouldn't allow it. The group traveled in separate cars, said Nancy, "living like gypsies." They criss-crossed the country, one week in Pittsburgh, the next in Omaha. While in El Paso the group crossed the border to Juarez and enjoyed a nightclub. On their return, after an argument, Flo tried to barge inside McCarthy's room. She kicked the door down and McCarthy "slapped her around." Nancy and Flo sent a telegram to Joe Dunn. They were "through with the Carnival." But Flo regretted it, "Maybe we can get something out of Dunn." Joe McCarthy told them to pack. He drove them to a rented bungalow in Ocean City, Califor-nia. Dunn arrived, and a heated argument ensued. McCarthy informed the women he was the new boss. The women were watched closer than ever. Asked if she was afraid, Nancy responded: "I'll say I was; we all were."

Nancy knew many underworld secrets. Before the trial, she had disclosed information that was never made public. At the Palace Hotel she had seen Joe

Wilson, the former warden of Great Meadows Prison. Waxey Gordon and Willie Weber spoke to Wilson. They handed him an envelope filled with money "to take care of the boys." Nancy talked to Wilson alone. He did favors for certain prisoners, he told her, one of whom was his chauffeur. Wilson said he was on the Parole Board. Not long afterward, Nancy saw a former prisoner, whom she did not name. The ex-con said Joe Wilson had "sprung him." He had a gun, showed it to Nancy and said it felt good. After Nancy Presser had finished her statement, she left the office and vanished.

Dewey discovered that the judge who permitted bail for Buchalter and Shapiro had been paid $25,000.[3] Louis Buchalter remained hidden in Brooklyn while FBI agents scoured the nation, creating intense heat for mobsters. J. Edgar Hoover was determined to apprehend the most wanted criminal in America. As FBI agents probed crime channels, the searchlight was pointed at Frank Costello, who passed the word to Buchalter to surrender or else face capture. On October 24, 1939, Louis Buchalter walked up to an automobile parked at Fifth Avenue and 28th Street. Inside was columnist Walter Winchell; J. Edgar Hoover approached in another car. Buchalter was tried for narcotics violations and sentenced to 14 years in prison. Dewey then prosecuted him for racketeering in the bakery industry. Buchalter was sentenced to serve 30 years to life. Buchalter was surprised there had been no deal to protect him. He blamed Frank Costello, angry he had been asked to surrender.

William O' Dwyer, a former judge, was now Brooklyn District Attorney. He had received a letter from the workhouse implicating Abe "Kid Twist" Reles in an unsolved murder. Burton Turkus, an Assistant Deputy District Attorney, was in charge of the felony and homicide squads. There were two hundred unsolved murders in Brooklyn. In March 1940, Abe Reles turned informant against *Murder, Inc.* Albert Tannenbaum, Charles Workman, and Louis Capone were arrested. Reles gave information that solved 57 murders. Reles was under constant police guard on the sixth floor of the Half Moon Hotel. Kid Twist's sensational information ended on November 12, 1941, when he was found dead. Police theorized he had fallen to his death while trying to escape. But the body was 20 feet from the building. There was immediate speculation that the police, and even District Attorney William O' Dwyer, allowed Abe Reles to be murdered. The next hoodlum who faced prosecution would have been Albert Anastasia. The case against Anastasia faded with Kid Twist's death, although there was evidence tying the gunman to 17 murders. When later asked about the strange death of Abe Reles, William O' Dwyer answered that he was in the military at the time but pointed out that he had prosecuted seven criminals who went to the electric chair. O'Dwyer was elected mayor of New York in November 1945.

As Lucky languished in jail, his former associates were arrested. In April 1940, Lorenzo "Chappie" Brescio was in the news.[4] Though Brescio called himself a union arbitrator, the owner of a fruit store called him an extortionist. Charges were later filed against Lucky's former bodyguard for extortion in the taxi industry. After being indicted, Chappie fled.

After four years in Sing Sing, Pete Balitzer was released. Not long after, Pete and Jojo returned to booking prostitutes. Police soon raided Pete's houses. In an apartment they arrested 2 women and 19 men. Pete and Jojo were playing cards when they were handcuffed and taken to jail.

While Luciano wasted in a jail cell, Dewey's political star was rising. Dewey was promoted as a presidential candidate in 1940, but at the Republican convention in June he lost the nomination to Wendell Wilkie. During the campaign Dewey attacked FDR for accepting support from corrupt political machines. Wilkie ran a disorganized bid that resulted in defeat by President Roosevelt by five million votes. Like most Americans, Dewey was worried about Hitler's rampage across Europe. However, Americans were wary of entering the war. Though America was officially neutral, Roosevelt was seeking ways to assist Britain. FDR introduced the Lend-Lease Act whereby Britain and its allies would receive seven billion dollars in armaments. Dewey supported the aid but hoped the U.S. could avoid war. In the spring, Louis "Lepke" Buchalter was arraigned on a five-year murder charge in Brooklyn by D.A. William O' Dwyer. Buchalter, still serving time serving for narcotics and racketeering charges, tried to make a deal with Dewey and claimed to have incriminating information about Sidney Hillerman of the Amalgamated Clothing Workers. Dewey rejected Buchalter's plea as an attempt to save himself. Buchalter was tried for the murder of Joseph Rosen, a union truck driver, and sentenced to the electric chair.

On December 7, 1941, Japanese planes bombed Pearl Harbor. When America declared war on the Axis powers, Lucky Luciano moved a step closer to freedom. The security of the Port of New York worried President Roosevelt and the Secretary of the Navy, especially after the *Normandie* burned at its pier in February. Government agents feared sabotage, but the Normandie fire was judged to be an accident, started by careless workers; nevertheless, 71 merchant ships had been sunk by Nazi submarines lurking in the Atlantic. In March, Captain Roscoe McFall met with District Attorney Frank Hogan at 155 Leonard Street. Also present was Lieutenant James O'Malley of naval intelligence. James O'Malley had served for four years as an attorney in the homicide bureau before joining the Navy. Murray Gurfein, another criminal investigator, was also present. At a subsequent meeting they discussed a plan to use underworld informants to prevent sabotage and submarine refueling. Lieutenant Commander Charles Radcliffe Haffenden suggested that crime bosses be contacted, so counterespionage could start. Hogan assigned Gurfein to contact the underworld.[5]

Mobsters controlled union longshoremen, many of whom were Italians. Socks Lanza exerted influence in the fishing industry. But Lanza was under indictment for extortion, accused of demanding kickbacks from union members, and having them beaten if they disobeyed.

The City Democratic Club was the meeting place of the waterfront syndicate. Club members included Vincent Mangano, Joe Profaci, Joe Adonis, and other mobsters. Albert Anastasia was a club member. His brother, "Tough Tony" Anastasia, was a union official with Longshoreman's Local 1814. The International Longshoremen's Association controlled the Hudson River piers, and ILA locals controlled the Brooklyn wharfs.

Murray Gurfein, with Frank Hogan's approval, contacted Joseph Guerin, attorney for Socks Lanza. The trio arranged a meeting at the corner of Broadway and 103rd Street and entered a taxi. Murray Gurfein told Lanza his assistance would be an act of patriotism, but there would be no consideration for his pending indictment. Lanza agreed to cooperate. He met Commander Haffenden at the Astor Hotel. Haffenden wanted his agents in coastal fishing fleets. Socks agreed to furnish union cards. Word was passed to hundreds of fishermen to report anything suspicious, such as captains purchasing excess fuel or supplies. Though Lanza obtained the cooperation of fishermen, the longshoremen resisted. Lanza was apologetic, but only Charley could handle the longshoremen. Murray Gurfein telephoned Moses Polakoff, who agreed to a meeting. Polakoff told Gurfein he didn't know Luciano well enough to make the request, but he did know someone Lucky trusted — Meyer Lansky. Frank Hogan approved the arrangement and contacted John A. Lyons, the state commissioner of correction. Socks Lanza was given permission to confer with Lucky.

On May 12, Lyons transferred Lucky to Great Meadows Prison at Comstock, near Albany. Moses Polakoff and Meyer Lansky met with Lucky. They explained the request by naval intelligence. Due to the deportation order, Lucky hesitated, fearful that if he were deported to Italy at the end of the war, he would face reprisals. Finally, he agreed to cooperate. Word went out to the ILA bosses to assist naval intelligence. Lucky met with mobsters Mike Lascari, Frank Costello, and Mike Miranda. Prison employees were concerned over the unofficial visitors.

Frank Hogan obtained a court order to wiretap telephones in a hotel at 117 South Street, as part of a criminal investigation. Socks Lanza kept an office in the hotel. The telephone taps revealed that Socks Lanza and the naval intelligence agents were hard at work.[6] On June 13, four Nazi saboteurs landed on Long Island. The men were soon captured and the incident validated the Navy's concern over sabotage.

Due to the large Italian population of the city, plans were made by the District Intelligence Organization to obtain information about the Mediterranean area which might be useful for future operations, especially the invasion of Sicily. McFall and Haffenden began gathering information from Sicilians and others who had traveled to the region. Joe Adonis and Vincent Mangano sent native-born Sicilians to Naval Intelligence. Thousands of reports were assembled. These were especially helpful to military mapmakers. Haffenden had a rather fanciful idea. He suggested to his superior in Washington that Lucky be released from prison and infiltrated into Sicily, to prepare the way for an invasion. The idea was rejected.

Socks Lanza entered a guilty plea for extortion and conspiracy. He was sentenced to prison for 7 to 15 years. Hogan's wiretap revealed that Haffenden had approached the sentencing judge about leniency for Socks Lanza, and Haffenden intended to speak with an unidentified commissioner in Albany about helping Socks. Lanza had assisted the war effort and was entitled to consideration, believed Haffenden.

On November 3, 1942, at age 42, Thomas E. Dewey, was elected governor of New York by 647,000 votes, the first Republican governor in 20 years. There was already talk Dewey would challenge President Roosevelt in the next election. The salary was $25,000 a year, considerably less that Dewey could earn in the private sector. The new governor now faced problems in a state with 10 percent of the nation's population. The effects of the Depression lingered; citizens still lacked regular work. New York had 1,167 welfare agencies and 5,000 employees on the state payroll. In a speech Governor Dewey said he would try to achieve economic security. Unexpectedly, Dewey and Lucky again made headlines.

In February 1943, an application for the suspension of the two 15-year terms Charles Luciano was serving was made before Justice McCook. George Wolf said his client had been of assistance to military authorities. In addition, Wolf provided records indicating that Lucky had been a model prisoner and was worthy of freedom.[7] But D.A. Frank Hogan opposed release. Lucky's attorney asked Haffenden and Gurfein to confer with Justice McCook in private. Wolf said the details of Lucky's help could not be made public.[8] Justice McCook agreed that Lucky had been of service, but that was insufficient for release, due to his "cruel and extortionate crimes." If he continued to aid the war effort, and remained a model prisoner, then it was likely, said McCook, that executive clemency would be appropriate at a later date. Lucky had requested release in the care of his two brothers and sister. McCook had investigated the relatives and found them to be "respectable people."[9] Ironically, explained McCook, the outcome would be decided by Governor Dewey. While Lucky's counsel was busy trying to win him release, a hoodlum friend, Jacob

Shapiro, pleaded guilty to one charge of extortion in the garment and bakery industries. He was sentenced to life in prison.

In May 1943, Frank Hogan obtained a court order to place a wiretap on the telephone of Frank Costello, "the prime minister of the underworld." Costello lived in a seven-room penthouse apartment on the 18th floor of 115 Central Park West. He owned buildings on Wall Street, and his influence was so great that he arranged for Michael J. Kennedy to be elected leader of Tammany Hall. In August, Hogan revealed that candidate Thomas Aurelio was backed by Frank Costello. Aurelio was a respected city magistrate, endorsed by both political parties, and a prospective nominee for state Supreme Court justice. The wiretap caught Frank Costello expressing joy over Aurelio's nomination, as if he were a political boss, a puppet master pulling strings. Appointed by Mayor Jimmy Walker, Aurelio had a reputation for honesty. Frank Costello had advised the magistrate to obtain the endorsement of Italian organizations and have the groups contact Michael Kennedy at Tammany Hall. It was evident that Costello was a political kingpin.

Frank Hogan called Frank Costello to testify in court. Hogan had two months of wiretaps. Costello discussed his past. Costello's admission that he knew mobsters around the country and Tammany district leaders shocked the courtroom. But Costello had broken no laws. Citizens asked Governor Dewey to stop Aurelio. But Dewey said it was up to voters to decide at the electoral booth. Aurelio won the election, and the controversy died.

By August 1943, Sicily was secure. The Third Naval District in New York believed the information it had gathered was beneficial. With the collapse of fascism in Italy, Vito Genovese suddenly surfaced and offered to be an interpreter for the United States Army. Orange C. Dickey, an agent for the Army's Criminal Intelligence Division, determined that Genovese was involved in thefts from Army bases. Stolen goods had been sold on the black market. Genovese was arrested. Dickey discovered his prisoner was wanted for the murder of Ferdinand Boccia, a fellow conspirator in fleecing a victim in a crooked card game. Genovese offered Dickey a bribe of $250,000 to set him free. Dickey refused the bribe and turned Genovese over to the district attorney in Brooklyn. Peter La Tempa, a key witness, was so frightened he asked to be placed in the Brooklyn Jail. La Tempa suffered from gallstones. After drinking medicinal tablets, La Tempa mysteriously died. With him went the case against Genovese. There was speculation that La Tempa was murdered.

Meyer Lansky was caught in the glare of publicity when gambling in the Piping Rock Restaurant in Saratoga was exposed.[10] A detective noticed several *spotters* who watched a passageway; the corridor led from the restaurant to a casino in the rear. The spotters controlled who was allowed in the casino. George Heidt, the policeman Dewey suspected of lying for the defense during

As a special prosecutor, Thomas E. Dewey restored citizen confidence in the government by sending racketeers to prison. He was elected governor by grateful New Yorkers and served three terms from 1943 until 1955 (courtesy New York State Archives).

the trial, was employed at the casino. Joe Adonis was in the gambling casino every night, playing gin rummy with entertainer Joe E. Lewis. Testimony tied the Piping Rock to the management staff of the Copacabana nightclub in New York, where Frank Costello had secret interests. On March 5, 1944, Louis Buchalter was strapped in the electric chair at Sing Sing. "No one deserved it more," commented Governor Dewey.[11]

The Republican Party nominated Thomas E. Dewey as their presidential candidate. Since the nation was still at war, Dewey tempered his criticism of the actual conduct of military operations. But Dewey cited General George C. Marshall, who admitted the army was not prepared for war in 1940. Dewey also believed that Roosevelt had neglected to properly warn military commanders in Pearl Harbor about the dire threat. But to maintain national unity he never unleashed his strong condemnation. Voters went to the polls in November. Roosevelt won. The defeat was crushing for Dewey. But he was thankful the war was coming to an end. The next election would be in time of peace; perhaps he had chance in four years. Although a conservative, Dewey was a maverick. He supported the Ives-Quinn bill, a measure that prohibited discrimination in the workplace, subject to a $500 fine or a year in jail. Dewey believed that no one should be deprived of the chance to earn a living due to skin color. Such sweeping social legislation was far in advance of the civil rights laws that would be enacted decades later. Railroads soon eliminated the "coloreds only" cars. On April 12, FDR died. As the nation mourned, Governor Dewey offered his support to Harry Truman, the new president. Dewey was especially worried about Soviet aggression in Europe.

In May 1945, while Commander Haffenden recuperated from a stomach operation in the Brooklyn Navy Hospital, Moses Polakoff came to see him. Polakoff solicited a letter verifying his client's war service. Without official permission, Haffenden wrote the letter. Four days later, Polakoff publicly announced he had applied to the state parole board for executive clemency for Charles Luciano. His client had aided the war effort, the attorney assured reporters. The announcement was astounding. There was puzzlement by the public. How could a mobster assist the war effort from a jail cell? Naval officials were appalled by the disclosure. The Office of Naval Intelligence panicked and destroyed Haffenden's file. Haffenden was denied permission to speak with reporters. He was threatened with a court martial for the unauthorized letter and placed on inactive status due to poor health. When an investigator from the parole board spoke with Moses Polakoff, the attorney insisted his client had helped naval intelligence. Meyer Lansky confirmed that he had been an intermediary. Frederick Moran, Chairman of the Parole Board, personally interviewed Lucky, Socks Lanza, and John Lyons, Commissioner of Corrections. The report stated that Luciano was regarded as a model prisoner, though he did not attend chapel or school classes. The parole board recommended commutation of Lucky's sentence and immediate deportation.

On January 3, 1946, Governor Dewey announced that he was commuting the sentence of Charles Luciano and six alien felons. All seven would be deported to their native countries. From Albany, Dewey released a statement: "Upon the entry of the United States into the war, Luciano's aid was sought by the armed services in inducing others to provide information concerning possible enemy attack. It appears that he cooperated in such effort though the actual value of the information procured is not clear. His record in prison is reported as wholly satisfactory." The deportations were the first by a governor in New York since 1938, but there was widespread skepticism about Lucky's war efforts. Moses Polakoff told reporters his client had aided military authorities for two years as preparation for the invasion of Sicily. Lucky gave the names of Sicilian-born Italians who could provide information.

The following week, Lucky shielded his face from photographers as he left Great Meadow Prison for Sing Sing. He carried a large bag filled with personal items. At age 48, he faced exile to Italy. Any attempt to return would result in immediate imprisonment, and he would be forced to serve the remainder of his sentence. Governor Dewey commuted the prison sentence of Joe Bendix, who was released on life parole. Bendix refused to speak with reporters.

Reports surfaced that Gay Orlova would join Lucky in Italy. She lived in Paris at the exclusive Hotel Hausman. During the war she had been questioned by the Nazis and was suspected of being a Communist spy but was released. French officials denied her request to travel across the French border, and she faded from sight.

Lucky was transported to Ellis Island, confined to a room with only a toilet, bed, and chair. On the afternoon of February 2, he was scheduled to receive visitors. This was the custom for deportees, in order for their affairs to be arranged. Since early morning a reporter for the *Daily News* had been at the barge office, unsuccessfully attempting to obtain a pass to Ellis Island for an interview with Lucky. The reporter observed the arrival of Moses Polakoff, Frank Costello, Meyer Lansky, and a fourth unknown man. Polakoff told officials the men were with him. They boarded the ferry, but when the reporter tried to go aboard, a guard ordered him to leave.

On Ellis Island Lucky greeted his friends in a public room. A guard who spoke Italian stood within listening range. Costello produced luggage and personal belongings. According to federal law, only 60 dollars in currency could be removed from the country. Costello gave Lucky $2,500 in traveler's checks, which were unregulated. Lucky was desperate to remain in America, but Polakoff could do nothing. After less than an hour, the meeting ended.

The following afternoon, agents of the immigration service escorted Lucky aboard the *Laura Keene,* a freighter moored at Pier Seven in Brooklyn's Bush Terminal. The sole passenger arrived as stevedores, many of whom were Italians, loaded a cargo of sugar. They crowded about him, greeting him warmly, cheering him with "Attaboy Charlie!"[12] The following morning, reporters gathered at ten, but were disappointed that Lucky was already aboard. They wanted to speak with him before the ship sailed at noon. The press had been invited by immigration officials. But hostile stevedores barred the 18 reporters from setting foot on the ship. Near the pier entrance, a boss stevedore came forward. He said the group could not get any closer. Harry Ratzke, an immigration security official drove up and told the reporters he would see them aboard, but 25 longshoremen threatened the group. Ratzke went aboard alone. An INS guard stood in the passageway leading to Lucky's cabin; five other agents stood nearby. In the cabin Lucky sat with the first mate, who had been assigned by the ship's captain to watch him. When Ratzke suggested an interview, Lucky refused; the press had not treated him well in the past, so he had nothing to say. Rain halted the loading of flour, and the sailing was delayed until the following day.

A newspaper story reported that at 8:00 P.M. Albert Anastasia arrived with five men. According to the article, they carried steaming pots of spaghetti and bottles of red wine. On Sunday morning, February 10, the *Laura Keene* sailed. "Old Lady Liberty wore a contented smile," wrote reporter Art Smith in the *Daily News.*[13] Mayor La Guardia was furious to read of stevedores threatening reporters; INS officials appeared helpless. The day Lucky sailed, La Guardia gave his "Talk to the People" radio broadcast. He blasted Frank Costello as "nothing but a bum." As for the intimidation on Pier Seven, La Guardia blamed Attorney General Tom Clark: "Did you get word from Tammany Hall that the courtesy of the ports should be extended to Frank Costello?" La Guardia made a transcript of the address and sent copies to Attorney General Clark and J. Edgar Hoover.

FBI agents conducted an investigation. It was determined that Moses Polakoff had received passes to Ellis Island for himself and "three relatives." The immigration agents did not recognize Costello and assumed he was a family member. Ellis Island has always been forbidden to the press, explained an INS representative. Aboard the *Laura Keene*, Lucky had been watched by six immigration officials in pairs. They denied Lucky had any visitors during the entire period he was in custody aboard ship, from 2:45 P.M. Friday until Sunday, when the ship sailed. Nor was there any liquor aboard. Lucky ate meals at regular times in the ship's mess hall, where only guards and crew members were present. Saturday night he was served baked macaroni and steak for dinner, asked for tea but, as none was available, Lucky drank milk. Since his cabin was small, five feet by eight, Lucky and his guards spent hours in the mess hall listening to the radio. Lucky was quiet, but Saturday evening he told the guards he would be glad to get away from America and all the publicity he had created. The Italian-speaking guards observed Lucky exchanging greetings in Italian with stevedores, "about 20 of these individuals whom Luciano called by their first names." There was no prolonged conversation, nor was anyone allowed in his cabin.

New York police also interviewed the INS guards; photographs of Albert Anastasia were submitted. They denied having seen Anastasia and insisted Lucky had no visitors. The detectives were concerned because the police had assigned two agents to keep the ship under surveillance. As for the source of the Anastasia story, one guard smiled, "It's not too good." Either the guards were lying or, most likely, a reporter invented the story, disgruntled over being snubbed by Lucky and threatened by the stevedores.

An official at Bush Terminal said the pier was private property and that allowing reporters aboard ship would have delayed loading and subjected the company to liability for possible personal injury. Ratze was interviewed at length. He was uncertain who actually gave the orders barring the reporters from boarding. It could have been the pier superintendent or Luciano. But Ratze was certain that if the reporters had tried to board the ship "there would have been bloodshed."

After 17 days at sea, the *Laura Keene* arrived in Naples. Lucky was taken to police headquarters. He showed his documents and informed police his plans were to visit relatives in Naples and Sicily. His movements were immediately scrutinized by U.S. counterintelligence agents. The Department of State asked the American Consulate General in Naples to file a report on his activities.

In Rome, Lucky found a home at No. 37 Via Basurto. He avoided reporters, but was occasionally seen in nightclubs, sitting alone. He sipped wine as Italian bands played American jazz. He was allowed to travel freely. Lucky went to Palermo with his girlfriend, Virginia Massa; the couple stayed at the luxurious Hotel delle Palme. On June 26, Lucky drove to Settecannoli, to meet his sister, Rosa, at the Gargano Farm. Gabriel Celetta, a special agent, observed that "known members of the Mafia visited Luciano" at the Hotel delle Palme.[14] In August, Ralph Liguori was deported to Italy aboard the *Gripsholm* with 21 others. Like Lucky, Ralph had never applied for American citizenship. Surveillance reports reached America that Lucky would relocate to Mexico. Unexpectedly, he vanished.

CHAPTER FIFTEEN

Cuba

From now on he is going to be a has been

Reports reached American authorities that Lucky had been spotted placing bets at a race track in Havana. While Lucky savored his new freedom in Cuba, the FBI was curious about his release. J. Edgar Hoover initiated a discreet inquiry. As Hoover wrote, "This is an amazing and fantastic case. We should get all the facts for it looks rotten to me from several angles."[1]

A confidential report centered on Charles Haffenden. An FBI investigation revealed that an anonymous letter, mailed in July 1945 and sent to the Office of Naval Intelligence, disclosed Haffenden supported Lucky's release. Commander Haffenden "on his own initiative and at the request of Moses Polakoff" had sent a letter to Charles Brietel, counsel to Governor Dewey in Albany, indicating that Luciano had been made available for interview by ONI a number of informants who furnished information assisting in the invasion of Sicily and Italy.[2] "ONI files do not reflect any information backing up Haffenden's claims. Information has been received that Haffenden, who was appointed Commissioner of Marine and Aviation at New York City on January 1, 1946, by Mayor O'Dwyer is a close friend and golfing companion of Frank Costello and he is also a good friend of Moses Polakoff." The FBI had obtained copies of the confidential ONI communications, including Haffenden's letter to Breitel, which stated in part: "I am confident that the greater part of the intelligence developed in the Sicilian campaign was directly responsible to the number of Sicilians that emanated from the Charley Lucky contact." Haffenden said he had kept a record of all informants, many of whom were Sicilians who could not speak English, but were interviewed at 50 Church Street, and provided information and photographs. When waterfront strikes by stevedores took place in Brooklyn, interfering in shipping,

243

Haffenden discussed the problem with Moses Polakoff, and the strikes immediately stopped, attesting to the influence of the Mafia, asserted investigators.

The FBI learned that Commander Haffenden had been transferred out of New York, to the Coast Patrol in California and subsequently participated in limited action on Okinawa, where he was awarded a purple heart. On his return to the States, Haffenden regaled friends with stories about how he had organized and led landings at Okinawa. The FBI located the officer who had pinned the medal on Haffenden. He said Haffenden had received no wounds but was hospitalized when a large cannon fired near him and aggravated a stomach ailment.

An FBI informant had casually spoken with Haffenden about Frank Costello. At first, he was evasive and would not admit knowing Costello until asked if he had played golf with Costello at the Pomonok Country Club in Flushing: "Haffenden then suddenly acted as though his memory had been refreshed and stated he was friendly with Frank Costello and had played golf with him." According to the FBI report: "Confidential Informant T-1 further advised that it was apparent that Frank Costello had Haffenden appointed as Commissioner of Marine and Aviation although he could not prove how it came about except that it is generally felt that Frank Costello had considerable control in the present administration." Haffenden's appointment was sponsored by Congressman Jim Roe, Democratic leader of King's County, a neighbor who lived across the street.

Charles Haffenden was unexpectedly dismissed. Mayor O'Dwyer told the press he was dissatisfied with Haffenden's administration of the Marine and Aviation Department. FBI investigators reported that Haffenden's office controlled not only the docks of New York but also had jurisdiction over airports. The FBI informant learned that Mayor O'Dwyer had issued a memorandum to Haffenden on May 31. He was instructed to submit his resignation or be fired. According to Informant T-1: "One of the rumored reasons for his resignation is the allegation that Haffenden formed a corporation with two congressmen from Brooklyn, for the purpose of getting a monopoly of all the concessions at Idlewild Airport now under construction."

The FBI made a request to the parole board for access to Lucky's file.

In a report J. Edgar Hoover acidly commented: "A shocking example of misuse of Navy authority in interest of a hoodlum. It surprises me they didn't give Luciano the Navy Cross."

Agents determined that Lucky boarded a flight in Mont Mario and arrived in Camaguey on October 29, 1946. His Italian passport listed his occupation as merchant. Customs officials were shown a six-month visa, issued by the Cuban charge d' affaires in Rome. Foreign consuls in Rome had provided visas for Venezuela, Colombia, and Bolivia.

Lucky lived in the fashionable Miramar section, at Calle 30. He passed his time at the racetrack, seated at a table in the Jockey Club, placing bets and conversing with American tourists and prominent Cubans. During the holidays his sister, Fanny, came to see him.

On November 5, Dewey was again elected governor. The state legislature was controlled by a Republican majority. Dewey supported a law that banned state strikes but resisted banning communists. Dewey publicly supported President Truman and George Marshall's plan to provide billions in economic assistance to Europe. Despite Stalin's promises at Yalta, Russian troops remained in occupied countries; it was unlikely the communists would leave. A nationwide poll revealed that 73 percent of Americans regarded communists as a threat at home. Though concerned, Dewey spoke against banning communists, since this would merely drive them underground.

In January, Meyer Lansky flew to Cuba from Florida. Lansky was well known in Cuban gambling circles. Lansky supervised casinos in Hallandale, Florida, and made frequent trips to Havana. Lansky was affiliated with the only two government licensed gambling spots in Cuba, the Casino Nacional and the Oriental Race Track. There were reports that Frank Costello had paid casino directors $150,000 to operate a roulette wheel and a card table in the Casino Nacional. Costello had his own illegal casino on the sixth floor of the President Hotel. Costello planned to construct a beach hotel. The project would include Lucky, Meyer Lansky and Cuban politicians. But there was a serious problem. Costello had sunk a great deal of mob money into the Flamingo Hotel in Las Vegas, which appeared to be a financial disaster. Underworld investors were blaming Costello and Meyer Lansky for the Flamingo fiasco. Lucky advised Frank Costello to pay the outstanding bills.

"What happens to Bugsy?" asked Costello.[3]

"Him I can't help," answered Lucky.

Lucky enjoyed the Cuban sunshine and deal making but his idyll was soon to end. In the latter part of January 1947, FBI agents began shadowing him. Reports were forwarded to Washington that he lived under an assumed name and was backing gambling at the Casino Nacional and in the Jockey Club at the racetrack. An investigation disclosed that his visa had been obtained with the assistance of a Cuban congressman. A letter affirmed he knew Luciano personally and guaranteed him to be "a person of democratic ideals." The American Embassy in Havana was fearful that Lucky was attempting to establish himself in Cuba for narcotic trafficking.

Frank Sinatra arrived in Havana with Joe Fischetti, the cousin of Al Capone. The singer was introduced to Lucky at the Casino Nacional. Robert Ruark, a syndicated columnist, happened to be in the nightclub. Ruark expressed his astonishment in a newspaper article: "The weedy warbler has been having a high old time in Havana. He was here for four days last week, and during that time, his companion in public and private was Luciano, Luciano's bodyguard, and a rich collection of gamblers and highbinders. The friendship was beautiful. They were seen together at the racetrack, gambling casino, and at special parties."[4] Americans were shocked by the crooner and the mobster socializing. Cubans were also disturbed.

Lucky's presence in Havana was made public by Ronaldo Masferrer, editor of the weekly magazine *Tiempo En Cuba*. He accused Indalecio Pertierra of operating the Casino Nacional and Jockey Club with Lucky and Meyer Lansky: "Surrounded by killers, bouncers, and gorillas, the cheaters are dividing thousands of dollars every night. Any time that a police official dares to intervene, he will be immediately transferred to another district." Pertierra was a lawyer whose wealthy family owned the company that controlled gambling concessions. The story revealed how American tourists had won at roulette tables in the Jockey Club but were cheated in the payout after they complained: "The killers were called and recommended that they leave." Baccarat, roulette, and 21 were rigged. At the craps tables, the dice were palmed by crooked dealers, Americans who ran the games. The FBI obtained the article.

Cuban agents followed Lucky to the El Jardin café in the suburb of Vedado. While he sipped his breakfast coffee, the police arrested him. He was taken to Interior Minister Alfred Pequeno's private office and questioned, then escorted to the Tiscornia Immigration Center. A reporter from the *Havana Post* appeared. Luciano was back in the news. "This is terrible," he said. "I came here to live quietly and now all this blows up in my face."[5]

Lucky was informed he was being detained because on entry he perjured himself, by swearing that he was of good moral character. Lucky said he was in Cuba to be closer to relatives in America. The Italian government was embarrassed, since Lucky had left the country secretly, by using a false name. But Lucky replied that he had given his true name to obtain the passport. There was further Italian embarrassment after it was shown the passport had indeed been issued by the Foreign Ministry in Rome, in the name of Salvatore Lucania. Lucky protested that he had come to Cuba for a vacation, not to transact business.

Pertierra told reporters Lucky had paid his debt and was being persecuted. Another politician, displaying wounded national pride, announced plans to have the Cuban president stop all sugar shipments to the United States, until a black market dealer living in Miami was ejected.

George Collins, U.S. Chief of Customs, accused Lucky of directing a drug ring that smuggled heroin to the United States. Colonel Garland Williams, director of narcotic enforcement for the Treasury Department, announced that as long as Lucky was in Cuba there would be no shipment of medicinal narcotics from America. Lucky had to leave Cuba and fast. Alfred Pequeno assured the American Embassy Luciano would be deported to Italy for his "previous activities."[6] Italian officials insisted he would be arrested on his return. Luciano's presence in Cuba had become an international incident.

American narcotics agents were certain he was scheming to distribute drugs globally. James P. McMahon, U.S. Legal Attache in Cuba, reported the case facts directly to J. Edgar Hoover. Agents in Rome had kept Lucky under surveillance. However, in October he had disappeared, but reports circulated that he boarded a freighter to Mexico.

In the midst of the uproar, Democratic politicians seized the moment to attack Governor Dewey. Assemblyman Owen McGivern asked the New York legislature to investigate the entire question of Lucky's parole.[7] He charged the commutation originated in Governor Dewey's office, that Luciano's release was premature by a decade. Dewey's secretary, Paul Lockwood, responded that it was a common practice of New York governors to commute the sentences of deportable aliens.

The controversy grew when Charles Haffenden came forward. Lucky and Socks Lanza had cooperated with naval intelligence. "They sent the old padrones to see me," he told reporters.[8] He had never met Lucky. Haffenden was described as a businessman, an official with the Executives Association of Greater New York. Haffenden had been a member of the naval reserve since 1917. In July 1940, he was assigned to ONI. Felix Sacco defended naval surveillance, since Lucky, "being head of the Unione Siciliana made it easy for me to get to Sicilians." Those who hesitated to talk were told Lucky's men would deal with them. "We had to use every method and subterfuge," said Sacco, a specialist in naval intelligence and, during the war, an OSS member.

Nothing extraordinary came from Lucky, admitted Haffenden; many imprisoned felons who came from Axis countries also cooperated. The Navy Department was embarrassed by the mob connection. Rear Admiral Monroe Kelly, Commandant of the Third Naval District, said there was nothing in the files to indicate Lucky did any service whatsoever. Nevertheless, unofficial sources agreed with Haffenden, that Luciano had been useful in supplying the names of Sicilian criminals deported from the U.S.

Murray Gurfein contradicted the naval denials. He had joined the military in 1943 and served with General Eisenhower's staff in Paris. He was a lieutenant colonel in the Army's psychological warfare division. Gurfein acknowledged that Lucky used his contacts with underworld leaders in American port cities to assist the military. Gurfein had received a request from Polakoff for affirmation of Lucky's assistance. Gurfein agreed and provided an affidavit on June 12, 1945, but asked Hogan to clear it with naval intelligence. Naval authorities were ashamed of the mob connection and refused to confirm Gurfein's affidavit.

Frank Sinatra's association with Lucky created a firestorm. Wrote Frank Conniff: "Mr. Sinatra has been preaching tolerance to the younger generation and had practiced what he preached by consorting openly with Mr. Luciano, they were buddy buddy chum pals all over Havana."[9] Even more scathing was Westbrook Pegler, who denounced a sycophantic press for creating fake heroes: "An uncommonly nasty guttersnipe has been built into a sort of pied piper of the United States and a leader of American youth but leading them in the direction of the juvenile courts."[10]

About Sinatra, said Lucky: "I met him in Cuba. I didn't know him in New York. What the hell are you going to do? I'm getting bad write-ups. I don't understand this whole God damned thing."[11] When asked how much money he had with him, Lucky was evasive: "Some here and some there." He said he had purchased four thousand dollars in travelers checks in Cuba, from money his friends had brought to him. FBI agents speculated that Sinatra may have delivered mob money to Lucky, though it was never proven. From Acapulco, Sinatra replied through his representative George Evans: "Any report that I fraternize with goons and racketeers is a vicious lie."[12] Sinatra protested that he had merely shaken hands with Lucky in a Havana nightclub.

The U.S. Narcotic Bureau's threat to end the supply of legal drugs until Lucky was expelled made headlines in Cuban newspapers, with the case becoming "a political football," noted American officials.

In Havana the legal attaché, an FBI agent serving overseas as liaison with local law agencies, reported that there was no concrete information that Lucky Luciano was engaging in illegal drug traffic. A narcotic agent from the Treasury Department disagreed and flew to Havana to establish proof. Colonel George White of the Narcotics Bureau announced that Lucky had hired executioners who killed drug peddler Carl Carramuse, a criminal who was shotgunned to death in front of his Chicago home in June 1945, as well as Ignatio Anatanori, murdered in Tampa weeks earlier.

Benito Herrera, chief of the secret police, complained that he had been prematurely forced to arrest Lucky, before leads had been developed. The affair ended when President Ramon Grau San Martin signed an expulsion decree that classified Lucky as an undesirable alien. The president ordered his deportation to Italy.[13] The American Embassy was advised of the decision on the same day. Embassy officials informed the Cuban Ministry of State that no actual embargo had ever been initiated. Garland Williams was elated. Lucky had been internationally humiliated. Lucky had retained mob prestige while in prison, but no longer. "From now on he is going to be a has been," said Williams.[14]

Alfonso Suarez, a Communist attorney, filed a petition for habeas corpus on Lucky's behalf, without his authorization. Suarez said Lucky was the victim of "a vicious prosecution by pro–Nazi elements in the United States."[15] The Luciano controversy became so heated that a fist fight broke out on the floor of the Cuban Senate. The day before he was deported, Lucky was interviewed at the Tiscornia Immigration Center, where he had been held since his arrest. He was resigned to the fact he would have to return to Italy. His only complaint was about the immense publicity. Lucky said he would have departed voluntarily if anyone had made the request. He maintained his original intention in coming to Cuba was to be near his friends and relatives in the States. Yet, he admitted he had planned to buy a share in the gambling concession at the Casino Nacional and Oriental Park Race Track but changed his mind after realizing that gambling in Cuba was deeply connected to politics. He said he had no intention of selling narcotics. He hoped to proceed to South America from Italy, if possible. Lucky admitted that Meyer Lansky, Benjamin Siegel, and Frank Costello had paid him visits. As for his commutation, it was true he had given information during the war.

The Cuban press supported the government's deportation, although newspapers pointed out that the American government could have handled the matter in a more diplomatic manner. Anti-administration papers complained of outright bullying, and the Communist newspaper *Hoy* said it was another example of "imperialism and intervention into the affairs of small nations."[16]

When the Turkish merchant steamer *Bakir* left Havana, enroute to the Canary Islands and Genoa, Lucky was onboard. He had paid $300 for a first class cabin but was a despondent passenger. The trip had been a fiasco. In the aftermath of the visit, Indalecio Pertierra denied any connection to Lucky. FBI agents found no evidence that Lucky engaged in narcotic trafficking while in Cuba.

Benito Herrera claimed Lucky had been under surveillance for months and had been interrogated, but, as his papers were in order, he was released. Herrera said there was only a thousand dollars in Lucky's bank account when he was arrested. Herrera surmised that his sister, friends, and business associates had brought him money, since his lifestyle was expensive, and he still had money. Telephone calls were traced. The secret police questioned neighbors. Nothing strange was reported; women were never seen entering his home. FBI officers reported that no records were kept on those entering Cuba as tourists, so any suspicious meetings with mobsters was unclear.

At dawn on April 11, as the *Bakir* approached the Italian coast, police prepared to arrest internationally notorious Lucky Luciano. At dawn, officials came aboard, and charged him with clandestine departure without official government permission. Lucky was put in a launch. A crowd of journalists and photographers swarmed around him at the port.

In Marassi Prison Lucky gave police several small gold ingots, a belt with his name in diamonds, a hundred neckties, several bank books, and a large diamond set in white gold. During his 19 days in prison, reporters remained close, hearing from guards that he smoked heavily, refused alcoholic beverages and read five books, including Dumas. Luigi Ferrari, Chief of Police in Rome, publicly complained that American authorities had never informed him of Lucky's lengthy record.

Lucky emerged from the prison unshaven. He wore a light gray suit, dark glasses, and a cap. Flashbulbs popped, and Lucky cursed photographers. Four suitcases and golf clubs trailed after him to the Stazione Brignole, where he boarded a train with five armed guards. Around midnight, the prisoner arrived in Palermo and was taken to a local prison. Officials were satisfied with his passport explanations but warned him to stay out of trouble. When finally released, he drove off with his lawyers and later accused newspapers of creating untrue stories about him. Described by police as a menace to the public, he was temporarily restricted to his residence.

If Lucky's life seemed chaotic, at least he was still breathing. After dinner, Ben Siegel returned to 810 North Linden Drive in Beverly Hills, the residence of his girlfriend, Virginia Hill. As he sat on a sofa, two bullets ripped through the window and into his face and ended his life at age 41. Days after Bugsy's death, columnist Lee Mortimer wrote that "Luciano ordered Bugsy rubbed out." Mortimer claimed there had been a conference in Havana, to discuss the Las Vegas Flamingo's drain of syndicate money. According to Mortimer, Bugsy was asked to transfer the debt-ridden casino to a Mafia committee. Siegel voiced threats of his own, saying he would disclose information about them, if necessary. After Siegel's death, Frank Costello regained his power and prestige, said underworld sources.

In Palermo, Lucky stayed at the Hotel delle Palme, in a luxury suite. At month's end, he arrived in Rome. Reporters flocked to the fashionable Savoia Hotel. Dressed in a light sports jacket and gabardine slacks, Lucky faced reporters and sarcastically responded to questions. When asked to comment on reports that he ordered Bugsy's death from Havana, He sneered: "Sure, I had Siegel rubbed out."[17] What about stories of an international drug ring? "Sure, my territory's to be Europe and the Middle East-Russia, too, if I can get in there.... Anything more they say I did? No snatching, no baby killings, no ax murders, no clubbing old women to death? If they need anybody for them, send them to me. I'll take the rap for them all. I always do."

As Lucky angrily jeered at the international press, Gay Orlova was the focus of news stories in France. Gay was questioned by American military police about her boyfriend, an American major who had been arrested as a member of a black market ring. Gay dropped from sight; rumors circulated she had killed herself.

In late August, Lucky was spotted in Rome with Igea Lissoni. A native of Milan, Igea was 26, a former ballet dancer, with dark hair and blue eyes. They had met in Capri. When news of the romance reached her family, they shunned her. Igea became his constant companion. Lucky was recognized in Palermo during the summer. He was easy to spot, since he drove a red Dodge with New York license plates, Igea by his side.

Ralph Liguori realized that Lucky was an international figure and tried to capitalize on the notoriety. Ralph managed two nightclubs in Rome that featured dozens of women as entertainers. Liguori announced that he and Lucky wanted to sell exclusive film rights to their life story—*How We Was Framed*. Their nemesis made no response to Liguori's proposed film. Dewey was too busy contemplating a presidential bid. After war hero Dwight Eisenhower said he would not run as the GOP presidential candidate, Dewey decided to challenge Harry Truman in the November election. Lucky made no comment about the election. But he stayed in the detested public glare, trying to improve his image.

Lucky reluctantly decided to meet with reporters to refute published stories that he controlled 90 million dollars in former racket money. He hired a press agent, Major James Edmonds, a former assistant to the commander of the American army in Italy. Foreign correspondents were invited to a luxury hotel. Lucky was introduced by Major Edmonds. Lucky appeared relaxed and smiled for photographers. He removed newspaper clippings from his pocket. He scoffed at the story he hid millions and denied reports that he was involved in nightclubs with Ralph Liguori. He acknowledged he had received offers to invest in the film industry in Italy. He owned a small pastry and liqueur shop in Lercara Friddi, a business he operated with a cousin. As for selling dope: "There's a hell of a lot of easier ways to make money. I'm not crazy."[18]

Though Lucky tried to improve his image, the attempt was futile. His name was linked with every international narcotic arrest. When heroin, valued at $400,000, was discovered in false bulkheads in the crew's quarters of the *Vulcania*, customs officials blamed him for the shipment. A longtime friend, "Trigger Mike" Coppola, had been sentenced to prison on narcotic charges. Commissioner Anslinger of the U.S. Narcotics Bureau was convinced Lucky was involved in drug trafficking. Lucky angrily denounced drug smuggling stories, but surveillance agencies pointed to his lavish lifestyle and that he didn't work. Italian authorities were goaded to act. Only weeks after his press conference, Lucky was taken into police custody and questioned about his association with Mafia figures in Sicily.

Governor Thomas E. Dewey meets with Boys Club members in 1947 (courtesy New York State Archives).

In America the presidential race was underway. Dewey was once again the nominee of the Republican Party. Dewey advocated a civil rights program and crisscrossed the nation by train, along with Earl Warren, his vice-presidential nominee. Dewey had his supporters, including boxing champion Joe Lewis and famed musician W.C. Handy. Dewey tried to resist the hysteria over Communism. In a nationwide radio broadcast millions had listened to Dewey debate Harold Stassen concerning a proposal to outlaw the Communist Party. Dewey was forceful in his assertions: "I am unalterably, wholeheartedly, and unswervingly against any scheme to write laws outlawing people because of their religion, political, social, or economic ideas. I am against it because it is a violation of the Constitution in the United States and the Bill of Rights, and clearly so. I am against it because it is immoral and nothing but totalitarianism itself [...] the proposal wouldn't work [...] this is nothing but the method of Hitler and Stalin."[19]

Despite early polls that showed Dewey to be the frontrunner, the last two weeks of the race witnessed the erosion of Dewey support. On November 3, 1948, Harry Truman won by two million votes. The defeat was a bitter disappointment for Dewey. The following year, Governor Dewey responded to public opinion and endorsed the Feinberg Law. The State Board of Regents in New York was empowered to list subversive organizations in which membership might warrant dismissal from sensitive university teaching assignments.

When Meyer Lansky and his wife announced a cruise to Europe, the trip became a disaster. Before departure, narcotics agents asked Lansky if he intended to visit his old friend Charley. It was possible, he admitted. The couple booked passage on the *Italia*. They occupied a regal suite, priced at $2,600.

In July 1949, Lucky and Igea were escorted by police from their comfortable apartment in Rome's Parioli district. While detained at police headquarters, the police searched the apartment. Police sought connections to Vincent Trupia, an American arrested at Rome's Ciampino Airport ten days earlier. Trupia had been caught with 18 pounds of cocaine in his luggage, valued at a half million dollars. Igea was released, but Lucky was transferred to Regina Coeli Prison, a former convent built in the 14th century. A thousand inmates were housed in tiny cells with straw mattresses. Also imprisoned was Ralph Liguori. Neither prisoner was able to satisfactorily explain his source of income. Bank accounts were too small to support their lifestyle. *L'Unità*, a communist newspaper, published Lucky's picture with the caption: "Shipped to Italy as a supplement to the Marshall plan."[20]

No drugs were found in Lucky's apartment, but there were incriminating notebooks. The address of a restaurant on Houston Street was the known hangout of Tommy Lucchese. There were addresses for Willie Moretti, Joe Biondo, Mike Coppola, Joe Profaci, Gyp De Carlo, Anthony Bonasira, and Philip Mangano, brother of Vincent Mangano. Igea met with reporters in the penthouse she shared with Lucky in Via Lima. Dressed in only a negligee, Igea complained her boyfriend was being persecuted. After a week, Lucky was released, but the police banned him from Rome, since he had no visible means of support. He was issued a *foglio di via obbligatoria,* an order requiring him to live in the town of his birth. He had four days to return to Lercara Friddi in Sicily. Meyer Lansky and his wife arrived in Naples.[21] They stayed at the luxurious Excelsior Hotel, but Lansky never tried to see his old friend.

In Sicily, Lucky endured the suffocating summer heat, which he hated. In the fall he was allowed to go to Naples. He spoke with an American reporter by phone, only to deny a story that he had wed Igea. Marriage wasn't for him, he snapped. He complained that he was bored with the races and hoped to return to Rome, which he had earlier called a dump. There were reports that Virginia Hill was coming to Italy to talk to him. He denied ever meeting her or that he was responsible for the death of Ben "Bugsy" Siegel.

Life in exile had become a nightmare. Cuba had been a disaster. Everywhere he turned, someone watched his every move. The boss had once strutted down Mulberry Street, but no longer did Lucky Luciano have the anonymity and power he craved. As the months passed Lucky Luciano feared he would never return to New York City.

CHAPTER SIXTEEN

The Final Years

I'm barred from all the world

Lucky Luciano was now described in the world press as an international drug czar. On January 5, 1950, Senator Estes Kefauver announced a resolution to establish a special senate committee to investigate organized crime. Hearings were scheduled in 14 cities. Senator Kefauver criticized Luciano's release from prison and wanted a full explanation. Narcotics agents were incensed by Lucky's lavish lifestyle, though he had no visible means of support; frustrated agents were convinced he was involved in drug dealing but had difficulty gathering solid evidence. In Washington there was a proposal to provide the death penalty to those convicted of narcotics peddling. Italy was asked to pass stricter laws against heroin dealers. Italian officials scrutinized Lucky's every move; investigators determined Lucky paid $450 a month for a lavish apartment in Rome, but how did he obtain money?[1] Giuliano Oliva, Director of the Financial Police, estimated that during Lucky's five years in Italy he spent $80,000. Italian agents observed that Lucky had met drug dealers Giovanni Schillaci and Dominic "Gyp the Gap" Petrilli at the Hotel Turistico in Naples, but agents were unable to establish a direct link to drug smuggling.

Lucky was injected into the governor's race in New York. Democratic candidate Walter A. Lynch questioned Dewey's commutation of Lucky's sentence. Lynch claimed Frank Costello knew all the details of the Luciano release. On CBS Radio, Dewey defended himself against Lynch's accusations: "I am the guy who spent a year and a half of his life in convicting Luciano. He and his mob were nurtured at the breast of Tammany Hall."[2] Dewey repudiated Lynch's remarks that he was the first governor to commute the sentence of a convicted alien to allow deportation; there had been 51 cases in 22 years, including 20 when Roosevelt was governor, 23 during Governor

Lehman's tenure but only eight during his own administration. On WNBC Radio Dewey gave a succinct explanation: "He was shipped out of the country like the rat he is for the rest of his life."

Frederick A. Moran, Parole Board chairman and a prominent Democrat, came to Dewey's defense. Governor Dewey merely followed the parole board's recommendation, said Moran, a public official who had served under Roosevelt, Lehman, and Dewey.[3] Frederick Moran explained that the parole board was always independent; no one had exerted pressure on him to release Luciano. Moran responded because the parole board's activities had been subjected to reckless criticism. Moran said Lucky's minimum term should have been commuted, so he could be deported. Dewey was re-elected by over a half million votes. Dewey was now the titular head of the Republican Party, widely admired by the American public, even though he had failed in two presidential bids. Republicans had a plan to make Dwight Eisenhower, the former commander of allied forces, the party's nominee in 1952. When the time came, the messenger was Thomas E. Dewey. Eisenhower would end the long reign of the Democrats. But on the national scene, the spectre of gangsters mesmerized the citizenry. Estes Kefauver, chairman of the Senate Crime Committee, had captured the nation's attention. Kefauver maintained there was a secret crime government, with two commissions, one in New York and the other in Chicago. Lucky was described as an arbiter of disputes between the two syndicates. Reached in Milan, while he and Igea stayed at the Manin Hotel, Lucky denied any syndicate contact and demanded to be returned to America, to defend himself before the Senate Crime Committee.

In April, Frank Callace, "Chick 99," arrived in Palermo. Callace and his uncle boarded a flight to Milan, where Joe Pici met them. On a second trip to Milan, the Callaces bought three kilos of heroin from Pici. They departed by plane for Palermo, but in Rome an anonymous informant informed the police that heroin was in Frank Callace's suitcase. Police discovered Joe Pici had made telephone calls to Lucky. The international drug smugglers were active and controlled by Luciano, authorities asserted. Citizens were fascinated by the televised crime hearings. One session featured narcotics agent Charles Siragusa, whose face was never shown. Siragusa criticized Lucky's lavish lifestyle and discussed the arrest of Frank Callace.[4] Lucky was a high-ranking member of the Mafia, said Siragusa, with the title of *Don*.

Dewey's crime commission probed illegal activity on the waterfront in New York City. There were 900 piers and 40,000 longshoremen. Besides cargo theft, bribes were expected to be paid to corrupt union officials; if not, there were delays. Tony Bender Strollo was called as a witness before the New York State Crime Commission. Strollo denied being a notorious underworld character. He identified himself as a real estate broker. When Theodore Kiendl,

Special Assistant Attorney General, asked him about Albert Anastasia, the witness shrugged, "I don't understand what they mean, Murder Inc."[5]

Kiendl told the committee how Mayor Kenny had ordered Dominick Strollo, Tony's brother, off the piers as night hiring boss, but Tony threatened a strike. The mayor wanted to keep known criminals from Jersey City waterfronts. Tony Strollo conceded he had met with Mayor Kenny in the apartment of entertainer Phil Regan but refused to provide details. "Vincent Mauro is familiar to you. Did you know that he was an important narcotic violator?"

"No, I didn't have the slightest idea," said Tony, even though he had known Mauro since childhood and they were partners in a company that manufactured pinball machines. Tony admitted knowing Lucky and Vito Genovese. Not only Lucky was in the crime news but Ralph Liguori was as well. He was arrested for violating a 10:00 P.M. curfew. Ralph claimed his girlfriend was sick and his watch had stopped. The violation brought a sentence of two months in prison.

In June 1951, Pasquale "Patsy" Matranga arrived in Naples with a 1948 Oldsmobile with New Jersey license plates. Lucky's friend, Joe Sabio, had purchased the car in Matranga's name. Lucky took possession of his new car on the dock. Police watched Lucky's every move.[6]

Columnist Earl Wilson interviewed Lucky at the Zia Teresa restaurant. "I'm in no Mafia," said Lucky.[7] He spoke bitterly of the campaign to keep him in the spotlight. "Every wire is tapped. My corresponding is all censored." Wilson remarked that maybe Lucky was paying for something he once did. But Lucky corrected him. "Anything I ever did I was justified doing," he replied.

Lucky's mob friends were marked for death. There was a murder contract on Willie Moretti, issued by Vito Genovese. Moretti was talking too much. Willie Moretti walked inside Joe's Restaurant in Cliffside Park, New Jersey. His companion was Johnny Roberts Robilotto, the triggerman who had once terrified Nancy and Thelma. When the waitress left the table, Moretti was riddled with bullets by four men who vanished, but Robilotto was untouched. Police suspected Robilotto had arranged the execution. Though charged with homicide, Robilotto was released due to insufficient evidence. Robilotto was later murdered, supposedly by Carlo Gambino's gang.[8]

Another name from the old days made the newspapers. Waxey Gordon was arrested as part of a nationwide heroin ring. Waxey was sentenced to serve 25 years to life in Sing Sing. Police arrested Lucky for importation of a foreign vehicle without a license. In addition, he was caught with $27,000 in American currency. Lucky finally confessed that during his stay in Italy $30,000 had been brought to him by friends. He had brought $20,000 from

Cuba, which he claimed he had won by gambling. In March 1952, Treasury Minister Giuseppe Pella fined him $4,000.

Lucky was now followed by the *paparazzi*. Lucky and Igea were photographed in nightclubs. Often they posed with Bambi, their pet miniature pinscher, who was dressed in a custom-made plaid vest. In April, Lucky flew from Naples to Palermo. The previous day, police had arrested Serafino Mancuso, a former drug dealer in America. Lucky stayed at the plush Delle Palme Hotel. A call was traced to Umberto Alessi, an American expatriate who represented the Moxie soft drink company. The men met in Mondello for a discussion. Lucky's friendship with Alessi was the subject of interest, but Alessi simply wanted to write Lucky's biography. The American Consul General in Palermo sent a foreign service dispatch about the two men to the Department of State in Washington.

Sylvester Carollo was arrested in Sicily. Police determined Carollo had plans to refine drugs from raw opium in Sicily. Maurice W. Alttaffer, American Consul General, reported the narcotics gang had perhaps as many as 150 members "sheltered and assisted at every turn in Sicily by the vast network of the Mafia."[9] While in Palermo, Lucky realized he was being followed and immediately left for Naples.

The next month, the Italian Government canceled the 1950 Italian passport of Salvatore Lucania. This was prompted by a request from the United Nations Narcotics Commission. Lucky was furious and blamed Gene Giannini, a heroin dealer. Arrested in 1942, Giannini had served time and became an informant for the Bureau of Narcotics. But Giannini remained in the drug trade. He met Lucky in Naples. Giannini assured agents Lucky was involved in international drug smuggling. When Giannini was arrested in Italy for handling counterfeit currency, he wrote a letter from prison to Charles Siragusa about Lucky's drug trafficking. Giannini had already double-crossed associates in a heroin deal. Lucky ordered Giannini's death. Lucky sent word to Vito Genovese, who passed along the execution order to Tony Bender Strollo. Valachi came to Rocco's, a Greenwich Village restaurant, where Tony gave him the contract. For the gunmen, Valachi hired his nephew and two accomplices. On September 20, 1952, Gene Giannini was found dead in a gutter.[10] Luciano was identified in news accounts as an international drug smuggler.[11]

In December, Tony Bender Strollo again testified before the New York State Crime Commission. He had nothing to hide, he boasted, then refused to answer most questions on grounds that "it may lead to incriminate me."[12] Tony admitted being friends with Frank Costello, Albert Anastasia, Willie Moretti, Joe Adonis, Vito Genovese, and Lucky Luciano.

Albert Anastasia appeared before the committee.[13] He refused to answer most questions. When asked about his occupation, he said he was a dress contractor but couldn't recall his occupation between 1919 and 1942. He acknowledged he had four brothers. When asked if one was a priest in Italy, he became angry. Anastasia was questioned about crimes and murders. He admitted knowing Anthony Romeo, who had extorted thousands of dollars from Local 929 and had subsequently been murdered. Vincent Mangano was a member of the City Democratic Club, until he had been murdered. Louis Capone, a friend, had been executed in the electric chair in 1943. Emil Camarda was an ILA vice president and organizer, a union official who had also been murdered.

Lucky made an attempt to improve his notorious image. *Epoca* magazine published a story that Lucky financed a children's hospital in San Sebastiano, a small village outside of Naples. But Lucky's idle life was secretly documented. Lucky was daily observed at the Naples racetrack, where he kept his thoroughbreds. He also owned property in the summer resort of Santa Marinella, outside Rome. He bought a six-room suite in a new building atop a mountain at the northern end of the Bay of Naples. Nearby was the home of NATO's American commander and the summer villa of director Roberto Rosellini and Ingrid Bergman. Lucky's suite had a stunning view of Mount Vesuvius. The furniture had been in Igea's apartment in Rome; living room chairs were white with pink flowers; there was a piano in the study, and an American refrigerator was in the kitchen. Police calculated Lucky's expenses were several hundred dollars per week, but Lucky claimed expenses only amounted to eight hundred dollars a month. The police attempted to prove he was living on the proceeds of crime.

When Egidio Calascibetta, the director of a Milan drug firm, was arrested for diverting licensed heroin into illegal activities, the police discovered an association with Lucky Luciano.[14] The director denied knowing Lucky, but Lucky admitted knowing Calascibetta. Lucky had introduced him to Joe Biondo of Jackson Heights because Biondo wanted to import "acetic acid." Biondo told the police he represented three American pharmaceutical firms. Charles Siragusa investigated Biondo's claims, and all three firms denied he worked for them. Joe Pici had been convicted of drug smuggling in Italy. Lucky admitted Pici approached him about a drug deal, but he told him, "To go away from me as far as you can get."[15]

Newspapers reported that Hollywood producer Bill Tucker negotiated with Lucky for a film biography. Journalist Llewellyn Miller managed an interview with Lucky in the hillside apartment. Far below, the lights of Naples twinkled. The American writer was given a tour of the marble-floored apartment, including the bedroom where Lucky and Igea slept. Over the bed was a painting of the Madonna and Child. Igea wore a violet dress, gold bracelet, and pearl necklace. She sat near "Sharlie." Bodyguard Benny Dusso was also present. Lucky was dapper in a tailored-made suit. At 55, he wore gold-rimmed glasses, and his eyes were wary, just as his answers. "No matter what I say, you won't print anything favorable," he scoffed.[16]

Lucky was bored in Naples. There wasn't much to do except see a movie. When asked about the film biography, he grimaced: "Some guy writes and asks me to put up 75 grand. A laugh! What does he think I am, a sucker?" As for Hollywood, "I never got out there." He didn't want to discuss his family but did discuss J. Edgar Hoover: "He does his job no matter who it hurts." As for Estes Kefauver's crime investigation, Lucky was angry: "Strictly persecution and politics. Kefauver stopped high-class casinos. That's all he stopped," snapped Lucky. "Instead of gambling in beautiful casinos where they give you a show, Kefauver's got them gambling in cellars." What happened to all the money he made? asked the reporter.

"I like gambling and I like women, those are two things that make money go fast. It came and it went." And he liked Bambi. "Do you wanna go ride?" he asked the little pinscher.

J. Edgar Hoover was now convinced Lucky's release was standard procedure. In January 1953, Hoover sent a letter to Governor Dewey, along with confidential FBI reports about Charles Haffenden. Hoover had been informed that "Governor Dewey wanted it understood that his actions in paroling Luciano was not predicated upon any grounds to the effect that Luciano had been or could be of service to the American authorities in Italy but predicated upon entirely different grounds."[17] When writer Michael Stern made an appearance on singer Kate Smith's radio show, he claimed Lucky and his friends had paid large sums of money to Governor Dewey for the release. Dewey hired an attorney in New York and threatened to sue for defamation. The radio station issued a retraction.

In October, Frank Costello was released from a federal penitentiary in Michigan. Costello had served a year for contempt of Congress, the result of walking out of the Kefauver hearing; a trial for tax evasion soon sent Costello back to prison with a five-year sentence.

On a cold December night in the Bronx, Dominick "Gyp the Gap" Petrilli played cards at Mauriello's Bar and Grill.[18] After serving five years on a narcotics charge, he had been deported to Italy, but Petrilli had secretly returned seven weeks earlier. Tony Bender Strollo told Valachi that Gyp had turned informant. At 3:50 A.M. three men wearing dark glasses walked inside the bar at 634 East 183rd Street. Gyp the Gap was shot seven times. Word reached detectives that Petrilli had bragged to friends that he once slapped Lucky and knocked him down during a fight in Italy.

Lucky's wartime assistance once again flared into a controversy, after disclosure was made of Lucky's prison visitors. In January 1954, Edward J. Donovan, commissioner of corrections, said 35 visitors had seen Lucky while he was imprisoned.[19] The visitors included mobsters: Michael Lascari, Longie Zwillman, Joe Adonis, Frank Costello, Meyer Lansky, Socks Lanza, Mike Miranda, Bugs Siegel, and the late Willie Moretti. Other visitors were family members, attorneys, police officials but no politicians.

Governor Dewey said the visits had been made at the request of Governor Lehman before he took office. Dewey defended Governor Lehman's administration for the arrangement, since it was in the darkest days of the war, but Herbert Lehman denied knowledge or consent regarding the visits. Dewey said the late Corrections Commissioner John Lyons had approved the mobsters' visits to Lucky. In Italy Lucky said he couldn't remember who had visited him.

At a Democratic rally, assemblyman Louis Cioffi said a $300,000 bribe had been involved in Lucky's commutation; the charge was later expunged from the record. Walter Lynch, defeated by Dewey four years earlier, spoke before three hundred dinner guests in the National Democratic Club on Madison Avenue. Lynch said Dewey could be ousted "on the basis of corruption alone."[20]

Estes Kefauver probed the commutation. Before the senate crime committee, Charles Haffenden testified that in 1945 he had sent a letter to the governor's office, recommending Lucky's release. The letter had been solicited by Charles D. Breitel, the governor's counsel. If Haffenden so testified, then he was a liar, Dewey told newsmen.

In February, Lucky finally discussed his wartime help: "I did not remember where Sicily was on the map, but I talked to some of my influential friends."[21] He scoffed at any deal for a pardon arranged through Frank Costello. Finally William B. Herlands, State Commissioner of Investigation, conducted a formal inquiry into Lucky's release. Herlands had worked with Dewey in the prostitution and restaurant cases and later became an investigator for Mayor La Guardia. For several months, Herlands interviewed numerous witnesses and examined files. The investigation established that Lucky had indeed contributed help. The Navy requested that the final report not be released to the public, to prevent compromising surveillance agents and jeopardize similar operations.

The Herlands Investigation probed former controversies. When Moses Polakoff was interviewed he claimed he had unexpectedly met Frank Costello at Moore's Restaurant the night before Lucky was deported. He had *no idea* how Costello happened to be at the ferry terminal the following day.

In November 1954, a Naples court described Lucky as socially dangerous. This was the result of an investigation by Giorgio Florita, Naples police chief.[22] The report described him as a member of the international under-world and a narcotics trafficker. Lucky protested. He claimed his money came from a business in America. Lucky was ordered to remain at his apartment between dusk and dawn for two years. In daylight hours he could not travel more than 16 miles from his home. He blamed American authorities, and spoke of his greatest fear, that he would never see America again. Though exiled in Italy, at least he had a life, unlike many hoodlums. Frank Callace was found shot to death in a parked car near St. Raymond's Cemetery in the Bronx. "He was a bad egg," said Lucky.[23]

In January 1955, The McKay Publishing Company sent a copy of *The Luciano Story* to J. Edgar Hoover, at the suggestion of author Sid Feder. Hoover recognized Feder's name, and he wasn't pleased. *Murder, Inc.* by Sid Feder and Burton Turkus had not been favorably received at the Bureau because the book "contained derogatory remarks concerning the FBI and attributed false statements to the Director." But an FBI reviewer found the Luciano biography "a readable account," pleased that it had no derogatory comments about the Director. Co-author Joachim Joesten claimed Dewey delayed publication to put himself in a more favorable light. The publisher submitted the galley to Dewey; pertinent facts were missing, said Dewey. He gave Sid Feder access to files in Albany. Chapter 9 was rewritten to discuss the roles of Moses Polakoff, Murray Guerin, and Frank Hogan in Lucky's release. Joesten was not happy, saying the book became "a eulogy of Dewey."[24] But Sid Feder, a former newspaper reporter, disagreed; Feder admitted the delay was due to reviews of secret sworn testimony, but the delay improved the book.

The same month, Lucky allowed a photographer inside the apartment overlooking the Bay of Naples. Dressed in a silk dressing gown and necktie, he and Igea posed for domestic photographs, Lucky at the stove and with Bambi in his lap. The deported mobster only succeeded in appearing ridiculous. Senator Lina Merlin, the sole female member of Italy's senate, charged that Lucky was involved in international prostitution, but she produced no evidence. Senator Merlin proposed a law to ban Italy's government-licensed brothels. In Rome there were 18 houses alone.

Newspaper columnist Leonard Lyons interviewed Lucky in his apartment. Lucky was bitter about the restrictions on his freedom. Lyons asked about rumors he had paid $300,000 to get him released from jail. "Baloney, Dewey owed me my liberty," he responded.[25] "I was never mixed up in that." Lyons noticed faded New York newspapers. "I don't care how old the papers," said Lucky, "I read 'em." The same week Lyon's interview was published, Tommy Pennochio was charged with fraudulently obtaining a driver's license. Tommy had given his name as Tom Penny and claimed he had never been convicted of a crime. Like other combination members, Tommy faded from the public eye.

In December, Lucky's name was lettered in gold on a shop at 54 Via Chiatamone. Desperate to prove a livelihood, he now boasted he sold electrical appliances and medical equipment. The Bureau of Narcotics determined Lucky secretly owned the California Restaurant and the Royal Art Studio; both businesses were operated by deportee "Cockeyed Johnny" Raimondo.

Lucky was joined by more deported mobsters: Sam Accardi, Mike Spinella, and Joe Profaci. Frank Costello faced deportation. He was accused of fraudulently obtaining his citizenship. After defense attorneys demonstrated the evidence had been obtained by an illegal wiretap, the case died. Costello was released from prison and appealed the tax evasion conviction. Frank Costello would never return to Italy.

After 11 men were arrested for heroin trafficking, James C. Ryan, District Director of the Federal Bureau of Narcotics, said the dope rings were tied to Lucky Luciano, but there was no direct evidence. The bureau always linked each narcotics arrest to Lucky, whether there was evidence or not, but Lucky was never prosecuted. The publicity was likely designed to neuter Luciano and make him *persona non grata* with drug traffickers.

On May 2, 1957, Frank Costello arrived in a cab at the Majestic Apartments at 115 Central Park West. As he entered the lobby a gunshot rang out, and a bullet grazed his head. Vincent "the chin" Gigante was arrested. Word spread in the underworld that Vito Genovese was taking over. At the trial, Costello claimed innocence over the near execution. The jury found Gigante not guilty, but Costello was sent to 30 days in the workhouse, for refusing to answer trial questions.

On June 17, 1957, Bronx police answered an emergency call to Mazzaro's Market on Arthur Avenue. Frank Scalise shopped at a market, dressed in yellow shirt and slacks. Scalise had just bought 90 cents worth of peaches, when two gunmen pumped four bullets in him. The previous day, Scalise had been questioned about several killings, including the car trunk murder of Vincent Macri and the disappearance of his brother Benedetto. Scalise was the father of five married daughters and the vice president of a plastering company. In Scalise's home police found over 50 photographs taken with Lucky in Naples and letters in Lucky's handwriting. Informants claimed Frank Scalise was the number two *capo* in the Albert Anastasia regime, a crime boss who controlled the Bronx construction trades and was involved in drug shipments. According to Joe Valachi, Scalise was selling Mafia memberships for $50,000. When Anastasia heard about it, he wasn't happy. Joe Scalise vowed to avenge his brother's death. In September, Joe Scalise disappeared.[26]

The same month, Albert Anastasia vacationed in Hot Springs. Owen Madden and Alfred Raso held a banquet in Anastasia's honor at the Villanova. A month later, Anastasia went for a shave in the Park Sheraton Hotel. While sitting in a barber chair, a steaming towel on his face, two gunmen murdered *the executioner*. John Cusack, District Supervisor of the Narcotics Bureau, said Anastasia was shot on orders from Santos Trafficante in a dispute over gambling concessions in Havana. But the underworld whispered that Vito Genovese was merely consolidating power.

Only three weeks later, Genovese arranged a meeting of mob bosses in Apalachin, New York. An observant state trooper, Edgar L. Crosswell, noted the activity at the mansion of Joseph Barbara. A roadblock was arranged, and 58 crime bosses were identified. They had come to see their old pal Joe Barbara, who had a heart condition, said most of the visitors. John Cusack said Lucky had probably sent orders to the gathering concerning the trade in illicit narcotics. As a result, Lucky was summoned to court in Italy and questioned about the Apalachin gathering. He denied he sent any message whatsoever.

In July, a federal indictment accused Vito Genovese and 36 accomplices of conspiracy to import and sell narcotics. Vito's protégé, 30-year-old Vincent Gigante, the alleged assassin of Frank Costello, was also taken into custody. Two weeks later, Christopher Rubino, a mobster waiting to testify before a grand jury, was murdered. Assistant U.S. Attorney Joseph Soviero issued a statement. "Rubino was Luciano's courier and was telling all to save his own neck."[27]

Soon after, columnist Leonard Lyons dined with Lucky.[28] A recent court decision had revoked the police measures restricting Lucky. However, the police still questioned him about his association with Joe Adonis and other deported gangsters. In a restaurant on the bay, Lucky admitted he was a tourist attraction. He sported a large diamond ring, which he said was 28 years old but had been in hock with *guys*. Now he was a legitimate businessman, selling hospital furniture with partner Sam Zager. He joked he should be selling souvenir hats to tourists. He defended Vito Genovese and asserted his innocence. When asked about Senator McClellan's racket committee, Lucky said he would never submit to any questions about the Mafia.

In October, Igea Lissoni died of ovarian cancer at 37. Lucky attended the funeral in Milan, dressed in black, accompanied by her father. On his return to Naples, he found a court summons to explain the source of his money. In January 1959, *Europeo* featured a sensational article that claimed Lucky was involved in the disappearance of Lorenzo Rago, the Mayor of Battipaglia. The mayor's overcoat was found in his empty vehicle. The mayor financed cigarette smuggling. After Rago complained about illegal contraband being dumped in the sea, he suddenly disappeared. U.S. Narcotic Chief Charles

Siragusa said Lucky was to blame. The source of the allegation was an informer who was eventually indicted for libel. When asked if he wanted to file a slander lawsuit, Lucky declined. In March 1959, Ralph Liguori was arrested for exporting dancers to the Middle East, but the girls found themselves forced into prostitution. Liguori denied any knowledge about prostitution.

The Bureau of Narcotics arranged for an undercover agent to be introduced to Lucky in the San Francisco Bar and Grill.[29] The nightclub was supposedly owned by Lucky, but Frankie "Skeets" Culla, a deportee, fronted it for him, believed the Bureau. John Cusack had personally asked agent Sal Vizzini to accept a risky mission. Vizzini pretended to be an American air force serviceman. Lucky befriended "Major Mike Cerra." The undercover agent frequently visited Naples and always went to see his pal Lucky. The operation established that ships' pursers were smuggling American dollars to Lucky. But Vizzini uncovered no solid connections to narcotics transactions.

By 1960 reports circulated that Lucky had a heart condition, but health problems didn't stop him from dating Adriana Risso, an attractive 24-year-old brunette who soon shared Lucky's apartment. Lucky announced he was planning to sell his life story, since it was inevitable someone would bring it to the screen, so he may as well take advantage of an offer. Lucky wanted George Raft as the star. In the California Restaurant Lucky was interviewed by British writer Roderick Mann. Lucky was upset by a recent film about his friend Al Capone: "Al wasn't like that. I knew him better than anybody. He wasn't no murdering roughneck."[30] Lucky feared he would be treated the same way. Apparently, Lucky forgot his court testimony, when he denied ever knowing Capone.

In August, Lucky spoke to Louis Sobol.[31] The journalist noted that Lucky spoke in a whisper and never smiled. There would be no film, conceded Lucky, at least not while he was alive. He admitted he suffered from a heart condition and had been ill for two months. Despite the Sobol interview, Lucky signed a contract in 1961 with Martin Gosch and Barnett Glassman for an authorized film. Glassman was the co-producer of *John Paul Jones.* But the Luciano film would only cover his life after the deportation. The contract called for Lucky to receive $100,000 on the first day of principal photography and 10 percent of the producer's profit.

In January 1962, Martin Gosch telephoned Lucky from his Madrid home with the news that he had signed actor Cameron Mitchell for the lead. Gosch was coming to Naples to discuss the project. On January 26, Lucky went to the Capodichino Airport in the late afternoon. He was being watched by Cesare Resta, an English-speaking surveillance officer. A few minutes after the arrival of Gosch, the men walked toward the parking lot, Lucky's eyes began to roll.

He fell toward Gosch without saying a word. Aware of Lucky's heart condition, Gosch frantically searched Lucky's pockets for pills. He placed a pill in Lucky's mouth, but Lucky Luciano was dead of a massive heart attack at age 65. Among the personal effects police found a photograph of Igea, a hundred dollars, a prescription from a heart specialist, and a religious medallion.[32]

Unknown to Gosch, three fugitives had been arrested in Spain. They had fled after being accused of importing heroin. One of the trio was Vincent Mauro, the business partner of Tony Bender Strollo. Henry Giordano, a narcotics commissioner, described the trio as "Mafia gangsters" who were tied to Lucky.[33] Gosch was interrogated by Henry Manfredi, an American narcotics agent but released.

Lucky's body was removed from the morgue and transported to Santissima Trinita' Church. Four candles were lit near the casket, and the doors were locked for the night. The following day, over a 150 cameramen hovered outside the church. Many newsmen were actually surveillance agents. Joe Adonis was late due to a flat tire, but the Fischetti brothers came. Photographers closely watched the three hundred mourners as they filed inside the church. When one tried to photograph black-veiled Adrianna Risso, thugs knocked him to the ground and kicked him.

Once inside the church, Adrianna sobbed into a handkerchief. Lucky was to marry her within two months, she claimed. *So long, pal* was emblazoned on a wreath. A priest recited a funeral mass but delivered no eulogy. Adriana kissed the casket as it was carried from the church. The casket was placed inside a black hearse drawn by eight black horses. The body was temporarily interned in the English Cemetery at Poggioreale.

Rumors circulated that Lucky had been poisoned. Bystanders had indeed witnessed a pill being placed in Lucky's mouth. A Rome newspaper said Lucky had swallowed potassium cyanide. "Lucky wouldn't have the guts to do it," said Charles Siragusa.[34] An autopsy had been conducted by Professor Pietro Verga of Naples University. There was no poison in his system.

An official at the American Embassy filed a report with J. Edgar Hoover. The report refuted the tale about poisoning. A later report joked there were "more police than mourners" at the funeral.

On February 22, Martin Gosch held a press conference in New York. The producer complained of threats in Naples. "Luciano hoodlums" wanted to stop the film, but the production would go forward, Gosch announced. The Secretary of State received a report from the American Embassy in Rome; it disclosed details of Manfredi's interrogation: "Gosch denied that he had been threatened," stated the report, also intended for Harry Anslinger, the Chief of the U.S. Narcotics Bureau.[35] It described Martin Gosch as "diabolical and his conniving methods will stop at nothing ... obviously Gosch shrewdly planting story that underworld forces did not want to see production go through." Though embassy officials and narcotics agents viewed Gosch as a liar and an opportunist, the FBI noted that Pasquale "Pat" Eboli, a *caporegima* in the Genovese crime family, had visited Lucky in 1960, to discuss the proposed film. Journalist Jack Anderson reported Eboli had been sent by Tony Bender Strollo, who feared the publicity would jeopardize business. According to FBI reports, Pat Eboli asked Gosch in Naples if Lucky had said anything from the time of his heart attack until he died. "Gosch advised that he truthfully told Eboli that Luciano had said nothing."

After 16 years in exile, Lucky Luciano was finally allowed to return home. In February, Joe and Bart Lucania watched as a large wooden crate was unloaded from a cargo plane. Fifty law enforcement officials were also present. The casket bore a metal plate with the name Salvatore Lucania. The hearse was followed by a single mourner's car, but two dozen vehicles filled with drug agents and reporters trailed the cortege. Lucky Luciano was interred in the family vault at St. John's Cemetery, Middle Village, Queens.

In April, Lucky's crime associate Tony Bender Strollo went out for a walk and never returned. Several months after Lucky's death, government agents arrested 11 men. Reports stated the narcotics ring was "directly linked to Lucky Luciano's underworld heirs in Italy. Lucky escaped the net because he fell dead of a heart attack."[36] Even in death, Lucky was still a drug kingpin. Though Lucky was gone, his memory would strike fear in citizens for decades. Joe Valachi talked to FBI agents. The mob assassin had been sentenced to federal prison for heroin trafficking. Though imprisoned in the U.S. penitentiary in Atlanta, Valachi feared Vito Genovese would arrange his death, just like Tony Bender Strollo's disappearance. On June 22, 1962, in a blind panic Valachi killed inmate John Saupp, mistakenly believing he was a killer. The cornered murderer negotiated a deal and pleaded guilty to second degree murder. As promised, Valachi revealed mob secrets. In September, Valachi testified before a senate subcommittee chaired by John McClellan. The once loyal executioner revealed the operation and organization of crime families, each ruled by a boss engaged in notorious activities. Over time, America's obsession with the shadowy Mafia would grow and grow. Lucky's past emerged to haunt the present.

Martin Gosch published *The Last Testament of Lucky Luciano* in 1974. Gosch said it was Lucky's long hidden memoir. The FBI examined two installments and called it "a complete fraud, along the lines of Clifford Irving's alleged memoirs of Howard Hughes."

By then, Dewey was gone. He had died of a heart attack in 1971. The players in the vice underworld had long faded from the pages of history. What became of them? In *Twenty Against the Underworld*, Dewey's posthumous autobiography, he wrote that one of the trio "settled down to a decent living and, after a year, got married." Dewey never disclosed the woman's identity, but it was Nancy.

Moses Polakoff practiced law until 1989. He died at his Manhattan apartment in 1993, at the age of 97. Though he defended many notorious criminals, Polakoff was respected by his peers. Was there any truth to Nancy Presser's statement that Polakoff attempted to entrap Harold Cole? Nancy was told to lure the attorney to a hotel room where Dictaphones were hidden. Did Polakoff attempt to arrange a frame-up? It is likely. Polakoff did indeed know of Flo and Mildred's drug addiction when they lied during the recanting affidavits. Although they swore they were not on narcotics, Polakoff knew they were addicts and arranged for them to enter the Town Hospital. Is it credible that the lead attorney in Luciano's defense strategy would fail to read all the recanting affidavits? To save himself, Polakoff had to claim ignorance, which made him look like a complete fool. Jojo Weintraub manipulated the recanters, at the behest of Moses Polakoff. Jojo removed the women from the sanitarium, and it is likely that he was the drug conduit. Jojo made the initial approach for Flo and Mildred to recant. Jojo needed money. If Harold Cole had been lured to the hotel, it would have been quite easy for Nancy to engage in a conversation, as if they had been sexually intimate.

What was Nancy's motive for confessing the scheme to Frank Hogan, the district attorney in 1939? She had nothing to gain by reappearing. Nancy's credibility had been shattered. Did she want to clear her conscience? Nancy's comments alone provide a clear picture of what had occurred during Luciano's appeal process. Joseph McCarthy undoubtedly knew Flo and Mildred were injecting drugs. With McCarthy as the trio's handler, Polakoff had *plausible deniability* if anything went wrong, which it did. But the evidence discredits Moses Polakoff. Nancy was the bait. She was afraid of being murdered. Harold Cole avoided entrapment. However, it was Polakoff who engineered the use of secret Dictaphones. The weight of the argument is in Nancy Presser's favor. Polakoff never offered any Dictaphone evidence in Lucky's appeal motion, not even the alleged comments of Thelma Jordan. The secret Dictaphones were smoke but no fire. Thelma Jordan remained a loyal witness for the prosecution.

And who was the unnamed informant whose clear knowledge of the combination sharpened Dewey's picture of the vice ring? It may have been Nancy Brooks, Danny Caputo's bigamist wife. When Jimmy Fredericks abandoned Danny in prison, she threatened to go to Dewey, and she may have done so previously. Danny's early warning to Dewey allowed the special prosecutor to prepare for the battle ahead. Dewey triumphed.

The participants in the Luciano prosecution are gone; however, in 2009,

I spoke with Nancy Presser's sister-in-law: "Oh, yes, we knew about her past life in the family, but I never knew her as Nancy. She was always Gen to me, short for Genevieve. She was a beautiful blonde. I married into the family in 1946. Gen was married to a fellow named Walter, a Polish-American steel-worker. They had a happy marriage until they died, although they didn't have children, something she disliked. I heard they had threatened to kill her and the family. I corresponded with her and finally met her. I asked her about what had happened. She told me that she was never a real hooker. Gen had once been in love with Lucky, she said. She came home with him. They had visited a home he kept nearby called 'the storehouse.' They stayed a night at the family home. Lucky borrowed a pair of pajamas from Pa and never returned them. Gen told me his main operation was drugs." In later years, Genevieve spoke out against the prevalence of drug use but never discussed her own past addiction. In fact, she denied ever taking any drugs herself. There was never any mention of Ralph Liguori.[37]

So the prodigal daughter had returned to her family. Genevieve spoke of her past, at least what she chose to discuss. Had there been an early romance with Luciano, or was he just a client? Although she denied being "a real hooker," Nancy had told the investigators the same thing when she was questioned. During the Luciano prosecution she viewed herself as "an escort," while Dewey's staff regarded her as a high-price call girl. As for drug use, Nancy had once been a morphine addict. So it appears Gen glossed over the life she had lived in New York City.

Genevieve and Walter resided in Syracuse for 30 years. As a young man, Walter had served time in prison for assault. Despite their shady pasts, both became churchgoers. Yet, according to her sister-in-law, "Pa and Ma were somewhat embarrassed by her. If anyone asked about Gen, they were quiet, looked down, and didn't say much."

Nevertheless, Genevieve was no longer the same person but had reformed and needed the support and esteem of her family, all of whom were solid citizens, religious and upstanding; reformed sinners who disclose too much risk being shunned. As previously noted, Nancy had nothing to gain when she unexpectedly appeared and disclosed to authorities what had occurred after the trio recanted. The disclosure seems to be a turning point in her life. The extensive archival files document Nancy's involvement with Waxey Gordon and the Luciano mob. How she chose to portray her past life to the family was a delicate matter. In fact, even Justice McCook had raised the issue with the prostitutes before their release.

Genevieve likely informed Dewey that she was happily wed. The fact that she had turned her life around would have pleased Justice McCook; at least one lost soul had escaped the underworld. But what became of the other women

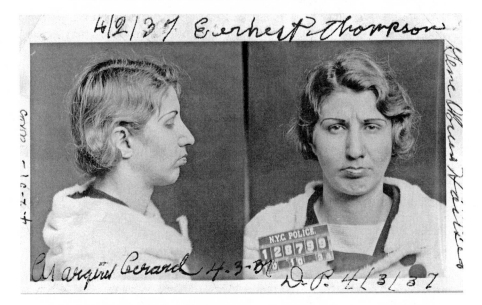

Lost soul. Florence Brown, police photograph, 1934. Nancy Presser reformed and married, but what became of Flo and the other prostitutes who testified against Lucky? (Courtesy NYC Municipal Archives.)

who were arrested and released? Did any return to *the trade*? Their fate remains unknown. Records reveal that Genevieve died in 1984, at age 74. Walter, her husband, died four years later. They were married for over 40 years. Their obituaries were published, and they faded from this world as respectable citizens.

Fate linked the careers of Lucky and Dewey. The rackets prosecution made Dewey the most famous special prosecutor in American history. Dewey restored the confidence of the average citizen in the legal system. He prosecuted mobsters and politicians alike, despite threats to his life. But Lucky's release cast a long shadow over Dewey's career. Political enemies smeared Dewey's reputation with stories of payoffs. But money had never been the goal for Dewey. As a Wall Street lawyer he could have earned much more than a public servant. Was he politically ambitious? Certainly. But corrupt? No. In 1939, when Dewey purchased Dapplemere Farm for $30,000, he could only afford a $3,000 down payment, a sum that was borrowed from his cousin, Leonard Reid. If Dewey had been corrupt, Dutch Schultz, Waxey Gordon, and Lucky Luciano would have gladly offered bribes to stay out of prison. There is no indication that Dewey lived a lavish life. Only when he left public office in 1955 and entered private law practice did he earn high sums. According to his political biographer, Richard Norton Smith, Dewey was worth three million dollars at his death.

Dewey had inflicted the greatest punishment possible when he deported Lucky to Italy. Dewey deprived him of the city he loved. Lucky Luciano never again enjoyed the streets of New York City. The deposed sultan of vice surely cursed the day when Tommy and Davie had urged him to take over the pimps and girls; they assured him he couldn't lose. But Charley Lucky tossed the dice and lost.

Notes

NYCMA = New York City Municipal Archives

Introduction: Charley Lucky

1. "Luciano Kidnapped," *New York Times*, October 18, 1929.
2. "Don't you cops...." Ibid.
3. "Have you...." NYCMA: Charles Luciano, Grand Jury Testimony, October 29, 1929.

One. City of Vice

1. George Kneeland's *Commercialized Prostitution in New York* and *The Social Evil* by the Committee of Fourteen provide invaluable insight, statistics, and narrative. Though unacknowledged, Kneeland was also involved in research for *The Social Evil*.
2. "Prowling Prostitutes." Edward Crapsey, *The Nether Side of New York* (New York: Sheldon, 1872).
3. "I am what...." Ibid.
4. "Their faces...." Timothy J. Gilfoyle, *City of Eros* (New York: W.W. Norton, 1992).
5. "Run for...." Jimmy Durante and Jack Kofoed, *Night Clubs* (New York: Knopf, 1931).
6. "He owned...." Louis J. Beck, *New York's Chinatown* (New York: Bohemia, 1898).

Two. Rise to Power

1. "Italian Immigration." Donald Tri-

carico, *The Italians of Greenwich Village* (Staten Island: Center for Migration Studies, 1984).
2. "For years the Mafia...." *New Orleans Times Picayune*, May 15, 1891. Humbert S. Nelli presents a fine analysis of the Hennessy murder in *The Business of Crime*.
3. "Joseph Petrosino." Andrew Roth, *Infamous Manhattan* (New York: Citadel, 1996).
4. "Italian blackhanders...." Ibid.
5. Lansky meeting. Robert Lacey, *Little Man* (Boston: Little, Brown, 1991).
6. Charley Lucky and morphine. NYCMA: Luciano Police File.
7. "Satan's Seat." Graham Nown, *The English Godfather* (Ward Lock: London, 1987).
8. "Francesco Costiglia and Prohibition." George Wolf and Joseph DiMona, *Frank Costello* (New York: Morrow, 1974).
9. Giuseppe Masseria. Luciano Police File.
10. "The Monster," *Daily Mirror*, October 29, 1930.
11. Valenti and Mauro deaths. *New York Times*, April 15, 1931.
12. Luciano and Betty Cook. NYCMA: Luciano Investigation, Nancy Presser File.
13. Luciano criminal activities. NYCMA: Luciano Police File.
14. Stolen jewelry. Joe Bendix. NYCMA: Grand Jury Testimony, June 2, 1936.

15. Police surveillance. NYCMA: Luciano Police File.

16. "Legs Diamond," *Daily Mirror*, October 10, 1931.

17. Shooting pheasants. NYCMA: Luciano Police File.

18. "From now on...." Wolf and DiMona, *Frank Costello.*

19. High stake card game. NYCMA: Undated newspaper article, Luciano Police File.

20. "Cut In," *Daily Mirror*, October 27, 1930.

21. "Members of the national...." Ibid.

22. "Jewish-dope...." *Daily Mirror*, April 16, 1931.

23. "And Charley...." *Daily Mirror*, April 20, 1931.

24. "Little is known...." *Daily Mirror*, April 23, 1931.

25. "On Suspicion." Ed Reid, *The Shame of New York* (New York: Random House, 1953).

26. "The Sicilian...." *Daily Mirror*, Sept. 9, 1931.

27. "Scarpato Death," *Sun*, September 15, 1932.

28. Reggione murder. Peter Maas, *The Valachi Papers* (New York: Bantam, 1968).

29. Betillo hangout. NYCMA: Luciano Police File.

Three. Love's Illusion

1. "Fifteen Luscious Peaches." Stephen Graham, *New York Nights* (New York: Doran, 1927).

2. "Hello Suckers." Stanley Walker, *The Night Club Era* (New York: Stokes, 1933).

3. "The benefit...." NYCMA: Luciano Investigation, White Slave Report, June 25, 1931.

4. "Hello, Louie...." NYCMA: Luciano Investigation, Wiretap Transcripts.

Four. Sex Underworld

1. "Will you...." NYCMA: Statement of Renee Gallo (alias Rose Cohen), undated.

2. "Would you like...." NYCMA: Statement of Ellen Grosso, May 5, 1936.

3. "A better selection...." NYCMA: Molly Leonard, Grand Jury Testimony, March 25, 1936.

4. "You have heard...." NYCMA: Statement of Jennie Benjamin, undated.

5. "Double...." Polly Adler, *A House Is Not A Home* (New York: Rinehart, 1953).

6. "Come on up...." NYCMA: Florence Brown, Trial Testimony.

7. "Meet my boss...." NYCMA: Mildred Balitzer, Grand Jury Testimony, March 6, April 1, 1936.

8. "Two way girl...." NYCMA: Statement of Helen Kelly Horvath, undated.

9. "Take the tubes...." NYCMA: Nancy Presser, Trial Testimony.

10. "Plain, honest...." NYCMA: Thelma Jordan, Trial Testimony.

Five. The Takeover

1. "See Little Davie...." NYCMA: Charley Berner (alias Sam Warner), Grand Jury Testimony, April 22, 1936.

2. "A benefactor." NYCMA: Memo of Anthony E. Mancuso, February 17, 1936.

3. "A little...." NYCMA: Statement of Rose Lerner, February 17, 1936.

4. "Millie, meet Charles...." NYCMA: Statement of Mildred Curtis, May 20, 1936.

5. "I'm waiting...." NYCMA: Statement of Mildred Curtis, May 4, 1936.

6. "I got about...." NYCMA: Statement of Mildred Curtis, May 20, 1936.

7. "Too bad...." NYCMA: Pete Balitzer, Grand Jury Testimony, March 26–27, 1936.

8. "Stickups...." NYCMA: Eddie Balitzer, Grand Jury Testimony, February 19, 1936.

9. "Lucky is behind it." NYCMA: Mollie Glick, Trial Testimony.

10. "I came to collect...." NYCMA: Joan Martin, Trial Testimony.

11. "Why didn't you...." NYCMA: Statement of Peter Tach, May 4, 1936.

12. "What the hell...." NYCMA: Pete Balitzer, Supplement No. 1, report No. 17.

13. "You have...." NYCMA: Dave Marcus, Trial Testimony.

14. "I had orders...." NYCMA: Statement of Nancy Presser, May 6, 1936.

15. "Sweetheart." NYCMA: Henry Seligman, Grand Jury Testimony, February 7, 1936.

16. "This is...." NYCMA: Danny Caputo, Trial Testimony.

17. "A lot of bunk." NYCMA: Shirley Mason, Grand Jury Testimony, February 11, 1936.

18. "Where is that money?" NYCMA: Statement of Danny Caputo, April 30, 1936.

19. "A bankroll interest." Mark Palmer, January 18, 1995.

20. "Mr. Gee." Ibid.

21. "Meet the bondsman." NYCMA: Statement of Florence Brown, May 20, 1936.

22. "I think...." Ibid.

23. "We'll close them...." NYCMA: Statement of Nancy Presser, May 1936.

Six. Rotten to the Core

1. "Boss Tweed." Warren Moscow, *What Have You Done For Me Lately?* (Englewood-Cliffs, NJ: Prentice Hall, 1967).

2. "The best...." Ibid.

3. "You stand...." Paul Sann, *The Lawless Years* (New York: Bonanza, 1958).

4. "I have never...." Stanley, *The Night Club Era.*

5. "Vice Fiends...." *Daily Mirror*, October 25, 1930.

6. "Body Snatchers." Emanuel H. Lavine, *Stand and Deliver* (London: Routledge, 1931).

7. "Get out...." Ibid.

8. "Lucky has a...." Ibid.

9. Socks Lanza. NYCMA: Luciano Investigation.

10. Samuel Seabury. *Daily Mirror*, October 9, 1931.

11. "Helped to throw out...." Alan Block, *East Side, West Side* (Cardiff, Wales: University College Cardiff Press, 1980).

12. "Two-thirds." *Sun*, October 26, 1942.

13. Albert Anastasia. Sid Feder and Burton B. Turkus, *Murder, Inc* (New York: Da Capo Press, 1992).

14. Dutch Schultz. *New York Times, Tribune, Journal, World-Telegram*, October 1935; Paul Sann, *Kill the Dutchman.*

15. Leo Linderman. *World-Telegram*, February 5, 1937.

16. Thomas E. Dewey. Rupert Hughes, *The Story of Thomas E. Dewey* (New York: Grosset and Dunlap, 1944); newspaper accounts.

17. "Tammany represents...." Ibid.

18. James A. McQuade. Alfred Connable and Edward Silverfarb, *Tigers of Tammany* (Holt: New York: 1967).

19. "Here and There." Ibid.

20. "Break the coppers...." NYCMA: Statement of Nancy Presser, April 22, 1936.

21. "Didn't I tell you...." NYCMA: Pete Balitzer, Trial Testimony.

22. "What is this...." NYCMA: Mildred Balitzer, Trial testimony.

Seven. Soulless Creatures

1. "Do you know...." NYCMA: Mildred Balitzer, Trial Testimony.

2. "I just okayed...." NYCMA: Dave Marcus, Trial testimony.

3. "We'll come...." NYCMA: Statement of Al Weiner, March 17, 1936.

4. Weinberg. Paul Sann. *Kill the Dutchman* (New York: Da Capo, 1991); newspaper accounts.

5. Scholtz, Fletcher. NYCMA: Siegel. Trial Testimony.

6. "When Pete pays...." NYCMA: Mildred Balitzer, Grand Jury Testimony, April 1, 1936.

7. "She and all...." NYCMA: Statement of Nancy Presser, May 6, 1936.

8. "This is Charley...." NYCMA: Nancy Presser, Grand Jury Testimony, April 6, 1936.

9. "I'm going to take...." Ibid.

10. "No less than...." Block, *East Side, West Side.*

11. Dewey's appointment. *New York Times*, June 28, July 2, July 7, 1935; Hughes, *The Story of Thomas E. Dewey.*

12. "He is the treasurer...." NYCMA: Danny Caputo, Trial Testimony

13. "Who is going...." Ibid.

14. "For operatives...." NYCMA: Letter, July 3, 1935.

15. "Streetboys." NYCMA: Letter, July 7, 1935.

16. "Hot Nuts Club." NYCMA: Letter, July 15, 1935.

17. "I got protection." NYCMA: Statement of John Romano, August 26, 1935.

18. "I am so deeply...." NYCMA: Letter, August 29, 1935.

19. "Just for...." NYCMA: Letter, August 30, 1935.

20. "You can get...." NYCMA: Letter, September 3, 1935.

21. "All these girls...." NYCMA: Letter, December 21, 1935.

22. "Mrs. Gay." NYCMA: Letter, November 7, 1935.

23. "You know, Joe...." NYCMA: Joe Bendix (John Bower), Grand Jury Testimony, April 22, 1936.

24. "I told you...." NYCMA: Statement of Florence Brown, May 20, 1936.

25. "Jesus...." NYCMA: Statement of Nancy Brooks, undated.

26. Saratoga Club. NYCMA: Robert Crawford, Trial Testimony.

27. Anastasia wanted Dewey murdered. Joseph Bonanno, *A Man of Honor* (New York: Pocket Books, 1983).

28. "A largely Jewish...." Ibid.

29. "We have had...." NYCMA: Statement of Al Weiner, March 17, 1936.

30. "I am tired...." NYCMA: Flo Brown, Trial Testimony.

31. "Max Rachlin...." NYCMA: Report of Eunice Carter, November 22, 1935.

Eight. Lamster

1. Schultz death. Costello. *New York Times*, October 24, 25, 26, 1935; *Miami Herald*, October 24, 25, 26, 1935.

2. "I don't...." *New York Times*, October 25, 1935.

3. "This is the...." *Journal*, October 24. 1935.

4. "Don't let Satan...." *Journal*, October 25, 1935.

5. "The most powerful...." *Tarrytown News*, October 24, 1935.

6. "How long...." NYCMA: Frank Gregory, Grand Jury Testimony, April 9, 1936.

7. "Subject is at...." NYCMA: Report, November 20, 1935. The statement refutes the claim in *Hot Toddy* that Lucky Luciano was in Los Angeles and murdered actress Thelma Todd. Luciano was under police surveillance when Todd died in December 1935.

8. "About time." NYCMA: Michael Redmond, Grand Jury Testimony, February 6, 1936.

9. "Benny can't...." NYCMA: Thelma Jordan, Trial Testimony.

10. "This is my...." NYCMA: Statement of Nancy Presser, May 6, 1936.

11. "I'm Tommy Bull...." NYCMA: Statement of Nancy Brooks, undated.

12. "Pinches...." NYCMA: Malcolm Bailey, Grand Jury Testimony, February 26, 1936.

13. "How do you...." NYCMA: Dave Marcus, Trial Testimony.

14. "Two Million...." *Evening Journal*, December 10, 1935.

Nine. The Big Pinch

1. Police raid. Luciano Investigation.

2. "Sir, I...." *Herald,* February 5, 1936.

3. "Informant told...." NYCMA: Luciano Investigation, Supplement No. 1, reports No. 1–4.

4. "Detectives...." Ibid.

5. "He is in reality...." NYCMA: Memorandum, Anthony E. Mancuso, February 17, 1936. Box 27.

6. "How long...." NYCMA: Statement of Jenny White, February 6, 1936.

7. "From an accident...." NYCMA: Dave Markowitz, Grand Jury Testimony, February 17, 1936.

8. "The downtown...." NYCMA: Statement of Harold Cole, April 17, 1937.

9. "Not only in...." Ibid.

10. "You remember...." NYCMA: Nancy Presser, Trial Testimony.

11. "If Ralph doesn't...." NYCMA: Anna Liguori, Trial Testimony.

12. "That certain party...." NYCMA: Harold Cole Memo, April 22, 1936.

13. "Fear of...." *People's Brief.*

14. "I may not...." *Sentinel-Record,* April 2, 1936.

15. I am amply...." *Sentinel-Record,* April 4, 1936.

16. "Get more...." *Arkansas Gazette,* April 7, 1936.

17. "Greasy men." NYCMA: Statement of Pauline Fletcher, April 17, 1936.

18. "Lucky's a perfect...." *Mirror,* April 21, 1936.

19. "Slept with Lucky...." NYCMA: Surveillance Report, undated.

20. Flo Brown. NYCMA: Letter, Luciano Investigation.

21. "I am going to advise...." NYCMA: Dewey examination, Louis Weiner, Grand Jury Testimony, April 30, 1936.

22. NYCMA: "You fellows...." Sam Warner (Sam Berner), Grand Jury Testimony, April 22, 1936.

Ten. The Trial

1. "In order...." *Sun,* May 12, 1936.

2. "I don't know...." NYCMA: Statement of Antoinette Napolitano, May 6, 1936.

3. "Now as I...." NYCMA: Statement of Florence Brown, May 20, 1936.

4. "I'm ready for...." *Journal,* June 2, 1936.

Eleven. The Verdict

1. Luciano et al. NYCMA: Trial Testimony.
2. "Where do you live...." *Mirror*, June 8, 1936.
3. "This, of course...." *Tribune*, June 8, 1936.
4. "As for you...." NYCMA: Philip J. McCook, Investigation of the Material Witnesses, June 8, 1936.
5. "A Super Pimp." *Sun*, June 19, 1936.
6. "Proved nothing...." *Sun*, June 8, 1936.
7. "Through a relative...." Ibid.
8. "Swanky...." *New York Enquirer*, June 27, 1936.
9. "Absolutely groundless...." NYCMA: Statement of Bernard Thompson, July 10, 1936.
10. "I just married...." *Journal American*, April 22, 1937.

Twelve. Betrayal

1. "I got up...." NYCMA: *People's Brief.*
2. "Yes...." NYCMA: Statement of Thelma Jordan, Match 12, 1937.
3. "Learning the truth...." NYCMA: Statement of Joseph E.P. Dunn, March 8, 1937.
4. "In the main...." NYCMA: Statement of Mildred Balitzer, March 8, 1937.
5. "While Thelma...." NYCMA: Statement of Joseph McCarthy, March 8, 1937.
6. "Put it on...." NYCMA: Statement of Helen Horvath, March 10, 1937.
7. "I was furnished...." NYCMA: Statement of Nancy Presser, March 8, 1937.
8. "He seemed...." NYCMA: Statement of Muriel Weiss, March 2, 1937.
9. "Unless it...." NYCMA: Notes on Moving Papers.

Thirteen. Poisonously False

1. "I have known...." *Journal*, March 11, 1937.
2. "But you did not...." NYCMA: Statement of Nancy Presser, June 17, 1936.
3. "I heard you...." NYCMA: Statement of Florence Brown, May 8, 1936.
4. "All we would...." NYCMA: Statement of Thelma Jordan, March 12, 1937.
5. "Was a liar." NYCMA: Statement of Emma Brogan, April 8, 1937.

6. "They were unfriendly...." NYCMA: Statement of William Cunningham, April 8, 1937.
7. "Which required...." NYCMA: Statement of Robert J. Quinn, April 8, 1937.
8. "At no...." NYCMA: Statement of Harold Cole, April 17, 1937.
9. "Miss Wilson." NYCMA: Statement of Ann Kenneth, April 6, 1937.
10. "Lay off...." *Brooklyn Citizen*, March 26, 1937.
11. "The District...." *Journal*, April 20, 1937.
12. "I regard...." NYCMA: *People vs. Luciano*, April 20, 1937.
13. "The picture...." *Daily News*, April 12, 1937.
14. John Foster Dulles offer. Richard Norton Smith, *Thomas E. Dewey and His Times* (New York: Simon and Schuster, 1982).
15. John Masseria death. *American*, June 23, 1937.
16. Dewey radio address. NYCMA: Luciano Investigation.
17. Dapplemere Farm. Smith, *Thomas E. Dewey and His Times.*

Fourteen. No. 92168

1. "My lawyers...." *Post*, October 19, 1938.
2. "Mr. McArthur." NYCMA: Statement of Nancy Presser, May 9, 1939.
3. Buchalter and Reles. Feder and Turkus, *Murder, Inc.*
4. Brescio arrest. *New York Times*, April 13, 1940.
5. Haffenden. *Daily Compass*, September 4, 7, 9, 1951; Luciano FBI File.
6. Lanza. *World Telegram*, February 26, 1947.
7. Wolf application to suspend sentence. *Sun*, February 10, 1943.
8. Gurfein. *Journal*, January 29, 1954.
9. "Respectable people." Ibid.
10. Piping Rock Restaurant. *New York Times*, September 16, 1944.
11. "No man...." Thomas E. Dewey, *Twenty Against the Underworld* (New York: Doubleday, 1974).
12. "Attaboy...." *World-Telegram*, February 9, 1946.
13. "Old lady...." *Daily News*, February 11, 1946.

14. "Known members...." Charles Luciano, FBI file.

Fifteen. Cuba

1. "This is an amazing...." Charles Luciano, FBI File. Hoover Memo to Mr. Tamm, May 17, 1946.
2. "Haffenden then suddenly...." Charles Luciano, FBI File, NY File No. 62-8768, March 13, 1946.
3. "What happens...." Wolf and DiMona, *Frank Costello.*
4. "The weedy warbler...." *World Telegram,* February 20, 1947.
5. "This is terrible...." *Havana Post,* February 23, 1947.
6. "Previous activities...." *New York Times,* Feb. 25, 1947.
7. Owen McGivern. *Journal American,* March 5, 1947.
8. "They sent...." *World Telegram,* February 26, 1947.
9. "Mr. Sinatra...." *Journal American,* February 27, 1947.
10. "An uncommonly...." *Los Angeles Examiner,* March 25, 1947.
11. "I met him...." *Daily News,* February 24, 1947.
12. "Any report...." *World Telegram,* February 25, 1947.
13. Luciano deported. *Daily Mirror,* June 28, 1947.
14. "From now on...." *Journal American,* February 26, 1947.
15. "A vicious prosecution...." Charles Luciano, FBI File.
16. "Imperialism...." Ibid.
17. "Sure...." *Daily News,* July 1, 1947.
18. "There's a hell...." *Sun,* June 21, 1948.
19. "I am unalterably...." Smith, *Thomas E. Dewey and His Times.*
20. "Shipped to Italy...." *Sun,* July 8, 1949.
21. Lansky trip. Ibid.

Sixteen. The Final Years

1. Luciano's life in Italy. *Tribune,* January 30, 1951; October 20, 1952.
2. "I am the guy...." *Journal American,* November 4, 1950.
3. Moran and parole board. *New York Times,* October 24, 1950; *Tribune,* October 25, 1950.

4. Callace death. *Mirror,* November 15, 1954.
5. "I don't understand...." Commission Hearings, Anthony Strollo Testimony, May 8, 1952.
6. Foreign vehicle. *New York Times,* June 27, 1951.
7. "I'm in no Mafia...." *Post,* August 13, 1951.
8. Robilotto murdered. Maas, *The Valachi Papers.*
9. "Sheltered and assisted." Foreign Service Dispatch No. 59, July 23, 1952.
10. Giannini death. *Journal American,* September 22, 1952; Maas, *The Valachi Papers.*
11. International drug smuggling. *Journal American,* September 28, 1952.
12. "It may...." New York State Crime Commission, Anthony Strollo Testimony, December 17, 1952.
13. Anastasia. New York State Crime Commission, Albert Anastasia Testimony, December 19, 1952.
14. Calascibetta arrest. *Tribune,* October 19, 1952.
15. "To go...." *Tribune,* October 19, 1952.
16. "No matter...." *American Weekly,* December 14, 1952.
17. Michael Stern. J. Edgar Hoover, FBI Memo, March 10, 1953.
18. "Gyp the Gap." *Mirror,* December 11, 1953.
19. Edward J. Donovan. *Journal,* January 27, 1954.
20. "On the basis...." *Post,* January 29, 1954.
21. "I did not...." *Herald Tribune,* February 3, 1954.
22. Giorgio Florita. *New York Times,* November 20, 1954; *Journal American,* January 9, 1955.
23. "He was a bad...." *Journal American,* November 23, 1954.
24. "A eulogy...." *Post,* January 12, 1955.
25. "Baloney...." *Post,* May 31, 1955.
26. Scalise death. *Tribune,* June 19, 1957; *Journal American,* April 7, 1959.
27. "Rubino...." *Sun,* July 20, 1958.
28. Lyons interview. *Post,* July 20, 1958.
29. San Francisco Bar and Grill. Sal Vizzini, *Vizzini* (New York: Pinnacle, 1972).
30. "Al wasn't...." *World Telegram,* July 2, 1960.
31. Sobol interview. *Journal American,* August 3, 1960.

32. Luciano death. Luciano FBI File; *New York Times*, January 27, 1962; *World Telegram*, January 26, 33. 1962; *Mirror*, January 27, 1962.

33. "Mafia gangsters." *News*, February 3, 1962.

34. "Lucky wouldn't...." *Post*, February 9, 1962.

35. "Gosch denied...." Department of State, No. 2520, February 23, 1962.

36. "Directly linked...." *Journal American*, August 10, 1962.

37. D.F., interview, June 13 and July 25, 2009. D.F., age 87, asked that her name and the family name remain private. D. F. said her Polish father-in-law was strict, a trait that possibly made his only daughter rebellious. Genevieve had five brothers. "They were fine people, but Pa could be strict. My husband said he punished the boys by making them lie on lumps of coal, like they did in the old country. Gen once told me, 'I had enough of Pa, so I saved some money and took a bus to New York City.'"

Bibliography

Abbot, Shirley. *The Bookmaker's Daughter.* New York: Ticknor and Fields, 1991.

Adler, Polly. *A House Is Not a Home.* New York: Rinehart, 1953.

Albini, Joseph. *The American Mafia.* New York: Irvington, 1979.

Anslinger, Harry J., and Will Oursler. *The Murderers.* New York: Farrar, Strauss, 1961.

Asbury, Herbert. *The Gangs of New York.* New York: Paragon House, 1990.

Auburn, City of. *200 Years of History.* Auburn: Auburn Bicentennial Commission, 1992.

Beck, Louis J. *New York's Chinatown.* New York: Bohemia, 1898.

Block, Alan. *East Side, West Side.* Cardiff, Wales: University College Cardiff Press, 1980.

Bonanno, Joseph. *A Man of Honor.* New York: Pocket Books, 1983.

Brecher, Edward M. *Licit and Illicit Drugs.* Boston: Little, Brown, 1972.

Brennan, Bill. *The Frank Costello Story.* Derby, CT: Monarch, 1962.

Campbell, Rodney. *The Luciano Project.* New York: McGraw-Hill, 1977.

Chandler, David. *Brothers in Blood.* New York: Dutton, 1975.

Chase, Parker. *New York the Wonder City.* New York: Wonder City, 1932.

Connable, Alfred, and Edward Silberfarb. *Tigers of Tammany.* Holt: New York: 1967.

Conrad, Harold. *Dear Muffo. Thirty-five Years in the Fast Lane.* Briarcliff Manor, NY: Stein and Day, 1982.

Cook, Fred J. *Mafia.* Greenwich, CT: Fawcett, 1973.

Crapsey, Edward. *The Nether Side of New York.* New York: Sheldon, 1872.

Demaris, Ovid. *The Last Mafioso.* New York: Bantam, 1981.

Denman, L.N. *The Social Evil in New York City.* New York: Kellogg, 1910.

Dewey, Thomas E. *Twenty Against the Underworld.* New York: Doubleday, 1974.

Durante, Jimmy, and Jack Kofoed. *Night Clubs.* New York: Knopf, 1931.

Erenberg, Lewis A. *Steppin' Out.* Westport, CT: Greenwood, 1981.

Feder, Sid, and Burton B. Turkus. *Murder, Inc.* New York: Da Capo Press, 1992.

Federal Writers Project. *New York City Guide.* New York: Random House, 1939.

Fowler, Gene. *The Great Mouthpiece.* New York: Bantam, 1946.

Garrett, Charles. *The La Guardia Years.* New Brunswick, NJ: Rutgers University Press, 1961.

Giancana, Antoinette. *Mafia Princess.* New York: Avon, 1984.

Gilfoyle, Timothy J. *City of Eros.* New York: W.W. Norton, 1992.

Gold, Michael. *Jews Without Money.* Garden City, NY: Sundial Press, 1930.

Graham, Stephen. *New York Nights.* New York: Doran, 1927.

Helbrant, Maurice. *Narcotic Agent.* New York: Vanguard Press, 1941.

Howe, Irving. *World of Our Fathers.* New York: Harcourt, Brace, 1976.

Hueffer, Oliver Madox. *A Vagabond in New York.* New York: Lane, 1913.

Hughes, Rupert. *The Story of Thomas E. Dewey.* New York: Grosset and Dunlap, 1944.

Huneker, James. *New Cosmopolis.* New York: Scribners, 1915.

James, Rian. *All About New York.* New York: Day, 1931.

_____. *Dining in New York.* New York: Day, 1931.

Jennings, Dean. *We Only Kill Each Other.* New York: Pocket Books, 1992.

King, Moses. *Handbook of New York City 1893.* New York: Blom, 1972.

Kisselhoff, Jeff. *You Must Remember This.* New York: Harcourt, Brace, 1989.

Kneeland, George. *Commercialized Prostitution in New York.* New York: 1917.

Kogan, Herman, and Lloyd Wendt. *Lords of the Levee.* New York: Bobbs-Merrill, 1943.

Lacey, Robert. *Little Man.* Boston: Little, Brown, 1991.

Lait, Jack, and Lee Mortimer. *Chicago Confidential.* New York: Crown, 1950.

_____. *New York Confidential.* New York: Crown, 1951.

Lavine, Emanuel H. *Stand and Deliver.* London: Routledge, 1931.

Maas, Peter. *The Valachi Papers.* New York: Bantam, 1968.

Moscow, Warren. *What Have You Done for Me Lately?* Englewood-Cliffs, NJ: Prentice Hall, 1967.

Nelli, Humber S. *The Business of Crime.* New York: Oxford University Press, 1976.

Nown, Graham. *The English Godfather.* Ward Lock: London, 1987.

Oursler, Will, and Lawrence Smith. *Narcotics: America's Peril.* New York: Doubleday, 1952.

Rappleye, Charles, and Ed Becker. *All American Mafioso.* New York: Doubleday, 1951.

Reid, Ed. *Mafia.* New York: Random House, 1952.

_____. *The Shame of New York.* New York: Random House, 1953.

Roth, Andrew. *Infamous Manhattan.* New York: Citadel, 1996.

Sann, Paul. *Kill the Dutchman.* New York: Da Capo, 1991.

_____. *The Lawless Years.* New York: Bonanza, 1958.

Shackleton, Robert. *The Book of New York.* New York.

Silver, Gary. *The Dope Chronicles.* San Francisco: Harper and Row, 1979.

Siragusa, Charles. *The Trail of the Poppy.* Englewood-Cliffs, NJ: Prentice Hall, 1966.

Smith, Dwight C. *The Mafia Mystique.* New York: Basic Books, 1975.

Smith, Richard Norton. *Thomas E. Dewey and His Times.* New York: Simon and Schuster, 1982.

Stern, Zelda. *Ethic New York.* New York: St. Martins, 1980.

Stowers, Carlton. *The Unsinkable Titanic Thompson.* New York: Paperjacks, 1988.

Trager, James. *West of Fifth.* New York: Atheneum, 1987.

Tricarico, Donald. *The Italians of Greenwich Village.* Staten Island: Center for Migration Studies, 1984.

U.S. Bureau of Narcotics. *Traffic in Opium and Other Dangerous Drugs.* Washington: U.S. Printing Office, 1936.

Vizzini, Sal. *Vizzini.* New York: Pinnacle, 1972.

Walker, Stanley. *Dewey: An American of This Century.* New York: Whittlesey House, 1944.

_____. *The Night Club Era.* New York: Stokes, 1933.

Wolf, George, and Joseph DiMona. *Frank Costello.* New York: Morrow, 1974.

Worden, Helen. *Here Is New York.* New York: Doubleday, 1939.

_____. *The Real New York.* Indianapolis: Bobbs-Merrill, 1932.

Index

283